D1072157

Cultures in Motion

PUBLICATIONS IN PARTNERSHIP WITH THE SHELBY CULLOM DAVIS
CENTER AT PRINCETON UNIVERSITY

Daniel T. Rodgers, Bhavani Raman, and Helmut Reimitz, eds.,
Cultures in Motion

Cultures in Motion

EDITED BY

Daniel T. Rodgers, Bhavani Raman, and Helmut Reimitz

PRINCETON UNIVERSITY PRESS

Princeton and Oxford

Contents

Acknowledgments   vii

CULTURES IN MOTION: An Introduction

    Daniel T. Rodgers   1

PART I: *The Circulation of Cultural Practices*   21

CHAPTER ONE: The Challenge Dance:
Black-Irish Exchange in Antebellum America
April F. Masten   23

CHAPTER TWO: Musical Itinerancy in a World of Nations:
Germany, Its Music, and Its Musicians
Celia Applegate   60

CHAPTER THREE: From *Patriae Amator* to *Amator
Pauperum* and Back Again:
Social Imagination and Social Change in the West between Late
Antiquity and the Early Middle Ages, ca. 300–600
Peter Brown   87

PART II: *Objects in Transit*   107

CHAPTER FOUR: Knowledge in Motion:
Following Itineraries of Matter in the
Early Modern World
Pamela H. Smith   109

CHAPTER FIVE: Fashioning a Market:
The Singer Sewing Machine in Colonial Lanka
Nira Wickramasinghe   134

CHAPTER SIX: Speed Metal, Slow Tropics, Cold War:
Alcoa in the Caribbean
Mimi Sheller   165

PART III: *Translations*   195

CHAPTER SEVEN: The True Story of Ah Jake:
Language, Labor, and Justice in Late-Nineteenth-Century
Sierra County, California
Mae M. Ngai   197

CHAPTER EIGHT: Creative Misunderstandings:
    Chinese Medicine in Seventeenth-Century Europe
    Harold J. Cook   215

CHAPTER NINE: Transnational Feminism:
    Event, Temporality, and Performance at the 1975
    International Women's Year Conference
    Jocelyn Olcott   241

AFTERWORDS   *267–278*

Itinerancy and Power
    Bhavani Raman   267

From Cultures to Cultural Practices and Back Again
    Helmut Reimitz   270

List of Papers   279

List of Contributors   283

Notes   285

Index   357

Acknowledgments

THIS VOLUME GREW OUT of seminars and colloquia organized by the Shelby Cullom Davis Center for Historical Studies at Princeton University under its program from 2008 to 2010 titled "Cultures and Institutions in Motion."

Since 1968 the center has undertaken the exploration of topics at the cutting edge of the historical profession. At the weekly Davis Seminar, the center's selected resident fellows join with faculty and graduate students in intensive discussion of a broad, preselected theme.

The starting points for the discussions involving the authors of this volume were the new global and transnational histories that have so profoundly reshaped historical practice in recent times. Related to the current experience of globalization but reaching back deep into the past, these inquiries have begun to map worlds in which ideas, institutions, objects, and practices were in constant motion across social and geographic space. Taken together, they challenge the premise of stable, functionally integrated cultural systems that has long been core to the historical profession. They describe worlds of trespass, boundary crossing, itinerancy, translation, and exchange that historians are just beginning to plumb.

The essays assembled here represent only a fraction of the four dozen papers presented by the center's resident fellows and others over the course of these two years. Each sparked vigorous and wide-ranging discussion of the sort for which the Davis Seminar has long been known. A full list of papers is appended. To all those who presented their work to the seminar, with a richness that we can only partially tap here, we are extremely grateful. We are grateful, too, to the seminar participants—fellows, faculty members, graduate students, discussants, and others—who week by week tackled these issues, pressed our theme of "Cultures in Motion" forward, and probed its depths and complexities. Not the least we are grateful to the resident fellows, whose intellectual energy, inquisitiveness, and comradeship reverberated all through Dickinson Hall.

The Davis Center's manager, Jennifer Houle Goldman, deserves particular thanks for her efficient and gracious management of the center and the well-being of its fellows. Sarah Brooks edited the initial drafts of these essays with intelligence and care. At Princeton University Press, Peter Dougherty, director, Brigitta van Rheinberg, editor in chief, Larissa Klein, and Jenny Wolkowicki have been staunch supporters of the center's work and publishing projects.

Daniel T. Rodgers, Bhavani Raman, and Helmut Reimitz, *Editors*

Cultures in Motion

Cultures in Motion

AN INTRODUCTION

Daniel T. Rodgers

FOR HISTORIANS, place has been almost as foundational as gravity is to physics. A sense of bounded, stable location frames most of their professional identities and still saturates most of their work. Ask most historians what they do, and they answer geographically. They are historians of early-modern Europe, the preconquest Americas, ancient Rome, or modern Japan. Time provides the adjective; but the noun is place. The site in question may be a nation (France, Brazil), a continent (Africa), a city (London), a region (the American West), an empire (Roman, Soviet), or any of the precisely drawn and variegated locales of microhistory. But whatever the case, a sense of place as culturally set apart, with traditions, social organization, and ways of life sharply distinct from other places, still dominates most historical work.

Across those boundaries of place, external forces may intrude and disrupt, sometimes with massive consequences, but the narrative and analytical threads stay close to location. At focus is the culture of *this* nation, the experiences of *this* indigenous people, the social customs of *this* locale. This rooted sense of time and place distinguishes history from the social sciences that imagine that their general laws of economic or political behavior can be set down virtually anywhere with equally illuminating results.

And yet, place is not as stable or as neatly bounded as it once seemed to be. It has been almost two decades since history's sister discipline, anthropology, was overwhelmed by crisis over the match between culture and location. The axiom of Boasian anthropology, that if one got far enough from modernity one could find stable, largely homogenous culture islands, mapped neatly onto space, waiting for the ethnographic field worker to decode them, gave way to an unnerving realization that all those culture regions were, like the anthropologists' own societies, porous, heterogeneous, and interconnected. They were meeting places of cultures, entrepôts of goods and practices, nodes of translation and accommodation. Only the sleight of hand of the anthropologist had ever made them seem otherwise.

In its desire to classify and stabilize the spatially distinct cultures of the world, James Clifford wrote in the new critical vein, anthropology had failed to appreciate the real world's "restless movements of peoples and things." Cultures overflowed their fixed locations. They were not divided up "cleanly at the joints," even Clifford Geertz admitted. Their connections were as salient as their distinctions and had, indeed, always been so. In this recognition of "the refusal of cultural products and practices to 'stay put,'" as Akhil Gupta and James Ferguson put it in 1992, the hope of constructing a human atlas of locationally differentiated cultures and folkways evaporated. In its place, contemporary anthropology has spawned an uprooted vocabulary of diasporas, transculturations, entanglements, and zones of cultural friction.[1]

More slowly, historians have begun to come to the same realization. In contemporary historical writing, older implicit historical geographies are increasingly being challenged by models of worlds in motion. In the fields of modern history, "transnational" is an agenda and a buzzword. Borderlands studies, diaspora studies, Atlantic, Pacific, and Indian Ocean studies, studies of cultural transfer, and studies of interwoven histories have loosened many of the assumptions of stable, place-grounded tradition or localized social character that were common not long ago. Goods and fashions have circulated widely for centuries, bringing with them new social distinctions and new understandings of community and self. Ideas and ideologies travel. So do technologies and the practices of everyday life. Early modern science, it is now widely suggested, was made not through the local genius of Galileo's Pisa or Isaac Newton's Cambridge, but in a confluence of ideas and practices that swept through the trade routes of the early modern world. Religious systems have circulated across vast distances, morphing continually as they moved. "For the historian who is willing to scratch beneath the surface of [the] sources," Sanjay Subrahmanyam writes, "nothing turns out to be quite what it seems in terms of fixity and local rootedness."[2]

Peoples and nations have resisted the motion that has swirled around them, of course. They have feared the invasion of external cultural practices as often as they have coveted the moving bits of culture. They have set up barriers to the strange and exotic. They have invented stories of themselves and their homeland ties, elaborated and fought over their claims, and instantiated them in nations and kingdoms. But their very construction of place and culture has occurred within larger worlds of motion.

All this is becoming increasingly familiar across the subfields of history. But because historians' second thoughts about cultures, place, and motion have come without the intense disciplinary self-interrogation of the anthropologists, the new impulses in the historical discipline remain scattered and ad hoc. The very vocabularies for thinking beyond older, more stable notions of location and culture are still in formation. Like all emerging fields, this one is in search of models, analytical tools, and frameworks.

It is into this ferment that the essays of *Cultures in Motion* are offered. Ranging widely across locations and times, they seek to open the core questions, explore the key motifs, and offer models for writing histories of societies and cultures when none of the older containers of place are what they once seemed to be. They vary in their emphases; they tackle different aspects of their core theme. But together they begin to mark out the dimensions of this emerging field, its challenge to historians, and the promise it contains. Our subject is not the new "transnational" history or world history, both of which have been discussed in many prominent forums. The porousness of place is much older than the nation or the "transnational," and the global stage is only one of many scales of cultural intersection.[3] Our focus is not on the movement of peoples across space, bringing (as best they could) their cultural practices with them—a rich and important subject in its own right, renewed now in an age of global refugees, migrants, and deterritorialized workers.[4] Our core focus is on the ways in which, from earliest to most recent times, cultural practices have crossed the boundaries of place that human communities have constructed, unsettling social and cultural relations, keeping even spatially rooted cultures in motion.

The essays collected here are ventures into this emerging field. They offer stories of intrusion, translation, resistance, and adaptation. They are experiments in writing histories of cultural motion where nothing—dance rhythms, alchemical formulas, practices of charity, feminist aspirations, medical techniques, sewing machines, or labor networks—stays fixed quite where we imagined it was supposed to be.

Two areas of study were critically important in helping to break apart older, simpler assumptions of place and culture. Together they shaped much of the vocabulary of this emerging field. And for better and for worse, their legacies hang over it still, sometimes as theory, more often as an unexamined phrase or premise.

The first was a striking renewal of historians' interest in empire. Some of the new interest in the histories of empire was the work of Asian, African, and Latin America historians seeking to rebalance the global historical formulas that had for so long placed the national histories of Europe and the United States at the center. Still more was generated by recognition that the age of empire was hardly past. Its legacies were written into postcolonial structures of power, economy, and culture throughout the once colonized and colonizing worlds. The migration of millions of workers from the reaches of the early-twentieth-century empires to their former metropoles could not but catch the attention of European historians who had let their focus turn inward onto domestic and national concerns. Even historians of the United States remembered that it, too, had an empire.[5]

In contrast to older histories of empire that had stressed trade and administration, the new histories of empire turned a much sharper gaze to interactions of culture. None of the new imperial historians doubted that empires' raison d'être was the mobilization and extraction of resources through a combination of projected force and domination. Nor did any of the new accounts minimize the ways in which the colonizers marked off the conquered and the colonized as radically other than themselves or imposed on those others, wherever they could, systems of racial difference and social subordination. And yet in the course of those imperial projects, and even across fiercely guarded boundaries of difference, cultural materials of all sorts were transported. Religious practices, gender constructs, manners, print, education, labor practices, notions of civilization and science, public health practices and biopolitics, ideas and ideologies were set in motion, where they collided and mixed with different cultural practices across the globe. From the fifteenth century onward, military conquest, massive movements of slave and semifree labor, and massive reroutings of plants, germs, animals, consumer goods, and raw materials literally reterritorialized the world. The peoples of the colonized world bore the massive brunt of the empires' impact, but it is an axiom of the new imperial history that the relations of empire also sharply unsettled social and cultural practices at the empires' Euro-American cores. Layered atop an older emphasis on systems and structures, the new histories of empire began to map a world of cultural trespass and continuous cultural motion.[6]

The empires these studies describe have virtually no resemblance to the uniform washes of color that the textbooks still routinely splash on their maps. The new histories have laid their stress, rather, on the mixtures and compounds, on the things out of place, on the "intermeshed transculturations" that empires made. They were complex and entangled worlds, with their middle grounds, contested borders, and contact zones. Brokers and intermediaries were essential to the administration of empire: persons and peoples, creoles and cultural métis, who found their niche, however anxiously and provisionally, in the empires' in-between places of culture and power.[7] The condition of postcoloniality, as cultural theorists now name it, maps a similarly uneven world of "migrant hybrids" and "in-between" cultural locations: a condition of space and time, as Homi Bhabha put it, where nothing is at "home."[8]

If the new inquiries into the relationship between culture and empire helped to break down older and more stable notions of place, the still stronger impetus in this direction has been the experience of contemporary globalization. Historians, it is fair to say, came to the debate over globalization with a certain professional skepticism. It was an axiom in most of the historians' forums on global economic integration that many of the characteristics that fell under the globalization rubric were not nearly as novel as the op-ed columns and the best-seller lists proclaimed. Dense patterns of exchange serving to integrate spatially distant economies were not novelties of the contemporary world order, most historians countered. They had left their mark on cultures from earliest times all over the globe.[9] But the intensity of talk about global integration, whether in the newspaper columns or in the anti–World Trade Organization street rallies in Seattle, had no precedent, and historians were hardly immune from its influences. When the clothes historians wore were now pieced together by workers across the globe, when they could download "world music" onto their iPods and roam worlds of referents on the Internet, when they could traverse a world of conferences without ever leaving the neighborhood of a sushi bar, a sharp new interest in goods, cultures, and peoples in motion could not but gather force in history faculties.

Part of what was at stake in the globalization debates was yet another reterritorialization of the world—a postnational order, some said, in which local, international, and transregional relations were more important arenas of power and culture than the nation-states. But the stronger motif in the globalization rhetoric was flux itself. Goods circled the world; finance capital moved at lightning speed; the new media penetrated even the most repressive of regimes. Cultural fashions moved virtually instantly from place to place, sometimes in the guise of liberation, sometimes as carriers of a new, mobile traditionalism. That very flux and instability, it was said, promoted reaction, as peoples caught in the tides of change struggled to create "traditional" religious or ethnic identities that they could imagine to be above the swirl of change. New forms of local consciousness were produced within these shifting fields of force. The dominant theme in the globalization debates, however, was the relentless pressure of external force and the porousness and vulnerabilities of place. If, as historians insisted, the phenomenon of contemporary globalization was a repetition (on a new scale and speed) of very old and familiar historical phenomena, then there was reason to think that place had always been more open to cultural materials in motion than they themselves had recognized.

Studies of empire and globalization not only helped, in these ways, to normalize and bring into focus the phenomenon of traveling cultures, loosening overbounded notions of place. They have also been, with mixed results, the principal sources of the analytical language with which historians have undertaken to describe what happens wherever cultural practices intersect.

There had been an older analytical language for these purposes, to be sure, borrowed from functionalist social theory. When pressed by new ideas, institutions, and social forces, it was routinely said, cultures "adapt" and "adjust." They react as Darwinian organisms react to invasions or to new environments, reorganizing themselves in response to pressures from outside. They incorporate the intruding elements into blends and adaptive cultural strategies, minimizing the cultural strain by folding elements of the new and the old together. Religious syncretism provided a paradigmatic example. The old gods did not capitulate even when massively challenged, writers in this vein suggested; they persisted, adaptively reclothed in the religious gestures and language of the new orthodoxies. The study of adaptive modernization strategies formed another well-worked example.[10] These strain-and-readjustment models were never very good models of cultural change, and they have now largely run their course. They homogenized societies too readily, elided questions of power and internal contest, stabilized too easily the products of these disruptions, and trivialized the productive cultural capacities at work.

The historian interested in cultural influences now talks not of functional adaptation but, in a more sophisticated and subtle analytical language, of hybridity, métissage, creole cultures, cultures of the middle ground, or "third spaces." All of these are now keywords in contemporary historical studies. They foreground the productive, the unstable, and the unexpected consequences of cultural collision and exchange. They speak to the liminal geographies of cultural intersection and to the plurality and fluidity of its outcomes. They foreground the absence of neat fit between the cultural elements fused together, the "unhomeliness," in Bhabha's words, of the phenomenon's extraordinarily varied products.

But *sotto voce* many of the new terms also speak of empire. They threaten to reproduce, even in their critique, the imperializers' way of seeing. The idea of the "middle ground" that Richard White made famous in his luminous history of the upper Great Lakes region in early North American history is a case in point. It is not clear that indigenous peoples mapped the landscape just beyond the edges of the European empires in this distinctive way, but the colonizers certainly did. Middle grounds were places where the power of empire unraveled enough that preponderance of violence or military force could no longer be relied on, and trade, negotiation, and brokered and ad hoc arrangements came to the fore. For both the native peoples and the French, White makes clear, they were sites of fluid social arrangements and creative cultural misunderstandings, where kin, gender, commerce, and authority relations were all in a degree of flux. But for native peoples, in-between spaces of this sort were certainly far more common than for the French. They were a normal and ubiquitous part of the social and cultural landscape wherever indigenous societies met and rubbed up against one another. Only for the French invaders was this a distinctive "middle" ground where strategies of war and trade had to be fundamentally reconceived. "Middle" can be conceived only between poles. Explicitly or tacitly, monoliths border and define it. The presence of empire hangs, in this way, over the very effort to think beyond and outside it.[11]

If the imperializers, pressing their way into others' territory through conquest, conversion, and resource hunger, carried with them distinctive ways of mapping space, still more they brought distinctly imperial ways of mapping peoples. Colonizers and indigenous peoples, racialized Selves and racialized Others, were the key binaries in these imperial anthropologies. The colonizers imposed these categories of difference with a fiercely anxious determination. What made it all the more anxious was that the categories never fit with anything near the clarity—us/them, ruler/ruled, civilized/savage—that the imperializers desired. On the conditions that they themselves created, the imperializers were surrounded by peoples in between. The creole populations produced by the sexual interpenetration of colonizers with the colonized were indispensable to the imperializers' projects of labor management and governance. But they were also, at the same time, objects of the colonizers' fearful fantasy and desire. The collaborators who moved into the cultural gap between colonized and colonizers as interpreters and functionaries, occupiers of the in-between spaces of power that the empires offered, were often no less feared. When Rudyard Kipling wrote of Hurree Babu, the strange, shape-shifting Bengali who spouts yards of queerly ornamented English, who scorns the British imperial Raj even as he joins Kim in gathering intelligence for the British and yearns for acknowledgment by the British Royal Society, his cultural patchwork marked him as a "monstrous hybridism."[12]

The initial appearance of that now-ubiquitous term "hybrid" into historical-cultural studies was designed precisely to underline that eruptive appearance of "monstrosity" at the sites where colonial power hoped, but disconcertingly failed, to reproduce itself. "The display of hybridity . . . terrorizes authority with the *ruse* of recognition, its mimicry, its mockery," Homi Bhabha wrote in his widely influential essay, "Signs Taken for Wonders," in 1985. Mimicry threatened the very chasm of difference—the "almost the same but not quite"—that the colonists had imposed. It laid claim to a promise of modernity and civilization that was meant, in fact, to be radically deferred. To stress the "hybrid" productions of empire, in these formulations, was not to stress the multicultural possibilities of interplay and fusion that the in-between spaces of empire enabled. It was, rather, to stress the way in which the discourse of the colonizers "split," became "deformed" and "undecidable," the way in which "the mimetic or narcissistic demands of colonial power" were effected but realized in barely recognizable, menacing form. To bring the hybrid productions of empire back into focus was to stand in the anxious shoes of the colonizers, within their own terrifyingly subversive ambivalence.[13]

It is safe to say that as the term "hybrid" has spread and naturalized in historical discourse, the disruptive, postmodern edge that the term possessed a decade and a half ago has almost completely dulled. It stands for variety now, for the uncountable, productive capacities where cultures meet, wash into each other, and collide. Luther Burbank, the plant hybridist who gave the world a new cornucopia of cultivars, is more often the implied reference than Homi Bhabha. Like the term "middle ground" as it escaped White's original use, it has grown soft, metaphorical, and celebratory. But even if the presence of empire is unspoken, it haunts the analytical language that has descended from it. To write of creole cultures, of métissage or mestizaje, of hybrid economies and hybrid cultures is to write not only within the language of the imperializers' binaries of difference but within the hard, racial logics that rode with them. These were the colonizers' terms for the "mixed-race" products of empire, its threatening, accidental, and racially polluted upshots: for the peoples and cultures that could never be of the same value as the pure, unmixed sources that generated them. The "strange and disquieting ramifications of [their] . . . forgotten past," as Robert Young puts it, may not haunt these terms forever. But the assumption lodged deep in their very structure is hard to scrub out of them, that what the historian is observing is a collision, however rife with possibilities, between two fully formed and mutually exclusive cultural communities, so integral and autonomous that they slip easily into the linguistic space where nineteenth-century anthropologists would have used "races."[14]

To write of "hybridities" depends on the historians' willingness to imagine purities. But what if no such purity ever existed outside the racial imaginations and terrors of the colonizers? What if every piece in these encounters was already an unstable amalgam, a hybrid from birth, already in motion?

It is at this point that the geographers' and social theorists' language of globalization sweeps confidently in. Exuberantly and without hesitation it declares everything in motion. "Flow" is the keyword in this literature. Information, capital, concepts, persons, and goods all flow through the models of contemporary globalization with a speed that David Harvey and others call radical "time-space compression." Bits of culture, broken apart like detachable objects, are carried along in these streams, coming together temporarily in all manner of combinations, only to rush on again. Hip-hop, gangster tags, designer clothing, fusion cuisine, and sampled and recombined musical styles all move through the world in this way; so do religious identifications, human rights discourses, and powerful political ideologies. In a fully networked world, Manuel Castells wrote in his influential *The Rise of the Network Society*, one would no longer speak of places at all but of temporary intersections on "the space of flows." Sequence would give way to "timeless time." Motion in these models is not wholly unchecked or unchanneled. Arjun Appadurai, whose writing casts a very long shadow across these formulations, suggested in his early work on the global cultural economy that persons, capital, media, and ideas should be imagined as flowing across different "scapes," disjunct from each other and eruptive at the edges where their misalignments were most jarring. Locality, too, was produced, however unstably. But the more dominant language, including Appadurai's own when globalization talk was at its height, was more insistently formless. One spoke of rhizomes, fractals, chaos, flows.[15]

Not many historians have fully embraced the terms that course through globalization talk. The notion of a global "dance of the flows and the fragments," as the historian Frederick Cooper forcefully put it, radically underrepresents the place of power, the stark unevenness of the actual historical landscapes, the institutional channels through which economic and political forces move. In writing loosely of flows, he insists, "Crucial questions don't get asked: about the limits of interconnection, about the areas where capital cannot go, and about the specificity of the structures necessary to make connections work."[16] Real historical space, many historians now suggest, was not flat or smoothly liquid but deeply grooved; persons and things moved on long but carefully defined circuits. The Jesuit missionaries in East and Southeast Asia in the seventeenth century sluiced bits of early modern science between nodal points across half the globe, but their circuits never touched down on most of it. Merchants and artisans who depended on mobility for their living in the early modern world moved along similarly well-inscribed itineraries. So did early medieval monarchs in the mobile display of power and presence. The mobility of some depended on the immobilizing of the lives and labors of others. The actual historical landscape of power and influence was, in Cooper's terms, "lumpy."

Mapping these terrains of connection and discontinuity has been an important, ongoing project. In German historiography in the 1990s there was a move to constitute a new domain of inquiry called *Transfergeschichte*. With its linguistic roots in the French term *transferts* for transfers of money and tangible property and its social science methodology, *Kulturtransfergeschichte* might have posed an alternative to the more formless language of flows; but locked in a heated battle with German social historians for whom stress on external cultural influences threatened to distract from the primacy of internal dynamics in German history, *Transfergeschichte* has not had much influence outside of Germany.[17] A more recent effort in this direction, Michael Werner and Bénédicte Zimmermann's agenda for intermeshed and interwoven histories, or *histoire croisée*, bids to lay across the landscape of the modern nation-states what might be imagined as overlay maps of culture zones.[18] Other efforts to articulate space have pulled in still different directions. Networks have been specified: made finite and discreet. The oceans and their ports and shore lands—Atlantic, Pacific, and Indian—have become active spaces of study. "Connected histories" of all sorts are being actively written. The term "exchange," employed so brilliantly by Alfred Crosby, is now everywhere. Routes and circuits are terms of active potential: trade routes, tourist routes, pilgrim circuits, labor migrant routes.[19]

And yet, historians seeking to get beyond notions of bounded place and cultures have not found it easy fully to resist the more watery language of flows or the Facebook language of infinitely ramifying networks. Complex and discontinuous as many of these new models of space and networks are, the terrains they map remain relatively flat. Cultural practices move through them with relative ease. Like all the analytical terms descended from the globalization debates, the language of fractals and flows makes connections easier to understand than blockages, mistranslations, impositions, and resistance. In this literature, the "monstrous hybridism" of Kipling's imagination is whisked from sight. The anxious, fearful collision of recognition with denial that, in Bhabha's terms, threatened the very project of domination, wilts into innocuousness. Questions of radical incommensurability between cultural languages and practices, which framed White's concept of the middle ground and made its products so fragile and unexpected, are rarely broached. Negotiation and translation are tacitly flattened out. Power dissolves into acts of communication and exchange. Anna Lowenhaupt Tsing's emphasis on "zones of cultural friction"—"zones of awkward engagement, where words mean something different across a divide even as people agree to speak"—tags these deficits. Everything we know as culture, she writes, is "co-produced in the interactions I call 'friction': the awkward, unequal, unstable, and creative qualities of interconnection across difference."[20]

Like the analytical terms descended from the discourses of empire, the globalization-derived language of circuits and flows, networks and connectivity, fluid cultures and intermeshed relationships has much to offer historians. But its very geniality and looseness poses a trap and a temptation. For in sober truth, cultures don't "flow" into one another; they don't "mix" like kitchen ingredients, or "borrow" from each other with obligations to pay things back, or "exchange" like merchants at a trade fair. Within this family of metaphors, historians face a tortuously difficult task if they are to embrace fully the features that Tsing calls "friction."

What might an alternative analytical vocabulary look like that was pinned not to the hydraulic rhetoric of flows, the fractals of networks, the boundaries of empire, or the race-inflected language of hybridities? What are the resources for writing about "the refusal of cultural products and practices to 'stay put'" that preserves the power, the multiplicity of possibilities, and the frictions in those acts of displacement? How might historians come closer to the grounds of cultural experience now that place no longer seems as bounded or impermeable as we once imagined it to be? Distilling two years of wide-ranging discussion at Princeton University's Shelby Cullom Davis Center for Historical Studies, we offer not a formula but a list of suggestions.

From Place-Rooted Cultures to Cultural Practices. The big block cultures that once dominated the anthropological textbooks, integrated in function and rooted in place, were an artifice of late-nineteenth- and early-twentieth-century social science. Except for an occasional reappearance in discussions of world politics (where a unitary Islam still haunts some imaginations) or comparative policy analysis (where unchanging national values may still be brought in as a last resort to explain what other variables leave a muddle), they have disappeared from the social science vocabulary. Cultures are constituted of practices; they are made and remade continuously in performance. What moves between sites are never whole systems of value but the semidetachable parts of practice.

Practices in this sense are not acts merely, but actions laden with meaning. Music, dance, artisanal crafts, social rituals, acts of charity, practices of justice, health and medical regimes, protest movements, and gender performances have carried with them complex, shifting significance as they moved from site to site. Goods have traversed the world not as things in themselves but through practices of use and consumption, of social claims and signification. Religions, a classic case of cultural displacement, have traveled in the same way, not as block units but as practices of piety and behavior, rituals of empowerment and purification, social systems of authority, read texts and retold stories—the glue between them never altogether solid. Political cultures are made mobile as texts and performances. In recognizing cultures as complex amalgams of practices, constantly in reproduction, assumptions of simple one-to-one correspondence between place and culture, nation and *Geist*, dissolve. The incessant movement of cultural goods and practices between societies becomes imaginable.[21]

Disembeddings and Displacements. Setting a cultural practice in motion, however, is never simply an act of transfer. Not everything can be extracted from place, and nothing can be extracted unchanged. For a cultural practice to move from one setting to another, it first has to be disembedded from its contexts. At times, goods and practices, set in motion, have carried complex structures of meaning with them. Elements of sacred ritual moved in this way between many of the native peoples of the Americas. Folkloric motifs were transported across local settings. Sacred relics traveled through early Christendom as "portable parcels" of Christianity. Alchemical practices moved across early modern Europe in the company of elaborate meaning systems of metallurgy and cosmology.[22]

In other instances, cultural practices were set in motion first by stripping away layers of meaning to leave something sparer and more portable, more mechanical, perhaps, or more abstract. The paring down of missionary teaching to a more easily exportable parcel is a classic example; the rapid circulation of technical information in the modern world is another. Other acts of disembedding work in just the opposite way, by emptying out one set of meanings and reinfusing another. When early European voyagers in the Pacific eagerly plucked up the fauna and flora that were new and exotic to them, shipping them home for cataloging and display, their first act of displacement was their translation of their living cargo into botanical objects. Objects in the European trade with India, as Sanjay Subrahmanyam has shown, were infused with radically novel aesthetic significance in the very act of making their transportation worthwhile. The brass and steel sewing machine arrived in colonial Sri Lanka, Nira Wickramasinghe demonstrates, already elaborately clothed as "modernity."[23]

Are some cultural practices too "sticky," too firmly set in context, to be disembedded from place? Are others in their nature somehow infinitely malleable, like the graffiti tags that one can find everywhere in the contemporary globe? Do some move as "modules," kits of pretested practice that can be reassembled anywhere, as Benedict Anderson once suggested was the case of modern nationalism?[24] Or is it wiser to think of every movement of cultural practice across space as entailing inescapably an uprooting, a potentially radical disembedding that was, from the first, infused with friction?

Routes and Itineraries. Just as no element of cultural practice moves intact, like a sealed parcel, none moves everywhere. The space through which cultural bits and pieces have moved was defined and routed by tracks that other practices made. New fashions in art and theater were carried along the itineraries of traveling artisans and itinerant production companies. Itinerant musicians, Celia Applegate shows, created the landscape of modern Western music. The labor strike traveled from its shipboard beginnings, when seamen had "struck" the sails rather than accept a bad bargain for the voyage, across the routes that sailors and, later, the new wage-laboring class voyaged. Captive peoples and coerced laborers carried cultural practices into distant settings. Trade routes, both widely flung and close at hand, were everywhere powerful conduits of cultural practices.[25]

Routes such as these were constantly under construction—expanding, contracting, and shifting location. But whether the historical reconstruction is of correspondence chains, trade networks, book distribution patterns, itinerant labor routes, or credit relationships, their patterns display both an astonishing extent of connection and striking unevenness. There were places of terrific centripetal force: Paris in the first years of the twentieth century and London in the 1930s were filled, as Susan Pennybacker has shown, by a world of radicals and exiles.[26] There are just as striking absences, multiple, nonintersecting networks, and disconnections. Even the oceans, as many scholars have shown, were anything but featureless, watery places. Inscribed by lines of trade and power, the space through which cultural practices moved was never flat but, rather, broken and uneven.

Fields of Contest and Collision. Set in motion along these routes, cultural practices collided with others. At times the result was violent imposition. The cultural projects of empire were saturated with coercion, from the erection of modernity's new iron cages of race to the hope of pious late-nineteenth-century American reformers to "kill" the cultural Indian within the indigenous Americans. The Inquisition and the *Kulturkampf*, repeated in endless variation, punctuate the history of modernity.[27] But still more common were the ways in which each new, traveling cultural practice generated a new arena of contest. This is Partha Chatterjee's reading of the ways in which the home-rule ambitions of the urban Indian bourgeoisie, rather than opening up as the modular, mail-order tool kit they may have envisioned, precipitated in subaltern India instead a vast and dense new field of struggle.[28] The very character of the gifts that the wealthy bestowed on their fellows in late antique Europe, as Peter Brown shows, was a field of contest. Elephants for the urban crowd or alms for the poor? Worlds of politics and cosmology hung on the difference. The American-made material goods that began to pour into Europe in the twentieth century, as Mary Nolan, Victoria de Grazia, and others have shown, set off not only new desires but also new anxieties and intense new rivalries.[29]

Out of those collisions of cultural practices came, finally, an astonishing variety of new cultural productions. Focused, as their sources often lead them to be, on efforts to police, contain, or resist the intruding cultural forms, historians are still learning to appreciate how generative

these collisions were. Irish and African dance forms, constructed continents apart, met in early-nineteenth-century New York City, as April
Masten shows, to create not a new common dance practice but a new
space of cultural contest, competition, display, betting, and even (at times)
racial cross-identification that was powerfully productive of cultural possibilities. Similarly, zoot suit fashions ricocheted through African American and Latino neighborhoods in the 1940s; reworked designer clothing
traveled from Paris to Central Africa; rock music invaded the world and
hip-hop has become a field of competition virtually everywhere.[30] These
instances of contest were not outliers. In churches and music halls, the
new moving materials—forms of piety, styles of preaching, virtuosities of
performance—sustained a field of ongoing and continuous competition. In
Peter Brown's late antique cities, centuries-long collision zones of classical,
Jewish, and Christian practices of justice, gift, and charity, what emerged
was an utterly novel social imagination of economy and belonging.

The fields where cultural practices collided, in short, were not merely
contact zones: middle grounds of accommodation, compromise, and
amalgamation. They were not merely sites of syncretic, functional reintegration; nor fields of fertile cross-pollination; nor occasions where dominant discourses might be disrupted—though they could be all of these.
Above all they were sites of assertion, rivalry, and contention, sometimes
violent and astonishingly generative.

Translations and Misunderstandings. As cultural practices trespassed
into new terrain, as new fields of contest formed, there came not only a
suddenly expanded field of possibilities but also the need for translation
and the possibilities of radical misunderstandings. Here, too, friction was
ubiquitous. Brokers and in-between figures, the *passeurs culturels* who
stood between competing worlds of practice, were critically important
figures. Translation, in its literal sense, was essential work as well, as
Douglas Howland has shown in the incorporation of nineteenth-century
liberal ideas into Japan—all the more so because it was necessarily imperfect, contested, and incomplete. Trading languages and pidgins developed everywhere, as Mae Ngai emphasizes, in efforts to fill in the gaps of
incomprehension; but they were only partly successful, as she shows, in
bridging the distance between competing words and meanings. In these
worlds of friction, the struggle for commensurability was part and parcel
of the phenomena of displacement.[31]

Sometimes the most potent forms of communication came through misreadings and misunderstandings. "Creative misunderstandings" played
a key role in the making of early modern science. They were the bridge-
work over which religious conversion often proceeded. They helped
shape the anxious core of "mimicry." At times, an event itself unfolded
on a stage so saturated with misreadings that they became a constitutive

part of the event itself. This is William Sewell's frame for what came to be called the fall of the Bastille. In Jocelyn Olcott's work, it helps us see the international gatherings of women's advocates not only as sites for alliances and disputes but also as theaters of translation and mistranslation as a world of feminist practices converged.[32]

Power and Structures. Finally, just as cultural practices moved across articulated space, and through the frictions of contest and translation, they moved across articulated relationships of power. Making visible those systems of power is one of the tasks of the new histories of cultures in motion. Imported cultural practices could be profoundly destructive, as the history of indigenous peoples in the Americas and Australasia gives so powerful a witnesses. They could be used as instruments of coercion and governance, as pawns in class and status rivalry, as entry wedges for the formation of new economies and markets, or as markers of state control. Asymmetries in power were the rule. When missionaries in nineteenth-century China sat for photographs in native dress and Chinese wage laborers put on trousers, there was no simple equivalence in these two, overtly parallel acts. When African or Asian householders began to purchase European-made products or American-made sewing machines as items of domestic display, both local and transnational systems of power came into play. Appropriation of the goods and practices of another could be an act of aggression, of surrender, of subversion, of alliance, or of satire. But it was never a neutral act of exchange.

The systems that put cultural practices in motion, finally, demobilized others within them. The ships and caravans of trade required not only enormous capital accumulation and fixed investments but also elaborate systems of slave and bound labor to make the global circulation of goods possible. The Pacific mining diaspora that Mae Ngai describes and the postslavery systems of global cotton production, whose rise Sven Beckert and Andrew Zimmerman have traced, depended on moving forms of semifree labor. In modern times, cultural practices would be carried by conscript armies and the flotillas of war. The very liberation of aluminum from the ground to become the post–World War II era's facilitator of speed and mobility, Mimi Sheller shows, depended on systems of immobility that limited labor movements in the Caribbean and sought to represent the region as fixed in the past. These structures of immobilization are not always easy to discern. But as in a modern airport, or in the warehouses of a globe-spanning Walmart, motion and structure, systems of cultural interaction and systems of power, have always been all intricately interlinked.[33]

Practices, disembeddings, routes, fields of contest, translations, and power: these do not exhaust the possibilities for a still richer and more adequate language for the displacements of culture. But they open potential avenues and provocations at a time when place and the conventional place-bound identities of historians have both become more problematic than before.

The essays of this volume are offered in a similar spirit: as examples, forays, and experiments in the interpretation of cultures in motion. The volume opens with three rich and suggestive essays on the circulation of cultural practices. In the first of them, "The Challenge Dance," April Masten looks at the ways in which Irish and African dance forms unexpected converged and collided in the taverns of New York City in the early nineteenth century. The virulent racism of the new nation's social order hangs over these settings, and Masten does not dismiss it. But racist minstrelsy was not the only phenomenon at work. What she shows, rather, is a cultural space and moment in which working-class blacks and whites saw enough likeness in their dance traditions to frame a space of public, popular competition: fierce in its intensity and fiercely productive of new cultural forms. In these licks and flings, in the hammering of these feet on a sounding shingle, in the dancers' stolen moves and the betting crowds she shows us, graphically, cultures in motion.

Across the continent of Europe, too, music was made in travel. Celia Applegate's "Musical Itinerancy in a World of Nations" probes a different world of cultural motion: that of the traveling musicians who produced European musical culture and haunted its literary imagination. Disparaged often as rootless musical peddlers, traveling performers carted new musical styles, forms, and techniques between local musical settings. By the end of the nineteenth century monstrously large choral festivals drew professionals and amateurs by the thousands. Out of all of this came new fields of rivalry and new forms of identity (even Brahms registered himself in his summer village as an "itinerant musician"), but also, she shows, the lineaments of a new German cultural nationalism, etched by these travels on the European landscape.

In the last essay in this section, "From *Patriae Amator* to *Amator Pauperum* and Back Again," Peter Brown explores the ways in which classical, Christian, and Jewish practices of public-spirited gifts, justice, and civic charity swirled together in the cities of late-antique Europe. Gift giving was a continuing obligation throughout these centuries; donation was part of the obligations of wealth. But over time, the forms and recipients of gift-giving practices changed dramatically. The poor displaced the citizenry; the horizons of charity expanded out beyond the locality; its social terms grew bleaker even as its spirit grew more exalted. In these shifting practices, Brown shows, new forms of "pastoral" power came into being. More than that, a classical form of social imagination was displaced by an understanding of wealth, poverty, and society that heralded the beginnings of Western modernity.

The next section turns to "itineraries of matter," as Pamela Smith calls it: to objects as traveling carriers of cultural practice and meaning. Smith's essay, "Knowledge in Motion," opens by plunging us into the heat and dangers of vermillion production in early modern Europe: the hours of firing, stirring, stoking, hammering, chemical manipulation, and anxious waiting, out of which came the red pigment so valued by painters and illuminators to bring blood to life. It was dangerous and exacting, like many artisanal practices, and the friction and resistance of materials were built into it. And yet the techniques of vermillion production traveled rapidly across early modern Europe (and beyond) together with the webs of interlinked homologies—an entourage of lizards, blood, gold, alchemical formulas, and vernacular knowledge—which formed, from matter and artisan labor up, the foundations of early modern science. Arabic texts and Aztec glass figure, too, in the global span of Smith's essay, as practices and ideas literally swirled through the early modern world.

Nira Wickramasinghe's "Fashioning a Market" turns the focus to an iconic object in the global commerce of the late nineteenth and early twentieth centuries. The American-made Singer machine was not only an early case of mass production for a global market, but one of the first cases in which a corporation tried to standardize the very sale and meaning of its products around the world. The sewing machine instantiated modernity, or tried to. Wickramasinghe's essay explores the success but also the deflections of that process, as colonial Sri Lankans incorporated the Singer machine into their society and culture. The sewing machine altered gender and commercial practices. It introduced a new market imaginary. But it also created a new field of contest over the very meaning of time and the multiple possibilities of modernity itself.

Mimi Sheller's exploration of the production and marketing of aluminum as a carrier of uneven global modernities drills down to the ways in which mobility and immobilization were simultaneously produced in the world of traveling commodities, transport systems, and tourism. Aluminum, the "speed metal," was packaged from the first as a perfectly liquid product whose gleaming surface would carry humans into a bold new frictionless era. Aluminum streamlined the world, even as it fed into infrastructures of transport, electrical power, labor, and communication. The very processes of its production were rooted in producing place, especially in the Caribbean where Alco and Alcan mined bauxite, transshipped alumina, and, surprisingly, also brought tourists on cruises through the region. Following the Aluminum Corporation of America's attempts to bridge the symbolic gap between its raw material sources and its seemingly placeless, modern product, "Speed Metal, Slow Tropics, Cold War" probes the ways in which in which circulation and structure were not only intertwined in these itineraries of matters but radically dependent on each other.

Our third section turns to the friction of translation and mistranslation across the contact zones of cultural difference. In "The True Story of Ah Jake," Mae Ngai takes us into a familiar site of cross-cultural tension: the gold fields of nineteenth-century California, where wealth hunger, violence, and escalating racist tension among Chinese, Anglo, and Mexican laborers seared the social landscape of the Pacific slope. All of these haunted the trial of the placer mine laborer Ah Jake. But behind a story of botched justice, Ngai shows us more: a traveling set of labor and social practices carried by Chinese workers across the nineteenth-century Chinese mining diaspora, the competing practices of justice that swirled around each other in the courtroom like rivers of fog, and, most importantly, the struggle to create a trading language between those cultures, a pidgin through which their incommensurability could be partially overcome. The truth of Ah Jake's story turns out to lie not in his guilt or innocence, Ngai suggests, but in taking seriously the frictions of translation into which he found himself flung.

The stakes in Harold Cook's "Creative Misunderstandings" were different, but they were no less serious. Sensing the "pulse" of an ailing person went back deep into the pasts of both European and Chinese medical practices, but on such radically different terms that historians of science and medicine have set them apart as independent developments. To sense the *mo* and to palpitate the pulse were wholly different ventures. Sir John Floyer, the British inventor of a "pulse watch" accurate enough to quantify and arithmeticize pulse counting, might be imagined only to have widened that disconnection. But in uncovering the texts and travels through which observations of Chinese sensing of the *mo* came into the ken of early modern medical innovators like Floyer, Cook shows us a much more arresting and nuanced picture. Following accounts of Chinese medical practices as they move through the writings of Jesuit missionaries and Dutch imperial administrators in Asia, imperfect translation layered upon imperfect translation, Cook shows that "creative misunderstandings" can travel, too, and often just as potently.

In the last essay of this section, the processes of translation spill out on a still more crowded stage. In "Transnational Feminism," Jocelyn Olcott reads the international women's year gathering at Mexico City in 1975 not simply as a place of alliance making, as feminists found voice and agenda across the world in the 1970s. It was also, she shows, a stage across which feminists moved with highly different understandings of time, event, and selves, a theater in which the problems of translating these into a common project were thickly present. Even the great confrontation between "first-" and "third-world" feminism that was said to define the conference turns out to have been a misreading. The generative force of the Mexico City gathering for modern global feminism does not dissolve in Olcott's reading. But she helps us see the conference not only as a struggle for power and unity but as a struggle between these globally gathered feminists for commensurability itself.

We conclude with two brief afterwords, opening out the themes of the volume. Bhavani Raman reminds us that the metaphors of reciprocal exchange that energize histories of the itinerant and the peripatetic must not keep the historian from recognizing the violence that also haunts encounters of culture. Helmut Reimitz, drawing on the work of the German sociologist Niklas Luhmann, reflects on the culture concept itself and the ways in which it, too, needs to be implicated in the moving practices that this volume explores.

To offer these essays as evidence of the dynamics of traveling cultural practices or the radical porousness of place might seem to suggest a field bound up in abstractions. To the contrary, the gift of these essays is to make these worlds of motion vivid, tangible, and, we hope, unforgettable.

PART I

The Circulation of Cultural Practices

CHAPTER 1

The Challenge Dance

BLACK-IRISH EXCHANGE IN ANTEBELLUM AMERICA

April F. Masten

IN HIS 1843 EDITION of *Traits and Stories of the Irish Peasantry*, Irish writer William Carleton described the accomplishments of Bob M'Cann, whom he encountered in a "remote and isolated" part of Ireland.[1] "Bob's crack feat," Carleton recalled, "was performing the *Screw-pin Dance*, of which we have only this to say, that by whatsoever means he became acquainted with it, it is precisely the same dance which is said to have been exhibited by some strolling Moor before the late Queen Caroline."[2] It is not surprising that Carleton recorded Bob's screw-pin dance in his volume since the love of dancing was considered a typical Irish trait, but his speculation that it had African roots was exceptional.

Carleton was unable to pinpoint a site of exchange—that time or place where African and Irish dancers shared steps, yet his details suggest multiple possibilities. He identifies the dance as "Bob's crack feat," which means it was his signature step, the humorous "brag" dance he performed to show off or compete with other dancers.[3] Bob might have made it up himself, but the name "screw-pin dance" suggests he learned it in a waterfront parish. Screw-pins were wooden spindles with which sailors and dockworkers tightened the bales of cotton they stowed in the holds of ships. Negro stevedores used to sing as they pushed the spindles around, and these *jack-screw* shanties were transposed into dance tunes by shipboard and dockside musicians. Sailors hailing from England, Ireland, Europe, Africa, and the Americas traded dances on sea and in port towns where ships docked and whites and blacks mixed freely.[4] By the 1840s, the U.S. South was the largest producer and exporter of cotton in the world. So Bob's step could have been an American dance transported to the coastal regions of Ireland in the body memory of ship passengers.

Or it might have been a Mediterranean hybrid transmitted straight from North Africa, another cotton-producing region, where the notorious Queen Caroline spent the early 1800s carousing with her Italian servants and a black dancer named Mahomet. During her trial for adultery in 1820, Caroline's defenders compared Mahomet's dance to "the Spanish bolero or the negro dance" performed at theaters in London and Dublin since the 1790s.[5] Censored by the Spanish aristocracy, the bolero was a sensuous peasant dance characterized by syncopated percussive steps, castanet clicks, and the pelvic twists common to many African dances.[6] Then again, Mahomet's dance could have been like Bob's and incorporated the steps of sailors and actors visiting North Africa. In any case, by linking the brag dance of an Irish rube to that of a strolling Moor, Carleton was not denying its Irishness. Rather, his observation suggests a contemporary awareness that peasant traditions were being produced around the globe by intercultural mixing and a diaspora that sent millions of Irish immigrants and African slaves to America.

This essay recovers the transnational origins of a distinctly American tradition of brag dancing—the challenge dance. Part theater, part sport, challenge dances were jigging contests got up among and between white and black men, and sometimes women. Emerging in the antebellum era alongside boxing, scores of elaborate and impromptu jig-dance competitions enlivened riverfront and port cities from New Orleans to Toronto. They took place on streets, docksides, and plantations, in market squares, taverns, and town halls, and in theaters and circus rings as part of white and blackface shows. Spontaneous and planned, spread by word of mouth or announced in print, dance matches drew large raucous crowds and were viewed, judged, and bet on like prizefights. Repeat winners of large wagers claimed the title, or named themselves, "Champion Dancer of the World." These matches were the product of the intersecting diasporas and cultural exchange of Irish and African emigrants moving through the Atlantic world.

Antebellum America's most famous rivals were a young African American dancer called Master Juba and a young Irish American dancer called Master Diamond who engaged in a series of challenge dances between 1843 and 1846. Master Juba, stage name of William Henry Lane, is a familiar figure in the history of American dance. Visiting New York in 1842, Charles Dickens saw him perform at Pete Williams's tavern in Five Points and immortalized him in his travelogue, *American Notes for General Circulation*. John Diamond (Dimond) is less well known. P. T. Barnum found him dancing about the wharves of New York in 1839, signed a contract with his father, and put him in the hands of a theatrical agent. After 1843 both men traveled with blackface minstrel troupes, and their challenge dancing is usually studied in that context, with Juba's moves providing evidence of African influences on American dance and Diamond's proving that white minstrels stole black material.[7] But scant attention has been paid to challenge dancing as a popular social practice engaged in by ordinary folk for sociability, sport, entertainment, status, and profit. Promoted professional challenge dancing relied on this practice as a source for dancers and point of access for audiences. What is obscured when the challenge dance is looked at solely through the lens of minstrelsy is the formative intertwining of Irish and African culture that brought Diamond and Juba into competition.

The jig dancing parodied in blackface minstrel shows of the postbellum era was quite different from that which emerged earlier in a variety of settings. Challenge dancers swirled across racial and ethnic boundaries, not erasing those lines but helping to construct new social practices and spaces. Even when they blacked up, their steps were called "a wonder," "beautiful," and "intricate," words rarely used to describe low comedy. Using the influences at hand, black and white challenge dancers studied, adopted, and transformed each other's steps and moves, jointly forging a distinctive dance style and tradition. Their matches conveyed a national identity shared by lower-class whites and blacks that later forms of blackface minstrelsy erased.

White influences on black dance are rarely explored, despite the fact that Irish jigging was pervasive among slaves and free blacks in early America. The spread of European language, food, music, dance, and religion to Africans is usually dismissed as the inevitable consequence of racial slavery.[8] But as Hazel Carby reminds us, "the migratory histories and cultures of other peoples . . . are sometimes carried by and sometimes expressed through political and cultural vessels marked as black."[9] Master Juba was hailed as an exceptional jig dancer and Master Diamond as an outstanding Negro dancer, designations that suggest pervasive, inextricable black-Irish exchange. Nowhere better can this magnificent global crosscurrent be seen than in the steps, movements, rhythms, musical accompaniments, dress, stage names, advertisements, venues, and vocabulary of challenge dancers.

The term "jig" originally referred to a dance of Irish origins, yet in nineteenth-century America it became synonymous with Negro dancing. Negro jig dancers were blacks who adapted Celtic culture to their own purposes; they were also whites, sometimes called "nigger dancers," who wore blackface or adopted the black jigging style. Such monikers were not simply demeaning; they were denotative. Negro jigging pervaded the Northeast in the 1830s, by which time gradual emancipation laws had ended slavery in the region and an agricultural depression after the Napoleonic War had forced over 800,000 people to leave Ireland for America.[10] Thrown together in the slum districts of port towns, these black and Irish migrants enjoyed and developed creolized styles of music and dance. In this context, newspapers, playbills, market books, urban guides, and other texts employed the term "nigger dancer" to describe anyone whose movement and musical style asserted slave-like characteristics, that is, a mixture of African and Celtic or English elements.[11] Beyond referring to African Americans, the term incorporated prejudice against lower-class whites, particularly Irish immigrants. It signified the sort of lowborn whites whom blacks interacted with and vice versa, and the way they were both elevated and disadvantaged by their connection to each other. Masters Diamond and Juba matured and met as dancers in this complex, symbiotic world. But as suggested by William Carleton, Bob M'Cann, and Mahomet, the blending of Irish and African culture that produced their dancing rivalry began much earlier and elsewhere.

SHARED TRADITIONS

It is impossible to know the first time an African captive shuffled to a Celtic tune or an Irish sailor reeled to an African beat, voluntarily or under duress. Such exchanges began on sea and land, in Africa and the British Isles, and in every metropole and colonial outpost where blacks interacted with whites.[12] They flourished throughout the transatlantic world, but most spectacularly in Jacksonian America where dancing was pervasive among all classes. Journalist George Foster in 1849 called it "a universal human instinct." Almost every militia group, firemen's company, art association, trade union, neighborhood tavern, upscale brothel, and political organization regularly held balls or shindigs, and these social dances often ended with a dancing match, called a breakdown or dance for eels.[13] During the financial recession of 1837–43, these informal dance matches proliferated alongside commercial acts financed and promoted by saloon and theater managers. In this environment, incoming dance practices collided with local traditions, creating something fresh and exciting.[14]

Underlying this cultural exchange was not just the poverty and migration that brought black and Irish groups together but compatibilities in their two dance traditions. Across Africa and Ireland, people danced with regional differences in their movement and musical styles, but they maintained a conceptual approach to the arts that created commonalities.[15] Irish and African emigrants shared a love of dancing, complex rhythmic patterns in their music, similar dance formats and techniques, and an emphasis on training with a master, improvisation, and competition. Dancing was also universal among common people—young and old, male and female—who danced for entertainment, ritual, and sport at weddings, funerals, feasts, holy days, and other celebrations.[16] These similarities made it easier for Irish and African migrants to creatively merge their dance practices.

But their traditions also included formal differences (figure 1.1). In African dance the action is falling, while in Irish it is rising. African dancers are pulled to the earth; the dancer works with gravity using the body's weight to accent the rhythmic beats of the dance. Irish dancers rebound from the earth; the dancer dances underneath the body, trapping each note of the music on the floor as if the body were weightless. Nineteenth-century African dancers emphasized angulated postures and gestures, performing with relaxed knees and separating hip, torso, and shoulder moves. Nineteenth-century Irish dancers accentuated foot and legwork, keeping the upper body erect and moving from the hips down with relaxed arms.[17] These differences were important to challenge dancers, whose success depended on not just precision in performing traditional steps but also an aptitude for improvisation. They represented new moves with which to create novel steps. They gave black and Irish dancers a reason to interact.

Competitive dance can be traced to many societies, but the dominant features of antebellum challenge dancing came from western Africa and Ireland.[18] In both places, dance competitions took place between men and women, or sometimes dancers of the same sex, within a circle of potential dancers and musicians. The *nzuba* or juba was a dance of skill and courting brought to the Americas by African slaves.[19] In a customary juba witnessed in 1844 Cuba, a female dancer advanced and "commencing a slow dance, made up of shuffling of the feet and various contortions of the body; thus challenges a rival from among the men. One of these, bolder than the rest, after awhile steps out, and the two then strive which shall first tire the other; the woman performing many feats which the man attempts to rival, often excelling them, amid the shouts of the rest. A woman will sometimes drive two or three successive beaux from the ring, yielding her place at length to some impatient belle, who has been meanwhile looking on with envy at her success."[20]

The juba was absorbed and altered by white competitive dancers who lived alongside slaves in North America. "Towards the close of an evening," observed an Englishman traveling through Virginia in 1775, "when the company are pretty well tired with country-dances, it is usual to dance jigs; a practice originally borrowed, I am informed, from the Negroes. . . . These dances are without any method or regularity: a gentleman and lady stand up, and dance about the room, one of them retiring, the other pursuing, then perhaps meeting, in an irregular fantastical manner. After some time, another lady gets up, and then the first lady must sit down, she being, as they term it, cut out: the second lady acts the same part which the first did, till somebody cuts her out. The gentlemen perform in the same manner."[21] Unfamiliar with challenge dancing,

FIGURE 1.1: Although these figures are only "stock" images used to decorate play-bills and programs, the similar poses are striking, as is the difference in the upper body, with the African American dancer's chest curving toward the earth and the Irishman's chest extending toward the sky. *Specimens of Theatrical Cuts: Being Facsimiles, in Miniature, of Poster Cuts; Comprising Colored and Plain Designs, Suitable for Theatrical, Variety and Circus Business* [Philadelphia: Ledger Job Printing Establishment, ca. 1869], Harvard Theatre Collection, Houghton Library, Harvard University.

FIGURE 1.2: *Moín* is Irish for "turf, peat, bog-land or moor," on which jigs were often danced by country folk. The *Moínín* dancer may have lifted her skirts to keep them dry as well as to show off her steps. From Sampson Towgood Roch, [1757-1847], *A piper plays for a couple dancing.* The collections of Ulster Folk and Transport Museum, Northern Ireland, © National Museums Northern Ireland. Reproduced with permission of National Museums Northern Ireland.

the observer did not recognize the dancers' "irregular fantastical" movements as the formal steps of a dance, but Irish jig dancers did.

All nineteenth-century Irish jigs were competitive, but Ireland's counterpart to the juba was the *moínín* or moneen jig (figure 1.2). According to contemporary accounts, the dancing couple faced each other inside a circle of spectator-dancers "scarcely more than two yards each way." The footwork was lively, and the woman held up her skirts to facilitate the steps. After each step, "the dancers changed places, and moving slowly for a few seconds, commenced another which threw the proceeding one quite into the shade, and, as a matter of course, called out a louder 'bravo!' and a wilder 'hurro!' " Without causing any interruption, "doors were slipped under the feet of the dancers, which now beat an accompaniment to the music, as if a couple of expert drummers had suddenly joined the orchestra." Like the juba, Irish jigs required stamina, as one factor was tiring out or "dancing down" one's partner or fellow couples. One Irishman described the dancing as "so violent . . . the very recollection of it makes me feel as if the barometer was some two hundred in the shade." Another said that "the girls danced the jig facing the boys and that the lads couldn't stop dancing 'on point of honour.' "[22] Carried to North America by the Irish diaspora, this dance was taken up and altered by African American dancers for whom such violent freedom was a familiar element of dance.

When new popular dances or dancing styles reach people with strong dance and music traditions, they are merged into the repertoire and subtly changed by each dancer's knowledge of steps, body type, and musical tastes. Dance and music were inextricably intertwined in Irish and African dance practice. In Ireland melodies distinguished dances just as rhythms differentiated them in Africa. Irish dancers *felt* the melody; African dancers *danced* the drums. Good dancers did not just follow the music; they embellished it with their rhythms; they played a duet with the musician. Nor did good musicians just keep time by playing the tune; they responded to the dancer, inserting rhythmic and melodic passages of their own. In Ireland and Africa a friendly rivalry between dancers and musicians could be heard in the increased tempo and intricate patterns of their embellishments.[23] The musical instruments and techniques used to accompany challenge dancing in America were products of both regions. Fiddles (played against the chest) and banjos had African precursors (figure 1.3). Irish dancers also whistled or hummed the tune, a *sean nós* (old style) technique known as "lilting," and black dancers created rhythmic sounds by striking the body with the hands and the foot on the floor, an African American technique known as "patting" juba. These accompaniments were passed from one group to the other. In the 1830s, a travel writer in Buffalo noted that "the beaten jig time" of the Irish boys dancing on the wharves "was a rapid patting on the fore thighs," while a journalist at a Philadelphia market observed New Jersey slaves dancing "while some darkies whistle."[24]

Despite its ubiquity in both communities, dancing was an acquired rather than natural skill. Almost everyone in nineteenth-century Ireland and Africa trained with a dancing master, and not everyone who danced well was considered "a dancer." In Africa, the dancing master held a high social position and as the chosen representative of his people was responsible for their prestige. Expert dancers identified their status through body adornment, drawing from their environment whatever finery it offered them—animal skins, feathers, shells, pigments—with which they costumed and colored their bodies. But only "title holders" held the privilege of wearing the "cloth" of their clan or dancing society.[25]

In Ireland, the dancing master, although itinerant, represented the district in which he taught and respected the territory of others. Irish brag dancers polished their shoes and converged on patterns (patron saint's day fairs) in the shabby vests, wide cravats, or other raiment identified with their local gang or faction. The dancing master advertised his station with a "castor or Caroline hat" above and "pumps and stockings" below.

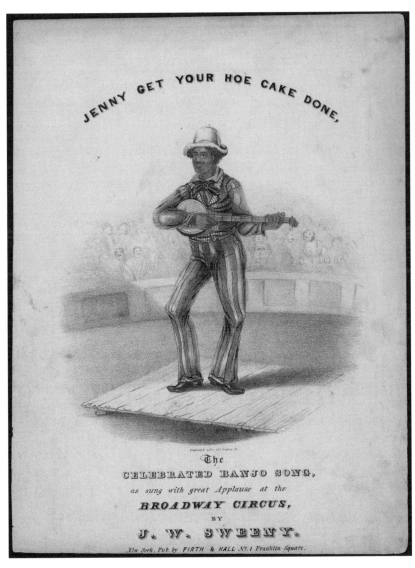

FIGURE 1.3: Banjo player Joel Walker Sweeny is depicted standing on a dancer's shingle ballast inside a circus ring. That shingle and his heeled boots suggest that he accompanied his playing with percussive dance steps. Dancers preferred musicians who knew how to dance, and musicians liked dancers who could play. From J. W. Sweeny, "Jenny Get Your Hoe Cake Done" [New York, 1840], Sheet Music—Negro Minstrels. Courtesy of American Antiquarian Society.

"A friendly rivalry existed between all dancing masters," observed historian Brendán Breathnach. "Casual meetings at fairs and sporting events would lead to challenges when both would dance it out in public to the joy and edification of the spectators and, frequently, without any eventual decision." Victors called out "Who dar spoil?" and held their place until beaten. Only when two dancers were "wieing" for a parish did the competition demand a final decision.[26]

Competitiveness was an attitude instilled in young dancers by African and Irish teachers. Many African dances incorporated martial skills appropriate to age and sex, such as the control and discipline young men needed in warfare. In Central Africa, fighter-dancers trained inside a ring of singers, noted historian T.J. Desch Obi, "dancing and swaying to the music as they squared off." Some young African women also became masters of the "art of combat."[27] Similarly, youths in Ireland learned martial games or sports along with dancing and deportment and, according to eyewitness accounts, bold Irish girls responded with exuberance to their triumphs: "'Whoo! Judy, that's the girl; handle your feet, avourneen; that's it, acushla! stand to me! Hurroo for our side of the house!'" Both Irish and African boys were also taught stick fighting (or cudgel play) to encourage physical and mental agility and nerve.[28] This prowess was evident in their every step and encouraged bragging and teasing, which often led to fighting among male dancers.

The challenge element in dance represented self-assertion and communal identity to both groups. In Ireland it was "not unusual for crack-dancers from opposite parishes, or from distant parts of the same parish, to meet and dance against each other for the victory," affirmed Carleton. "But as the judges in those cases consist of the respective friends or factions of the champions, . . . many a battle is fought in consequence of such challenges." Young Irish men danced and fought to impress each other and attract the girls. In fact, the African American word "shin-dig" for dance came from the shin-kicking brawl or "shindy" that often ended an Irish ball.[29]

Group dances were more common in western Africa, but in some regions large numbers of dancers met to compete in a *Bantaba*, or area cleared for dancing. One dancer entered the ring, danced for a few minutes, and was challenged by another who took over. Such spirited displays singled out the best dancers among the young men, who often became leaders of their peers in other social and political contexts. They also gave each dancer a chance to show off for the young women. However, the skill and swagger important to African dance could lead to humiliation (if the dancer could not back up his claims) and aggression, or even violence.[30]

While competitive dancing was a social recreation, exceptional dancers were sometimes rewarded for their expertise. Sketches of Ireland written between 1682 and 1850 describe adjudicated jigging contests called "cake dances," which were held in some rural regions until the late nineteenth century. It was customary among the poor whose usual fare was "potatoes and milk" to spare "some few halfpence" from the household purse to dance for a cake made of oatmeal and sugar. Cake dances were held in an open area or crossroads next to an alehouse. Young and old of both sexes, for miles around, came to enjoy "the pleasures of the cake," which might include "dancing, courting, coshering [chatting], whiskey-drinking, card-playing, fighting, and sometimes a little ribbonism [anti-landlord-class agitation]." The alewife, whose trade was enhanced by the festivities, often provided the cake, but the dancers paid the piper (a penny a jig). The cake was won by the dancing couple who held out the longest or by the best dancer, who presented it to "his favourite *cailín*" to cut up and divide among all the company. In North America, African slaves carried on the tradition of jig dancing for a cake (made of cornmeal and cabbage) long after their Irish counterparts gave it up. They also turned African-style competitions, such as promenading with a pail of water held on the head, into "cakewalks" to entertain the master and mistress (who sometimes provided the cake).[31]

All types of aesthetic dueling could be found in Africa and Ireland. Singing, dancing, music making, storytelling, and joking contests were used to entertain, teach, and test. Dancing was a mental competition with the body. Both African and Irish dancers observed, imitated, and responded to physical movements with inventions of their own. One competitive strategy used by both was the combining of skill and wit. A difficult, out-of-the-ordinary move (like Bob's crack feat) communicated humor and, if it provoked laughter, could tilt the balance of support in a dancer's favor. At dance contests in Ireland sometimes "the best dancer, and sometimes the archest wag" took the cake. In Africa, poking fun could be done respectfully or could be harsh or vulgar (like Mahomet's dance), depending on the context.[32] Meeting at Atlantic crossroads in the old world and new, artistic competitive dancers incorporated hornpipes into African jubas and hip thrusts into Irish jigs to provoke hilarity and vanquish their opponents.

GENEALOGY OF CHALLENGE DANCING

Nineteenth-century travelers interested in seeing America's peasant dance were taken to sugar houses in the South and oyster cellars in the North to watch African Americans dancing Irish sets, sometimes called jubas (figure 1.4). In a "set dance" four couples faced off and performed the same steps for three changes of music or figures. Each "step" lasted eight bars of music or sixteen if doubled, that is, repeated on the other foot.

FIGURE 1.4: Men and women dancing a "set" or "juba" at Pete Williams's tavern dance house. A.B. Frost illustration from Charles Dickens, *American Notes* [London: Chapman & Hall, 1871].

The dances were jigs, reels, and hornpipes. Jigs were considered Irish and danced to tunes in 6/8 time; reels Scottish, danced to 2/2 or 4/4 time; and hornpipes English, danced to 2/4 or reel time. A set combined two or more of these dance tunes, thereby encouraging the dancers to think in both jig and reel time, which share a duple downbeat but have syncopated internal rhythms. Black dancers and musicians already versed in polyrhythm heard the step dancer cross the fiddler's 2s with his 3s or vice versa and added their own complexities and syncopations to the percussive footwork they learned from affable sailors, young mistresses, and fellow servants.[33] They then shared these steps with white dancers, who revised them yet again, and so on, back and forth.

Challenges came at the end of the set or night of dancing. British dancers called all step dances that featured the percussive accompaniment of the dancer's feet to the music, regardless of the measure, hornpipes, while Americans often called them jigs. They shared the term "breakdown," which referred to "a riotous dance, with which balls are often terminated" and "a dance in the peculiar style of the negroes." During the final change of a set, usually a hornpipe, the favored local step dancer or couple (figure 1.5) came forward to exhibit his or her prowess and compete with their peer group. The woman usually danced with a "delicate vivacity that is equally gentle and animated," while the man "could express his joy of dancing through vigorous and agile movements."[34] Because the improvisational part of the set allowed the couple to separate and dance with more rhythmic and physical freedom, African Americans related it to "breaking the beat or breaking the pattern," which is used in Kongo dance "to break on into the world of the ancestors."[35] In 1841 a New York newspaper correspondent attended a "Ball" in New Brunswick, New Jersey, where he saw white couples performing sets: "The dancing—no light fantastic work—but good wholesome breaking down," he approvingly noted, "in which the great point seemed to be, who should the soonest tire the other down [in] a variety of shuffles, break-downs and jig steps."[36] With these three words the writer related the complex history of this competitive dance to his readers: shuffles referred to African style close-to-the-floor footwork, break-downs to the dynamic rhythmic moves of competitive dancers from both cultures, and jig steps to the lift-from-the-floor that characterized Irish dance.

Out of these couple dances leaped the professional challenge dancer, who specialized in exhibition hornpipes and breakdowns. In 1840, William Carleton described the male step dancer of his youth in County Tyrone, Ireland. After selecting "his own sweetheart," and assuming a station on the floor so "that both should face the fiddler," he commenced, "quietly at the outset; gradually he begins to move more sprightly." Then "Up he bounds in a fling or a caper—crack go the fingers—cut and treble

FIGURE 1.5: The dancing couple in "The Sabbath among Slaves" is in the third figure of a set, accompanied by banjo and another dancer/musician patting juba. Other festivities include a blend of Celtic and African entertainments—gambling, hurling, drinking, and wrestling. From *Narrative of the Life and Adventures of Henry Bibb, An American Slave, Written by Himself* [New York: 1849]. Courtesy of the American Antiquarian Society.

go the feet, heel and toe, right and left. Then he flings the right heel up to the ham, up again the left, the whole face in a furnace-heat of ecstatic delight."[37] Charles Dickens's 1842 description of the African American dancer (figure 1.6) he saw in Five Points, New York, was much the same. Impressed by the reserved demeanor of the mulatto female partners, he bemoans the languishing length of the set: "when suddenly the lively hero dashes in to the rescue. . . . Single shuffle, double shuffle, cut and cross-cut: snapping his fingers, rolling his eyes, turning in his knees, presenting the backs of his legs in front, spinning about on his toes and heels . . . dancing with all sorts of legs or no legs. . . . [Until], having danced his partner off her feet, and himself too, he finishes by leaping gloriously on the bar-counter, and calling for something to drink."[38] This sort of dancing, this combining of Irish crosscuts and African turned-in knees, is what made Diamond and Juba jig-dance champions.

STREET CHALLENGES

Before the 1830s, dance matches in America were mostly casual, spontaneous events at private social gatherings and public assemblies such as fairs, militia training days, and horse races, which generally included an outdoor "frolic" with drinking, eating, dancing, gambling, and fight-

FIGURE 1.6: Master Juba blacked up for an "American dance" at Royal Vauxhall Gardens in London, where he performed Negro breakdowns as "Boz's Juba" with Pell's Serenaders. But in this image, his attire (he wore a canary yellow vest and jacket) and the position of his arms (down by his sides) suggest he was dancing an exhibition hornpipe choreographed to impress his overwhelmingly female British audience. *Illustrated London News*, August 5, 1848. An American paper claimed, "An Englishman never dances above his waist. His feet may cut pigeon wings, or his legs go into vibrations, but the head and heart of the man never gets above prose and buttons." *Life in Boston and New York*, October 1, 1853, 3. Harvard Theatre Collection, Houghton Library, Harvard University.

ing.[39] Following 1808, with gradual manumission and rising immigration, these public festivities drew an increasing number of blacks and lower-class whites in small towns and cities across the Northeast. Clergymen, politicians, industrialists, and mobs of white nativists curtailed this interracial capering through sermons, laws, and violence.[40] But rather than disappear altogether, it coalesced into particular forms and moved to particular venues. Until the Civil War, black and white competitive dancers met and worked in the streets, theaters, and taverns of lower-class districts throughout the United States.

The first reported instances of "public 'negro dancing' " or challenge dancing as a trade, as opposed to "one of their pastimes at home on the barn-floor, or in a frolic," took place at dockside markets in New York, Boston, Philadelphia, Buffalo, and other port and riverfront cities. According to municipal histories and market books, slaves who had leave of their masters for "Pinkster" or some other festival would gather up and bring to market in their skiffs anything they could sell for a few pence or shillings—"roots, berries, herbs, yellow or other birds, fish, clams, oysters, &c.," recorded historian Thomas De Voe in 1862. And "as they had usually three days holiday, they were ever ready, by their 'negro sayings or doings,' to make a few shillings more. So they would be hired by some joking butcher or individual to engage in a jig or break-down . . . and those that could and would dance soon raised a collection." The preferred dancing place in New York City was a cleared space at Catherine Slip east of the fish market in front of Burnel Brown's Ship Chandlery where passengers gathered to catch the ferry to Brooklyn and sailors came to buy provisions. In Philadelphia it was Callohill Street in the Northern Liberties, where "shipcarpenters from Kensington" battled with "butchers from Spring Garden" on Saturday nights and "Jersey niggers [danced] against Philadelphia darkies" on Sunday mornings.[41]

Slave or free, market dancers were not strangers to city residents. They were regular hucksters known by name to the German butchers, Irish fishmongers, and other vendors and shoppers who purchased their goods. "Among the most famous in their day was '*Ned*' (Francis), a little wiry negro slave, belonging to Martin Ryerson," a New York butcher told De Voe, and "another named Bob Rowley, who called himself '*Bobolink Bob*,' belonging to William Bennett, and *Jack*, belonging to Frederick De Voo, all farmers on Long Island." Performing music, dance, or other feats in public for small change, called "busking" in Europe, was not peculiar to American blacks. Two Irish American boys—Dick Sliter, "precocious as a jig dancer," and George Harrington, who "beat time with his hands expertly"—haunted the steamboat wharves of Buffalo in the 1830s, exhibiting "their peculiar talent to admiring crowds, who would strew small coin around the feet of the dancer." Produce vendors and tavern keepers patronized street dancers for their own entertainment and to draw in potential customers. This public dancing developed over time into contests set up by the participants. "The large amount collected in this way after a time produced some excellent 'dancers,' " said De Voe, "in fact, it raised a sort of strife for the highest honors, *i.e.*, the most cheering and the most collected in the 'hat.' "[42] Favorite dancers came again and again to exhibit their skills, which encouraged competition. Then dancers from other regions, seeing that there was money to be made, arrived to contend for the prizes.

Street dancers could be seen almost any day of the week, but their numbers swelled on Sundays as black people congregated "with their trifles to sell, and their friends to meet or visit." Irish immigrants and their children were there too, enjoying the familiar format and unusual content of the dancing competition. To demonstrate their skill, all the dancers who participated in "the regular 'shake-down' " at Catharine Market had to confine their steps to a "board" or "shingle" of five to six feet long and of large width. They worked "several together in parties," each bringing along a favorite shingle ("with its particular spring in it") as part of his or her stock in trade. "Their music or time was usually given by one of their party, which was done by beating their hands on the sides of their legs and the noise of the heel."[43] While patting juba was an African American technique, dancing on a board was an Irish practice used to demonstrate the dancer's agility and enhance the sound of the percussive steps. "The great effort was to exhibit all varieties of steps and dances, without once quitting the prostrate door on which the exhibitor took his stand," recalled Irish writer Shelton Mackenzie in 1854: "The jumps, the 'cuttings' in the air, the bends, the dives, the wrigglings, the hops." In Ireland and America, people danced on ship decks, cart boards, tabletops, cellar doors, wooden ballasts, and hogshead barrels because of their small size.[44]

Market dancers identified themselves regionally by their appearance and style of dance. Long Islanders at Catherine Market tied their hair "up in a cue, with dried eel-skin" (harvested on Long Island) or "combed it about their heads and shoulders, in the form of a wig, then all the fashion." These dancers were "placed 'up head' in this great and nimble art" by their close association with white musicians and dancers, as demonstrated by their excellent use of shingles and the genre paintings of William Sydney Mount (figure 1.7). New Jersey contenders were "known by their suppleness and plaited forelocks tied up with tea-lead." These dancers were successful too, observed De Voe, but "not so early accomplished as their Long Island friends."[45] Mostly from Tappan, they were probably

FIGURE 1.7: Black and white dancers and musicians in a barn on Long Island enjoying a breakdown. In the heat of the moment the white dancer throws his arms above his head, while the mulatto gentleman on the sidelines closely watches his feet and the child adds his own rhythms. William Sydney Mount, *Dance of the Haymakers*, 1845. Reproduced with permission from The Long Island Museum of American Art, History, & Carriages. Gift of Mr. and Mrs. Ward Melville, 1950.

house slaves who had access to such amenities as dancing lessons (and bags of tea tied with lead).

Former house slave, tavern keeper, and competitive dancer Sylvia Dubois learned to jig in the 1810s at weekly frolics in the homes of plantation owners and from her grandfather, a master dancer from Princeton. Her prize steps were "the eleven times, the twelve times, and the thirteen times. . . . These were the steps my grandfather, Harry Compton, used to like, and all other good dancers," she explained to C. W. Larison in 1883. The names of the steps represented the difficult intricacy of the footwork. "Why, when I was young, I'd cross my feet ninety-nine times in a minute and never miss the time, strike heel or toe with equal ease, and go through the figures as nimble as a witch." She disapproved of the "stomp and jump and hop and run" and turning "heels over head" of younger blacks, just as Irish dancing masters discouraged their students from "flinging the hands about" or "the cutting of such acrobatic steps as *léim an bhradáin* (the salmon leap)." Dubois's favorite step, a rapid crossing of one foot over the other called "cutting" or "cover the buckle," figured prominently in old Irish jigs.[46]

"House-slaves," like Dubois, "wielded considerable influence on the others," recalled ex-slave Austin Steward. But not all New Jersey competitors danced the same way. Field-hand-style steps were conspicuous among public dancers too. On Sunday mornings in 1839, "troops" of Jersey slaves from the countryside danced against city blacks at Philadelphia's Callowhill Street Market, where as many as sixty contestants assembled along with an integrated crowd of spectators. "They have different styles of dancing from our darkies," reported a New York correspondent, but the "big licks" (combinations of moves) and "flat foot heel" work put in by these dancers "was no way slow I can tell you." These steps developed into the style known in the United States as flatfoot and in Ireland as sean nós dancing. Unlike step dancers who featured a rapid striking of the toe on the ground, these dancers worked heel and toe in a style much closer to the "gliding, dragging, or shuffling steps" of African dance.[47] Perceiving these steps like dialects, contemporaries could easily distinguish between the field hands' flatfoot breakdowns and the house slaves' fancy footwork.

The success of Long Island and New Jersey challengers at Catharine Market (figure 1.8), where "in the end, an equal division of the proceeds took place," brought "our city negroes down there," recalled a partisan New Yorker, "who, after a time, even exceeded them both." But unlike their country-based counterparts, "if money was not to be had 'they would dance for a bunch of eels or fish.'" It was sensible for city blacks with no access to domestic garden produce or wild fish and game to dance for eels, popular fare among country people in England and America. Working for food was common among performers of every ilk. At the Pantheon, a tavern on Houston Street, white professionals received "a frying of eels in compensation" for their songs and dances, one patron recalled, as that was "the habitual recompense at that time in the places of this class in New York." In fact out west in the 1830s, "Eels" was the nickname for all Yankees black and white.[48]

Dancing for eels and fish was the urban equivalent of cake dancing. "The stakes were catfish [in Philadelphia] . . . placed in a basket those that were skinned, and those that were not, in tubs, and as fast as either party won, were carried off by the wenches and sold, and the proceeds divided." This division of the winnings replicated the trade economy of many lower-class families whose survival depended on keeping and circulating any money acquired within their communities. "Most of those who have families, save up their odd change thro' the week, and then on Sundays proceed to the market, purchase the largest bunch they can find

DANCING FOR EELS, 1820 CATHARINE MARKET.

FIGURE 1.8: The musician keeps time by patting juba for the dancer, whose arm positions and clothes suggest he is performing a sailor's hornpipe. There is no need for a shingle as he is dancing on the wooden dock. The man kneeling behind the performers is possibly a judge counting steps. An interracial crowd of spectators cheers from the back, while the butcher-sponsors enjoy watching the dance upfront. Folk drawing of "Dancing for Eels, 1820 Catherine Market." © 1973 Sotheby's, Inc. 23.

and challenge the first darkey they see with a similar bunch, to dance the best in three trials, who take both. They then appoint judges—take off their coats, and generally give another darkey two eels each out of the bunches to beat the juber for them. And then the sport commences."[49] By providing the eels themselves, market dancers became their own sponsors. *They* paid the musician and held the stakes, thereby controlling the performance, the betting around the matches, and the divvying of the proceeds among all who participated.

Written as a humorous urban "travelogue" in 1842, this account of "Dancing for Eels" unwittingly recovered the training (teaching and testing) of black challenge dancers. "The next trial of moment" took place between a couple of youths while "their daddies being their backers" sang and beat time for them. The great "deal of sweating" and "some new and mighty big licks put in by both of the young ones" poised them to face, eventually, the present champion: a professional dancer who called himself Caesar. "Never been known to lose" and "generally winning enough to last him thro' the week," Caesar "makes his appearance with a shingle under his arm," expecting to show "his science" to anyone interested "for the sum of three cents." Young women were among the challengers too: "at the same time two wenches engaged in a similar dance, a young nigger beating time to the tune of take your time, Miss Lucy." The tune's name called to mind male "wench dancers" who warbled and danced to "Lucy Long" in blackface and women's clothes. However, in the end, what the story conjures up by including young men and old, women, and boys is more than racist or sexist humor. It is the picture of several generations of African Americans passing on the jig-dance trade.

This image enriches our limited knowledge of African American dancers like William Henry Lane, who was said to have learned much of his art from a master dancer named "Uncle Jim" Lowe, "a natural jig and reel dancer of extra-ordinary skill," and whose stepfather Zachary Reed also danced at Pete Williams's tavern.[50] Like their dances, Lane, Lowe, and Reed had Irish names, which suggests Master Juba and his mentors considered themselves black-Irish. Although whites identified African Americans by race and race largely determined their lives, many blacks with European forebears retained a sense of ethnic identity along with cultural practices. Free blacks often named themselves, and it is possible these surnames came from unions between black men and Irish women, a not uncommon coupling in lower-class districts of antebellum cities.[51] But even if they represented the residue of slavery, such retentions suggest that black-Irish alliances were important to African American dancers. They were also important to the careers of Irish American dancers.

THE CIRCULATION OF STEPS

These challengers captivated young Diamond, who began "Negro Dancing" at theaters in New York, Boston, and Philadelphia in 1839. He also performed for Welch & Bartlett's Circus, an equestrian troupe that erected wooden walls and a canvas roof in a vacant lot on Broadway.[52] Diamond was born in 1823, probably to first-generation Irish immigrants, as his father did not speak English. Juba was a few years younger, probably born free and raised by his African American mother and stepfather. Both dancers were in their teens when they first competed, and promoters drew attention to their age and their skill by calling them "Master." The title also denoted their "dependency" on parents or guardians, with whom troupe or theater managers contracted for their services.[53] Child performers (figure 1.9 and 1.10) were common, celebrated sights in North American cities where working life began early and over half the population was younger than twenty in 1840. These young dancers attracted young, diverse audiences to their shows.

Master Diamond's signature step was the "Camp Town Hornpipe," named after a suburb of Philadelphia (bordered by the Delaware River and Callohill Street to the south) notorious for its taverns, brothels, and clans of "rough and tumble" fighters.[54] Among the "UNHEARD-OF, OUT-LANDISH and INIMITABLE LICKS" touted in his playbills were the "regular double shuffle" (three beats made by a step and two strokes with the opposite foot, moving out and back), "locomotive imitations" (sounds created by sliding or dragging the feet along the floor), "rattling" (rapid-fire toe and heel taps), and running on his heels. Called "[t]he very beau ideal of a little Long Island darkie," Diamond also reproduced the format of market competitions in his "extravaganzas" with young Irish dancer-actor Barney Williams, who patted juba while he jigged on a shingle.[55]

Itinerant circus and theater dancers spread these creolized steps throughout North America. "About 1842 John Diamond came with a circus" to Nashville, recalled James Thomas, an ex-slave and barber turned Tennessee businessman. "Toward the close of the performance a platform was brought out and Diamond, [who] came in black, asked the Master in the band to play 'Camptown Hornpipe' (figure 1.11) or some other dance. He would walk around the board, then jump on it, and dance in a manner as though he would pick it up with his feet, jump-off, again walk around, and say something nigger like and dance again. The people thought that the best part of the show." Sitting in the stands beside Thomas were Irish immigrants (who moved inland digging the canals and south by way of the Illinois River) and East Coast slaves (carried up the Mississippi into the west by the cotton boom) who understood the meaning of the dance.[56] To signal an exhibition the Irish hornpipe dancer "circumnavigated the floor twice, in opposite directions, and then with arms crossed, or poised, or whirled as he pleased, he went through his stock performances."[57] So Diamond walked around then jumped on the shingle to demonstrate his champion steps, and he "came in black" and talked like a slave to transform those steps into "Negro dancing," the product of exchange between blacks and whites in the United States.

The challenge dancer's audience was well aware that jigs were Irish and hornpipes English. But if a black man danced them they were American. Diamond's board and blackface allowed a broader spectrum of people to appreciate the brilliance of his dancing. They also distinguished his steps from more pristine black dances, which Thomas saw in New Orleans: "All the country over, where there were any blacks, they were dancing 'Rubin Rede,' Juba, and 'Jumping Jim Crow.' Judging from the

Figure 1.9 AND 1.10: R.M. Carroll ("Mast. Marks. The Celebrated Dancer") and
William Henry Lane ("Boz's. Juba.") in their prime. Carroll trained under Master Juba
at White's Melodeon in New York. Portrait of Boz's Juba from the Royal Vauxhall
Gardens playbill, 1848, Joseph N. Ireland scrapbook, Harvard Theatre Collection,
Houghton Library, Harvard University; portrait of Master Marks from the cover of
"Ethiopian Melodies of White's Serenaders" [New York, 1849], Sheet Music—Negro
Minstrels. Courtesy of the American Antiquarian Society.

FIGURE 1.11: "Camp towns" were integrated suburbs that began as military encampments on the outskirts of cities during the Revolutionary War. "Camp Town Hornpipe, as danced by Master Dimond" [New York: William Hall & Son, 1840], Sheet Music by Title. Courtesy of the American Antiquarian Society.

antics of those blacks on congo green . . . their dances, Juber and Partner, were imported from Africa, modified slightly. I don't remember ever seeing a white man dancing Juber. They dance the Jig."[58] African "antics" like juber and partner were more alien to native-born African Americans than the hybrid jubas, jigs, and Jim Crows captivating the nation.

Long before 1843, when blackface minstrels began forming their own companies, traveling circuses were hiring one or two whites to imitate "the Negro in all his peculiarity of dance or shouting songs" and one or two African Americans as drivers and fiddlers. These workers learned from each other and from dancers and musicians who joined their troupes along the way. At Broadway Circus, Diamond honed the "Ole Wirginny Breakdown" with banjo player Joe Sweeney (J. W. Sweeny), who cultivated his own music and dancing talents among "plantation and corn-field" slaves in Virginia. And en route with Barnum's troupe, he traded steps to a black fiddler's tunes with a young jig dancer picked up in Troy, New York (which contained a large Irish community).[59]

Landing in hundreds of small towns and cities, these companies circulated knowledge and skills developed in northeastern cities and carried away local styles formed wherever whites and blacks worked or lived in close proximity. As itinerant dancers traversed their region, slaves in Kentucky turned their African shuffles into tapping steps: "We danced some of the dances the white folks danced, the minuette, the reels, and other dances common in those days," recalled ex-slave Robert Anderson, "but we liked better the dances of our own particular race." These were "individual dances, consisting of shuffling of the feet, and swinging of the arms and shoulders in a peculiar rhythm of time [which] developed into what is known today as the Double Shuffle, Heel and Toe, Buck and Wing, Juba, etc." The slaves became proficient at such dances, "and could play a tune with their feet, dancing largely to an inward music, a music that was felt, but not heard."[60] Taken together, the routes of traveling troupes, mixed audiences attending their shows, and dance names shared by slaves and blackface performers indicate swaps were made when the circus came to town.

Challenge dancers employed by theaters as entr'acte variety perpetuated the interracial exchange of dance practices onstage and off. Following the eighteenth-century British custom, North American playhouses often engaged dancers and other popular performers to amuse their patrons between the acts or after the plays. Most of them came from the ranks of local talent or itinerant troupes working the low stages outside "legitimate" theaters, and who diverted from the theaters "a certain class of patrons." Their acts included horse handling, music playing, dancing, comic storytelling, balancing, and other "working or holiday accomplishments of the audience, carried to a pitch they had not leisure to attain but which they would directly and by experience be able to judge and appreciate," explains theater scholar J. S. Bratton. The hornpipe, danced on the stage in hard shoes by men and women, was a favorite entr'acte due to its widespread familiarity among spectators of all kinds. Even the upper classes learned hornpipes as part of etiquette training. But as ever-increasing numbers of young first-generation workers swamped urban theaters in the early nineteenth century, the meaning and character of hornpipes changed. These audiences viewed every hornpipe on the stage as a kind of challenge. They came to see dancers reputedly better than their local heroes and expected them to be astonishing.[61]

Outstanding dancers responded by inserting new and difficult steps into their hornpipes, adding novelties such as dancing them in fetters or on a slack rope, or performing them in character or a particular style.

FIGURE 1.12: Sailor's Hornpipe costume. Theatrical print of T.P. Cooke in D.W. Jerrold's *Black-Ey'd Susan* [London: G. Skelt, 1829].

They also cut comic parodies of each other and joined forces to compete in trials of skill. Sailor's hornpipes, distinguished by costume (figure 1.12) and arm movements, prevailed throughout the Atlantic world, as seamen on leave sought out dockside theaters for entertainment.[62] But on North American stages they were soon challenged by Negro hornpipes and breakdowns. For his benefit night at Boston's National Theatre in June 1840, Master Diamond danced "the Sailor's Hornpipe" in proper attire as entr'acte, and played three parts—Henry Smith, Patrick, and Dinah Crow—in a "new after entertainment" entitled "JOHN SMITH! OR, BLACK AND WHITE!" written expressly for his "extraordinary and peculiar talent." But he saved his most popular steps for the finale: "Diamond in the Negro Camptown Hornpipe, Ole Wirginny Breakdown, Smoke-House Movement, and Five Miles out of Town Dance."[63]

Diamond's bill reflected his spectators. Most early-nineteenth-century theaters, North and South, catered to all ages, colors, and classes. Not until the Astor Place Riot in 1849 did New York's elite break away from popular fare and defend a separate theatrical culture. Large theaters (figure 1.13) had pit, box, and second tier seats for middle-class white patrons, a third tier for prostitutes, and a gallery for the motley crew of working-class citizens. Some offered "Colored Boxes"; others reserved

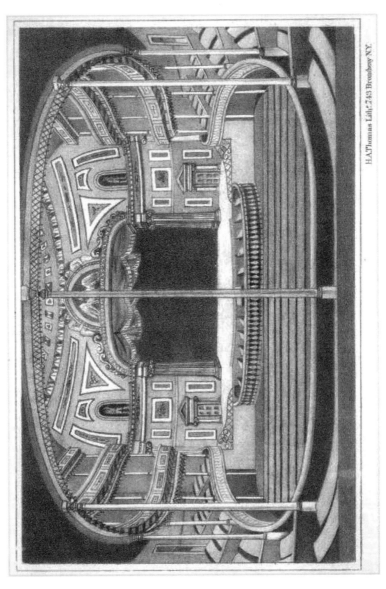

H.AThomas Lith.º 243 Broadway NY

FIGURE 1.13: View of seats, tiers, gallery, and stage at New York's Chatham Theatre from the parquet. George C.D. Odell, *Annals of the New York Stage*, 6 vols. [New York, 1928], 3:120.

the parquet (or wooden floor behind the seats) for blacks and lower-class whites, sometimes divided, sometimes not. White, black, and mulatto men and women, plump girls, nursing mothers, newsboys, "young sailors, Hanover-street shopmen, mechanics, and other people of that kidney" mingled as well (outside the "most aristocratic part of the house") in theaters specifically "for the middling and lower classes."[64]

Many white performers counted on black theatergoers to round out their audiences. In 1833, when the District of Columbia placed a curfew on African Americans out after nine o'clock, an actor who had hired a popular theater complained. "A great proportion of our audience consists of persons of this caste," he insisted, "and they are consequently deterred from giving us that support that they would otherwise do." Fortunately, most theater managers were "sporting" men well accustomed to the likes and dislikes of integrated gatherings. For Diamond's shows manager James Caldwell sat "Free colored People" and "Colored Servants" with "a pass from their owners" on the right hand third tier of the St. Charles in New Orleans and New Theatre in Mobile (figure 1.14); John Tyron set apart "Places . . . for colored persons" at New York's Bowery Amphitheatre; and several managers in Philadelphia turned the third tier of their theaters into a "colored gallery."[65] A few critics regretted that legitimate theaters "sullied" their boards with "the rude and uncouth dancing of a Diamond or a Pierce." But they agreed it was good for business.[66]

FIGURE 1.14: Master Diamond shown mocking renowned ballerina Fanny Elssler and challenging "any person" to a trial of skill in "Negro Dancing, in all its varieties." Admission prices include seats for black patrons. New Theatre playbill, Mobile, February 22, 1841. New Theatre folder, OS Posters box, Harvard Theatre Collection, Houghton Library, Harvard University.

Negro hornpipes gave these audiences a sense of importance, as they watched experts perform dances they felt were their own. But what drew people to Diamond's act was the way he captured and complicated the unfamiliar moves of dancers in the regions he was touring "with the greatest fidelity," according to the *Picayune*. During his sojourns in New Orleans, explained the New York *Whip*, Diamond "could daily be found on wharves, freely distributing his 'pic's.' [picayunes, or 6¼-cent coins] among the darkeys, [and] nightly did he give proofs of his knowledge of levee nigger. In short, he can dance more steps and give a more perfect delineation of the negro character than any man in this profession." Through this exchange, Diamond transformed camptown hornpipes and levee breakdowns into professional performances that could be judged by local spectators. He therefore provoked strong performer-audience identification wherever he danced. That was how he filled the gallery seats, reserved for colored people and "the lowest class of the white population," from Boston to New Orleans.[67]

Challenge dancing was ideal for drawing a crowd as it upped the ante of the already competitive performer-audience relationship, and because "women as well [as] male bipeds enjoyed the sport with a relish keen and delightful."[68] The first dancing match promoted and covered in the popular press took place at New York's Chatham Theatre on February 13, 1840, between Master Diamond and R. W. Pelham, recently attached to Broadway Circus. To distinguish the competition from an ordinary "trial of skill" (which did not demand a victor) and assure the audience of its authenticity, the *New York Herald* ad stated that judges would "award the stake to the successful competitor on the stage, and in the presence of the audience." An enthusiastic follow-up report in *Spirit of the Times* captured the excitement of the event: "On Thursday last, a match for $500 a side (we wish they may get it!) came off between the rival negro dancers, Diamond and Pelham. The house was so crowded at 10 o'clock, that a friend of ours could not obtain sight of the stage. Master Diamond is said to have 'flaxed out' young Pelham, who claims to be 'de mos science nigga!' The tunes 'chawed up' on the occasion, were 'Juba'—'For I'm gwine to the Alabarme'—'Go way, nigga'—'Jimmy, is yer hoe-cake done!'—'Shinbone Alley,' etc., etc."[69] From these details— the overflowing crowd, pugilistic language, and long list of blackface tunes—knowledgeable readers could imagine the speed and character of the dancing.

Those readers came from the self-appointed "sporting community," among whom "jig dancin' was thought to be a big thing, as it was," recalled an old aficionado, and who bet on "favorite jig-dancers, just as they [did] on favorite horses or walkers."[70] Whenever he toured, Diamond frequented city districts where African Americans lived and worked and sporting people congregated to drink, gamble, dance, and carouse.[71] This leisure activity was the source of his success. Diamond's "style of dancing is peculiarly his own," stated the *Whip* in 1843, "having ever since his first appearance made the habits of the negro his study," while the dancing of Pelham, his foremost opponent, has fallen "somewhat 'behind the times.' . . . [H]is steps are too old to take in this age of modern improvement."[72] According to their contemporaries, professional challenge dancers kept up with the game by jigging in mixed company at the tavern down the block.

TAVERN MATCHES

Stage challenges were actually part of a much larger world of sport that often merged the races and classes. Contests of skill, strength, speed, and endurance among men (and women) and their animals were ubiquitous in antebellum America. Dancers, fiddlers, newspaper folders, plowmen, and myriad others made challenges because games and friendly wagers were a common form of sociability and recreation.[73] As fellow circus performers, Diamond and Pelham would have been just such companionable rivals. They also would have frequented the same "resorts" where members of their audience challenged each other to jigging contests, singing matches, card games, and other competitions. In fact, most champion dancers made their names competing in the heat and sweat immediacy of neighborhood taverns.

Tavern matches ranged from informal bouts organized on the spur of the moment to prearranged contests with carefully outlined terms of engagement. A dancer usually made the challenge and specified the terms, which another dancer either accepted or countered. Challenges might be oral or written, with the latter appearing in newspaper columns as an advertisement for the match. It was also common for the dancers' friends or seconds to sponsor the match and for tavern keepers or other trustworthy men to "hold the stakes." Diamond and Juba's first match was arranged by "some fellows" who wanted "to see who could dance the longest and this match made quite an excitement." The excitement came from the dancers' exhibition of their "Art" and the lively sport (i.e., bets made among the performers and spectators) surrounding the match. "The stake is large and an unparalleled display will be the result," announced the *New York Sporting Whip*, which also predicted that Diamond would "conquer" his opponent.[74]

Even more than street and theater challenges, tavern matches brought Irish and African Americans into the same arena as participants and observers. The close proximity of the stages on which Diamond and Juba were currently performing, and the fame each dancer had garnered, brought them together in 1843. Diamond was in New York working for Barnum, who had offered to pay him a "good salary" and make him "a kind of star" at his new venue, the American Museum on Ann Street, "which was all the go then," recalled another entrepreneur, "and where the girls and boys used to go meet each other in the 'Lecture Room,' and enjoy themselves generally." Juba "was then dancin' at Pete Williams' dance house" on Orange Street, which became "one of the show places or sights of New York" because "Charles Dickens went there once, and enjoyed himself, and that kind of made it fashionable." The only surviving account of the contest, which came off at Williams's place, is an interview conducted some years later with a white tavern keeper who described himself as equally fond of "colored people" and "burnt-cork people": "this bein', perhaps, the only case in which I am as fond of the make-believe article as of the genuine. I really like colored people, as I have said elsewhere, and I like those who can take 'em off, provided they imitate 'em well."[75]

Pete Williams was an African American tavern landlord who, like our informant and many other proprietors in Lower Manhattan, welcomed the custom of both black and white men and women. Middle-class outsiders often commented on the presence of interracial trade in lower-class districts of growing cities as if it was unusual. But it wasn't.[76] Williams's tavern was "connected to at least three white businesses—one above it and two on either side—as well as an interracial shanty colony in the back."[77] To people living within those communities race did not always determine the status of a business or its clientele. More often people chose to patronize the establishments of men and women they knew and respected, black or white. Racial prejudice did segregate people, but needs and interests also led to the kind of cross-racial support expressed in an article written in defense of Thomas Downing, an eminently respectable oyster saloonkeeper who, "although black, holds a station among his friends," against the slander of the notoriously racist journalist "Tom Nichols," who called on Downing "and to his utter surprise found that he had to pay for what he called for, while at any other oyster shop he could get drunk on any body else's expense but his own."[78]

Sites of exchange and leisure, many liquor sellers provided a place for collective forms of entertainment—from drinking, storytelling, and music making, to singing, dancing, and gambling—depending on their size. Customers came to Free-and-Easys to sing and hear others sing. At Evans's on Cedar Street even "the good natured host" could be heard offering some favorite air with "touching sweetness," while up the block black patrons sang "soul-stirring" hymns, pleasing "the landlord behind the bar" and causing confusion in passers-by.[79] Dancers and musicians met at the Branch in the Bowery, Three Tuns Tavern in Baltimore, and Canadian

FIGURE 1.15: White and black, male and female, old and young met and mixed in many lower-class neighborhood businesses. From Junius Henri Browne, *The Great Metropolis: A Mirror of New York* [Hartford, 1869], 659.

House in Toronto to show off, share ideas, and compete.[80] Some taverns kept open floor space or provided platforms where amateurs and professionals could present their special talents for a drink, a plate of food, or "for free gratis for nothin', just for fun of the thing." Challenge dancers waited for a purse to be raised before entertaining the crowd with a show of their amazing or comical steps.[81] On these nights, when the customers provided the entertainment, taverns did not charge admission. But proprietors who paid musicians to call the sets and accompany the dances did. They also hired professional jig dancers to get on the floor and liven things up.

The communal rather than male sociability that characterized taverns and groggeries in integrated neighborhoods is unmistakable in visual and written representations from the time (figure 1.15), despite their intent. An 1840 account of a police raid on a New York "gambling house," while clearly crafted to amuse readers and fuel middle-class dread of amalgamation, offered a glimpse into one of these taverns. Sharing an evening of drink and leisure activities were about twenty men, women, and children "of all sizes and colors." The place seemed well run, for directing the attention of the crowd was "a master of ceremonies, an out-and-out darkey." In one corner a circle of juvenile spectators applauded the exertions of a tiny black dancer "who was jumping 'Jim Crow.'" Other patrons entertained themselves "free and easy" style. Sitting at a table, "a little black rascal of twelve years, assisted by two little white ones of eleven or under, were roaring a love song." When the police burst in the patrons protected each other: chairs, tables, "glasses and tumblers went crash, crash, crash, in all directions—and to crown the whole, two feminine blocks of ebony and a little Irish woman set up a pullaloo that was equal to the keen of a Munster funeral."[82] Hidden within the reporter's picture of lower-class mayhem is a scene of easy exchange between blacks and whites, a place where young dancers like Juba and Diamond met to perfect their steps and practice their trade.

Challenge dancing at legitimate theaters attracted middle-class spectators to working-class venues where jig dancers regularly performed. After the publication of *American Notes*, flocks of curious writers, "gay fellows," and betting men sought out Williams's place to get a peek at the dancers. "The best in the profession danced there," recalled theater critic T. Allston Brown, "as well as Juba." They called it Almack's, as had Dickens facetiously to bring to mind England's Almack's, where "powerful women of influence" got up exclusive subscription balls. Newspaperman Nathaniel P. Willis, who visited the London version in 1836, used the name as a more earnest comparison in 1846: the "grand subterranean Almacks of the Five Points looked very clean and cheerful. It was a spacious room, with a low ceiling, excessively white-washed, nicely sanded and well-lit, and the black proprietor and his ministering spirits were well-dressed and well-mannered people." Williams's dance house was about twenty-five feet square with wooden benches along the walls, a bar at one end, and a raised platform for the musicians, providing dancing room for about one dozen couples. Circus ringmaster Robert Ellingham sometimes acted as master of ceremonies, while onlookers filled the corners of the room "waiting for their chance to enter the swirling, foot-stomping throng." Admission was ten cents, and three cents for a glass of whiskey.[83]

Characterized by mixed sociability and an ethic of reciprocity, neighborhood taverns supported communal diversions and customs increasingly opposed by the market mentality of more commercialized saloons, which separated working-class culture from its practitioners and sold it back to them as spectacle. Even the bets and wagers that accompanied tavern challenges acted as mutual exchange, for "as long as poor people gambled among themselves in honest games money would return."[84] At dance competitions in Ireland the champion treated "all the company" to a glass of whiskey; "he who 'took the sway' having to maintain the dignity of his position by lavish spending, instead of being both socially and financially a winner."[85] A similar circulation of funds took place on the night of Diamond and Juba's match. "After the show was over at Barnum's Jack Diamond and his gang came down to Pete Williams' and took dinner all round. The boy, Juba, had his friends too, who jested him about

the match, and told him to go in and do his best."[86] These two factions provided the stake money and laid bets with each other. They also supported Williams's establishment with purchases of food and drink before, during, and after the match, in return for which Williams provided an honest, comfortable space for their contest.

While the dancers were taking their suppers, "'Boss' Harrington came in to look at the match, and he was warmly greeted by the boys, for the Boss had lots of friends." Bill "Liverhead" Harrington was a butcher and bare-knuckle boxer who became a local hero in 1832.[87] His presence at the match signified jig dancing's close association with pugilism, another popular form of leisure and gambling. Jig dancers began incorporating the trappings of the prizefighting ring into their contests in the 1830s, after a number of English boxers immigrated to the United States.[88] They adopted the lingo of pugilists, gave themselves stage names and regional affiliations, held trials and exhibitions tours, and introduced "scientific" steps into their repertoires. On his National Theatre playbill, June 5, 1840 (figure 1.16), Master Diamond

FIGURE 1.16: There is no evidence that Diamond limited his challenges to whites. Detail from National Theatre playbill, Boston, July 5, 1840. Diamond Minstrels & Master Diamond folder, box 5 (Co-Du), Harvard Theatre Collection, Houghton Library, Harvard University.

invited all comers to "TOE DE MARK," a boxing phrase that referred to a line scratched in the dirt to divide the ring. At the beginning of each round, the fighters were required to put their toes up against the line—to come up to scratch, or to the mark—to prove they were fit enough for the bout. Diamond's challenge was made in blackface language to identify his style of jigging, but it was not directed to theatrical dancers whom he would burlesque elsewhere in the show. Rather, it invited "any man" (black or white) willing and able to match the wager to compete.[89] As a formal sport, bare-knuckle boxing commenced in Britain, and most contenders in early America came from England or Ireland; there were few American-born prizefighters at the time. Prominent among those few were several black champions. In fact, the first U.S.-born boxers to compete for the English championship were Bill Richmond and his protégé Tom Molyneaux, both black men.[90] So when the juvenile king of diamonds blacked up for his challenge dances, he not only identified his jigs and hornpipes as American, he announced his champion status!

Fighters danced, and dancers fought. And as in boxing, it was training, body type, and style that made two dancers a good matchup. "There were a lot of jig-dancers [who competed] in those days—Inyard, Wooly Moon, Jack Diamond and others." Some were professionals; many were not. "Juba was a little negro, about fourteen years old, and spry and not so bad lookin'." Diamond was closer to twenty; "Small of stature, he executed in an extremely neat and slow fashion." He also "thought a heap of himself," as did most dancers. Pride in physical ability was common among journeymen, and despite repeated references to the "Art" and "Science" of their trade, jig dancers remained working class. After all, they supported themselves with their bodies and sweat. Joe Miles was "one of the roughest chaps, but with a soft heart under his hard hide," admitted our interviewee. "He was quite a jig-dancer, and very proud of his legs; as well he might be, for those legs of his made him his livin'." John Diamond may have "looked neat" in his "white stockings and boots with high heels, . . . but it was his movin' and not his lookin' that did the business."[91]

Actually, looks and moves were closely connected for jig dancers. In Africa and Ireland, "brilliance of phrasing and vividness of enactment" were enhanced by a dancer's "strikingly attractive use of style," which was associated with "notions of preening and making of the person sexually attractive."[92] Upper-class observers felt continually annoyed by "uppity blacks" and "insolent Irish" who audaciously stepped out in fancy clothes. They assumed such people were pretending to hold a higher social station. But like their betters, working people dressed to announce group identity and individual accomplishments. In early America, champion jig dancers "posed about attired in a velvet coat, flashy, flowing necktie, glazed cap, tight pants, [and] patent leather shoes with old cop-per pennies fastened to the heels."[93] People with low funds worked with what they had. Market dancers tied up their hair with eel skin or tea lead to identify their expertise through style, just as Diamond chose high-heeled boots over pumps, clogs, or brogans to mark his particular genius.

Because the terms of the bout included length of time, five fiddlers and a tambourine were on hand at Williams's place that night.[94] No one fiddler could have played for the whole time. "The match began about eleven o'clock, and Juba went at it first, and went at it with a will. One of the fiddlers played a reel for him, and he shuffled, and twisted, and walked around, and danced on for one hour and fifteen minutes by the watch. Then he brought his left foot down with a bang and went and took a drink, while the boys cheered him tremendous." Clean entrances and exits were part of the competition. They showed that the dancer knew where he was in the music.[95] Juba gave the floor a stomp to end his final flourish and signal the close of his dance.

Tavern dancers performed in the center of the room, in among the spectators who paid close attention to their footwork and called out to encourage them on. "The negroes around [went] wild over the dancin' of Juba, and they had bet all their coppers on their champion. Many of the white folks present, too, thought that the colored boy would win, but they changed their tune when they looked at Jack a while. Jack never danced so well as he did that night. It was quantity and quality both. He outstepped Juba [surpassed his time], and then he put in a lot of fancy work besides—got in lots of fine touches." Juba, who watched with open mouth and staring eyes, seemed astonished to our informant, but the dancer's expression more likely reflected his concentration as he intently watched Diamond's feet. A panel was sometimes placed between the dancers at tournaments to keep the second contestant from memorizing and adding the first dancer's steps to his own for the win. This ability would make Juba the champion the next time he met Diamond. In fact, the finale of his shows became his imitation dance, during which he per-formed all the current challengers' prize steps, including his own.[96]

Tavern matches had personal and professional significance for the dancers. "Jack Diamond didn't pretend to care much, but he did, for all his careless way. Jig-dancers have their pride like other people, and Jack had his position to maintain, and he knew that the match would get wind among the boys. . . . So, when it came Diamond's turn to dance, he danced." The tavern keeper stops here to give the competition one more meaning: "You see it was not only a case of Barnum's Museum against Pete Williams' dance-house, but it was a case of white against black. So Jack Diamond went at his dancin' with double energy—first, for his place, next, for his color." Looking back, our witness situates the racial antipathy of the times in the two competing venues, which plainly represented white against black. But the scene he described was far more ambiguous. Inside the tavern, where Diamond danced "for his place" among a cohort that included black dancers like Juba, color did not come first.

In America's newly forming middle-class society, which condemned dancing (not in itself but as an incitement to sin and rowdyism) and censored racial mingling (as the source of amalgamation and degradation), this match would never have taken place, and if it did it probably would have been about class or racial domination. But in a context where interracial exchange was the norm, and the two best dancers in town—one black, one Irish—danced the same dance, the stakes were very different. This match was about which dancer owned the steps. "Even the negroes gave Juba the go-bye soon, and threw up the sponge, and wished they had their money back. One of the colored boys yelled out 'He's a white man, sure,' lookin' at Diamond, 'but he's got a nigger in his heel.'"[97]

Racial fear and hatred permeated antebellum America, but it did not wholly define everyday life in mixed communities. Sometimes shared traditions, professional camaraderie, or mutual benefit trumped race. In July 1844, Masters Diamond and Juba hired the Bowery Theatre for their next challenge, announcing it in the *New York Herald* as a "GREAT PUBLIC CONTEST" to see which will "bear the Title of the Champion Dancer of the World." Five judges were chosen, the wager set at $200, and the terms laid down ("three Jigs, two Reels, and the Camptown Hornpipe").[98] This time Juba prevailed, and they would meet again in other matches and tournaments.

Like Bob's crack feat, the challenge dance cannot be traced to one originating culture. Neither the theft of African dance forms by whites nor the appropriation of Irish dance forms by blacks adequately describes the complex consensual and combative exchange that shaped the competition between Diamond and Juba. Its origins lay in the aesthetic movements and global migrations of white and black men and women loosed from their cultural moorings, sharing the bottom rungs of society, and remaking their traditions in the interest of survival in a new world.

CHAPTER 2

Musical Itinerancy in a World of Nations

GERMANY, ITS MUSIC, AND ITS MUSICIANS

Celia Applegate

IN NOVEMBER 1862, Johannes Brahms wrote an anguished letter to Clara Schumann about being passed over as conductor of the Hamburg Philharmonic—"where may I and can I [go now]?" he wrote. "[I am] set loose to fly about all alone in empty space." Two decades later, in 1884, he composed five songs (Opus 94), the fifth of which was a bleak setting of a poem by Friedrich Halm: "No house, no homeland, no wife and no child; thus I am whirled like a straw in storm and wind." That same summer, he identified himself, when registering with the police for his (usual) summer sojourn in the Austrian mountain village of Mürzzuschlag, as "itinerant musician."[1] At age fifty he saw himself as a refugee, a man without place, a vagabond with only his music to recommend him. For Brahms's biographers, these documents allow speculation about his psychology. For the cultural historian, their appeal lies in his illumination, deliberate at times, of the relationship of the musician to society. His description of himself to the settled folk of Mürzzuschlag as itinerant musician may have represented Brahmsian irony, but the irony derived from the contrast between this portly, portmanteaued professional man and a folkloric figure of dubious musical skills and doubtful morals. It invites us to explore the historical reality of both musicians, the legendary scapegrace evoked by Brahms and the professional musician Brahms himself embodied, along with the lines of development that stretch in both directions from them.

Itinerancy was, and continues to be, one of the persistent features of the musical life. Evidence for the existence of musical travelers of one kind or another dates back to as far as evidence for music making can be confirmed. In every time and place for which a history can be written, one can find musicians on the move. In the modern period, European musicians traveled to all places that Europeans lived and colonized.[2] If we adopt Brahms's tongue-in-cheek use of the term "itinerant musician," then we observe a great range of musical people—professionals and amateurs, early moderns and moderns, stars and worker bees, men and women, composers, performers, writers about music, and those who traveled simply to listen to music. And if we further stretch the term "itinerancy" to include the travels of not only musicians but also their music, then one comes quickly to the conclusion that movement represents the defining characteristic of the art form itself in Western culture and thus of its practitioners.

This essay provides glimpses of the long history of musical itinerancy and travel, mainly in the places of German-speaking Europe, in order to illuminate the means by which Germans shaped and expressed their collective identity. Itinerant musicians and music making formed the German nation, not in the sense of determining its borders or shaping its politics but in the sense of making it a lived experience. That musical travel of any sort, whether constant or occasional, should have anything to teach us about nationhood is not, however, immediately apparent. All cultures are "travelling cultures," wrote James Clifford in his essays on how "culture makes itself at home in motion," but the claim is much easier to substantiate in postcolonial, globalizing cultural development than in the age of nationalism.[3] National cultures seem on the face of them to be the opposite of traveling ones, located in bounded spaces and rooted, at least in the minds of their creators and adherents, in the very soil itself. Music, for its part, is different from some of the more obvious markers of nation making, like monuments, museums, and memorials, paintings, poems, and parks. Its participation in nation making cannot be described through metaphors of construction, because the work music does exists in the moment of its performance and, like Renan's daily plebiscite, relies on repetition and continual recreation. Even after the advent of the age of mechanical reproduction, music still involves continual production and reproduction to exist in the world.

Yet this momentary quality of music, its "dying fall," its immediacy, and its accompanying demand to be made again and again, is precisely what has made it so powerful an agent in the making of national cultures and, by the same token, made travel and circulation so fundamental to its social effectiveness. The movements of musicians thus become a central element in any history of music in national cultures, which involve, just as much as do contemporary globalizing cultures, displacement and "tangled cultural experiences," as well as "impure, unruly processes of collective invention."[4] Traveling musicians, of all stripes, dramatize the generalized placeness of the nation by moving across all parts of the nation and representing it outside its borders. The sections that follow suggest answers to two kinds of questions about musical travel and the making of nation-states—first, musical travel's effects on social groups within and among nations and, second, its changing meaning. The first draws our attention to the way in which musical practices formed a transnational space that was itself predicated on the existence and recognition of national cultures. The phrase "the musical world," which came into circulation in the latter decades of the eighteenth century, was thus a world not of courts, religious communities, and the road itself but of musical nations.[5]

First, travel transmitted knowledge, practical and theoretical, among people in many places, and that transmission of musical knowledge in turn brought about the development of new musical styles, instruments, and institutions. Music has so often been called a universal language that the very sentence practically writes itself. Even though ethnomusicologists have long since debunked this cliché and a new cultural history of music has tried to bring its insights to bear on Western music, it remains the case that the social processes of musical transfer and exchange, how they were both limited and promoted by the existence of national and nationalizing states, remain less well understood than the musical evidence that such processes were at work. Bach's French suites were called that because they followed the sequence of dance forms common to seventeenth-century instrumental suites by French composers; Mozart's Piano Sonata no. 11 (*alla Turka*) represented his homage to Turkish Janissary bands then fashionable in the capitals of Europe; and Bizet made *Carmen* sound both Spanish and gypsy-ish without ever meeting a gypsy or traveling to Spain ("that would only confuse me").[6] These examples are all manifestations of successive "cultural waves" across the ethnic and national boundaries of Europe and beyond, the movement of which we have only begun to map.[7]

Second, these cultural waves were themselves signs of how musical travel helped to form a variety of identities, each of which reflected people's sense of belonging to communities larger than the locality to which the traveler came and in which he or she performed. Europe was one such community, though we need to specify its meaning in earlier times. Musical travel and traveling music certainly reinforced pan-European confessional identities—even while some music, Bach's for instance, was capable of crossing confessional boundaries. But by the nineteenth century, national communities, even and perhaps especially before they were nation-states, were the most important of the supralocal identities that musical travel helped to form. To call such communities imagined is to diminish the importance of musical practices themselves in making them real—practices, moreover, made possible and sustained by the incessant travel of musicians. Musical interchange, within and among nations, may have been all the more rapid and pervasive because of the nonlinguistic nature of music—that "fatal diversity of human language," on which Benedict Anderson put so much conceptual weight. But it still required—or perhaps better, created—feelings of mutual understanding among those who undertook such acts of cultural transfer. In 1988, Akira Iriye asked, rhetorically, "Who can deny that thinkers, artists, and musicians . . . have contributed decisively to the making of contemporary history?" His main interest lay in the "alternative community of nations and peoples" that could emerge from their activities, but cultural interchanges are relevant to the history of national communities as well.[8] Such exchanges illuminate, moreover, the strange nature of national boundaries. Some, in Prasenjit Duara's formulation, are hard and cannot be crossed without violating the integrity of the community, and others are soft and easily blurred.[9] Among the soft boundaries, one would certainly include music. The history of how it functioned, or not, as a boundary among nations, of how its practitioners were and were not representatives of their nations, promises to clarify what nations were, and remain.

The second question that informs this essay is that of the meaning of itinerancy and travel. If we wish productively to revise the conceptual behemoths of modernization, nationalization, and imperialism, we need to disaggregate them and see how people experienced the changes of past centuries in their everyday lives. Musical life provides a wide field for such investigations precisely because it is pervasive, various, dispersed, and unstable. From concert hall and opera house to parlor piano and factory brass band, music making helped to condition people's adjustment to rapid, relentless alterations in their social worlds. It may not be the most sensitive barometer of change, nor should we seek only the sounds of upheaval and transformation. But to account for the reasons that musicians have traveled and how those have changed or to draw out the views that people have held about musical travelers and see how they changed is to illuminate constitutive experiences of the human, and in this case especially national, community. In a period that stretches from the end of one Thirty Years' War in the mid-seventeenth century to the end of another in the mid-twentieth, the ties that bound such a German community together broke and re-formed dozens of times, but it came to seem to its members that the music would always be there.

ON THE ROAD: EARLY MODERN MUSICIANS
AND THEIR WORLDS

In 2009, the *New York Times* ran a human interest story about Gerry Niewood and Coleman Mellett, two men killed in the crash of Continental Flight 3407, under the headline "For Two Jazzmen, Work Meant Life on the Road." For both, "flying in a cramped turboprop plane to play a show in Buffalo in February was not an unfamiliar routine," yet both also had, according to the article, a "middle-class existence": as a friend said of Mellett, he "loved his wife, he loved his home, he loved the town where they lived" in his "ranch-style house."[10] Bland though these remarks may be, they echo, faintly but discernibly, a centuries-old prejudice held by settled people about the musicians and players who moved from place to place. As long as people have written about musicians as a group, they have been accusing them of immorality or defending them against such accusations. To explore the long history of perceptions of itinerant musicians is to illuminate processes of Christianization, urbanization, and the uneven development of law and sovereignty across disparate territorial arrangements (among other things). Terminology alone presents a daunting problem, with much of the acrimony over the centuries centered on titles and their consequences.[11] The baroque writer and musician Johann Beer dramatized this in his picaresque novel *German Winter Nights* (1681) by staging a brawl between courtiers and musicians over whether the latter would be called *Stadtpfeiffer* or *Spielmann*.[12]

And for centuries this had been a distinction that made a difference. The *Spielmann* (and similar names) was someone who had neither regular employment—in a court or a town or a church or some combination of all those—nor fixed abode and who thus wandered around picking up work when he could. He belonged to the category of "un-honorable people" (*unehrliche Leute*), along with executioners, sheep shearers, grave diggers, linen weavers, and unmarried daughters.[13] Many of these positions required that people live semipermanently on the road, and as a result only with difficulty can we separate their movement from their work in explaining their lack of honor. Because of their violation of the mimetic taboo, their association with the libidinous, ecstatic, and unruly powers of music, *and* their lack of settled place, traveling musicians lacked honor and with it rights—to be witness or juror or to win damages as plaintiff in a trial, to hold civic office, to own land, to be a member of a guild.[14]

Not surprisingly, for townsmen this last became the nub of the matter. One might regard the traveling musicians as those left over after long-term processes of institutional growth had regularized the ways in which people composed, performed, and heard music in Europe, but that would be to diminish the dynamic force they represented in the development of musical styles *and* institutions. In the history of the musical profession, town employment of musicians was the last kind of employment to emerge, after centuries in which the mainstay of musical life had been the church, supported and increasingly rivaled by royal and noble establishments that required larger and more ambitious musical programming. But as towns too sought to formalize their soundscape—bells calling people to church, trumpets announcing the arrival of people and goods at the city gates, pipers and drums accompanying civic ceremonials—musicians were able to settle down in towns and train their children in their profession.[15] They were still Johnny-come-latelies in the money and moral economy of early modern towns and cities. Musicians' guilds date probably to the fourteenth century, and town records of localities all across Europe are filled, from then until the near total disappearance of musicians' guilds in the early nineteenth century, with evidence of endless bickering over who did and did not belong to a guild, or deserve to belong to one, or perform services that should be restricted to one. In 1593, Bartoldt Snider and Peter Gerken, a pair of traveling musicians perhaps similar in their partnership to Niewood and Mellett, were ejected from the city of Bremen for playing at a wedding without authorization, that is to say, without membership in the local musicians' guild. They unsuccessfully defended themselves by claiming that they had been playing without harassment in many places—"Saxonland, Braunswig, Westphalia, Hamburg, Lünenborg, Magdeburg, the state of Lyppe Schomburg, and many other honorable cities."[16]

But in fact, pursuit of the guild strategy by musicians who had managed to find positions as town trumpeters never entirely worked. Henry Raynor has written that "there was never a period in their history when the town musicians were not engaged in a bitter struggle to preserve their monopoly," and, one might add, to maintain their place among existing and higher ranking guilds in the towns and cities.[17] Even before the loosening of guild cohesion in the eighteenth century, other guilds regularly challenged their presence among them, a circumstance that in 1653 led to an unusual supralocal effort on the part of German musicians to obtain imperial approval for uniform standards within communities. The Saxon Town Musician Articles, which the emperor himself confirmed, consisted of twenty-five specifications of musicians' guild privileges, ranging from a monopoly over local performances to moral instruction of journeymen.[18] And although scores of musicians signed onto them, the articles did not represent a step toward gradual unification of musical employment across Central Europe but only an attempt to strengthen the position of musicians in a handful of localities. Moreover, the guilding of musicians did not work because even guilds could not ensure that the salary of a town trumpeter would support a family, thus guaranteeing that all musicians, whether in guilds or not, would compete for occasional work at weddings and wakes. The search for supplementary work also meant that travel always beckoned—travel especially to courts, of which Germany had, of course, many.

The limited effectiveness of musicians' guilds raises the question of whether one ought indeed to regard traveling musicians merely as the throwbacks in a modernizing musical world.[19] Such a perspective obscures the extent to which even musicians with regular employment in court, church, and town continued to travel throughout those long stretches of time in which Europeans were settling down and mostly staying put. One can distinguish between different types of travel, between the true vagabond and the purposeful traveler, but in both cases, traveling musicians did the cultural work that created and sustained the European musical world. The spread of styles and genres—monophony, polyphony, functional harmony; plainchant, organum, motet, madrigal, opera, concerto grosso—is one of explorations and elaborations of patterns in sound, which depended on the creation of a system of musical notation that could record exact pitch and time and thus provide the possibility of building on the explorations and elaborations that had come before. Musical notation was portable, and thus the very development of musical style in the Western tradition resulted from travel, among monasteries, courts, and towns, and by musicians, whether monks or minstrels, saints or scoundrels, and all those in between. Conditions of service accounted for most travel, as for that of all musicians in court employment. When the papacy itself went on the road in the fourteenth century, this had rippling effects on patterns of training and recruiting musicians.

Musicologists have never ignored the existence of travel, of cultural transfers and networks—the spread of "northern polyphony" and the contributions of the Franco-Flemish school to the development of the motet, for instance, are staples of music history, as are the multiple interactions between German and Italian musicians that defined the transition from Renaissance to baroque music. Nevertheless, the significance of musical travel to the crossing of social, not just geographical, boundaries and to the formation of national, not just musical, identities has necessarily remained out of focus in the picture musicologists have drawn. As to the first, the constant infusion of influences from popular music into church and court music relied in part on the movement of musicians without honor who traveled the roads of Europe in the company of beggars and thieves. So did developments in instruments and their technique: Georg Philipp Telemann greatly admired the Polish and Moravian fiddlers he heard on his own extensive travels, and the violinist Franz Benda wrote in his autobiography that he learned techniques from a Jewish tavern fiddler in Prague.[20] As to the second, the gradual stabilization of notions of what constituted German, French, or Italian musical styles came about through increasing familiarity with the work of musicians coming from these places and speaking these languages. And over the course of the late seventeenth and eighteenth centuries, the question of just where exactly musicians belonged in the increasingly dynamic social and political structures of European countries came more sharply into focus, generating not just anxiety and ambition among musicians but also considerable reflection in print about what role music and musicians played in European life.

After all, it was not so easy then—as now, looking back—to distinguish between the reputable and the disreputable travelers, between the Italian composing French music or the Bohemian composing Italian music or the German turned Englishman and composing German music now dubbed quintessentially English. All such distinctions were especially difficult to discern in places disrupted by warfare, expansionist states, and changing economic opportunities (often for the worse). Yet discerning such differences became, at the same time, all the more important, especially since the quickening circulation of new knowledge about the world had the effect of making it all the more important to possess a stable and legible identity. People needed, in other words, to read and to be read, especially if those people were travelers. In the last decades of the seventeenth century, a growing number of musicians in German-speaking Europe took up the pen to write prose about music and musicians, establishing a literary pendant to music making itself. Through novels and treatises, they made musicians legible to German literary culture.

This was also the only truly national culture in the German-speaking lands, constituting a social network of shared concerns that crossed geographical, social, and political barriers dividing one locality from another and the privileged aristocracy from all. It expressed the nationality of Germany, and in its products, whether they were comic accounts of imaginary travels or learned treatises on ecclesiastical law, nationality was a quality that grew ever more distinct in the contemplation and description of it. It was, in James Sheehan's words, "a culture of readers and writers for whom print had become the essential means of communication and printed matter the primary source and subject of cultural activity."[21] Its social core consisted of a mélange of the merchants, patriciates, and pastors of the burgher order alongside the new bureaucratic elites that served the prince, and from the late seventeenth century on, such people created a self-supporting, sustained, and secular reading public. Numbers of books and new periodicals rose dramatically, each feeding off the other.

The literary products of musician writers, less scrutinized today than their musical compositions, thus shed considerable light on the question of how musicians fit in to an emergent national culture in Germany; these writings show us how people infused the national into the German pursuit of the musical. And in much of the fictional writing in the decades before and after 1700, the traveling musician played a central role, becoming indeed a stock figure. The mother of all these works was the sprawling picaresque novel *The Adventures of Simplicius Simplicissimus the Vagabond* by Hans Jakob von Grimmelshausen, published in

1669 and celebrated for its depiction of the horrors of the Thirty Years' War. In one of its episodes, Simplicissimus poses as a musician in order to seduce a countess, and in one of the "Simplician" sequels to the original novel, *Der seltsame Springinsfeld* (The Odd Spring-into-Action), the main character is a musician of an exceedingly marginal sort, a one-legged mercenary turned beggar-fiddler, whose mother was Greek noblewoman turned itinerant singer and whose father was a Turkish tightrope walker. By the 1670s, thanks to the popularity of Grimmelshausen's writings, the pace of literary production began to pick up. In Johann Beer's fifteen or so novels, Daniel Speer's five, Wolfgang Caspar Printz's three, and Johann Kuhnau's three, all written between 1677 and 1704, not only are musicians usually the principal characters in the novels but the writers themselves were all principally musicians.[22] Between the musical experiences of the authors themselves and those of the characters they created, one encounters the range of musical travel, from penny-ante scoundrels to itinerant but honest entertainers to Kapellmeisters, cantors, city trumpeters, and a whole host of boys orphaned at a young age, whose musical training takes place on the road of life. The sites of education and performance consist of inns and castles, monasteries and bedrooms, cities and villages, places as exotic as Babylon and as provincial as Ulm.

Given the satirical tone of these works and the incoherence of their narratives, they might seem merely to confirm the poetic theory of Christian Weise (1642–1708), who held that literature had the power to dispel melancholy and depression (as did, of course, music).[23] But Weise also tried to bring an element of instructive social commentary into the so-called political novels he pioneered. Precursors of the more celebrated *Bildungsroman* and *Künstlerroman* a century later, these works adopted satire for the purpose of plain speaking. These were anti-court, anti-"alamode" works that expressed the need to find a literary language that could defend *alte teutsche Redlichkeit und Aufrichtigkeit* (old German integrity and honesty).[24] The "political" in this context—and one finds it often in the titles of books, e.g., Weise's *Der politische Näscher* (Political Climber) or Beer's *Der politische Bratenwender* (Political Sausage Roaster)—means something like prudent or worldly, hence the political met the picaresque in the journey, through which characters learn about the world and their place in it. And the world was, as these books showed, a dangerous and terrible place for young Germans on their own.

Literary historians have found in these works a kind of proto-realism, with dashes of magic thrown in, and preposterous though these characters and plot lines can be, nevertheless even the strangest of them remain powerfully grounded in the circumstances of the late seventeenth century. One does not have to believe that everything Simplicissimus experienced actually happened to Grimmelshausen, the one-time boy soldier and musketeer, in order to see in the novel a remarkable working through of the trauma of the Thirty Years' War—sinners in the hands of an indifferent God.[25] Likewise, in the musician novels, two closely related aspects of the musical world come to the fore repeatedly—the problems of the musician's social identity and national identity. Both problems are reflected in the lives of the authors themselves, and both are worked out through the theme of travel. In Johann Beer's *Der simplicianische Welt-Kucker oder der abentheuerliche Jan Rebhu* (The Simplician World-Observer or the Adventurous Jan Rebhu), the title character, an orphan of course, becomes a soprano at a court dominated by Italian musicians, is taught by a castrato, barely escapes becoming one himself, and then wanders in and out of more or less dangerous love affairs, getting into all kinds of trouble, including shipwrecks, near executions, and battles with Turks. In Daniel Speer's *Haspel-Hanss*, the main character, this time a deformed orphan, half learns the musical trade and proceeds to practice it badly in university towns all across Germany. In Speer's *Der Dacianische Simplicissimus*, the main character, this time a religiously persecuted orphan, takes to the road, learns to play the drum and the trumpet, then serves as a military musician in the wars against the Turks, traveling through Galicia, Bohemia, Hungary, and Austria, before moving on to Constantinople and the Middle East in the book's sequel, *Der Türckische Vagrant*.

Beyond the book-selling exoticism of their adventures, the marginality of these characters serves a common admonitory purpose. All suffer from deficient musical training, and none is able to find a settled place in his native land. Buffeted by fate, exploited and abandoned by nobles and courtiers, they embody the displacements and sufferings of a Germany victimized by its more powerful neighbors and its selfish or incompetent rulers. Their travel, as much symptom as cause of their vulnerability, can produce no worldly experience that would make up for what it takes away; a life of adventure is no substitute for a craft well learned. Moreover, the problems they face, as Beer made explicit in the polemical pamphlets he wrote shortly after the *Jan Rebhu* series, were not moral ones arising from their musical profession. In 1696, a school rector and scholar named Gottfried Vockerodt had published an antimusical fulmination in which he suggested that music led people into lives of dissipation and evil deeds (being a classicist, his prime example was young Nero and his violin). Beer retorted that harmony was the very foundation of the universe (a familiar argument); the creation of harmony through music made this art the finest and most humanly important of all arts (an unfamiliar one); and the occasional rackety behavior associated with some musicians and music lovers could not be solved by the banning of music.[26] It could be solved, however, by thorough education in the musical craft, which would foster a deep understanding of the rules of harmony and composition. That in turn required that German musicians resist the siren call of foreign names and foreign ways, learn their trade, and practice it well.[27] It required, in short, not that musicians cease to travel but that they cease to wander aimlessly.

A declared enemy of musical scholasticism and someone who had led a rackety life himself before and during his successful career as concert master and singer for Duke August of Saxony-Weissenfels, Beer did not always see eye to eye with his fellow musician-authors. He attacked in print, among others, Wolfgang Caspar Printz, like him a successful and widely traveled court musician but a man less tolerant of disruptive behavior.[28] In writing style and professional experience, Beer also had little in common with fellow novelist Johann Kuhnau, Johann Sebastian Bach's immediate predecessor in the respectable position of cantor of the Thomaskirche in Leipzig. But viewed from our perspective, removed from the disputatious atmosphere of this emergent German public sphere, they shared a basic understanding of the importance of the role of the musician in German life. This was an understanding that went beyond a defense of the craft and honor of the guild musician against his roguish doppelgänger and beyond the *Untertan*'s ineffectual complaining about his noble employer—though to be sure the novels can be seen as expressive of pervasive anxiety about the insecurities of court employment and the possibility of a settled life in troubled times.[29] The kinds of social tensions these novels depict, and the kinds of resolutions they propose, go further and assert a new order, which their authors were simultaneously working to achieve in their musical activities. At the purely musical level, this period saw the full articulation of a system of functional harmony, by which, in the striking characterization of Joseph Kerman, "chords seem to be going where we expect them to, harmonies no longer seem to wander, detour, hesitate, or evaporate."[30] At a more broadly cultural level, these activities—composing, performing, organizing, writing, traveling—ultimately shaped a new transnational musical world, in which German musicians, *as* Germans and in both German-speaking lands and abroad, strove for recognition outside the older structures of guild and court and thereby helped to make Germany audible, legible, and real.

MUSIC AND NATIONALIZING CULTURE IN THE EIGHTEENTH CENTURY

The baroque musician-novelists of the late seventeenth century first posed the problem of who is the musician in the world, a theme that plays out in a rich set of variations over the course of the eighteenth century. To call eighteenth-century Germany a nationalizing culture is to acknowledge that many, indeed most, aspects of social, political, and cultural life were *not* nationalizing in this period and that signs of German consciousness must be seen within the complexity of milieus from which this nationalizing project emerged. Consider, for instance, the extent to which J. S. Bach, musical colossus that he was, straddled the interlocking spheres of worship, political display, learning, and sociability, each of which was marked by, in widely varying degrees, a consciousness of German national identity. In the period in which he worked, from January 1703 to his death in July 1750, he earned money, in descending order of importance to his income, from municipal authorities, noblemen, and the anonymous paying public, and he held gradually more prestigious posts as minor court musician, organist, music director, concertmaster, Kapellmeister, and finally (a lateral move to a different kind of prestige) cantor. The geographical spread of places where he held these positions is small, as scholars often point out, and the farthest extent of his own travels was to Lübeck in the north.

During this period, the most active and well-funded centers of musical life lay in the princely courts and residential cities, in which a distinctive courtly "institutionalization of music, following the French model and employing mainly Italian musicians, served to domesticate the nobility—through rituals, etiquettes, and entertainments, which Italian opera, with its elaborate plots and theatrical realizations, dominated."[31] This cultural milieu was cosmopolitan and its makers notoriously indifferent to anything like native cultural development. Princely preference for Italian or French musical culture did not reflect disdain for native German musical work as such but the function of art in connecting princes and nobility to their social and political counterparts across all of Europe. Italian-dominated communities of musical taste thus asserted an aristocratic identity over a national or local one. Moreover, even if they did not set the dominant musical style or fill the most prestigious courtly positions, many German musicians traveled to Italy to study music and subsequently found employment in the courts, as well as opportunities for modest social advancement within their ensembles. Bach worked this system as much as he was able, serving for extended periods in the ducal court at Weimar and the princely court of Anhalt-Cöthen, but his reputation was not made in the service of princes.

As for town musicians of the eighteenth century, the only independent and vibrant urban centers were the trading cities of Hamburg, Bremen, Frankfurt, and Leipzig. All managed to sustain astonishingly rich musical cultures well into the era when independent urban culture elsewhere declined in the face of the rising domination of princely states and their cities. Leipzig, although not an imperial free city, managed after 1648 to reclaim its position as the most important trade center of Central Europe by 1710.[32] Its renewed prosperity allowed it to spend some money on its cultural institutions, which thus enjoyed independence from princely intervention. The powerful city council of Leipzig, in concert with church authorities, controlled the Thomasschule and city churches. The university was a proudly self-governing corporation, with extensive (though not complete) control over its musical activities. This plethora of alternately competing and cooperative authorities characterized many a smaller German community, ensuring equilibrium, if not excellence or innovation. In Bach's frequent clashes with authorities, he usually deployed arguments about his rightful corporate privileges, never his needs as an artist. His career illustrated the profound differences between the local and courtly musical milieu. Bach, like many practicing musicians by the start of the eighteenth century, moved back and forth between these two, submitting at times to the contentious discipline of corporate town institutions and at other times to the humiliating servitude and insecure tenure of the court musician and struggling throughout to extract the best from both worlds.[33]

It is hard nevertheless to avoid the conclusion that court music provided more scope for creativity and individual achievement than did the "static dull complexities" and the "monotony and melancholy" of German town life.[34] Duke Johann Ernst of Weimar, for all that he is remembered as the patron who consigned Bach to a month in the local jail, made it possible for Bach to immerse himself in a great body of Italian instrumental music (Vivaldi, Corelli, et alia), in part by bringing back thousands of scores of the latest works from his own travels. To say that Bach, who had never been able to travel to Italy or anywhere outside of Germany himself, absorbed all this, worked on it, and synthesized it into works at once Italianate and wholly his own is an understatement. The circumstances that made possible the full expression of his musical potential thus included, prominently, networks of travel and cultural exchange linking European court cultures and rippling out from them into town and church milieu.

Finally, Bach's career reveals glimpses of the literary culture, to the growing significance of which the musician novels and musical polemics attested. The first printed reference to Bach—Johann Mattheson's (1681–1764) remark in 1717 that he had "seen things by the famous organist of Weimar, Mr. Joh. Sebastian Bach . . . that are certainly such as must make one esteem the man highly"—was a direct indication of this third culture's existence. So too was his request to Bach in 1720 for biographical information (never provided) for a planned dictionary of musicians. Likewise when the mayor of Leipzig pressed for Bach's appointment because he was eager to appoint a "famous man" to the cantorate in order to "bolster the attractiveness and reputation of the city," we sense the presence of a new set of cultural assumptions at work.[35] These moments all concern Bach's reputation—a simple enough concept, one would have thought, but in early eighteenth century Germany it was anything but. The milieu of locality and hometown, the one into which Bach was born and spent much of his life, understood reputation in terms of membership in the community, what Mack Walker once described as "a silhouette projected on community," which can be "rendered and reflected only by community."[36] Divorced from this community, individual artistic achievement made no sense. Reputation in court circles was by contrast a matter of virtuosity and display, the purpose of which was to cast not one's own shadow upon the world at large but rather that of the prince one served. And those who had it tended not to be Germans, or if they were Germans, they had become cosmopolitans, known for their extensive travels and conversant in many languages.[37]

Mattheson was deploying a third notion of reputation when he referred to the "esteem" in which Bach ought to be held. This kind was earned through striving and merit. It marked one out for notice from a larger world than a single community, and most important, it was both the product of the musician's circulation and a literary artifact, written about and discussed among the educated inhabitants of independent and princely cities. Historians have for the most part explored literary culture as a project that consisted of writing literature and developing the expressive capacities of the German language. As a result, the participation of musicians, including musicians writing about music, in the nationalizing project of literary culture is more obscure to us, even though the writings of musical novelists, scholars, and aesthetic philosophers, extracted from this context, have long drawn the attention of scholars in their respective disciplines. But musical matters were more central to the makers of this new nationalizing culture than we have acknowledged, and vice versa, the makers of this national culture contributed substantially to new developments in musical life in ways that may have been recognized, though not often in such terms.

Two major trends in musical life in the eighteenth century reflected the growth of nationalizing culture and the social groups defining it. The first was a trend toward a musical marketplace, separate from court institutions and free of guild restrictions, in which musicians could earn money—teaching and playing with growing numbers of amateurs, performing in the new phenomenon of public concerts, and participating as middlemen, copyists, publishers, sellers, and of course composers in the expanding commerce of music publishing. All these adjustments required movement, travel, flexibility, not unprecedented for musicians but now in a changed context. Inevitably, some commentators experienced this as loss—not just of security but of something more like standards, the craft itself. Klaus Hortschansky argues that by the latter half of the eighteenth century, a "latent crisis" existed in the music profession; music was doomed to become, in the words of composer J. W. Hässler in 1787, a "breadless art," in which no distinctions could any longer be maintained "between beer fiddlers, town musicians, and true artists."[38] A few years earlier, composer Johann Friedrich Reichardt lamented that "from the prince's *Oberkapellmeister* to the beer fiddler who drags operettas into the peasant pub, everyone has become an artisan producing cheap copies for the going market price."[39] Established institutions of court music themselves furthered the growth of this marketplace by opening court performances to a limited audience and supporting the development of national theaters.[40] Princely courts also stood behind the development of the social core of new audiences consisting of educated and culturally ambitious people who were often members of the bureaucratic elites. They consumed music in concerts, on their travels, in their own homes, commodifying music but at the same time establishing the beginnings of organized public interest in the arts.

The second trend, no less important in shaping the meaning of music and musical travel, was a slow accumulation of writings about music: critical, scholarly, imaginative, and concerned—far more than was the case with the baroque novelists like Johann Beer and others—with the question of music's role in the humanistic project of enlightenment and social improvement. In Johann Kuhnau's cheerful *Der musikalische Quacksalber* (Musical Charlatan), published in Dresden in 1700, the story begins in a prosperous, bustling market town, with substantial citizens and an educated cadre of town musicians engaged in musical and academic undertakings who consider themselves men of the world—all that is to say, the novel's setting is Leipzig.[41] But Kuhnau also invokes the broader milieu of literary culture with his greeting to the "amiable reader" and his references to antiquity, the "stage of our world," and the Leipzig Book Fair catalog. Finally he makes clear his purpose not to attack "the upright virtuosic *musici* who adorn not only foreign countries but also our own" but to show "how great a gulf exists between art and ignorance," "how much something splendid and delicate is to be preferred to that which is rustically wild and maladroit," and how much in the world is "good and moral."[42]

The assertion and defense of German identity is the undertow of the whole work, pulling the reader along through surface actions and distractions of his antihero, the musical charlatan. This "so-called Caraffa," a German from Swabia with a false name who "for approximately a year had carried the instruments of some famous musicians in Italy," returns to a town in Germany, sure that he will be able to fool people there as he could not in Italy. Caraffa considers most Germans to belong to "that silly company who think a composer or *musicus* who hasn't seen Italy is a foolish dunderhead" and believe "that the air of Italy can impregnate people with the most perfect skills."[43] He also counts on being unknown—Kuhnau's depiction of the limits of local knowledge amounts to a running commentary on German fragmentation, as Caraffa travels through Germany's provincial backwaters. There are, then, three kinds of fools in this novel: the ordinary fools, country bumpkins who know nothing and have spent their lives gossiping around the parish pump; the pretentious, insecure fools who have a little learning and no sense; and the fool Caraffa who thinks that all his fellow Germans are as ignorant of true learning, true art, and true music as is he.

We meet Kuhnau's heroes on the first page, the members of the *collegium musicum*. This characteristically German musical organization, of which Leipzig's was among the most famous, dated probably to the Reformation era and consisted of professional and amateur musicians, gathering for the pleasure of performing instrumental and vocal music. Under Kuhnau himself, and his successors Georg Philipp Telemann and J. S. Bach, the Leipzig Collegium Musicum began to perform weekly in public, usually at the storied Zimmerman's coffee house. Music historians regard it as one of several points of origin for the rise of the public concert and symphony orchestra; it represented a form of sociability through small-scale music making that proliferated from the late eighteenth century onward.[44] Kuhnau's account describes it as "indeed a praiseworthy undertaking, partly because [its members] thereby continue to improve themselves in their splendid profession and partly because from their pleasant harmony they also should learn an even, harmonious agreement among their personalities which from time to time must prevail among such people."[45] Music makes society, and in this case, the members of the group know how to act in concert. They quickly identify Caraffa as a fraud, through reports of a member who knows Swabia and so knows the "real" Caraffa (travelers' knowledge) and, more profoundly, by his inability to participate in their performance. The charlatan continually interrupts it by taking snuff, the marker of French affectation and equally as suspect as his Italian disguise.

Travel in this story represents, then, both a danger and a promise for Germans. On the one hand it clearly fosters trickery like Caraffa's; on the other it can enlighten and strengthen Germans in their craft, as we see in the members of the collegia musica, not bumpkins or fools but Germans of broad experience and "*alte teutsche Redlichkeit und Aufrichtigkeit.*" Their judgment on Caraffa is unequivocal. "All those who are ashamed of their German names and commit a fraud by changing them deserve to have Germany be ashamed of *them* and expel them from its borders along with other frauds," says one musician; another adds, "because he prefers the Italian language, manners, and names to the Swabian and thus disdains his good fatherland, I can't recognize him as an honest fellow."[46]

But piquant though *The Musical Charlatan* may be, Kuhnau himself was not the most important figure in defining and defending music to the German reading public of the eighteenth century. That status belongs to Mattheson of Hamburg, organist, composer, and the true founder of the tradition of musical writing in Central Europe. He was born, lived, and was buried in Hamburg, and his life's work reflected the ethos of this trading hub of enduring importance and this site for the absorption of English influences in German Europe. Though he lived only briefly in England, Mattheson was a conduit of such influences, a tutor to the English ambassador's son, then a fully invested diplomat attached to his entourage. He retained this post for much of his life, and it brought him income, elevated social status, and marriage to an Englishwoman. Mattheson's physical travels were limited; his was the traveling of the mind, by which he ranged across Europe, including the fractured, musically scattered landscape of Germany. He extended the possibilities of music writing in several directions: a pedagogic one, by providing useful aids to fellow musicians, which in turn circulated widely even into the nineteenth century; a learned one, by writing treatises for the scholarly community; and a public, political one, by translating from English numerous political and economic tracts, and by writing quite a few himself, often commenting on the musical scene.[47] Not of course the first to bring music into such discursive contexts, his contributions were wide-ranging, substantial, and timely. They ensured that discussions of music in Germany would for the next two and a half centuries implicate and debate nationality. Otto Dann has called Hamburg the "point of departure for modern patriotism in Germany," and because of Mattheson we can add, for modern musical patriotism as well.[48]

In 1713, Mattheson published his first sustained work on music, *Das neu-eröffnete Orchestre* (The Newly-Established Orchestra), a "universal and fundamental guide" for the "educated gentleman" to understand "fully the greatness and worth of noble music." The first musical compendium for nonmusicians in Germany, it included information, in nontechnical terms, about musical qualities and terminology, as well as rules and national schools (Italian, French, English, and German) of composition. His book was at once useful and critical, universalizing and comparative, and he used it to point out the urgent need for musical composition to develop with changing times, something that would never happen in Germany without improving the deplorable educational and economic condition of German musicians.[49] In 1722, Mattheson's first venture in musical journalism, *Critica Musica*, became the first musical periodical in Europe, modeled explicitly on the scholarly periodicals and moral weeklies of literary culture, including that of England.[50] In 1728 he began a second periodical, called *Der musicalische Patriot*, to signal its kinship with *Der Patriot*, a journal aimed at the "German-speaking community" of Hamburg and beyond. A number of further treatises on the principles of harmony and melody followed, liberally sprinkled with his views on the wretched state of musical Germany (operatic music, church music, instrumental music, courts, cantorates, universities). His crowning achievements came close on each other's heels, in 1739 and 1741. The first and most famous was *Der vollkommene Capellmeister*, containing "the fundamental information about all those matters that anyone who would preside over an ensemble with honor and competence must know, be able to do, and completely master."[51] The second was his *Grundlage einer Ehrenpforte* (Foundations for a Gateway of Honor), a biographical encyclopedia of the 148 "most excellent" musicians of his day (not including J. S. Bach, though that was possibly Bach's own fault). The latter in its essential nature and the former in its digressions both constituted documents of a nationalizing culture. Both were widely read in their day and influential long after it; both attest to an understanding of music as a vital part of European life, in which Germany could, with considerable effort at reforming itself musically, be playing a more substantial role.

Might we then consider Mattheson a nation builder and a nationalist? His was a nationalism grounded in the observation and emulation of other nations and in his efforts to experience and understand the rest of the world. Perhaps better than nationalist would be "patriot," the title of his periodical. In his day it carried overlapping connotations, including devotion to one's native land (a place of indeterminate boundaries but essentially local and limited) and consciousness of membership in an indeterminate entity called *Deutschland*. The word also evoked a discourse of "baroque language and cultural patriotism" and a search for the missing ground of national consciousness that dated back more than half a century.[52] "The unity of the citizenry," he wrote in a brief section of *Der Vollkommene Capellmeister* on "the use of music in the General Public," is the foundation of the "strongest nations," and what better way to achieve such unity than through the promotion of music. All great states, from the Greeks to the "present-day wise Chinese" to the French and the English, "have structured their inner life so admirably by means of music, still do so," as to bring about a "complete political body."[53] Mattheson's choice of the term "patriot" also reflected his belief in a common good, as well as defensiveness about Italian music (especially opera) and other influences from outside the communities to which the patriot belonged. Reinhart Koselleck has described this defensiveness as a "concrete fear of the cultural infiltration of foreigners [*Überfremdung*] and political powerlessness."[54] Literate people knew that German culture existed, but lacking the confident assertion of a deeply rooted existence for it that Herder would deliver half a century later, German culture seemed to them a vulnerable, elusive thing, too dependent on the changing fortunes of princes and easily lost through the bumbling ignorance of the people.

CHORAL SOCIETIES AND NATION BUILDING IN THE NINETEENTH CENTURY

Any consensus on what actually constituted German culture, as compared to, for instance, the German manners and German names that Kuhnau's learned musicians so confidently recognized, proved difficult to articulate. Mattheson himself danced around the problem, saying a great deal about canons and fugues, Italian and French styles of declamation, and problems like carpetbagging Italian musicians (they "make all the money and then return home"). But neither he nor anyone else managed to describe in words what Johann Philipp Praetorius called the "ingenious character of the German nation" that music alone expressed.[55] Putting aside, then, the further development of musical writing along the meandering paths that led eventually to the Romantics, we need to consider people in the act of making music, in order to illuminate further aspects of the work both music and travel did in a world of nations.

Choral activity formed a large a part of nineteenth-century music making in German-speaking Europe. It was simultaneously local, national, and transnational, and singing in choral groups and traveling to choral festivals probably did more to provide ways in which people understood and lived their nationality than did any number of canonizing composer biographies or concert and opera performances. Nevertheless, its rapid growth after 1815, and the large numbers of people it mobilized, poses a nagging "why" question for which neither social nor aesthetic nor political explanations suffice. The first large-scale choral performances, immediate ancestors of the sort that became widespread in the nineteenth century, took place not in Germany but in England. They took shape in midcentury in the Lenten performances of Handel's oratorios and had an early apotheosis in 1784, with the enormous centenary commemoration of Handel in Westminster Abbey. Apart from the composer's birthplace, little was peculiarly German about these origins.

Still, the British developed in a short amount of time a "social and musical ritual" that, in the words of William Weber, "proved remarkably appealing and adaptable," as well as portable.[56] It brought together large numbers of amateur and professional singers from a nationally extensive space to perform revered older or serious newer works. The nineteenth century added a degree of institutionalization to the spread of choral festivals, with the proliferation of musical societies.[57] Number, size, and purposes of festivals expanded apace, crowding the civic calendars with celebrations of composers, monarchs, events, and inventions. The Great Exhibition of 1851 included round-the-clock oratorio performances of the Anglo-German lineup of Handel's *Messiah*, Mendelssohn's *Elijah*, and Haydn's *Creation*, and thereafter, in the characteristic dynamic of imitation and amplification, thousands of singers descended on every world's fair for friendly international competition.[58] In short, nineteenth-century singers leave the impression of having spent their time in a state of constant motion and tireless enthusiasm.[59]

What is not so obvious is whether all this traveling and singing meant the same thing. The Handel festivals in England, says Weber, were national celebrations that stabilized the relationship among state, state church, and society.[60] The situation was otherwise in German Europe, where state and society were too decentralized and scattered for any music festival to have German-wide consequences. Still, this was not for want of aspirations. In 1786, Johann Adam Hiller, the first director of Leipzig's Gewandhaus concerts, organized the first full performance of *Messiah* in German-speaking Europe, imitating the British. It took place in the Berlin Cathedral, with an orchestra and chorus numbering in the hundreds. He followed it up with similarly large-scale performances in Leipzig in 1786 and 1787, then in Breslau in 1788—taking it on the road to the leading musical centers of north-central Germany. When Hiller moved to Leipzig in 1751, the year after Bach's death, he already had more in common with Mattheson, or indeed with Handel, than he did with Bach, and hoped his work would improve musical life beyond that of any single locality. Bringing Handel back to the Germans thus formed one part of a varied career as composer, theorist, pedagogue, and impresario, in which he traveled often from place to place.[61] He organized concert series, established musical societies for amateurs, ran a school for singers, and founded a musical periodical. His treatises on singing instruction were revolutionary, and his collections of songs for children and household music making reflected progressive ideas about music in the home and the enlightening sociability inherent to music making as a whole.

All these activities echo far into the nineteenth century, marking them as a point of origin for a number of key transformations in the musical culture of Germany, Europe, and North America—festivals, big groups, careful training regimens, easily accessible collections of songs for home and amateur singing, and attention to national traits and traditions. Yet his impact dissipated in the era of the French Revolution, when Germans became aware of models of choral activity at once more inspiring and more disturbing. After 1790, the open-air festivals of revolutionary and

Napoleonic Paris, which included massed choral singing and large military bands, recruited music to the cause of the new regimes. In German-speaking Central Europe, these French models implicitly competed with the English Handelian ones for the soul of the German choral movement, winning at least a few initial victories for what in the German context was a destabilizing nationalism. The first large-scale festival in Germany, in 1810 in the small Thuringian town of Frankenhausen, was not overtly political, but its place and time sounded themes of a nationalizing consciousness that became louder over the next decades. Its organizer, an obscure local cantor and court musician named G. F. Bischoff, was so encouraged by a performance of Haydn's *Creation* in his native Frankenhausen that he convinced Louis Spohr, then conductor of the court orchestra in nearby Gotha, to direct a larger-scale festival in his hometown.

Frankenhausen lies at the foot of the Kyffhäuser mountain, deep inside of which, according to German legend, the Emperor Frederick Barbarossa slept in a hidden chamber, waiting to arise and come to Germany's rescue in his country's hour of greatest need—a fanciful notion with surprising resonance. The participants in the festival did not cry "Wach' auf!" to the emperor or to their fellow Germans, like the townspeople of Wagner's *Meistersinger of Nuremberg* some sixty years later. Still, hundreds of German musicians, both amateur and professional, did gather to perform Haydn's *Creation* and Beethoven's Fifth Symphony. Five years later, even more gathered again, this time to commemorate the victory over Napoleon two years earlier at the Battle of the Nations in Leipzig. They sang Gottfried Weber's *Te Deum* as well as Spohr's newly composed cantata *Das befreite Deutschland* (Germany Liberated) and gave speeches consonant with the aggressive, even sacralized, nature of German nationalist discourse during the period of the Napoleonic Wars. In 1818, the first of what became the most musically ambitious of the German festivals, the Lower Rhine Festival, took place in Elberfeld, with a large orchestra and chorus from the surrounding area.[62] The emperor, it seems, had awoken.

The development of German nationalism after the monarchical restorations of 1815 takes one through many political detours and disappointments, but a concern for the cultural achievements of the German nation never disappeared. Nationally minded people of this era did not make neat distinctions between the cultural content of nationhood and its political implications; to believe that Germany existed as a cultural reality was also to believe in the political ideal of self-government and unified statehood.[63] But people expressed their consciousness of their nationality in different ways, and when the opportunities for political activism diminished, especially after 1819, the promotion of cultural unity and national fulfillment through the consumption of culture became more important, and not simply as a cover for forbidden political gatherings. Events like the Lower Rhine Festivals exemplified such activism with their performances of oratorios and symphonies by composers whose German nationality the organizers and participants found deeply satisfying. The international significance of these compositions was to them a truth they held to be self-evident, and hence the performance of such works asserted, in very public fashion, the existence of a German nation among nations. They were a cultural declaration of national independence.

We can also regard the Lower Rhine Festivals, and others like them, as the most public face of the many respectable singing societies that had developed in Central Europe since the founding of Carl Friedrich Fasch's Berlin Singakademie in 1791, the first permanent amateur singing organization in German Europe and accidental heir to the Handel tradition in Germany begun by Hiller. Fasch's Singakademie grew to more than a hundred singers by 1800 and more than two hundred by 1815. Under him and his successor, Carl Friedrich Zelter, it became known for its careful study of sacred choral music, much of it no longer regularly heard in either Catholic or Protestant churches. In January 1794, Fasch introduced J. S. Bach's double-chorus motet *Komm, Jesu, Komm* into rehearsals, setting the Singakademie off on its thirty-five-year journey to its celebrated revival of his *St. Matthew Passion* in 1829—an event, like the Lower Rhine Festivals, of profound national significance to performers and audiences alike.[64] Groups seeking a similar kind of musical experience soon began to appear all over German-speaking Europe. The Singakademie's first wave of imitators, starting with the Leipzig Singakademie (founded in 1800), included within a couple decades more than a dozen new choral societies from Stettin to Innsbruck.[65]

The German festival movement, with its large mixed-sex choruses, did not challenge established authority, but they did maintain a presence in the public eye. They adopted formal statutes, elected officials, held fund-raisers, and made claims on public space that were anything but modest.[66] The desire to assert themselves publically was even more the case with a rowdier strand of the choral-festival movement, that of male choruses. Starting in 1809, with Carl Friedrich Zelter's founding in Berlin of a singing group, or *Liedertafel*, for men only, hundreds of similar organizations sprang up all across German-speaking Europe. By the 1830s, these men's singing societies represented one of the most important outlets for the public participatory impulses of people whose political activism was virtually shut down. Frequent gatherings of singers in the years preceding the outbreak of revolution in 1848 were occasions for cautious speech making and unrestrained singing, both making a case for a single German nation as well as celebrating German nature and the German people.[67] Whether unveiling a monument (Gutenberg in Mainz in 1840,

Beethoven in Bonn in 1845), honoring a restored cathedral (two for the Cologne Cathedral in 1842), or celebrating the patriotic fellowship of song, these events mobilized several thousand male singers and drew even larger audiences from the city and surrounding towns. None of the festivals or groups contributed directly to the outbreak of the revolution, and they more or less ceased as a form of public activism in the revolutionary years themselves, thus making this kind of massed singing different from its French predecessors. Nevertheless, the men's singing movement of the pre-1848 period established its credentials as the authentic voice of the German nation.

The general tendency of the nineteenth century, no matter the country or the activity, was to consolidate and institutionalize, and singing everywhere was no exception. After the revolutionary period had faded away, massed singing returned to Central Europe, with greater numbers than before. In 1862, a German Singing Confederation (Deutsche Sängerbund) solidified the fluid ties among different localities, and soon an annual Confederation Festival became a regular, ever more staid event on the musical calendar of a soon-to-be-united German Empire. Yet the Liedertafel model, with its combination of small local groups and periodic large festivals, had not simply become establishment. It proved influential in showing Eastern European nationalities a way to express their sense of belonging together, and to give workers, students, and veterans a satisfying and relatively peaceful way to make noise. Workers' choruses, which began to form in large numbers in the 1860s, took the middle-class Liedertafel as both model and countermodel, adopting its earlier method of using singing as a way to pursue politics and consciousness raising through nonpolitical means. Especially after the new German Empire passed antisocialist laws in the 1870s, massed singing became, once again, as much a way to evade authority as to celebrate it.[68] Regardless of the political valence of German men's singing groups, all in one way or another served the cause of nation building. Germany and other modernizing nations became real to people because many thousands of them traveled around it, first by coach or horseback or on foot, later most often by train, meeting their fellow countrymen and singing together.[69]

Finally, all these choral groups, including ones in other European nations and in the United States, showed a lively, even maniacal interest in competition. By the latter half of the nineteenth century, neither a year nor an exposition went by without a choral competition taking place. For the exhibition organizers, this was a winning proposition, promising to bring "music-lovers in all parts of the country" to the event; for singers, this pursuit of war by other means brought the pleasure of travel and the thrill of defeating others. For all the differences between the development of choral singing and festivals in Germany, Great Britain, and the United

States, if one simply closed one's eyes and listened, one would have been hearing the same thing, and that held true over a surprisingly long period of time. There were exceptions of course: many of the individual choral societies that gathered at these mass events sang a wider European repertoire of choral works, and a number of non-German works made their way into the massed chorus festivals as well. The immense popularity and rapid dissemination of Verdi's *Requiem* in Germany after 1875 provides an intense, yet nevertheless characteristic, example of the porousness of national musical borders in practice.[70] Nevertheless, from Handel to Haydn to Mendelssohn and beyond, these societies converged on a repertoire that was largely the joint creation of German-English musical interaction, institutionally and compositionally. Probably the most notable difference between singing societies and choral festivals in England and Germany was not the music but the absence of alcohol at the former and its overindulgence at the latter. In contrast to the teetotaling temperance activists who filled the English choral societies, German festivals of local Liedertafeln had already by 1844 earned the reputation of being, in the words of the *Allgemeine Musikalische Zeitung*, "drinking bouts with shouting and tobacco smoke."[71]

The pleasures of participation in the public world were the hallmark of singing in big groups, but we should not allow the peremptory claims of publicity to blind us to more intimate forms of small-group singing that were just as important to nineteenth-century music lovers. Composers wrote for them; publishers catered to them; parents encouraged their older children to participate in them; likewise employers their employees and eventually all levels of schooling, from the elementary to the university, included them. Small-group singing was often, though not always, a single-sex activity. The German Liedertafel in Zelter's original formulation consisted of a small number (fifteen or so) of like-minded men, who would gather "with German gaiety (*Fröhlichkeit*) and conviviality (*Gemütlichkeit*)" for a "frugal repast" and sing songs that the members themselves had written. Within a decade of its founding, it had become stodgy enough that a rival organization, of *younger* like-minded men, had formed in Berlin. And so it went all across Germany and soon across America. The logic of the diffusion was the logic of sociability, that is, of finding people with whom one wanted to spend time. Some societies organized themselves around certain genres—madrigals, motets—and thus considered themselves chiefly motivated by the work of historical recovery. Others grew out of the isolation of immigrants in foreign lands or small-town people in big cities and so affirmed regional and local identities in unfamiliar places. The whole superstructure of festivals, competitions, and national dreams grew out of this basic experience of "keeping together in time" and also creating together in time. As McNeill put it, this togetherness constituted and reconstituted social bonds on a daily basis—it did not simply reflect the fact that society already existed.[72]

Take the Berlin Singakademie, for another instance. At the start of the century in which it became the model for so many other choruses, Zelter described it as "a kind of artistic corps" in which "every serious-minded friend of art" would find "as much satisfaction through serious art as is possible." Its gatherings encompassed "attentiveness without visible exertion, beauty without privilege, multiplicity of all estates, ages, and trades, without affectation; delight in a fine art without weariness; the young and the old, the aristocrat and the burgher; the joy and the discipline; the father and the daughter, the mother with her son, and every possible mixing of the sexes and the estates."[73] The musicologist Erich Valentin once wrote that groups of people singing in homes "formed the foundation on which public music life first began to constitute itself, radiating from within society to more outward forms."[74] Zelter's description, in which his group is a family, and indeed a rapidly growing one, confirms the truth of this. Many a choral society in the nineteenth century, especially those that began almost casually, as did the Singakademie, had their roots not in church practices or public, state-centered ceremonials, but in the semiprivate and private settings of domestic music making.

As a result, the organizational structures of this quasi-formal, quasi-private singing varied enormously, from occasional gatherings in someone's music room or parlor to highly organized groups with regular rehearsal space, statutes, dues, membership lists, and annual reports. Women's choruses in German-speaking Europe sometimes traced their activity to the singing that went on in the spinning rooms of premodern households, and there were plenty of folklorists who were willing to play the game of "find the origins" as well.[75] Richard Wagner gave the theory his own peculiar blessing in the "Spin, Spin, Fair Maiden" chorus that opens act 2 of *Der Fliegende Holländer*, and in the way of such things, versions of this popular scene in the opera circulated back into the women's chorus repertoire. Singing and spinning did go together naturally, as did song and work, song and edification, education and moral improvement, song and conviviality, with or without alcoholic lubrication. If one follows the yearly activities, for instance, of the University of Munich men's chorus in the late nineteenth century, one finds a group that maintained in its yearbook a list of all former members, honorary members, auxiliary members, and "philistines" (that is, community people who paid dues), thus constituting social bonds across time as well as in place. Rituals abounded in such groups. An annual party before Lent included elaborate shenanigans that usually involved cross-dressing (imagine a young Max Planck, future Nobel Prize winner, writing an operetta for this group, of which he was assistant director, about the unexpected arrival of a harem at the Vienna world's fair). An annual expedition took the group to some town in the surrounding country-side, where much wining, dining, and singing with the town men's chorus would take place, followed often by an early morning hike to the local promontory or castle ruin, where a patriotic song of some sort would ring forth, and then more wining and dining and singing.[76] Nature itself was inscribed with social and national significance in such practices, and the combination of movement and music created vital bonds of belonging that could be mobilized in other settings and for other purposes as well. To invoke again the biological and the anthropological, singing was work done together. It enacted the struggle to come together and the satisfaction of achieving it. It was the synchronization of individual bodies (ears, minds, eyes, lungs, arms holding music, legs standing and sitting). Particularly when one realizes that behind every performance lay months and years of weekly rehearsals, each with the warm-ups, the repetitions, the tea breaks with sweet cakes, the talking and exchanging of opinions and experiences, the coming together and leaving only to return again the next week, then one comes to acknowledge that singing together was a central experience of the quotidian for hundreds of thousands of Europeans and Americans, made all the more memorable by the unconscious effects, so impossible to measure, of the music itself.

IN CONCLUSION

Ethnomusicologist John Blacking wrote,

> Music cannot change societies, as can changes in technology and political organization. It cannot make people act unless they are already socially and culturally disposed to act. It cannot instill brotherhood, as Tolstoy hoped, or any other state or social value. If it can do anything to people, the best that it can do is to confirm situations that already exist. It cannot in itself generate thoughts that may benefit or harm mankind, as some writers have suggested; but it can make people more aware of feelings that they have experienced, or partly experienced, by reinforcing, narrowing or expanding their consciousness in a variety of ways.[77]

When thinking about the Germans and their music (if indeed we should even consider it "theirs"), this is bracing good sense to counteract the more vulgar notions of music's implication in the crimes of the German people. Still, in his effort to get past the sentimentalizing, heroizing, and demonizing discourses about music that are among the many legacies to Western culture from its musical past, Blacking may restrict too severely the historical contributions of musicians to society and underplay the centrality to collective life of the actions he does allow that music can perform. It is particularly easy to underestimate music's broader cultural importance if we regard it as something that can be neatly sorted into hierarchies of low, middle, and high, filed under genres of blues, Christian, classical, country, jazz, rap, and reggae, confined to certain times of the week or modes of leisure—in short, a kind of decorative motif carved onto the iron cages of our modern existence. The study of how musicians and music have moved around in the world can provide an escape from these interpretative cages. "Out into the world with you!" wrote Carl Maria von Weber in 1809, as the opening line of his unfinished novel, *A Musician's Life*, "for the world is the artist's true sphere. . . . What good does it do you to live with a petty clique and to earn the gracious applause of a patron. Out! A man's spirit must find itself in the spirits of his fellow creatures."[78] German musicians followed his exhortation in ever greater numbers in the centuries that followed, out of ambition, curiosity, idealism, restlessness, and every kind of necessity, including, of course, exile and flight. One result was the German nation itself.

CHAPTER 3

From *Patriae Amator* to *Amator Pauperum* and Back Again

SOCIAL IMAGINATION AND SOCIAL CHANGE IN THE WEST BETWEEN LATE ANTIQUITY AND THE EARLY MIDDLE AGES, CA. 300–600

Peter Brown

PATRIAEQUE SEMPER AMATOR: "ALWAYS A LOVER OF HIS HOMELAND"

THIS IS A STUDY OF THE BODY image of a society in motion—and in motion over time.[1] It traces changes in the social imagination of populations of the Roman and post-Roman, Latin West between 300 and 600 CE. It will describe (and attempt, if only in part, to explain) how a society that had been characterized by a "classical," pointedly civic notion of society moved to a Christianized, postclassical notion of the community. The classical model took the individual city as its primary unit. It stressed the distinction between citizens and noncitizens, in a manner that effectively excluded slaves, country folk, and even resident foreigners. Only citizens were entitled to the generosity that the wealthy were expected to lavish on the inhabitants of their city. This sharply defined civic model was replaced by a view of society that was, at one and the same time, more universal and more high-pitched. Christian preaching stressed the universal obligation of all believers to give alms to the poor—to citizens and noncitizens, in town and countryside alike. It also presented society in more bleakly "economic" terms—as universally divided between rich and poor. Society was made up of rich and poor, and no longer of citizens and noncitizens. It was expected to be held together, primarily, by the obligation of the rich to care for the poor. This was now seen as a religious obligation, which would bear consequences for the soul in the other world. Last but not least, the obligations of the rich to the poor were upheld by religious leaders, by the bishops of the Catholic Church.

In the course of three centuries, Western Europe moved from the one social model to the other. The change in the social imagination did not occur in the blink of an eye, nor did it grow insensibly out of the new conditions of society itself. It was, rather, the consequence of a protracted challenge between competing visions of society. Christian, Hebrew, and classical notions of community, charity, poverty, and wealth flowed together into late Roman society, only slowly to lay down a new, stable conglomerate of values. Ultimately, what was brought about by this change amounted to nothing less than the end of the ancient world and the beginning of the medieval society from which our own world eventually emerged. As it is a long story, it is best to begin at the end.

It is a thrill for a historian of the West Roman Empire in its last days to arrive (through rooms devoted to a clutter of Victorian chinaware) at the small exhibit of early medieval tombstones in the Museum of the Carmarthenshire Antiquarian Society, in southwestern Wales. The crude inscriptions, carved in local sandstone, speak of a region in western Britain that had already lost much of its Roman face. It is, therefore, a surprise to find, in the midst of monuments to early Welsh and Irish warlords, broken portions of a square stone tombstone, whose clumsy lettering and erratic spelling reveal, on closer inspection, a carefully composed Latin inscription:

Here lies Paulinus servatur fidaei patrieq[ue] semper
amator guardian of the faith and always a lover of his home land.[2]

Paulinus may well have been a mid-sixth-century bishop in an area (near Caio, Carmarthen) that still bears his name—Pant-y-Polion: "the Vale of Paulinus." Paulinus was praised "as always a lover of his *patria*"—of his homeland. It was a phrase that was also used by his contemporaries across the sea in Gaul. A century after the disappearance of the Roman Empire in the West (in 476), the bishops of the cities of Gaul continued to be praised in Roman terms. Each was hailed as *Decus Patriae*, an "Ornament of his Homeland," *Tutor Patriae*, a "Guardian of his Homeland," *Urbis Amator* , a "Lover of his City."[3] The message was plain. If a leading Roman was to love anything, it was his *patria*—his home town. The inscription of Paulinus, in distant Wales, shows that, as late as the 550s and beyond, the Christian bishop was expected to continue this deep-rooted Roman love for a specific community. But what had changed was how this patria was defined; what sort of love the patria would receive, who would show this love and who would be its principal recipients.

Those who used the term *amator patriae* of their bishops were the heirs of a long tradition. Two centuries before the title amator patriae had been used in faraway Libya on the southern shore of the Mediterranean. To take only one example, the term appears in around 300 on the base of a statue set up to honor Porphyrius, a rich citizen of Lepcis Magna.

Porphyrius had shown himself to be a "lover of the city and of his fellow-citizens." He had provided four live elephants for the circus games of his city. In Lepcis Magna and elsewhere, "lover of the city/of the homeland" was a common phrase, with long roots in the ancient world.[4]

One thing is certain, Paulinus of Pant-y-Polion and other sixth-century bishops were no longer expected to provide elephants in order to prove their love for the community. The change in what they were now expected to provide sums up the turning of an age. But what, exactly, had changed? One aspect of the change is obvious: Paulinus was also praised as a *servator fidei*, a "guardian of the faith." He was a religious leader. What is less obvious is the specific nature of the power that came from such leadership. As a Christian bishop, he wielded a "pastoral" power. Let us begin by lingering a little on the peculiarity of that kind of power, which had come to the fore in Roman society with the spread of Christianity in the fourth, fifth, and sixth centuries.

In a series of lectures to the Collège de France in 1977–78 (which have only recently been published), the French philosopher Michel Foucault drew attention to the oddity and to the long destiny in European thought of the notion of "pastoral" power. It had deep roots in the ancient Near East and in early Christian discourse. It was "absolutely specific and different from political power" as it had usually been conceived in the Greco-Roman world.[5] It was a power that was thought of as more than usually insistent, wide-ranging, and absorptive. It was "directed to all and each" member of a flock of believers.[6] The bishop was supposed to love all members of his flock, loving each one of them equally, up to the very edge of the human community, where the poor gathered like a black band on the far horizon, marking the extreme edges of society. For the bishop's "pastoral" love for his flock was thought of as no more than a specific, localized manifestation of the love of God himself for all humankind.[7]

Even in his own patria, the bishop's love was not cramped by traditional civic boundaries: it was expected to extend to all classes. It spilled over in such a way as to erase (or, at least, in practice, to erode) the primary distinction—for ancient city dwellers—between townsfolk as "citizens" and the people of the countryside, who lived in a faceless world effectively deprived of citizenship. Porphyrius, by contrast, like any other ancient civic benefactor, did not have to stretch his love so far. It was enough for him to love only the city of Lepcis Magna up to its city walls but not beyond. Within Lepcis Magna itself, he needed to love only the clearly defined core of the city, which consisted of his "fellow citizens." To strangers and to the poor he owed nothing.

More important still, the bishop's "pastoral" power was unique in one other respect. To use Foucault's words, it was a form of power shorn of "all those disturbing features that make men tremble before the power of kings."[8] The ideal relation of a bishop to his flock was that of a father to his children, of a shepherd coaxing his sheep and of a head intimately bound by innumerable strands of fellow feeling to the wider "body" of his fellow believers. Sixth-century persons did not need to be reminded by an alert French philosopher of this peculiar aspect of the power ascribed to their bishops. One need only turn to the poems written by Venantius Fortunatus in praise of bishop Leontius of Bordeaux (ca. 545–75). Leontius was a hardy relic of the ancien régime. He came from a Roman "senatorial" family. He was "second to none in nobility." But in his relations to his congregation he was not presented as a lord. He was a shepherd and a father: "One would say that he had begotten this people as their father. For he admonished them in so gentle a voice that you would think that he was speaking to parts of his own body."[9]

In reality, we know that the Christian clergy in East and West alike had their fair share of thugs, would-be warriors, and lordly rulers. Emergencies, such as sieges and food shortages, frequently pushed the bishop to the fore as the de facto head of the entire community.[10] But for a bishop to flaunt any power other than "soft" pastoral power, of the sort that was praised in bishop Leontius of Bordeaux, was to destroy the basis of his legitimacy.

In the 250 years between the conversion of Constantine (in 312) and the middle of the sixth century, the bishop and his clergy had found a niche for the exercise of just such soft power—for power that was not power—in the heart of every Christian city of the Roman and post-Roman world. This was a new development. The division between church and state had been unknown in the classical world. It emerged only slowly, and in very different ways in different regions, in late antiquity. But it amounted to a fissure in the ancient notion of the community that was made possible by a polarization of the social imagination that pitted nonviolent "pastoral" power against mere "worldly" power. It was a development that, in the year 300, had been unimaginable to persons such as Porphyrius as it was to the overwhelming majority of the population of the Roman world who were not yet Christian. How had this strange polarity between "pastoral" and "worldly" power come to be expressed—and with which consequences, if any, on the ground?

FROM *AMATOR PATRIAE* TO *AMATOR PAUPERUM*, CA. 300–450

The opening bout of this great change consisted in a challenge to the ancient, civic notion of the community. The traditional notion of the patria had always been expressed (in the manner of Porphyrius of Lepcis Magna with his precious elephants) in terms of the "love" of rich persons for their city and for their fellow citizens. In the fourth century, the rich "lovers of the city" were challenged by Christian preachers to look both further down the social scale and further afield. They were urged to become "lovers of the poor."

This was not simply a challenge to notice the misery that lay around them and to do something about it. What was at stake were two rival models of the community. The one saw the world in terms of a brittle honeycomb of "civic" institutions and "civic" entitlements. Christian preachers wished this model to give way to a vision of society that was as universal as human nature itself. In this new vision of society, the principal distinction was not that between "citizens" and "noncitizens," "free" and "slave," "city" and "countryside," but between the "rich" and the "poor." The cohesion of this society was supposed to depend on the love of the rich in general for the poor in general.

It is important to stress the momentous nature of these contrasting visions. Behind each stood an implied option for a specific type of community. The classical view had been fostered in the innumerable cities that were scattered like fairy dust across the entire length and breadth of the Roman Empire. (There were some two thousand in all of these, nine hundred of which were in the West). Each city liked to think of itself as a vivid oasis of civic entitlement upheld by the richer inhabitants, each of whom lavished amenities on a well-defined core of their "fellow citizens." These amenities ranged from occasional elephants to shipments of grain so as to provide free or cheap food, by means of a system that was known as the *annona civica*—the grain levy for the citizens of Rome. The annona caused entire armadas of grain ships to sail every year across the Mediterranean from Africa and Egypt so as to feed the privileged "citizens" of Rome as if from the hand of the emperor himself. The provision of the annona showed that the emperor (quite as much as a local magnate such as Porphyrius) was expected to be an amator patriae. By the year 400 CE, his superabundant love extended to the two greatest cities of the empire—both to Rome and to Constantinople. They were "his" cities and their inhabitants were "his" fellow citizens. (It is not for nothing that Constantinople is called Konstantinou Polis—Constantine's City. It was founded to be his very own city, and its inhabitants were spoiled by massive food supplies because they were Constantine's very own people.)[11]

Compared with this view, Christian preaching proposed a vision of society that was as featureless and as boundless as poverty itself. In terms of the buildup of the social imagination, it was a shift as challenging—and in many ways as unnerving—as was the early modern shift from a closed to an open universe. One passed from a view of society made up of a familiar patchwork of civic distinctions into a seemingly limitless social space, where human beings fell into a binary opposition of rich and poor that appeared to be as uniform as the sway of Newton's law of universal gravity. To move from the one model to the other (in the period between 300 and 600) was to move from the age of the classical city to what has recently been termed "a post-Roman late antiquity"—a world where the classical model of the city had lost its grip on the social imagination.[12]

Not surprisingly, scholars have thrilled to the audacious paradigm shift implied in the Christian social discourse of the fourth century. Paul Veyne and Evelyne Patlagean first drew attention to this momentous shift in the social imagination in the late 1970s. Their work has provoked some of the very best studies on the social history of the later empire. They raised the challenging possibility that this decisive change in the social imagi-nation was symptomatic of wider changes in late Roman society. They implied that the new Christian discourse of rich and poor betrayed (if at one remove) the real direction of the evolution of late Roman society. The Christian image of society was a demystified image. Its insistence on the primal division between rich and poor "removed the civic veil" that had swathed the Roman Empire of classical times. It was a disabused, non-civic image that seemed to reflect the general leveling of the classes within an autocratic empire, the growing polarization between rich and poor, the erosion of the privileges of the cities, and the erasure of the boundary between city and countryside—all developments we have tended to take as characteristic of the society of the Roman Empire in its last centuries. It was an image of society suited to a new, harsh age.[13]

Altogether, the work of Veyne and Patlagean presented us with a grand scenario of change. Yet it has struck me that it does not enter deeply enough into the phenomena whose general drift it categorizes so clearly. It offers a story of change that takes place between two mighty bookends. It starts with a crisp definition of a society divided according to a "civic" model, where the most esteemed forms of giving were directed to groups whose entitlements derived from their citizen status. It ends with a sad and sprawling world, in which degrees of misery alone formed the basis of entitlement, and where the generosity of the rich was expected to reach out, without distinction, to town and countryside alike. But the stages by which the one model changed into the other, and the pace of this change itself, are less well known than is the overall trajectory that led from the one to the other.[14]

Above all, the language of the postcivic, Christian bookend tends to be taken for granted. This is not surprising. Statements of a Christian's duties to the poor reached their classical form in the great preachers of the late fourth and early fifth centuries—in Ambrose and Augustine for the West, and Basil of Caesarea and John Chrysostom in the East. For the first time in the history of the ancient world, the poor are placed at the center of the picture of late Roman society. They are presented in a language tinged with pathos and scattered with hyper-realistic vignettes of suffering. But the imaginative building blocks of the Christian model of society were not assembled in a day. Many central themes of Christian preaching contained ambiguities that required resolution before a stable model could establish itself. This is particularly true in the case of the central theme of Christian preaching: the image of the poor themselves.

Preaching on the poor and on almsgiving to the poor has recently been studied with great care and intelligence, both by Richard Finn and by Christel Freu.[15] What has emerged from both books (and especially from the very sensitive study of Christel Freu, which has the merit of being devoted to the preaching of one region alone) is that the image of the poor swayed with dizzying zest between two poles—the poor were treated either as "others" or as "brothers." As a result, the view of what a Christian society should be differed greatly, according to the imaginative pole at which the image of the poor rested.

"MEN MAY HAVE NO USE FOR THEM, BUT GOD HAS": AGAINST RECIPROCITY

When we approach the imaginative play set loose by Christian preaching on the poor, it is sometimes easy to forget that Christianity, though we may study it in terms of its concrete impact on late Roman society, was, above all, a religious movement. Like the Buddhism that entered so dramatically into what had previously been the somewhat stolid world of imperial China (between the fifth and the seventh centuries), Christianity was a religion "avid for the incommensurable."[16] Christians needed to create their own image of society on a scale worthy of the vaulting spiritual ambition of their faith. We are dealing with a religion driven by the need to represent on earth the purposes of a starkly transcendent and universal God.

Hence a need to place in society itself a series of concrete, unmistakable—even shocking—"markers" that served to remind believers and outsiders alike of the unimaginably wide horizons opened up to humanity by the Christian message. For this reason, fourth-century Christianity fostered attention to extreme states of the human condition. It is no accident that the torrent of Christian preaching on outreach to the poor coincided with a sharp elevation of forms of total sexual renunciation—of virginity, of monastic withdrawal, and even, in certain circles, of clerical celibacy. Indeed, the preachers, writers, and organizers who advocated most vehemently the care of the poor were often the same persons who spoke out most passionately in favor of virginity and celibacy.[17]

These palpable markers brought the "incommensurable" into society. Both outreach to the poor and the adoption of virginity and celibacy were held, by their advocates, to go against the grain of human nature. Both were tinged with a sense of heroic *démesure* that bordered on the supernatural.

For this reason, giving to the poor was presented as an act of altruism in its purest and most challenging form. Late Roman society (like almost every other ancient society) was a world held together, at every level, by intense networks of reciprocal gifts. Society appeared to be ruled by iron laws of reciprocity. In such a world, it was considered bad to dream that one gave money to a beggar. The dream foretold death: "For Death is like a beggar, who takes and gives nothing in return."[18]

It is only against this background that we can understand the *frisson* attached by Christian writers and preachers to the ultimate, nonreciprocated gift—the gift to the poor. In the challenging words of Lactantius, who wrote around 310, such giving showed that "The only true and certain obligation is to feed the needy and useless. Men may have no use for them, but God has."[19]

In many ways, for Christian intellectuals such as Lactantius, charity to the poor was what the "gratuitous act" once was to existentialist writers of the 1950s. It was an almost terrifying statement of potential boundlessness. But it was also an act of appropriation. To claim the poor as part of the body of the Christian community was to claim society up to its furthest, darkest margin in the name of the church.

This melodramatic imaginative tilt downward toward the poor is not altogether surprising. We must remember that Christian preaching had sunk deep roots into what Seth Schwartz, in his recent book, *Were the Jews a Mediterranean Society? Reciprocity and Solidarity in Ancient Judaism*, has called "a Mediterranean counter-culture."[20] To problematize the social mechanisms of reciprocity and to toy with the notion of the pure, altruistic gift had kept philosophers, dropouts, the leaders of cults, and all those who listened to such persons engaged for centuries in various forms of countercultural stances.[21] Fourth-century Christian preaching merely turned up the volume of this licensed noise. For, as Schwartz has observed, "reciprocity-based societies normally validate a religious or political escape hatch."[22] Already by the year 300, the Christian churches had become the largest of such escape hatches ever to have been opened in the ancient world.

Christian preachers had to face the same problems as their Jewish and pagan predecessors and neighbors. Groups that emphasized "antireciprocal solidarity" at the expense of the traditional bonds of society had to recognize that, to be blunt, solidarity based on gratuitous acts of generosity alone might be astonishing and commendable. But it was unlikely to last. In this respect, the Christian churches of the fourth century found themselves in danger of having to replay the failure of Jewish society in the first century BC and the early first century CE. The religious elites of the period of the Herodian Temple had relied too much on an ideology of solidarity that was not undergirded by traditional social exchanges. As a result, they lacked the practices of rural patronage and urban euergetism (public benefactions by the rich as we have seen them practiced by figures such as Porphyrius) that might have provided a measure of social stability for some farmers and artisans, and instead practiced charity, which kept the poor alive, numerous, unhappy, and socially unmoored.[23]

Charity was not enough. Something had to be done about the image of the poor if this state of affairs was not to recur in the cities of the later empire. The Christian notion of community had to "thicken," as it were, by embracing more solidly established groups.

"NOT JUSTICE BUT A CRY": THE POOR OF THE OLD TESTAMENT IN A NEW AGE

For this reason we cannot underestimate the importance of the manner in which the Christians of the fourth and subsequent centuries began to breathe the air of a preclassical society. The Old Testament—the Hebrew Scriptures (but not, of course, in Hebrew)—had slowly but surely become part of the imaginative world of Roman Christians. These Scriptures presented a different model of society, based not on the classical city but on the social experience of the ancient Near East. In the Hebrew Scriptures, rich and poor faced each other directly, in the prayers of the Psalms, in the denunciations of the prophets, and in vivid incidents in the history of the kingdom of Israel. Christian preachers derived the fateful binary of rich and poor largely from the language of the Scriptures. But, in the Old Testament, the poor did not face the rich as beggars. Rather, in the manner of other ancient Near Eastern societies, the "poor" of Israel came, first and foremost, before the powerful in search of justice, not of alms. They did so as a self-styled "poor." They came as plaintiffs, not as beggars. They were "poor" because they had pointedly surrendered their own status so as to seek the judgment and protection of the powerful in their favor. Their cry was not for handouts. It was the cry for justice of free men and women, often of moderate—some even of considerable—means. It was the cry of victims. But they were not the victims of poverty so much as they were the victims of injustice, violence, and oppression, brought upon them by persons more powerful than themselves.[24] It was this relation of petition to justice that gave weight to the Hebrew assonance by which zeʾaqah—"the cry"—was expected to be met by zedeqah—by "righteousness."

He looked for justice, but, behold, bloodshed;
for righteousness (z^{e}deqah) but, behold, a cry (z^e'aqah). (Isaiah 5:7)

This "elegant juxtaposition of words" did not escape the alert eyes of the great Hebraist, Saint Jerome, in 408–10, as he commented on the classic phrase of the prophet Isaiah.[25]

The absorption of the language and historical narratives of the Hebrew Scriptures in the Christian communities of the later empire slowly added a rougher texture to the Christian discourse on poverty. It ensured that the poor were not simply seen as creatures who trembled on the margins of society, asking to be saved by the wealthy. Like the poor of Israel, they had the right to "cry out" for justice. They were as much a *populus*, a people, as was the citizen body to whose needs the amator patriae of the classical city was encouraged to pay such studious attention. This redefinition of the populus as the outraged "poor" placed the bishop at the head of a formidable constituency. In the sermons of Ambrose, in the 380s, the words "poor" and "people" merge ominously. The cry of the "poor" for justice was, in fact, the cry of the "Christian people" of Milan as a whole, mobilized in opposition to the avarice of courtiers and great landowners.[26]

Based on the model of the Old Testament, an "upward slippage" in the image of the poor gathered momentum in the course of the fifth century. Members of the plebeian classes of large cities such as Rome began to edge in around the Christian churches. They became, as it were, a "para-poor" in search of a "para-annona." These people were not the "others" constructed by a heady rhetoric of Christian altruism. They were brothers—brothers down in their luck; but fellow citizens nevertheless, entitled to support of every kind, from food to quick justice.

In the sermons of Leo the Great, in Rome, between 440 and 461, we find an image of the poor that had come to include not only paupers, but townsmen, free peasants, and the "shamefaced poor"—that is, well-to-do persons who had slipped into poverty. By the time of Gregory the Great (590–604) all of these persons were duly noted on the poor rolls of the churches. Three thousand refugee nuns in the city received, in cash, the equivalent of the corn dole once received by members of the citizen people of Rome as part of their annona.[27] Once the "poor" of the cities ceased to consist solely of outright paupers (consigned by Christian rhetoric to the charged, outer fringes of society) but had come to include a large number of the lesser townsfolk and even impoverished members of the upper classes, the Christian bishop could step forward, once again, if on different terms, as "always an amator patriae." His "fellow-citizens" had reinvented themselves as the "poor of the church."

"TREASURE IN HEAVEN":
THE JOINING OF HEAVEN AND EARTH

This "upward slippage" of the poor was a silent process, spread over a century. We catch only glimpses of it in our sources. I tried to trace its trajectory and to measure its consequences in my study *Poverty and Leadership in the Later Roman Empire*. What I stress now more than I did at that time was the nature of the givers. What was their social constituency? What were their notions of the nature and effects of their gifts?[28]

It is on the issue of the nature of the gift within the Christian churches that we find ourselves entering strange new territory. There is good reason for this feeling of strangeness. As long as we had been content to think of the changing social structures of late Roman society (as these changes were encoded in a new Christian discourse of rich and poor), as the central theme in the trajectory from the ancient to the proto-medieval world, we could assume that the givers remained much the same. The rich were still the rich. They had not changed. What had changed were the beneficiaries of their gifts, not the raw adrenaline of patronage and display that still ran in the veins of the givers.[29] When discussing almsgiving and the foundation of churches, it was enough to point to the novel shift in the direction of the flow of gifts. There seemed to be no need to probe the motives of the givers themselves, and still less to examine closely the imaginative associations that gathered around the gift.

Plus ça change, plus c'est la même chose is a reassuring phrase for students of the later empire. My friend Philip Rousseau, in his comments, has reminded me, rightly, not to neglect the elements of continuity in the styles and ideals of leadership exercised by local magnates and, then, by Christian bishops. But there is a danger that a one-sided emphasis on the continuity of old-world traditions of patronage and public benefaction within the Christian church can become a mantra rather than a tool of research. There is an implied teleology in such an approach. An air of all's well that ends well hangs over many narratives of the rise of Christianity in the late Roman Empire. As Kim Bowes has put it in her recent book, *Private Worship, Public Values and Religious Change in Late Antiquity*,

> Christianization narratives generally tend to formulate . . . social changes as a swap sale: they describe how the senator exchanged his consular robe for bishop's miter; how the civic bureaucracy was charged with building churches and hostels instead of amphitheaters and baths.[30]

In order to answer this "swap sale" model, I would draw attention to two considerations. First, it forgets that, in the fourth century, the Christian churches of the West were socially diverse bodies. As Hugo Jones pointed out long ago, in both East and West, "The main strength of Christianity lay in the lower and middle classes of the towns, the manual workers and clerks, the shopkeepers and merchants."[31] Though originally expressed somewhat in passing and in impressionistic terms, Jones's judgment on the diverse social constituency of Christian communities has been confirmed by all subsequent studies. It is far from certain that an elite discourse of patronage, gift giving, and civic benefaction was inevitably shared by all levels of society within the Christian churches, nor that such a discourse was prevalent in all regions of the West.[32]

Second, and more seriously, it underestimates the slow but sure development of a Christian consensus on the nature of the religious gift that had taken firm root alongside and often in competition with the Jewish synagogues. The bishops and their Christian patrons of the late fourth century did not step into an imaginative and ritual vacuum that their Roman habits—and their Roman habits alone—sufficed to fill. Far from it. By 300 Christianity was already an old religion. Its beginnings lay as far in the past as do the days of King George III in our own time. When it came to the obligations and rewards of almsgiving, the collective memory of the churches reached back for over half a millennium, through the Hebrew Scriptures, to the days of the Achaemenid Empire and to the Wisdom Literature of the Hellenistic period.[33]

The Christian churches certainly depended on the generosity of innumerable donors. But was this generosity invariably driven by the same motivations as had inspired the elite benefactors of old? The answer is no. We are dealing with a different sort of gift. The motivations of the gift were different. This is well known. It was a fixed component of all Christian and Jewish exhortation that obedience to the commands of God and compassion for the poor were what drove the believer to "works of mercy." The sheer, gross "rush" of the civic benefactor, who sought the acclaim of his community, was out of the question.[34]

But the more significant difference was not so much in the motivation of the giver as in the imagined working of the gift. As Augustine made plain, in a sermon on giving to the church and to the poor that has only recently been discovered, such gifts were described as *veneranda sanctorum commercia*—"reverend exchanges" among the saints exchanging earthly gifts for incalculable heavenly rewards.[35]

It was in this area more than in any other that late Roman Christianity showed that it was a religion "avid for the incommensurable." In some way or other, to give to the poor and to the Christian churches was to open a path to heaven. With vertiginous incongruity, any Christian gift—from the smallest to the greatest—was magnified out of all proportion in another world. It became "treasure in heaven." This was the conclusion that preachers drew insistently from the story of the rich young man (Matthew 9:21, with Mark 10:21 and Luke 18:22) and from the command of Christ:

> give to the poor; provide yourselves with a treasure in the heavens which does not fail. (Luke 12:33; cf. Matthew 6:19-20)

In some way or other, which few stopped to analyze, to give to the church and to the poor was to join heaven and earth. The Latin *commercia*, we must remember, was not as cold as our own word "commerce" suggests. Rather, *commercium* "implied a harmony within duality."[36] Two poles that had been kept far apart in the late antique imagination—the transient world beneath the Moon and the serene eternity of the heavens—had been brought together.

This late antique Christian and Jewish notion of a joining of heavenly and earthly riches has caused exquisite embarrassment to modern scholars. So much so that in no modern dictionary of the Christian church or of Judaism does the word "treasure" appear! We moderns have created two distinct spheres—the world of buying and selling and the world of religious actions. To join the language of one sphere—that of commerce and treasure—with the sphere of religion now strikes us as a joining of incompatibles so inappropriate as to seem, almost, an off-color joke. Yet, if we wish to understand the economic upsurge of the Christian churches at this time, it is important that we overcome a prudery that no late Roman Christian would have shared.

For late antique Christians, the issue was not whether gifts should happen without the expectation of a counter gift. What mattered was the speed of the return of the counter gift and the nature and location of that return. We are not dealing with two distinct spheres—commerce and religion—in which the ethos of the one is thought of as flatly contradictory to the ethos of the other. Rather, we are dealing with two different orbits of exchange.[37] Purely earthly gifts moved, as it were, on a quick circuit. Money exchanged hands. Clients and patrons exchanged favors and support. The grand gift of the amator patriae was greeted, instantly, by the roar of the counter gift of praise from "his" people in the theater and, a little later, by with the counter gift of statues and public honors from the town council.

All of these exchanges happened in this world only. The benefactors whose statues crowded the forum sought posthumous fame only "in the sweet air" of the living. They hoped that their glory might last on earth. (Porphyrius, for instance, would have been delighted to have found himself mentioned, yet again, at the Davis Center, on the strength of a great statue, which showed him driving a two horse chariot, standing above the crowds who passed every day through the marketplace of Lepcis Magna.) But no one thought that the gifts of urban benefactors to their city might follow them to heaven.

Gifts to the other world were different. They set off on an orbit so far distant and so divorced from human time as to leave the imagination haunted by thoughts of the incommensurability between the gift and its reward.

This was a notion not altogether ill fitted to the expectations of a socially diverse religious community. To place "treasure in heaven" by giving vastly raised the worth of the average giver. Heroic giving was no longer seen as the monopoly of the rich. Christian preaching played incessantly on the intriguing incongruity between the gift itself and its imagined reward. Confronted with the sayings of Christ in the Gospels—such as his words on the widow's mite (Mark 12:42; Luke 21:2) and his promised reward of heaven for a mere cup of cold water (Matthew 10:42; Mark 9:42)—Christian preachers developed a sharp aesthetic of disproportion. The smallest fragment conjured up the highest magnitude. A gift of copper coins and of basic food and clothing reverberated with the sense of its exact opposite, the immensity of Christ's reward in a heaven filled with golden treasure. The regular poor box in Augustine's Hippo was called "the Quadriga." It was thought of as a four-horse chariot that swung low to sweep the alms of the faithful (as it had once swept the prophet Elijah himself) far beyond the stars to heaven.[38]

Most important of all, the alms of rich and poor were held to be equal in value because they were given for the same reasons. We must remember that to give to the poor was always presented by Christian preachers as an act of compassion. We should not underestimate the sincerity with which preachers such as Ambrose, Augustine, and Leo attempted to "sensitize" their congregations to the spectacle of human misery around them. Nor should we be too hard-nosed about the sincerity of the many humble believers who internalized this call to compassion. What is more important, perhaps, than the creation of new habits of the heart was the equalizing effect of stress on this particular virtue. It was a virtue open to all. Compassion for the poor formed, as it were, a true democracy of tender hearts. For Christians, as for Jews, charity to the poor enjoyed the status of a "national virtue." It was asserted (if not always observed) by all members of the church, rich and poor alike.[39]

Many Christians took their almsgiving seriously. But they did not always reflect on what they were doing. Amid a high-pitched rhetoric of treasure in heaven gained by outreach to the abject poor, they simply kept on giving because God had commanded them to do so. Bishop Leo, from an unknown see in the neighborhood of Rome, wrote on a mausoleum that he had built for himself while still a pagan:

Coming to despise riches, I preferred to know Christ.
My care became to clothe the naked who begged of me,
To pour on the poor what each year's season yielded.[40]

In Tharros, in southern Sardinia, a table for the poor set up in a cemetery spoke of Karissimus

Who provided well for all his friends,
And kept the commandments concerning [care of] the poor.[41]

Beneath the inscription to Karissimus is an image of a circus horse. Flanked by a palm of victory, it trots briskly with the Chi-Rho ($\chi\rho$) monogram branded on its rump. Those who set up Karissimus's monument chose an image from the ancient mystique of the hippodrome to emphasize his victory over death and the good cheer that his modest foundation had offered.

Leo and Karissimus did not spin high-pitched ideological claims out of their day-to-day practice. They were unaware that they and those who acted like them would come to be regarded by modern scholars as bringing in the end of the ancient city. We know of them only through the chance finds of archaeologists, and not from any texts. What we read in the texts is a rhetoric of "treasure in heaven." But this rhetoric is lacking on their tombstones. Rather, they did their thing: they "kept the commandments." They were the Forrest Gumps of late antiquity.

PATRIMONIA PAUPERUM: "PATRIMONIES OF THE POOR"

But the regular, low-profile practice of giving provided a solid background to the emergence of a grandiose language of treasure in heaven gained through giving to the poor. This language played a crucial role in a further development. It defined the peculiar nature of the wealth of the church. By the year 500, the wealth of the church had increased appreciably in almost every region of the Latin West. Above all, it had become touched by a shimmer of sacrality. As Julianus Pomerius advised a bishop in Arles, the wealth of the church was not like any other wealth. It was sacred wealth. It had piled up like a coral reef from countless acts of giving by donors concerned to place treasure in heaven. The bishops and clergy

should know that the goods of the church are nothing other than the fruit of vows made by the faithful, the various prices which they offer for their sins, they are the *patrimonia pauperum*—the patrimonies of the poor.[42]

We should notice one thing. The properties of the church were not spoken of as sacred in themselves. They were sacred because the poor, on whose behalf these "patrimonies" were held in trust, were sacred. It is a strangely indirect but potent form of blessing. From the 400s onward, churches themselves had come to be treated as sacred buildings. Associated with the grand drama of the Eucharist reinforced by the increasing presence of relics, the physical space of churches became what temples had been—a place of sanctuary.[43] Not so church lands. Instead, their sacrality came from two centuries of rhetoric on the poor as the ultimate victims, to injure whose rights was tantamount to sacrilege. This was what generated the novel sound that accompanied the growing wealth of the church in postimperial Western Europe.

And with this we can conclude by returning to the sixth-century world of Paulinus of Pant-y-Polion. For the appeal to the notion of the poor as the victims par excellence of the misuse and appropriation of church wealth derived its power from concerns that were specific to the post-imperial West. In the canons of the councils of fifth- and sixth-century Gaul we can see the emergence of a discourse that linked the integrity of church property to the perpetual rights of the poor. Those who robbed the church of its lands—both those who directly appropriated church property and those who held back bequests made to the church by members of their family—were deemed to be *necatores pauperum*, "murderers of the poor."[44] They were solemnly cursed. At the council of Tours, in 567, bishops and their clergy were urged to gather together so as to chant in unison against such defaulters the solemn malediction of Psalm 108:

> Because he did not remember to show mercy but persecuted the poor and needy and sought to kill the broken hearted.[45]

Everyone knew who the *broken hearted* were. They were not the poor gathered in the courtyard of the church. They were the bishop and his clergy whose rights (exercised on behalf of the poor) had been flouted.

We are witnessing a characteristic mutation of an old Christian theme. In the fourth century, to give to the poor had been presented as a supremely counterfactual gesture. Christians who gave to the poor—rather than lavish comforts on the narrow core of their fellow citizens—were thought to have reached out to claim the furthest edges of society for the church. By the sixth century, this notion had hardened into a means to protect the fragile edges of the lands of the church. The notion that the poor were the "endangered species" of sixth-century society placed a cordon around the properties of the church. It wired a system of alarms calculated to go off at the slightest touch.

Furthermore, the notion of the poor as victims had gained in symbolic force from merging with more widespread anxieties in a postimperial world. In the fluid world of the so-called barbarian kingdoms, the honeycomb of carefully graded social statuses that had protected free Romans—as senators, as town councilors, as *honestiores*—had tended to collapse. What had survived best was the brutal binary model in which the rich and powerful faced the poor.

This model had been conjured up, now for two centuries, by Christian preaching. Over the years, as we have seen, it had subtly changed. It had been joined by a model of society derived from the Old Testament. On this Old Testament model, the "poor" were invariably thought of not as beggars, but rather as average persons who cried for justice. What they lacked was not money, but power. In the same way, the rich were not simply the wealthy. They were the powerful—the *potentes*. What they were expected to give to the poor were not alms, but justice.[46]

It was to that Old Testament model that bishops and lay statesmen alike now turned, so as to think about the proper treatment of subjects in the new, post-Roman states. It was easier to advise a king, a queen or a count to show mercy to the poor (in the manner of an Old Testament monarch) than to deliver a lecture on the complicated rights of Roman citizens.[47] Talk about the poor became a way to talk about the highly charged issue of what it was to be the subjects of new, non-Roman kings.

The decisions of the second council of Mâcon, in 585, made this plain:

> Those to whom the cares of great affairs have been entrusted [as royal governors] should not pass over as of little esteem the affairs of the very smallest persons. For it so happens that, when the smallest of the land are despised, matters slowly grow to a great evil.[48]

Put bluntly, to tread on the "poor" was to threaten to tread on everybody else. It was by their ability to crystallize intense feelings of victimhood around the figures of the poor, "who live beneath the veil" of episcopal protection, that the bishops of Gaul and elsewhere were able to bring to the surface the grievances of entire regions, and of groups of persons who were far from being beggars. The language mobilized for the protection of the poor had become the language of all potential victims of the power of kings and their representatives.[49] Furthermore, this language put the bishops at center stage. They were encouraged to draw on their "soft" power as advocates of the poor to act as spokesmen for entire regions (and, indeed, for entire kingdoms) on issues of oppression and clemency that affected the political community as a whole.

MAGNUM ET MIRABILE DONUM DEI: "A GREAT AND AMAZING GIFT OF GOD." WEALTH FOR THE OTHER WORLD

But advocacy was never enough. As in classical times, a "lover of the patria" had to put his money where his mouth was. He had to show his love through his use of wealth for the benefit of the community. So, to conclude, what does this trajectory of almost three centuries involve for the meaning of wealth itself?

Put briefly, wealth had been problematized. The Christian donor was not encouraged to experience the heady "rush" of generosity that had once set Porphyrius of Lepcis Magna literally on a pedestal high above the heads of his fellow citizens. But neither had wealth been demonized. It certainly had not evaporated. The very rhetoric that had insisted that wealth should flow to the poor ensured that, as the wealth of the church, it would be touched by the magic of perpetuity.

This still leaves us with a sociopsychological riddle. It is an observed fact that otherworldly religions—whether this be late antique Christianity or its exact contemporary at the other end of Eurasia, the Buddhism of Central Asia and western China—often managed to become very rich very quickly. As Chinese observers noted, with characteristic economy of words, there was a lot of wealth to be gotten from *fo-shih*—from "Buddha business."[50]

We can treat this fact (as many late antique Christians did) as sad evidence of the decline of the church from a first moment of imagined virtue. Or we can view it, either with pessimism or with a certain worldly wise snigger, as the inevitable working out of the relations between order and charisma in a religious movement. Idealism never lasts. Social mores tend to prevail. If these are the mores of a Roman aristocracy, we are somewhat relieved. It is comforting to think that the views of upholders of the good old Roman ways did not give way entirely to irresponsible Christian hotheads, who had urged the renunciation of all wealth. If we are historians of Christian thought, we can even ignore the phenomenon. We can be content to say that the wealth of the church—like the British Empire as described by Benjamin Disraeli—happened "in a fit of absence of mind." We do not need to study it, and still less to meditate on the paradox of its existence.

Yet it may still be possible to go further. We need to find some way to integrate the sincere otherworldliness of the Christian movement with its considerable worldly success in the late antique period. I would suggest that, faced by this problem, Buddhists and Christians may have found their way to a common solution. They knew that those who supped with the devil of wealth needed a long spoon. But it was, perhaps, precisely the length of the spoon that gave them an advantage. An ideal of detachment from worldly things took the glamour out of wealth. But it did not make wealth go away. Indeed, the ideal of detachment subtly reinforced the notion that, if wealth was there, it was there for a reason. It was there to be used—to be administered in a no-nonsense and effective manner for the good of the church. Bluntly, wealth was given a purpose. It was swept into the "pastoral" image of the church, to which Michel Foucault referred in his lectures to the Collège de France: it was made subject "to a power that guides towards an end and functions as an intermediary towards that end."[51]

We should not exaggerate the effect of this high view on the actual administration of the wealth of the churches in the sixth century, which was often slipshod and oppressive, like the administration of many other great estates. But it did affect the way in which this wealth was seen by those who approached the church as donors. The wealth of the church came to be viewed as wealth that radiated a future. Like the great Buddhist monasteries of northern India at the time of the Kushan Empire and the great age of Gandhara art, the wealth of the church had a certain magnetic quality. For donors, it was "beautiful" wealth.[52]

This was because the idea of the wealth of the church rested on a mighty paradox that had haunted the late antique imagination. As we have seen, even the smallest gift to the poor or to the church brought about a miraculous joining of heaven and earth. Time and eternity, usually thought of as antithetical, were joined. In the words of the donation of Palladius of Autun to the convent of St. Julian, in 635,

> It is a great and amazing gift of God—*magnum et mirabile donum Dei*—that with things bound by time and destined to bankruptcy prizes can be acquired in heaven that will last without end.[53]

And, as another charter put it (this time, a royal donation to Saint Denis in 627),

> The world perishes and those things that are in the world. (1 John 2:17)
>
> That, however, which has been transferred to the churches, to the shrines of saints, or to the poor never perishes.[54]

For such donors, wealth did not stand in the way of heaven. Rather, when given to the church, wealth opened a high road to a future that could be thought of as extensive on earth because it was bathed in the soft glow of the thought of perpetual treasure in heaven. The hopes expressed in the charters were almost proved right. The poor house founded in Le Mans by Bishop Bertram in 616 lasted until 1789; that founded in Trier by the rich deacon Adalgisel Grimo, in 634, lasted up to the time of Napoleon.[55] Not a bad innings.

With this last mutation of ancient Christianity, which took place between the years 500 and 650, a new conglomerate of notions about the nature of the community, about the use of wealth within it, about the symbolic role of the poor and about the destiny of the Christian soul after death insensibly came together. In later centuries, this became the "inherited conglomerate" of Latin Catholic Europe.

It was a conglomerate that Western Europeans were supposed to take with them wherever they went. Half a millennium later, in around 1020, the first European settler in Greenland to become a Christian, Thorstein, the son of Eric the Red, lay dying at Lysefjord (Ameralik in Greenland). He summoned his wife, Gudrid, just before he died. In a manner associated with Norse tales of prophecy, he sat up suddenly (as if returned to life) and gave her this advice: "He bade her beware of marrying a Greenlander and then he urged her to bestow their money upon the church or to give it to the poor; and then he sank back for the last time."[56]

Recounted some centuries later, in the Saga of the Greenlanders, the story carried with it the heavy weight of an inherited conglomerate of ideas concerning the Christian use of wealth. It was what any Christian, such as Thorstein Eiriksson, was expected to have carried with him even to the fringes of the Arctic. This essay has attempted to go back to a very ancient world and to the Christianity that grew up within it. It was in this world that the conglomerate of ideas that medieval persons took for granted was first formed. And yet it was from this world—a world before our world—that so many of our own views on wealth and poverty have derived.

PART II

Objects in Transit

CHAPTER 4

Knowledge in Motion

FOLLOWING ITINERARIES OF MATTER
IN THE EARLY MODERN WORLD

Pamela H. Smith

I BEGIN WITH RED . . .

RED IS THE COLOR OF BLOOD AND LIFE. Its symbolic power can be glimpsed in the practices of prehistory, when red pigment was used to paint human remains and cinnabar—the red ore of mercury—ornamented tombs from the Near and Middle East in the seventh millennium BCE to the sprawling *urbs* of Çatal Hüyük in the eleventh and tenth centuries BCE.[1] Red is primal, and it appears to have possessed symbolic significance—perhaps universally—across the globe. In early modern Europe, red pigment was produced by grinding red ochre clay or by boiling, drying, and grinding madder root, or through mashing kermes beetles from Poland and Armenia;[2] but a much more saturated red could be produced by grinding cinnabar (HgS, or mercury sulfide), mined since Roman times in Almaden, Spain; or, after the 1520s, by drying, compressing, then grinding the red cochineal beetle, which lived on Central and South American cacti.[3] Finally, sulfur and mercury were heated together to produce a "synthetic" cinnabar that yielded a bright vermilion pigment.

In this essay, red plays a role in the flow of knowledge back and forth among European vernacular practitioners and text-oriented scholars in their diverse practices of producing and reproducing knowledge about natural things. Red pigments also exemplify the crisscrossing flows of matter, practices, and knowledge across Eurasia. In focusing on red, I introduce a confounding variety of motions and pathways—the exchange of materials, the flows from matter to ideas, from producers to philosophers and back again, between different social groups, language groups, trading partners, and warring empires—that intersect, collide, and meld to produce new configurations that themselves incorporate disaggregating and re-forming parts. The material of red pigment forms my guiding thread in weaving together this multitude of strands. I do not thereby claim that it was the most significant item of trade, nor did it possess precisely the same meanings in the multiplicity of places I pass through in this essay. Other materials, incorporated in entirely distinctive (and non-European) complexes of knowledge and practice, could also have served as such a thread.

I begin with the matter of the red pigment itself and its manipulation by the human hand. Matter possesses certain properties that the human hand employs in transforming matter into objects—material objects of use, of desire, of study, as well as of thought and philosophizing. Only by appreciating this first station of the itinerary of matter, that is, the struggle of the human body with matter and the process of bodily labor and embodied reasoning by which the properties of materials come to be known and material objects emerge, can we understand how human intervention—both bodily and conceptual—in the flows of matter comes to constitute knowledge. I therefore begin with the materials and the bodily processes of making vermilion itself, before moving on to explore the systems of meaning that both informed and were formed by the material and conceptual uses of this object in the early modern world.

VERMILION

Making the red pigment vermilion was a dangerous and spectacular process. Evidence for this comes from a collection of recipes made in the last half of the seventeenth century by the Amsterdam paint seller Willem Pekstok (1635–91) and his wife Katalina Saragon (d. 1681). Among the instructions for sealing waxes, pigments, dyes, borax, eye remedies, fever and bladder stone remedies, brandy wine distillations, and the making of hippocras (spiced wine) is a long and extraordinarily detailed recipe for the large-scale production of vermilion.[4] Like other vermilion recipes available in Europe (at least in textual form) since the eighth century, the Pekstoks' recipe called for twice the amount of quicksilver (i.e., mercury) to every one part refined Italian sulfur.[5] The sulfur was melted in an iron pot, taken off the fire, and mixed with half the quicksilver. This mixture was stirred with an iron shovel and allowed to rest until covered with a thin film, at which point the other half of the quicksilver was added and stirred well until the two ingredients combined entirely and began to harden. The contents of the pot were emptied onto a wet iron slab and spread to a thickness of about two fingers. The worker had to be alert with his water and wet brush in case any flame broke out, and, as for safety procedures, he should have eaten a "thick piece of bread and butter" before beginning the mixing process to protect himself from the fumes.[6] The mixture eventually turned dark blue on the outside and an even silver color on the inside without any individual drops of quicksilver being visible. When the molten slab of metals had reached this dramatic stage, it was placed in a large wooden bowl and pounded with a pestle, then divided between eight or ten small pots.

A large pot was then hung in the furnace on its trivets, piled all around with bricks, and heated above the flame. The firing had to be even and carefully controlled so that the pot did not burst. When the pot and its surrounding bricks were heated to a glowing red (about five hours), it had to be sounded with an iron bar to ascertain that it had not cracked, and the bricks removed to halfway down the pot. Ash was then laid upon the top layers of bricks to keep the flame from reaching above the midpoint, the fire was stoked, and three of the small pots full of the mercury-sulfur mixture were added to the red-hot vessel. After a short time, a flame about three to four yards high shot out of the pot. When this began to die down, three more pots were added. This was repeated. The fire, which had been kept hot during this stage, was allowed to die down slightly and the pot was covered with an iron lid. The pot had to be watched for any sign of a "greasy mixture" rising to the top, a sign that the sulfur was not sufficiently burned to begin the sublimation process. If this occurred, the fire had to be stoked again until the "greasy inflammability" burned up.

The next stage of the process reached a culmination in the subliming process that produced the pigment:

> When a thick clear flame appears out of the bluish fire all full of slate-like glittering, this is the correct flame and indicates that the substance sublimes. Place your lid so that it is lighted up by the subliming flame. Now it is not greasy and goes out immediately. When a smooth dry red is shown on the lid shining out of the brown, and when this flame is present, then the pot has to remain covered because, if it remains open, the vermilion escapes constantly. But one has to take care that the lid remains constantly loose. When the flame comes out forcefully between the pot and the lid one must reduce the fire under the pot. By doing this the flame in the pot also diminishes and slowly starts to burn against the lid.

If the fire was not hot enough, "the flame in the pot reacts accordingly and turns into black smoke." This signified a complete loss of the quicksilver because it had evaporated without combining with the sulfur. If all was going well, the lid had to be removed in order to watch the process. If the lid became stuck to the top of the pot by the subliming vermilion, one had to "slam the pot so hard" that the lid might fly off, but the instructions admonished, "Do not be afraid, but put it back on again" and "Stoke the fire the right way (because when you allow the lid to bake too fast to the pot, which happened to me once, and when I knocked off the lid, the pot, the vermilion, and the lid flew about my ears in ten thousand pieces; that is why you may not be sleepy, but always be awake and careful)."

The sublimation process took about two hours, at which point the lid was removed and the sublimed cake stirred loose from the sides of the pot with an iron bar. A row of bricks was removed in order that sublimation would continue lower down in the pot. After firing for "seven, eight, or nine hours, depending on the number of little pots, each one taking about an hour, and on how well the fire reacted, one feels inside the pot with a broomstick. If it is empty, another 90 livres of the sulfur-mercury mixture should be added and the whole process repeated at least twice." If one wanted to make the cake really heavy, one could knock the top of the pot open with a pointed hammer ("rather dangerous," as the writer notes) and put in a last load of forty to sixty livres of the mixture. At the end of the last burning, the fire was to be put out and the covered pot allowed to cool and then set upside down on a slab. The pot was then chipped away from the cake of vermilion, and the bell-shaped cake of two to three hundred livres was bound with a hoop to prevent it from disintegrating.

This recipe makes clear the strenuous bodily labor,[7] the wide-awake attention, the keen and experienced eye, the ability to precisely control the fire and the speed of the chemical reaction, as well as the ability to improvise when materials behaved in unexpected and refractory ways that were all part of vermilion manufacture. But why was this pigment being manufactured in bulk by the seventeenth century?

BLOOD

In medieval and early modern Europe, red substances possessed powerful properties associated with blood and regeneration. Red coral, for example, had a variety of valuable qualities:

> And it has been found by experience that it is good against any sort of bleeding. It is even said that, worn around the neck, it is good against epilepsy and the problems of menstruation, and against storms, lightning, and hail. And if it is powdered and sprinkled with water on herbs and trees, it is reported to multiply their fruits. They also say that it speeds the beginning and end of any business.[8]

Vermilion was often employed by painters to depict deep red blood. In his painting manual *The Book of the Art* (late fourteenth century), Cennino d'Andrea Cennini seems to have equated vermilion with blood and with the life force that it carried. In "How to Paint Wounds," Cennino specified that a painter must "take straight vermilion; get it laid in wherever you want to do blood."[9] In a long passage, Cennino describes precisely how one is to lay in the flesh tones of living individuals in a fresco. He specifies that this flesh tone is never to be used on dead faces. Where this living flesh color in fresco is to be made from red ochre pigment, on panel vermilion is used. Cennino called this color *incarnazione*, and the process of applying it *incarnare*, drawing an analogy between its use by the painter and the incarnation of life in a body.[10] This giving life to (or "incarnating") an image clearly represented to Cennino a straightforward artisanal technique by which the abstract principle and profound miracle of the incarnation of God and the Word in human flesh could be imitated. Cennino's simultaneously material and spiritual understanding of the production of materials illustrates one component of the "theory" that underlay artisanal practices, although it was a lived and practiced "theory," rather than a written and abstracted one.

Vermilion was especially associated with the blood of Christ. Evidence for this can be found in the practice of scribes and illuminators, who marked the places where vermilion was to be used in their manuscripts with a cross.[11] Perhaps their use of the cross even referred to the making of vermilion in the *crucible*; the root of "crucible" in Latin is of course "crucis" (cross), and it was in the crucible that sulfur and mercury underwent their own passion and transformation to produce the blood red pigment.

In vernacular practices and high theology, blood brimmed with overlapping and contradictory meanings. It signified vitality, fertility, the material of conception, and the spirit of life, but at the same time, blood poured out could signify death, and of course that shed by Jesus signified death, life, and redemption, all at the same time.[12] Blood was regarded as an extremely powerful agent: it was often listed in recipes as the only means to soften or cut hard gemstones such as diamonds. Most such recipes called for the blood of a male goat or a ram:

> If you want to carve a piece of rock crystal, take a two- or three-year-old goat and bind its feet together and cut a hole between its breast and stomach, in the place where the heart is, and put the crystal in there, so that it lies in its blood until it is hot. At once take it out and engrave whatever you want on it, while this heat lasts. When it begins to cool and become hard, put it back in the goat's blood, take it out again when it is hot, and engrave it. Keep on doing so until you finish the carving. Finally, heat it again, take it out and rub it with a woolen cloth so that you may render it brilliant with the same blood.[13]

Recipes such as this one for rendering hard substances soft, and for the related processes of turning soft or volatile materials hard, are to be found in overwhelmingly large numbers in recipe collections up through the seventeenth century. Some do cause changes of state, such as dissolution in acid, or heating, or even tempering of steel, but many of them, such as this goat's blood recipe, are repeated over and over again, despite the fact they could not possibly have functioned as intended. It may be that the origin of this recipe was to crack crystals in order to allow dye penetration. However, it seems more likely that such recipes instead were reiterated because they reinforced the philosophical framework of the Hippocratic-Aristotelian-Galenic view of nature in which opposites must be combined (or "tempered") in order to bring the four elements/humors/qualities into equilibrium, which denoted good health. In this system, materials we now think of as inanimate were not regarded as such. Minerals and metals grew in the earth and, like living human bodies, they too had to be purged and tempered in order to bring them into a healthy state. Books of techniques often indiscriminately mix medical recipes for human health with instructions for pigment, dye, and metallurgical recipes, but this should not be seen as a necessarily random combination, for all these recipes operate on the basis of the same coordinates of the four humors and qualities and the same principles of tempering in order to bring about balance (and thus health). This is supported by the thirteenth-century cleric Albertus Magnus (1193?–1280) who commented that the diamond can be softened neither with fire nor with iron, but it can be destroyed by the blood and flesh of a goat, "especially if the goat has for a considerable time beforehand drunk wine with wild parsley or eaten mountain fenugreek; for the blood of such a goat is strong enough even to break up a stone in the bladder, in those afflicted with the gravel." Albertus moves easily from the stones to be worked by an artisan to those to be cured by a physician.

RED GOLD

Blood was the carrier of life heat, and gold was seen to have analogous properties, heating up the body and stimulating rejuvenation when prepared as the medicinal "potable gold" or even when worn on the body as jewelry.[14] Red components, such as the pigment vermilion, were often ingredients in recipes to produce gold pigment,[15] even when they have no practical effect on the actual chemical reaction. Red seems to have been considered an essential ingredient in processes that sought to generate and transform, especially related to the noble metal gold.[16] The materials of vermilion, sulfur and mercury, also often appear in recipes for gold pigments, such as that for mosaic gold (tin or stannic sulfide, SnS_2), a sparkling golden pigment that imitated pure gold. Cennino Cennini lists one such recipe, which calls for "sal ammoniac (ammonium chloride), tin, sulfur, quicksilver, in equal parts; except less of the quicksilver."[17] Art conservators have determined that the mercury in this recipe is not necessary to produce the gold pigment and instead appears to refer back to the homologies between red and gold.[18]

LIZARDS

This correspondence among blood, red, and gold is also of importance in a puzzling recipe set down by the twelfth-century metalworker Theophilus for what he called "Spanish gold," concocted from "red copper, basilisk powder, human blood, and vinegar." In order to produce the basilisk powder, two cocks twelve to fifteen years old were put into a cage, walled like a dungeon with stones all around. These cocks were to be well fed until they copulated and laid eggs, at which point toads should then replace the cocks to hatch the eggs, being fed bread throughout their confinement. Male chickens eventually emerged from the eggs, but after seven days they grew serpent tales. They were to be prevented from burrowing into the floor of their cage by the stones, and, to further reduce the possibility of escape, they were to be put into brass vessels "of great size, perforated all over and with narrow mouths." These were closed up with copper lids and buried in the ground. The serpent-chickens, or basilisks, feeding on the fine soil that fell through the perforations, were kept for six months, at which time, the vessels were to be uncovered and a fire lit under them to completely burn up the basilisks. Their ashes were finely ground and added to a third part of the dried and ground blood of a red-headed man, which was then tempered with sharp vinegar. Red copper was to be repeatedly smeared with this composition, heated until red hot, then quenched in the same mixture until the composition ate through the copper. It thereby "acquire[d] the weight and color of gold" and was "suitable for all kinds of work."[19]

Where Theophilus calls for basilisks, a later set of recipes calls for lizards. In a 1531 text that includes pigment-making and metalworking recipes, titled *Rechter Gebrauch der Alchimei*, there are several recipes for making noble metals through a process of catching, feeding, and burning lizards. As in the instructions for softening hard stones by means of goat's blood, this recipe opens with quite precise instructions on how to catch these lizards. It directs the reader to move very quietly in "felt slippers," to quickly snatch the lizards before they give off their poison, and to immediately plunge them into a pot of human blood. A recipe for making "lizard-rib gold" follows, calling for two pounds of filed brass and a quart of goat's milk, and it continues,

> In a pot wide at the bottom and narrow at the top, with a cover containing air holes, place nine lizards in the milk, put on the cover, and bury it in damp earth. Make sure the lizards have air so they do not die. Let it stand until the seventh day in the afternoon. The lizards will have eaten the brass from hunger, and their strong poison will have compelled the brass to "transform itself to gold." Heat the pot at a

low enough temperature to burn the lizards to ash but not to melt the brass. Cool the mixture, then pour the brass into a vessel, rinse it with water, then put it in a linen cloth and hang it in the smoke of sal ammoniac. Once it is washed and dried again, it will yield a "good calx solis," or powdered form of gold.[20]

Lizards were associated with processes of putrefaction and generation more generally, as could be observed in the natural world: lizards appeared seemingly spontaneously from putrefying matter, informing the commonsense principle that generation involved a process of decay. Furthermore, lizards regenerated their tails when severed, and lizards emerged fully grown from their places of hibernation after freezing winters. In other words, lizards were bound up with the mysterious processes of putrefaction, generation, and regeneration.[21] An ambivalent attitude to lizards as impure and associated with putrefaction, yet at the same time crucial in processes of transformation and generation seems to have been very ancient. This attitude appears to have continued until recently, when Jewish silversmiths in early-twentieth-century Morocco adorned birth amulets with naturalistic lizards and salamanders.[22]

KNOWLEDGE IN MOTION?

The foregoing brief survey reveals a kind of "vernacular science"[23] of matter and transformation, a relational web of interlinked homologies among red, blood, gold, and lizards that underlay artisanal practices and techniques and that generated meaning in their world. Their knowledge system was not a theory in the sense that it could be formulated as a set of propositions, but rather it was sometimes practiced and lived and sometimes expressed in writing. It related making practices to knowing nature, and it gave access to the powers of nature, transformation, and generation. Productive practices in early modern Europe did not just involve the handling and transformation of inert materials, but rather allowed the artisan to investigate and engage in life forces and in the relationship of matter to spirit, and even to imitate the most profound mysteries such as the incarnation. On the one hand, their practices were mundane and oriented to the production of goods, but, on the other, artisanal techniques gave access to the greater powers of the universe.

What does this vernacular knowledge system of early modern European metalworkers have to do with the movement of knowledge? Vermilion making also interested medieval European scholars, such as Albertus Magnus, because the pigment was produced by the combining of sulfur and mercury. Albertus believed that the "principles" of sulfur and mercury formed the underlying substratum of all metals. What he meant by "principles" was not the everyday material manifestation of sulfur and mercury; instead, the principles embodied the physical characteristics of these metals: In a pure form in nature, sulfur, being heated, turns a dark red color, and then, when cooled rapidly, forms a glassy red substance. Native mercury, on the other hand, is liquid at room temperature and possesses a silver glittering quality. In Albertus's theory of metals, these essential properties of mercury and sulfur accounted for the behavior of metals. He describes the principle of sulfur as the hot, fiery, and male, incorporating the qualities of fire and air and giving metals their combustibility. Mercury was wet, cold, and female, possessing the qualities of earth and water. Its liquidity conferred on metals the structure that allowed them to move from a solid to a liquid state when heated.[24]

Albertus's theory of metals had only just arrived in Europe; indeed, alchemical theory had broken like a storm over medieval scholars in Latin Christendom. Before the eleventh and twelfth centuries, European scholars knew of recipe collections such as the *Mappa clavicula* (A Small Key of Handiwork) for operations using gold, precious stones, and gems. Although these recipes contained fragments from earlier Greek alchemical writings, these mysterious interpolations had been detached from any sort of conceptual framework. In the twelfth century, however, books of alchemy began to be translated from Arabic into Latin. Alchemical theory, based on Aristotle's four elements, stretched back to a conglomeration of Greek matter theory and Gnostic spiritual practices found in texts of second- and third-century CE Hellenistic Egypt, but the sulfur-mercury theory of metals was an innovation of Arabic alchemical writers, worked into the older Hellenistic texts and appearing for the first time in the Latin West as an entirely new field of knowledge. One translator, impressed at the *novitas* of his subject, wrote, "Since the wisest men have sweated on the work of the philosophers, we have decided to treat a domain which the Latin world as a whole has not yet dealt with, like swimmers in the high seas, we have decided to explore alone the open sea."[25] The Arabic texts explicating this new domain of alchemy were translated into Latin helter-skelter,[26] often not distinguished from ancient Greek authors, especially Aristotle (indeed, the Arabic alchemical texts listed Socrates, Plato, and Aristotle as alchemists). This whole process of translation forms a fascinating case study of knowledge in motion, but one example, explicated by Robert Halleux, will have to suffice: At the end of book III of the *Meteorologica*, Aristotle promised a detailed exposition about metals and nonmetallic minerals, but he seems never to have written this exposition. Instead, a treatise on an entirely different subject was appended as book IV at some stage by the Greek tradition. The *Meteorologica* arrived in Western Europe in parts: first book IV was translated from Greek in 1156 by Henry Aristippus, then a few decades later, Gerard of Cremona put into Latin the first three books of the Arabic version of Aristotle's *Meteorologica*, using the version translated into Arabic from Greek two centuries before by Yahyā ibn al-Bitrīq (d. ca. 815).[27] In about 1200, Alfred of Sarashel, concerned that Aristotle had not fulfilled his promise in book IV, and finding that Abū 'Alī al-Husayn ibn Sīnā (ca. 980–1037, known to Latin Europe as Avicenna) had in fact authored the matter for this missing fourth book of Aristotle in his *Kitab al-Shifā* (Book of the Remedy), added three chapters to the *Meteorologica*'s book IV titled *De mineralibus*, which comprised a summarized translation of part of ibn Sīnā's work. These chapters continued to be viewed as the words of Aristotle up until the sixteenth century,[28] but they were not even original with ibn Sīnā, for it was Jābir ibn Hayyan (ca. 722–ca. 812, known as Geber) and his experimentally minded student Ab Bakr al-Rāzī (ca. 864–925, known as Rhazes),[29] whose work ibn Sīnā himself had made use of in adumbrating the idea that sulfur and mercury formed the basic components of all metals. This confusing situation was only intensified by a tenth-century Arabic *Kitāb al-Ahjār* (Book of Stones)—also believed to be a genuine work of Aristotle—which contained alchemical accretions as well as much information about stones and metals.[30]

For Albertus, these Arabic works supplied a theory of metals that he believed must have been contained in an entire lost book on minerals by Aristotle. Albertus was convinced that Aristotle had written such a text; however, when his years-long search failed to turn up anything, Albertus took matters into his own hands, composing his own book of minerals, with the model of Aristotle always before him: "And we shall make additions wherever books are incomplete, and wherever they have gaps in them, or are missing entirely—whether they were left unwritten by Aristotle or, if he did write them, they have not come down to us."[31] In order to remedy this troubling lacuna in Aristotle's corpus, Albertus made, as he said, "long journeys to mining districts, so that I could learn by observation the nature of metals. And for the same reason I have inquired into the transmutations of metals in alchemy, so as to learn from this, too, something of their nature and accidental properties."[32] He had much opportunity for such observations during his extraordinarily wide travels throughout Europe in various Church administrative positions. One of the practices he observed on his travels was vermilion making: the "manufacturers of minium [by which he means cinnabar] make it by subliming sulfur with quicksilver."[33]

Aspects of vermilion production and alchemical theory overlapped: most obviously, of course, in their common bases in the two metals, sulfur and mercury. In addition, a central component of the sulfur-mercury theory of metals was the possibility of transforming a base metal, such as lead, made from impure sulfur and mercury into noble silver or gold by eliminating the impurities from the two elemental metals. Such a process was described as subjecting the metal to a process of putrefaction and regeneration, which brought about a series of color changes not unlike those observed in the making of vermilion. The metal mass was described as black in the putrefaction stage and bright red just before it transformed into gold. Some alchemical writers believed that it might be possible to derive a substance that could effect this purification of base metals instantaneously. This "philosopher's stone," which was theoretically capable of transmuting a mass of base metal into shining gold through a dramatic series of color changes, was often described as a red powder, like vermilion. Thus, pigment making and alchemical theory appear to have been intimately related in more ways than one. Not only were the two principles of metals in alchemical theory also the ingredients of vermilion production, but the outward manifestations of both processes of combination involved spectacular transformations that bore strong resemblance to each other.

By the time Albertus avidly took up Arabic alchemical theory in the thirteenth century, craftspeople had already been combining mercury and sulfur to produce a red powder for at least four centuries.[34] Indeed, the practice of vermilion production everywhere predated the articulation in texts of a theory of metals. It appears probable that the sulfur-mercury theory of metals emerged from the practices of making vermilion—from the work of craftspeople and their productive activity. In other words, one of the most pervasive and enduring metallurgical theories of matter and its transformation—the alchemical sulfur-mercury theory—flowed from the making of a valuable material. Here is an instance of what can be called the "epistemic motion" of knowledge, in which matter and the practices of craftspeople shaped the theories of text-oriented scholars.

MOTION ACROSS SPACE

Besides suggesting the epistemic movement of knowledge between social groups and knowledge systems, vermilion manufacture also gives insight into the movement of knowledge in the more conventional sense of motion over geographic distance. As we have just seen, early European metalworkers oriented their practices through the red of vermilion and blood, and they believed lizards to be a key to transformative practices. At the same time, Albertus Magnus, relying upon the Arabic alchemical works that had come to him along a tortuous path of translation and compilation, and setting out to observe miners and metal workshops, also regarded red as central to transformation, based on the principles of mercury and sulfur. More evidence for the association of lizards and transformation comes from a book of secrets ascribed to Albertus Magnus, but probably a compilation of material from various sources written no later than the fourteenth century, which contains many "secrets" for lighting a house. One of these calls for cutting off the tail of a lizard and collecting the liquid that bleeds from it, "for it is like Quicksilver," and when it is put on a wick in a new lamp "the house shall seem bright and white, or gilded with silver."[35]

This recipe transports us to the other end of Eurasia, where lizards and red also appear to have had important powers ascribed to them. For, in the early twentieth century, anthropologists recorded recipes using reptiles to produce light in the oral culture of illiterate south Indian villagers.[36] In China, too, lizards are very interestingly implicated in transformation, indicated even by the very characters which make them up. Take for example the following passage from the *Bo wu zhi* (Comprehensive Record of Things) by Zhang Hua (232–300 CE), which illustrates this, while also drawing a direct connection between lizards and red pigment:

> Xi yi 蜥蜴 are also called yan yan 蝘蜓. If you keep it in a vessel and feed it cinnabar (zhu sha), its body will turn all red. After it has ingested seven *jin* of cinnabar, pound it into a pulp by ten thousand smashes with a pestle. Dot it on a woman's limbs and body and it will glow without extinguishing. If she has sexual intercourse, than it would extinguish. Therefore, it is called 守宮 shou gong (guard chamber).[37]

The historian of China Dorothy Ko has very kindly glossed this fascinating passage for me, explaining how deeply the concept of transformation is implicated in the Chinese names for lizards. According to the third-century dictionary *Shiming* (Explanation of Names), xi yi is so-called because its tail could detach (xi 析) (from the body) and its color could change (yi 易). Yi 易 is the word for change or transformation, as in the Yijing/I Ching 易經. The word yi 蜴 that made up the compound lizard is made up by adding the "insect" radical 虫 to 易. The former radical indicates that it is in the insect family, and the latter gives it its sound, *yi*. Thus, on this level the lizard is related to *yi*—transformation.[38]

Such conjunctures of practices and systems of meaning across these tremendous spans of time and space appear remarkable. But what happens if we shift our perspective from the local spectacle of vermilion making and take a more expansive view over the long-term and long-distance flows of the goods, knowledge, texts, practices, and people across the "Afro-Eurasian ecumene," as Marshall Hodgson called it? These flows seem to have moved with particular alacrity with regard to weapons technology, whether it was the alloying of copper and tin to create the strong but flexible metal of bronze in the fourth millennium BCE for weapons, or the horse chariots that spread throughout Middle Eurasia from about

4000 BCE,[39] taking the shape of war chariots from ca. 1600 BCE,[40] or the stirrup (widespread in China from the fifth century CE, then found in Persia and throughout the Islamic world by the seventh century and in Europe from the eighth),[41] or the gunpowder weaponry that shaped the Ottoman, Safavid, and Mogul "Gunpowder Empires" of the fourteenth to seventeenth centuries, and influenced the mining of copper and tin throughout Eurasia.[42] Like the physical instruments of power and destruction, the trappings, ceremonies, and techniques of staging power, such as the royal hunt carried out with noble animals and raptor birds, also spread very extensively throughout Afro-Eurasia.[43]

But less destructive objects and techniques also flowed across Africa and Eurasia: food crops probably traveled as swiftly as weapons, although the primary evidence for this comes from the period when New World foods entered into already well-established trade routes at the eastern end of Eurasia. A few examples indicate just how rapidly such crops could spread: the peanut, cultivated in the Chaco region of South America, could already be found growing as a food crop near Shanghai at the latest by the 1560s or 1570s; sweet potatoes arrived in China at least by the 1560s; New World maize was established there in 1555, where it was brought by Turkic frontiersmen, and along the Euphrates by 1574.[44] Food plants traveled in advance of recorded contact between peoples, carried by sailors and other anonymous intermediaries, and their cultivation in new soils must have occasioned much experimentation by their growers, both in the field and at the dinner table.

Food and weapons—the means of survival—perhaps traveled most rapidly, but rarities also moved along the same routes, such as the rock crystal vessels from India and the dancing elephants from Khotan, the red parrots and single white cockatoos that all arrived as tribute into eleventh-century Song China,[45] all manner of *materia medica* including the dragon's blood brought in to treat infantile fits in the Southern Song (1127–1279),[46] and the large quantities of sulfur flowing by the ton into Tang China from Indonesia and Japan between the seventh and tenth centuries CE. This sulfur went to concoct fireworks and to temper the constitution, as the minister of state Yuan Cai aimed to do when he "took his *hot* viands from porcelain utensils floating in cool water, [and] ate and drank *cold* preparations from sulfur bowls, aiming at the perfect balance between hot and cold influences thought to be necessary for bodily health."[47] All these rarities as well as the staples of silk and cotton textiles, glass ingots, ceramics, tea, salt, spices, aromatics, medicinal herbs, gold, and silver created a pathway along which, as Robert Hartwell noted, [t]echniques, ideas and institutions flowed in a constant stream."[48]

Sometimes this stream included organized exchanges of technologies and people, such as the Chinese physicians sent to Koryo in 1072, 1074, and 1103 to educate Korean doctors, and the forced migrations of crafts-people by the Mongols, as well as the ad hoc exchanges such as prison-ers of war, apparently always viewed as potential transmitters of tech-niques. The eleventh-century scholar Tha'ālibī, in his *Book of Curious and Entertaining Information*, reported that Chinese prisoners passed on the practices of paper making when they were captured by Islamic forces in the Battle of Talas in 751. As Tha'ālibī noted, "[A]mongst the Chi-nese prisoners-of-war . . . brought to Samarqand were some artisans who manufactured paper in Samarqand; then it was manufactured on a wide scale and passed into general use, until it became an important export commodity for the people of Samarqand. Its value was universally recog-nized and people everywhere used it."[49] Another Arabic author feared the potential for technology transfer:

> As for the flammable oils, they [the Franks] do not know them, nor do they know the *tarsim* [fitting gunpowder and explosive devices to weapons], nor do they know the [flying fire] arrows, or the com-position of the fuses, so understand this: If one is taken prisoner by them, God forbid, he must not give them any information because they will then ruin everything.[50]

Chinese institutional forms of the Song dynasty spread widely to Korea, Vietnam, Baghdad, and even Norman Sicily, which all adopted some elements of Chinese institutions such as the examination system, the relay postal system, granaries, famine relief, and techniques for man-aging fiscal monopolies. Roger II (r. 1132–54) of Norman Sicily gathered information and informants from all parts of the world, and his plan for training members of the court in three stages of education may have been based upon his knowledge of Chinese practices.[51]

Particularly intense periods of exchange occurred during the Bronze Age (ca. 3500–800 BCE) as societies fiercely competed and exchanged for the tin and copper to produce valued metal. Greater exchange across Eurasia often unfolded concurrently with the emergence of greater differ-entiation in culture and religion.[52] Corpora of texts began to form which would come to constitute the principal bases for remarkably durable lin-guistic, religious, and cultural identities. Trade, exchange, and competi-tion peaked during the simultaneous expansion of the Roman and Han Empires;[53] during the period of the Tang (618–906 CE) as the empire conquered lands to the west; again during the remarkable efflorescence of technological invention during the Song period (960–1279); across the extraordinary reach of the Abbasid Empire and its successor states from the eighth century; during the *pax Mongolica* of the thirteenth and four-teenth centuries; and again in the sixteenth through eighteenth centuries as Western Europe and the Americas entered into these well-established connective pathways.[54] From about 1500 BCE to about 1500 CE, much of the exchange across Eurasia was knit together by the web of land routes, known confusedly since the nineteenth century as the Silk Road, confusing because it was neither a single road, nor was silk by any means the primary good that traveled over it. Such flows continued further east and west around the globe as the Americas were forcibly incorporated within the Afro-Eurasian ecumene, and perhaps even continued on into the industrial revolution when William Kelly brought four "Chinese steel workers" to Kentucky in 1854 and produced what was then patented in 1856 by Henry Bessemer as the Bessemer converter, which made possible the mass production of steel from pig iron. Kelly claimed that Bessemer probably knew of his experiments.[55] As was made clear some years ago, high-quality steel had been made in China by Bessemer's method since the eleventh century.[56]

C. A. Bayly argues that the framework within which we should understand the global movement in the period before about 1600 is one in which "universal kingship," "cosmic religion," and a very widely shared system of humoral and astrological beliefs shaped economies and cultures.[57] He sees a shared Eurasian ideal of universal kingship in which rulers in various places claimed universal legitimacy, embarking upon long-distance conquests and bringing large quantities of goods and products into the treasury (often as "tribute" in the name of the ruler). This pattern of consumption emphasized the aggregation of a universal array of goods, with great value placed on the unique, the special, rare, and unusual object that could make real the qualities of distant parts of the realm. The simultaneously social, political, moral, and exchange economy in which such wonders were embedded extended downward and outward through the courts of regional nobles.[58]

At the same time, the emergence of continent-spanning religious communities, with their similar practices of prayer, sacrifice, and pilgrimage by which devotees pursued the signs and sites of the god scattered throughout the world, had by 1600 brought into existence a large infrastructure of transport, food, credit, and international trade to support their practices of devotion (spice for incense and Brahminical food restrictions, for example, and salted fish for Catholic fasting) and their extensive systems of pilgrimage.[59] The individuals traversing these various pilgrimage and trade routes shared both a common view of health and a common range of medicines. Central medical concepts, such as "life-breath," common to ancient Chinese, Stoic, and South Asian medical writers (*qi*, *pneuma*, and *prāna*), as well as general systems of health, informed care of the body throughout Afro-Eurasia. Both the Greco-Roman-Arabic-European system of the four humors and the Chinese system of *qi* and *yin/yang* had their origins in an overarching notion of balance and tempering in order to bring the body to a healthy state.[60] Moreover, many of the remedies by which a person's individual constitution (viewed throughout Eurasia as influenced by the heavenly bodies) could be tempered and balanced were transported over very long distances along the same trade routes by which staples and rarities alike traveled. Spices (wholly integrated into the health framework), medicinal plants (such as dragon's blood), animal parts (like rhinoceros horn), precious stones (for example, turquoise for eyesight; red coral to stop blood flow), and mineral-based concoctions (sulfur and mercury) all possessed medicinal virtues and commanded high exchange values throughout Afro-Eurasia.

A literature on "wonders," which began to codify and canonize these objects' marvelous qualities and simultaneously to stimulate desire for them, grew up around this exchange in rarities and medicines. In this literature, India was identified as the primary location of wonders and marvels, as well as the source of precious stones (which, along with Sri Lanka, it actually was).[61] Buzurg ibn Shahriyar, in his tenth-century *Kitab 'ajayib al-Hind* (The Wonders of India, ca. 960), recounts marvels of all sorts purportedly told to him on board merchant ships, including many involving fearsome snakes,[62] future-divining lizards as well as lizards with double sexual organs,[63] and especially crayfish—crayfish that detained ships by clasping the anchor between their pincers,[64] and crayfish that fell into the Sea of Senf, turned into stones, and were subsequently "carried into Iraq and all over, and used in making an ointment to cure eye complaints."[65] Such travelers' reports and sailors' yarns (best known perhaps are those of Sindbad the Sailor) spread exceedingly widely, forming the stuff of "folk tales" across Eurasia,[66] and might have generated the reptile stories of both the fourteenth-century European books of secrets and the oral culture of illiterate south Indian villagers in the early twentieth century.[67]

The foregoing section has done no more than gesture at the dense pathways of exchange that coursed across Eurasia since prehistoric times. The flows of goods and the people who mined, produced, transported, and consumed them helped to constitute the social, cultural, and medical complexes of belief that both structured and fostered this exchange. In this reciprocal process, the mundane production of material things (involving the manipulation of matter and nature) informed and transformed theoretical formulations of knowledge; the transfer of practical techniques across space fostered new ways of controlling both nature and other people; and the motion of goods and their trade gave rise to people telling oral tales, some of which were compiled, written down (only sometimes by identifiable authors), and translated into various vernacular and learned languages in texts that also moved across great distances and themselves stimulated the movement of yet further travelers, objects, and ideas.

RED AGAIN

One of the most important of these moving medicinal goods in China was cinnabar and its artificially produced substitute vermilion. Cinnabar had been extracted in China from a 100-kilometer-wide strip of deposits stretching "in a southwest-northeast direction some 700 km from northern Yunnan and southeastern Szechwan across Kweichow into western Hunan,"[68] from at least the fourth century BCE, and the pigment derived from it had come, on the one hand, to convey the power of the emperor in the bright red ink employed on particularly important documents of state,[69] and on the other to symbolize transformation. The *Baopuzi* (The Master Embracing Simplicity) of 320 CE by Ge Hong, for example, lists recipes for making artificial gold with red substances,[70] the same mosaic gold made by Cennino.[71] Ge Hong believed that the essence of cinnabar produced gold.[72]

A hoard of materia medica from between 741 and 756 CE containing cinnabar, red coral, gold powder, and gold leaf was uncovered recently.[73] This hoard indicates again the connections between red and gold, but also points to the widespread use in China of cinnabar in medicines and particularly in elixirs concocted to prolong life.[74] Cinnabar is listed in tribute texts back to the fifth century BCE, and these texts themselves go back to an oral tradition three hundred years older. The oldest text that definitively places cinnabar within a medical framework is from the second century BCE, and the use of cinnabar in this text is embedded in ritual practices.[75] Over time, this literature on the medicinal uses of cinnabar swelled into a veritable flood. In it cinnabar was viewed as far more efficacious for prolonging life than plant substances, but it could also be employed for seemingly contrary uses, such as abortifacients,[76] pointing to the ambiguous place of such a powerful transformative substance. Like lizards, cinnabar was implicated in death and putrefaction as well as regeneration.[77] For when struck with miners' tools, cinnabar sheds tears of mercury,[78] when heated and refined, cinnabar runs with living "quicksilver," and this mercury could revert again to cinnabar in the process of vermilion manufacture.[79] Much was made of mercury's quickening qualities in texts of the third century BCE, and, in the same period, channels in tomb chambers were constructed to run with liquid quicksilver. Indeed, one imperial tomb depicted the lands over which the emperor had ruled by means of a relief map, in which the rivers and streams flowed with liquid mercury, just as the emperor's veins had once flowed with blood.[80] The abundant texts of Chinese alchemy that grew up around the uses of cinnabar—one representative title from 712 CE being *The Mysterious Teachings on the Alchemical Preparation of Numinous Cinnabar*[81]—focus on the refining of cinnabar to mercury and from

mercury back to vermilion powder, prescribing repeated cyclical transformations both to produce the valuable elixirs and at the same time to
foster higher spiritual understanding in the adept.[82] Like the ninth- and
tenth-century Arabic literature (that so confused and excited its first Latin
translators), these texts are a combination of careful experimentation,
symbolism, and numerological speculation.[83] Sufi scholars and Chinese
alchemists regarded such productive knowledge not so much as a means
to useful materials (although they often produced them), but rather as the
way of personal and spiritual enlightenment.[84]

Although the links between Chinese and Arabic alchemical theories
have yet to be explored fully, the search for elixirs—such a prominent
feature of Chinese texts—is nowhere present in the late antique Greek
alchemical literature of the third through sixth centuries CE. In contrast,
Arabic alchemical literature is replete with elixirs, and, even more significantly, Arabic alchemy gives mercury and sulfur—which are absolutely
central to Chinese medical and alchemical practice—the foundational role
as generators of all metals. Moreover, the mercury trade in Islamic lands
during the eighth and ninth centuries stretched from the Almaden mines
to Alexandria and on to Fustat (in Egypt) via Tunisia, then through Aden
(in Yemen) perhaps as far as India.[85] The Arabic alchemical scholars Jābir
ibn Hayyan and especially Abū Bakr al-Rāzī both discuss in detail the process of vermilion making and other operations with mercury. Particularly
suggestive of the potential links between Chinese and Arabic alchemy is
al-Rāzī's remark, contained in instructions for making red and white mercury sublimate. About the white sublimate, he writes, "the substance will
coagulate in the phial like [the metal used to make] a Chinese mirror."[86]
Silvering mirrors by means of mercury in China can be traced definitively
back to the fifth or sixth century CE, but the process was probably known
as far back as the fourth century BCE.[87] Al-Rāzī was born and died in
Rayy, Persia, and he headed hospitals there and in Baghdad. He also
served at the Central Asian Sāmānid court in Bukhara where Chinese mirrors would undoubtedly have been available. All three cities in which he
worked were important trading zones between China and Central Asia.
The techniques of manufacture for such an object probably traveled with
people and goods, but it is not impossible that the mirrors themselves
formed the repository of information for their making. Objects like this
must have provided both a stimulus to imitation and experimentation as
well as information about their manufacture when "reverse engineered"
by practiced craftspeople and scholar-experimenters like al-Rāzī.[88]

Only recently have scholars made serious efforts to study Arabic
alchemical texts. Even so, as Robert Halleux notes, "everyone admits
today that Latin alchemy from the Middle Ages is all founded on Arabic
heritage, [but] the transmission mechanisms have not yet been studied.

The translations are not all discovered yet; their Arabic model is not always identified, their manuscript tradition is not known; the translator is only mentioned in a small number of cases."[89] Given this situation, it is perhaps premature to ask that the links between Arabic and Chinese alchemy be spelled out in any detail. From the suggestive work carried out so far, however, it appears that the transmission will not be found in texts, but rather in the movement of materials, such as sal ammoniac (ammonium chloride), an important export from Central Asia to China since the first millennium CE, which emerged after the Islamic inroads into this region as an essential material of Arabic alchemical and industrial practices and a central component of the Arabic alchemical theory of salts in the ninth century.[90] Materia medica also offer evidence of this flow from matter to ideas, for the remedies recorded in the Arabic and Persian pharmaceutical writings incorporated a hugely expanded range of medicinals from "as far away as China, Southeast Asia, the Himalayas, Southern India, and Africa."[91] Techniques traveled too, as we can see from an early ninth-century "how-to" manual in Arabic, which includes glue for broken porcelain, instructions on how to construct "Chinese saddles" (apparently an object of interest, as we also know that several were taken at the Battle of Talas River), a "Chinese cream" for polishing mirrors, and so on.[92] Such a text offers further evidence that it was by means of the motion of objects and techniques that new complexes of knowledge emerged in the contact zones of China and the lands of Islam.[93]

We will not be astounded, then, at the similar powers with which the materials cinnabar, quicksilver, vermilion, and lizards were endowed at opposite ends of Eurasia. For, when viewed against the background of the continuous flow of materials, people, technologies, practices, texts, and ideas back and forth across Eurasia, it is entirely plausible that the complex of ideas and practices surrounding lizards, vermilion, metals, and generation spread with the trade in pigments, materia medica, and health practices, and informed both metalworkers' vernacular beliefs and learned scholars seeking the lost books of Aristotle or the elixir for eternal life. The resulting amalgam of written and tacit knowledge and of theories and practices that made up this particular piece of knowledge about the natural world, I would argue, is characteristic of the making of knowledge,[94] including scientific knowledge.

Given this constant movement and exchange across Eurasia, it should perhaps become an automatic reflexive action for historians to look for connections, rather than assuming a trajectory of ideas and techniques confined within the artificial boundaries of "Europe" or "China."[95] An example from the more rarefied realms of the exact sciences is instructive here: Jamil Ragep and George Saliba have given insight into the ways in which the Arabic and Latinate communities of astronomers were all engaged in the same project during the fifteenth and sixteenth centuries, working with the same sets of textual and mathematical tools. It will not come as a surprise then that Nicholas Copernicus (1473–1543) could gain insight into the mathematical problems concerning the motions of the planets from the texts of the astronomers at the Maragha observatory (now East Azerbaijan, Iran), in particular that of Nasir al-Din al-Tusi (d. 1274).[96]

LET US TURN OUR BACKS NOW ON EURASIA
AND BRIEFLY CONSIDER MOVEMENT ACROSS
THE ATLANTIC AND PACIFIC OCEANS

Red in the New World was a color of sacred practice, desire, and trade. In the sixth century BCE, a "deep rusty blood red" dye was being used to color the wrappings of the dead in the high Andes, and, in the 1400s, the Inca depicted Mamahuaco, one of the progenitors of humankind, emerging from the Cave of Origin wearing a red dress.[97] With the Spanish destruction of the Inca Empire, the cochineal insect—called *nocheztli* in Central America and *macnu* in the Andes—cultivated on cactus to supply these pigments, became a commodity of great value to the Spanish Crown. In 1587, some 144,000 pounds were sent on Spanish ships across the Atlantic and then throughout Afro-Eurasia from their landing docks in Spain: to the Netherlands, France, and Venice and into the Ottoman Empire. With the advent of the Manila galleon trade in 1564, the red dye traveled on Spanish carracks from Acapulco across the Pacific to the Ming Empire, where, as we have seen, red possessed a ready market.[98] The dye was especially valuable at this moment in Europe because the *Murex* shell, which had produced the deep purple dye reserved to kings and cardinals, had reached near extinction due to overharvesting. Indeed, in "1464, Pope Paul II finally officially changed 'Cardinal's Purple' to red, which could be produced from insects rather than shellfish."[99] Spectacular attempts were made to break the Spanish Crown's monopoly on cochineal, including "scientific" exploratory voyages, like that of Nicolas-Joseph Thiéry de Menonville, sent on a voyage of industrial espionage in 1776 by the French king to bring live insects and cactus to Saint-Domingue.[100] Indeed many eighteenth-century scientific voyages had as their aim the discovery and mapping of commercial shipping routes, the surveying of new colonial lands, as well as the search (or espionage) for new commodities and medicines.[101] The generalizing global perspective afforded by such voyages could provide new scientific theories, such as those about global climactic patterns assembled by networks of botanists,[102] and it just as surely gave rise to a new science of ethnology employed by colonial administrators that helped establish a notion of "civilization" with its hierarchies of peoples and societies, such as that which resulted in preserving the "agrarian" Maori while fostering the hunting down and annihilation of the more "primitive" nomadic Australian aborigines.[103]

BUT LET US LEAVE THIS BLOOD RED AND TURN OUR ATTENTION TO GLISTENING BLACK . . .

When the famous Elizabethan scholar John Dee (1527–1608) wished to contact the spirit world to answer questions (which ranged from politics to natural philosophy to the best remedies for his wife's illnesses) and foretell the future, he brought an experienced "scryer" to look into a dark stone—his "scrying glass." With Dee anxiously standing beside him, the scryer saw and heard angels, the utterances of which he reported to Dee, who noted them in a special diary.[104] Dee's show stone, a black disc of stone 18.9 centimeters in diameter by 1.3 to 2.26 centimeters thick, believed until the early twentieth century to be a slab of a hard bituminous rock known as Kennel coal, had actually been shaped from black volcanic obsidian glass by a nameless Aztec artisan. We shall never know how Dee obtained this object (although there are a small number still extant in European museums, three of which form the supports of religious scenes painted in seventeenth-century Europe),[105] but its power was such that it has survived to the present, acquired by Horace Walpole and then by the British Museum.[106] Dee's use of this object is very suggestive, for it was a "smoking mirror," the name of Tezcatlipoca, the all-powerful Central American god of rulers, witches, and warriors, whose attribute, the glistening black obsidian mirror, had long been regarded as an instrument of divination and sorcery among the Aztecs.[107]

Dee's mirror launches us into the somewhat different world of exchange with the Americas, where, with the assistance of Eurasian microbes, European centralizing states were able to dominate existing empires very rapidly in a manner they were not able to realize in the Indian Ocean and the South China Sea until the nineteenth century. Recent scholars of this exchange have focused on the fact—strangely neglected by generations of historians of science—that European interest in nature in the New World, both natural-philosophical and practical, was always inextricably linked to interest in its commercial exploitation.[108] Or, as Richard Drayton has phrased it somewhat more bluntly, their motive for expansion, in common with any expansion into a foreign region, was "asset stripping" and "plunder."[109]

The Spaniard Pedro de Osma, wrote from Lima in 1568,

[C]onsider how many more herbs and plants possessing great virtues . . . our Indies must have. But they are out of our reach and knowledge because the Indians, being bad people and our enemies, will not reveal to us a secret, not a single virtue of a herb, even if they should see us die, or even if they be sawed in pieces. If we know anything of the matters I have treated, and of others, we learned it from the female Indians. Because they get involved with Spaniards, and reveal to them all that they know.

In the essay in which this passage appears, Daniela Bleichmar makes the point that "[t]he circulation of knowledge from the New World to the Old and back to the New was dependent on native knowledge yet unable to access and credit indigenous populations as sources. American natives were at the center of this cycle and at the same time excluded from it."[110] Indeed, Londa Schiebinger and Claudia Swan's *Colonial Botany*, Schiebinger's *Plants and Empire*, and Antonio Barrera-Osorio's *Experiencing Nature*, as well as the work of other scholars, with only a few exceptions, have demonstrated that local knowledge of the New World was translated, suppressed, ignored, or lost in its transition to Europe and to European scholars, where it went to form the stuff of the newly differentiating scientific disciplines like botany. These historians have argued that natural objects had to be stripped of their local significances and cultures in order to be incorporated into European natural history, medicine, and commerce. In *Matters of Exchange: Commerce, Medicine, and Science in the Dutch Golden Age*, Harold Cook has argued that this dynamic was central in the making of a new approach to nature in the period of European expansion. He contends that Dutch commerce in natural goods in the East and West Indies was central in the creation of new modes of valuing objects of nature and information about nature. By his account, commercial accumulation and exchange led to new ways of describing, measuring, and valuing objects as neutral quantum bits of information, which he views as giving rise to a new "objectivity" about natural things.[111]

While such accounts as those of Cook and Schiebinger provide important frameworks within which to understand an exchange that has left far fewer textual traces and objects out of which we can tease agglomerations of meaning, we should perhaps be wary of assuming Dee's ignorance about what he was doing when he called up spirits in the "smoking mirror" of Tezcatlipoca. A narrative at odds with that suggested by historians of science about the stripping of meaning from New World materials is suggested by Marcy Norton's study of chocolate in the Atlantic world, which instead demonstrates the reciprocal (we might say cathected) nature of this cultural exchange. She argues that the European taste for chocolate was not as simple as it has previously appeared to scholars, who viewed it as having been stripped of its Central American significance and ritual practices in order to be inserted into European medical beliefs, coffee drinking, or sugar consumption. In contrast, she demonstrates that Europeans consumed chocolate from very early on in much the same manner as native Americans, and the medical discourse that grew up around it aimed not to strip it of meaning, but rather to reconcile the meanings that this now firmly entrenched but still suspect taste raised for Europeans. As she elegantly concludes,

> In Spain and Spanish America, Europeans' taste for chocolate did not bolster a normative hierarchy that elevated European colonists over Indian subjects, or Christians over pagans. Instead, it brought unwanted attention to the failures of the colonial civilizing and evangelical project and revealed the civilizers' vulnerability to cultural metamorphosis and Christians' potential for internalizing idolatry.

Not quite so abstract as ideas and not so tangible as goods, taste—understood here as embodied habits and aesthetic dispositions—formed part of the "Columbian Exchange." These embodied habits and aesthetic dispositions have a history that exists in relation to—but is not dependent on—other historical phenomena. In the case of chocolate, particular social conditions, namely Spaniards' sustained proximity to Indian cultural milieus and the social integration of the Spanish Atlantic world, account for Europeans' acquisition of a new taste. This taste, rather than bolstering a monolithic imperial ideology, spotlighted its internal contradictions.[112]

Even in the Atlantic world, where a different dynamic of exchange than that in Eurasia occurred, it may be more fruitful to expect connections and creolizations (perhaps in the subtle ways that seemingly stable objects came to have new meanings or, as with chocolate, new tastes came into being)[113] rather than rushing too hastily to assume a blank slate, for, as we saw with Dee, the apparently natural slab of black rock into which he peered so intently was actually the made thing of another place entirely.

THE ITINERARIES OF MATTER, PRACTICES, AND IDEAS

This essay began in a consideration of matter—mercury and sulfur. These substances possess particular properties that enabled the manufacture of certain kinds of materials and objects by means of specialized practices and technologies. At different places and times, humans have assigned meanings to these practices and objects, and these meanings have been both embedded within and helped to extend systems of belief (or "theories) about the matter, practices, and objects they incorporated. This essay sought to illuminate the reciprocal processes by which matter gives rise to practices and objects, which themselves produce systems of belief that in their turn inform specific ideas about materials and practices.

All human societies interact in a variety of ways with their environment for survival, and, out of the experience gained through that interaction, certain skills and knowledge emerge.[114] We might consider the Neolithic Revolution by which humans manipulated animal and plant varieties to control nature in a spectacularly successful manner or the advent of bronze and glass making as part of a long, continuing interaction between humans and their environment—a long story of incremental developments at the interface of the human hand with the material world. Sometimes the practices, skills, and the theories that emerge out of this interaction with matter are accumulated and built upon, sometimes lost and rediscovered, and often just lost forever. The present development and accumulation of techniques and knowledge by means of the institutionalized natural sciences might be viewed as one phase of that very long enduring human engagement with the environment. There may be a difference in the volume and speed at which knowledge is accumulated today, as the system of knowledge production we now call "natural science" involves many people generously supported by the taxes of nation-states. Some observers might point to recent discoveries by individual scientists as evidence of new processes of knowledge production occurring since the so-called Scientific Revolution, a view that is reinforced by the institutional structures of modern science such as the Nobel Prize. Such a picture of the modern relationship of the human hand to the environment, however, grows out of a limited perspective on human history, perhaps arising from historians' overwhelming reliance upon the written word. The existence of a written record for the exceedingly short recent present of human history (only about 7,000 of the approximately 200,000-plus years since *Homo sapiens* emerged) gives historians the sense that they can pin discoveries and inventions to individuals, but on further investigation, many of these discoveries are found to have been the result of collective and collaborative processes,[115] much like those that produced bronze, writing, glass, and moveable type, to name only a few at random. Innovation, intelligence, and "creativity" (sometimes labeled "genius") have often been thought about as located in and manifested by individual minds, but they are better viewed as occurring within and emerging out of material, social, and cultural fields. Reliance by historians on written records and on identifiable individuals living in the recent human past (whose written works are still extant) has had the effect of misleading us about the collective and distributed nature by which all knowledge, but especially knowledge of our natural environment, is produced.

This essay attempts a kind of deep history of knowledge, one that seeks out "lost sciences"; which brings to the fore the role of that elusive human ability, skill; which follows matter and objects as well as texts along their routes of exchange; and which emphasizes the very gradual and often anonymous processes of amalgamation by which complexes of matter, skill, practices of production, formalized knowledge, and systems of meaning are accreted over time and across distance.

CHAPTER 5

Fashioning a Market

THE SINGER SEWING MACHINE IN COLONIAL LANKA

Nira Wickramasinghe

> Une machine Singer dans un foyer nègre
> Arabe, indien, malais, chinois, annamite
> Ou dans n'importe quelle maison
> Sans boussole du tiers monde
> C'était le dieu lare qui raccommodait
> Les mauvais jours de notre enfance.
>
> René Depestre

INTRODUCTION

Colonies were crucial markets for products such as the sewing machine. Consumption in the colony was, in consequence, an important site through which ideas about a global market came to be consolidated from the late nineteenth century, a period often termed as the age of international capitalism. Historians of international capitalism, however, have sparingly studied the experience and practices of this consumption and have paid scant attention to the market driven modernity sponsored by modern imperialism. Even Sidney Mintz's *Sweetness and Power*, which captures so well both the openness of local history and its conditioning by larger-scale structures, reinforces the distinction between the South as a site of sugar production and the North, in his case Britain, as a space of consumption.[1] One could go as far as to say that a consumption-production dichotomy between colonizer and colonized dominates the field of economic history, especially business history, where the consumer in the colony remains marginal to the operation of markets. In the spirit of countering such a conventional account of consumer goods, this essay focuses on the fashioning of a consumer market in a colonial setting through the itineraries of the sewing machine in Lanka, now known as Sri Lanka.

To write a history of consumption around the sewing machine (figure 5.1) in a colonial setting like Lanka is not without its difficulties.[2] Like

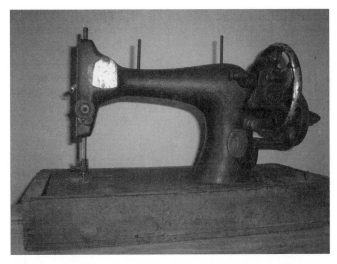

FIGURE 5.1: Sewing machine (ca. 1890), Historical Mansion Museum, Galle Fort. Author's private collection.

other questions that drive historical research in the colony, it is not easy to assess the reception of the sewing machine from the scattered details of purchase and use, even if official sources amply attest that the island of Lanka, like other Asian regions, saw the rapid emergence of consumer markets for manufactured goods in the early twentieth century. For instance, E. B. Denham, a colonial administrator in Lanka, commented authoritatively in his encyclopedic *Ceylon at the Census of 1911*, that "the 'habits and wants of the natives' have changed so considerably in the last hundred years that there is today a large and increasing demand for European goods."[3] Information on machines is, however, sparse. Successive volumes of *Ferguson's Directory* record the number of machines imported into the island, but we do not know where these stocks of machines were sent and who actually bought them. While we know that companies such as Singer and Pfaff set up agencies in many cities on the island, none of their agents left records or accounts of the daily life of the seller, in marked contrast to the situation in Japan.[4] Given how little is known about the lives of ordinary people during colonial rule, we lack the type of works mentioning tailors (*darzis*) that David Arnold relied upon for his recent study on the Indian sewing machine in India.[5]

Furthermore, visual traces of the machine remain sparse. We have neither drawings nor photographs of tailors or bourgeois women sitting in the comfort of their home instructing seamstresses sitting on the floor as in the Indonesian record.[6]

The simple paucity of data in the survey mode pales, however, in the face of a deeper conceptual challenge encountered in the official narratives about consumption in Lanka. Official commentary, such as that by the colonial administrator Denham, is a case in point. Denham argued that notwithstanding their appetite for goods, "the great mass of the inhabitants are quite unaware that *any movement* is taking place."[7] He conceded that a colonized subject could become a consumer, yet he denied the subject the ultimate gift of temporal consciousness, something that he implicitly associated with the market consumption. In fact, by asserting that consumption in Lanka was not coeval with a new perception of time, Denham could uphold both that time consciousness harbored the possibility of freedom from colonized status and that Lankans were incapable of becoming modern citizens. Such opinions were integral to liberal imperial ideologies of the market, for they enabled a variety of empire-sponsored agents, missionaries, and officials among them, to engage in a pedagogic exercise to teach inhabitants in the colony how to become proper modern consuming subjects. As Timothy Burke's work on commodities in Zimbabwe shows in the case of Lifebuoy soap, consumers in places like Zimbabwe played an active role in the commodity's history. Their acts of consumption, their desire for soap, redefined the use value of Western personal care products.[8] Schooling a desire for commodities articulated the political project of colonialism to a market-driven vision of modernity.

There is, however, something more at work. Consumers in the colony used commodities and their desire for commodities to define their own relation to modernity. The thrust of Denham's opinion on the inadequacies of Lankan consumption passes lightly over the opinion of a native chief headman recorded in the very same *Census Report*. "Today," declared the headman, "sewing machines and gramophones are the hallmark of respectability and wealth in the villages."[9] Undermining Denham's reading of natives as people incapable of conceiving themselves as "being in the world," these headman's words signal how the consciousness of contemporary lived experience, of the "now," was bound up with objects in colonial Lanka. Perhaps Denham cited the headman as evidence that the isolated Ceylonese village had indeed changed with the penetration and spread of new technologies. But perhaps more than a confirmation of the diffusion of particular goods and the entry of the market in the lives of common people, the words index a consciousness of the new, encapsulated in the figure of two machines that embodied "speed, shock and the spectacle of constant sensation."[10] Had Denham considered commodity fetishism, he would have realized that in a world dominated by capital, freedom for the former colonized subject would spawn other chains, the chains that come with unlimited desires!

The experience of modernity as desire installed through machines remains to be explored. Historians of Lanka have focused on other topics and used other methodologies. Recent scholarly work on colonial Lanka has paid much attention to the way male natives are represented, what Stoler calls "the representation machines,"[11] rather than how women and men negotiate with colonial state institutions and the market.[12] Furthermore, the frame of colonialism largely overdetermined accounts of the multiple spaces and times that continue over a "colonial period." Nationalist historiography in South Asia as well its critique have overlooked global connections in their refusal to see the colonized/disempowered as "consumers of modernity"[13] and in their eagerness to see the colonized moving in "uncontaminated autonomous cultures" that create "a reservoir of anti-colonialism."[14]

The life of the machine in this essay, then, is not a way to track the diffusion of consumption practices or its representation. My approach departs from that of contributors to a recent issue of *Modern Asian Studies* on everyday technology in South and Southeast Asia who try to "understand the role of technology as instrument and agent in the transformations affecting everyday life."[15] Rather, I seek to narrate the fashioning of a market imaginary, which indexed modernity as desire in Lanka. This imaginary takes shape at the intersection of the business archive and circuits of communication that channeled goods. An American company such as the Singer Sewing Machine Company operated through circuits distinct from those of the British Empire. The spatial imaginary of the business archive while attendant to imperial flows also traversed the boundaries of politically and culturally demarcated regions. To wit, the Singer Company papers deposited at the Wisconsin Historical Society Library contain boxes of correspondence between the headquarters and the agents arranged by region. The papers on Lanka, then Ceylon, are not treated as a separate territorial entity but as part of the Indian market sector. The collapse of the distance between Bombay and Colombo welded once disparate spaces. At the same time, their conjoining allowed for the development of nationally differentiated commodity cultures. The market imaginary also emerges as a freighted entity when it is considered through the circuits of mediation that enabled consumption. Here the market imaginary is revealed not just by Singer's efforts through the agency of its policy makers and sales staff, but also in advertisements and novels, discourses of Sinhalese modern nationalism, and the economy of the machines itself.

THE SINGER COMPANY AND THE MARKET FOR MACHINES

The sewing machine has been described as "one of the first standardized and mass marketed complex consumer goods to spread around the world." A single firm was predominantly responsible for its global diffusion: By 1912, Singer controlled 60 percent of the market share of family sewing machines in America and 90 percent in foreign markets.[16] If you bought a sewing machine outside the United States, you likely bought a Singer machine.

Like most other machines, a series of inventions and patents led to its development, rather than one person inventing it. The first Singer sewing machine was conceived in the early 1850s as a partnership between a mechanical genius, Isaac M. Singer, and a lawyer, Edward Clark. But the early history of the company, I. M. Singer, can be read as a maze of patent grabbing by a number of inventors—Howe, Grover, Baker, Wilson, and Singer were the most prominent—and subsequent litigation. No owner of a single patent could make a sewing machine without infringing on the patents of others. From the needle with a point and eye on one side (around 1755) to an abortive breakthrough by Barthélemy Thimonnier (1841), to the perfection of the shuttle principle by Elias Howe, Jr. and Isaac Merritt Singer, it took a century to turn these disparate innovations into a commercial success. Clark was instrumental in the creation of the Albany patent pool, where the holders of these key patents agreed to forgo litigation and to license their technology to one another. This led to a rapid development of the industry. That same year Singer began demonstrating and servicing its products in its own domestic sales rooms and selling on installments. Three years later it had fourteen branch sales offices in the United States.[17]

THE GLOBAL SPREAD OF SINGER

The mastery of the material world by nations of Western Europe and North America and the proliferation and flooding of African and Asian markets with cheap durable consumer goods in the last decades of the nineteenth century has been described in a number of excellent books.[18] Singer showed an early interest in the foreign side of the business. By 1864 it was exporting 40 percent of its output. In the next few years the company sold machines abroad using independent franchised agents in countries such as Mexico, Canada, Cuba, Germany, Venezuela, Uruguay, Peru, and Puerto Rico and employed a salaried representative in Glasgow and one in London. London soon replaced Glasgow as Singer's British sales center. The competition remained stiff: in England its main competitors were William Thomas and the American firm Wheeler & Wilson. Branch offices were established in Germany and Sweden. The first factory in Glasgow was initially a very small affair, an assembly operation. By 1869, however, the output had increased and another factory opened in Glasgow. By 1874 Singer was selling more than half its sewing machines abroad (126,694 of 241,679). In 1879 Singer's London headquarters had twenty-six central offices in the United Kingdom and one each in Paris,

Madrid, Brussels, Milan, Basel, Cape Town, Bombay, and Auckland. Each central office, in turn, had suboffices under its control. By 1890 Singer was selling 800,000 machines per year, three-quarters of all sewing machines sold in the world.[19]

THE ASIAN MARKET

In the late nineteenth century the desire of American entrepreneurs to sell in markets abroad spurred an interest in Asia. Asia had been, since American independence from Britain, conceived in America as a land of exotic wealth. In the eighteenth century the map of Asia encompassed a massive, vaguely defined area that included India, China, and the Arab world. For businessmen Asia was shaped into a succession of tempting markets: China, Japan, Korea, and the Philippines. Asia had made its debut in the American imaginary as a space of convergence between economic fact and fantasy. It was the space of romance.[20] It was during George Ross McKenzie's era at the helm of Singer (1882–89) that the company turned its eye toward Asia. In 1883, in response to a global economic downturn, he felt Asia would be "a commercial safety valve" to combat slow sales and to unload his warehoused stockpiles. His reasons for an all-out incursion in Asia were therefore purely practical.[21] A Singer Company publication suggested more noble reasons when it stated that whenever people substitute a machine for direct physical strength "they are so far uplifted in scale of being because they are enabled to make their lives more interesting as well as more productive . . . and a Singer sewing machine is one of the most conspicuous examples of this kind of invention which . . . elevates human nature."[22]

Singer sewing machines were being marketed in India, China, Japan, Burma, the Straits Settlements, Java, the Philippines, and Australia, exemplifying the "general expansionist behavior" of the New York office. However, apart from Davies's case studies of India and China and the work of Andrew Gordon on Japan, the sources on the Asian market are diffuse.[23] Davies shows how in each country Singer tried to use exactly the same sale techniques that had worked so well in the United States and Britain—traveling salesmen and generous selling terms—and attributes the failure in India to a combination of poverty, cultural barriers, and employee dishonesty. In China, after five years of attempting to capture the market, the company acknowledged it had failed; Davies attributes the failure in China to the single factor that Chinese people preferred their own loose stitching.[24] There were certainly other reasons. The disinclination of wealthier Chinese to permit their wives and daughters to use machines, which led to the adoption of Singer sewing machines mainly by tailors and shoemakers, was often mentioned in American consular reports.[25]

For the policy makers at the Singer headquarters, India, Burma, and Ceylon/Lanka constituted one single region. In this they followed the general approach seen in American consular reports, where Lankan companies were often but not always listed under the India heading.[26] They were quietly subverting the "geographies of empire" all the while the British were carefully demarcating their geographical zones according to constructed alliances and policies of caste, class, region. Either in blissful ignorance or perhaps cocking a snook at equally absurd but to them pragmatic British-constructed ways of envisioning an "Asian" market, Americans can in effect be seen as creating a counterreality—a capitalist "empire" operating as a counterflow to the political construct of empire. In this light the fact that Ceylon/Lanka was a distinct crown colony ruled separately from the Raj did not constitute a problem for American business. For all intents and purposes the geography of business did not have to follow geopolitical boundaries. This was the case not only in Asia but also in Europe, where "the Market Empire much preferred to have as its main interlocutor not the national state, but a generic entity called Europe."[27] The Singer Corporation was not different from other manufacturers and marketers.

The Indian market had been developed in the early 1870s, by George Woodruff, the general agent for Britain and its colonies who had divided the subcontinent into a southern district to be controlled by Bombay— Ceylon/Lanka would come under this—and a northern district to be worked from Calcutta. The imagined map of India on the part of Singer was quite distinct from the political map of the British administration. The Singer Corporation devised its own divisions in India that were clearly not based on any political template: Bombay, Ahmedabad, Allahabad, Belgaum, Calcutta and depots, Delhi and depots, Karachi, Lahore and depots, Madras and depots, Poona. Colombo was one of the Madras depots not distinct from Bangalore, Bellary, Cocanada, Conoor, Secundrabad, Trichinopoly, or Trivandrum and was perceived as another subdistrict of Madras.[28] In 1905–6 the district offices grew in number. The list offers a peculiar mix of important cities such as Aden, Allahabad, and Bombay and completely insignificant townships such as Belgaum, Jubbulpore, Indore, and Secundrabad. More than business opportunities or political boundaries, the criteria for the selection and opening of offices seemed more likely to have been dependent upon the whims and fancies of Mr. Nusserwanjee Merwanjee Patell, the Singer agent in India.

THE SINGER COMPANY IN CEYLON/LANKA

The first shop and office of the Singer Manufacturing Company was established in Colombo in 1877 at 27 Main Street, Pettah. There are records of a person in its employ—although the quality of the person remains doubtful—who looked after the Colombo operation. A Statement of Defalcations by Employees in India lists a G. Cronon as an employee in Colombo in December 1885 having embezzled a sum of 900 rupees.[29] Branches were next opened in Kandy, the capital of the central province and the second largest city in Lanka, and in Hatton, a small town in the hill country central to the tea plantation industry—on Bazaar Street. While the choice of Kandy seems logical, opening a branch at Hatton did not appear to be the most judicious choice.[30] There were teething problems. In 1893 Singer had to file a case against the Sewing Machine Company, a joint stock company registered and incorporated in India and also carrying on business in Colombo. Singer alleged that the Sewing Machine Company was using a sign board with the intention of deceiving people into believing that they were the authorized agents of Singer machines.[31] In 1899 the company had reputed agents in E. Cahill and Sons who advertised regularly in the English daily paper the *Lanka Independent*.[32] That year an advertisement for Singer sewing machines boasted that the company operated one hundred offices in India, Burma, and Lanka.[33] By 1906, another branch was opened in Galle, the second largest port in the island and a commercial hub in the southern province—at 28 High Street.[34] Thereafter the Singer Manufacturing Company established branches in many towns throughout the island. In 1915 an advertisement placed by Singer Company supervisor B. J. Keating and his assistant supervisor S. MacQueen claimed twenty-eight shops in Lanka and more to open.[35]

DIFFUSION OF THE SINGER SEWING MACHINE IN LANKA

There is no doubt that the peoples in Lanka were receptive to sewing machines, which they bought with a far greater zeal than their counterparts in India or China. In 1886 and 1887, early years for the company's offices in Lanka, figures for Singer sewing machines sold in Lanka are included under the category Madras and Depots—Bangalore, Bellary, Cocanada, Colombo, Conoor, Secundrabad, Trichinopoly, Trivandrum. All the depots were located in the southern part of India except for Colombo. The Madras office sold 558 machines and the depots 726 machines, still a very small figure. The Colombo office sold 81 machines in the space of twelve months (1886–87).[36] It is possible to estimate the number of machines in Lanka in 1930 as 113,309 machines, given the fact that machines are durable items and assuming that Singer captured 90 percent of the market.[37] Following Godley's method of assessing diffusion, the number of machines per household can be calculated with some accuracy. In a total population of Lanka amounting to 5,312,548, where each family can be assumed as constituting 4.7 members,[38] the number of families would be 1,130,329. The number of sewing machines per inhabitant can then be tallied as 1 per 47 persons (2 percent of the population) and 1 per 10 families (10 percent of households). As mentioned earlier, the diffusion of machines in Lanka offers a huge contrast to the Indian market, where in 1916 only 1 percent of households owned a machine. The diffusion in Lanka is more comparable to that in Turkey and Greece, where over 10 percent of households owned a machine before the First World War.[39]

It is not possible to prove beyond doubt that all these machines were Singer machines, although the Singer supervisor in 1915 claimed annual sales of 5,000 machines when he boasted that "at present with an imperfect selling organization our weekly sales average 150 machines."[40] He hoped to increase sales to 10,000 sewing machines in 1916. (This figure is probably exaggerated as it exceeds the number of machines imported into Lanka, but it reflects Singer's domination of the market and its ambition to expand exponentially.)

SALES STRATEGIES IN LANKA

The marketing strategies used by Singer in Lanka were closely linked to one individual, Nusserwanjee Merwanjee Patell (figure 5.2), until the beginning of the twentieth century. Patell left a deep imprint on the first thirty years of the history of the company in India as well as in Lanka.

He was appointed as Singer's agent in Bombay in June 1875, but visited his suboffices on occasion and communicated with Colombo quite frequently. Patell related the way in which he was recruited in the address he made at his retirement ceremony:

> One afternoon in 1875, when I was going to my father's office, I happened to pass by a show-window containing some Sewing Machines. Being of an inquisitive nature, I stood to look at them, when a gentleman named Mr. Leonard Cohn came to me and requested me to walk in. I did so reluctantly, because I had to attend my father's office and never meant to buy a machine. I inspected the machines and while leaving, I was asked if I was willing to take up buying agency. He was much after me and gave me all favourable terms as I wanted and I signed the agreement in 3 days.[41]

His account suggests that his recruitment was purely by chance and it simply may be that Mr. Leonard Cohn was immediately taken with the Westernized and eloquent young man. This would suggest a complete absence of any racial or cultural consideration on the part of American

FIGURE 5.2: N.M. Patell. *Report of the Proceedings at the Presentation of an Address to R.M. Patell, Esquire JP, Agent for India, Burmah and Ceylon, The Singer Manufacturing Company, on His Retirement.* Washington, DC: Smithsonian Institution Libraries, 1911.

staff of Singer and Patell's complete control of the way the corporation in India and Lanka was managed.

Patell's career spanned nearly four decades; he did not retire until 1911. In 1881 Singer president Edward Clark gave Patell charge of the whole of India, which included Ceylon/Lanka. During this time Patell was entirely responsible for developing the Indian market. As the general agent he had to remit the net weekly proceeds to London after "deducting all rents, salaries, advertisements, and other business related expenses." His salary amounted to three pounds per week plus a 5 percent commission on net cash proceeds up to 6,000 pounds, with an additional 2.5 percent commission on all monies remitted in excess of that amount.[42] Three years later he was granted a guaranteed yearly salary of 500 pounds.

The Singer Corporation followed the British colonial usage, appointing a member of the English-speaking minority as their representative, but instead of relying on Eurasians, Singer selected Patell, a member of the Parsee community.[43] Patell in turn chose his own cousin as his cashier. The Colombo office too had in 1888 a Parsee canvasser, Rastonji Nasserwanji, who was paid 30 rupees as a salary and collected 2 percent commission on sales.[44] Later, Singer appears to have recruited European agents in a consistent manner to look after the market in Lanka.

The exclusive use of Parsees as employees was questioned quite early. Notwithstanding the almost quasi-European status ascribed to Parsees, it was claimed that Parsees were not so well considered and integrated into society in Calcutta and Madras as in Bombay. The suggestion was that the Calcutta and Madras operations were large enough to have "a good

European management," but the issue was really one of "race"; "would a European work under a Parsee as general manager?" Edward Sang advised having separate districts dealing directly with London as the country was deemed too large to be under one single management, but his recommendation was not adopted.[45] Patell remained solely in charge.

For a time Patell did not follow the Singer model of selling that had been adopted all over the world. The canvasser-collector system used by Singer was the key innovation of the company. Canvassers were based in the retail stores, but they also approached the public directly in their homes to demonstrate the sewing machines and collect signed orders. To check on the work of the canvassers, the British office director, Woodruff, created a separate cadre of collectors while the retail branch manager doubled as the sales manager. Each canvasser was allocated a district and his responsibility was to knock on the door of every house every two years. He was supposed to befriend the family, offer advice and solicit introductions, and, if necessary, service the existing Singer machines. The collector intervened only once new accounts were opened: the collector delivered the machine and made the subsequent requests for the weekly installments to complete its purchase for up to two years. This was a very expensive method of selling, and a few years later, salesman-collectors replaced the separate cadre of canvassers and collectors. This system was expanded globally. By 1905 Singer employed 61,444 people in 4,552 branches throughout its global selling organization.[46] In contrast, Patell succeeded in recruiting one canvasser and only for a short time. The former canvasser then proceeded to join Singer's main competitor! After that no canvassers were used in India. Another reason was that the terms offered were so low that "no Europeans for canvassing among the people resident here, could be found on these terms."[47] It was firmly believed that only Europeans would be successful in selling machines to members of the British community in India, but the company was not prepared to change its policy on wages in order to attract potential candidates.

After a brief fall from grace due to a financial scandal, Patell was reinstated in 1887 and John Mitchell, the chief inspector in the London office, introduced a change of strategy after his visit to India. He authorized the appointment of resident commission agents who would advertise, secure orders, and collect market information to be used by the occasional traveling canvassers from city offices.[48] This change was based on the observation that local customers preferred to buy at a shop and pay in cash rather than make use of the hire purchase system. Often customers would pool their resources to buy a machine. Patell was authorized to sell at a lower price for cash. Adapting sales methods and management styles to India paid off but never quite matched the sales expectations Singer had for a country of 200 million people.

Davies explained the relative failure of Singer in India as related to India's culture: the caste system, the seclusion and widespread illiteracy of Indian women, the inaccessibility of homes to canvassers, the popular preference for cash sales, and the style of clothing that did not require a sewing machine stitch.[49] But the conclusion attributes too much to structural issues and not enough to flaws in the office in Bombay solely run by Patell. It seems that sewing machines as early as 1883 were popular, a fact pointed out by a Singer employee visiting from New York:

> When walking in the native quarters of the town, I was struck with the number of machines in use (the people always working at the open doors) but scarcely any of ours, something more must evidently be done.[50]

Another reason could be Patell's inability to cope with the effect of climate on stocks and his use of doubtful selling methods. When Edward Sang went to inspect the operations in Bombay and Calcutta, he noted with dismay the state of the stock. He suggested the use of nickel plating as a measure against dampness and deplored the "skeletons of machines rusty and stripped of parts" that he discovered in the warehouse. The selling techniques of Mr. Patell were also problematic since he was described as not having "the necessary patience" especially with "those of a lower caste."[51] Nor had he managed the stock keeping in a methodical way. Patell was warned not to advertise the sale of damaged items as this would create the idea that Singer sold old machines returned by hirers and would weaken the confidence of the public in the goods.[52]

If one follows Davies's argument to understand why Lankans consumed more sewing machines than Indians, certain cultural differences may be put forward: in a predominantly Buddhist country, the literacy of women was higher than it was in India, and women of the Sinhalese community enjoyed a relative freedom of movement, as homes were more open. Due to the influence of the Portuguese and Dutch, the style of clothing was already Europeanized, or sewn clothes were combined with draped clothing in many cities and coastal areas. Finally, Lanka had a less harsh climate. But common approaches to credit make up another important factor behind the different response; the people of Lanka already had formed a habit of borrowing from Chettiars, suggesting their familiarity with the idea of interest and installment purchase.[53]

People in Lanka had begun to buy sewing machines on installments, as Patell would discover during his visit to the island in 1901. His visit was motivated by the need to check on the Colombo office and their difficulties in controlling affairs in the suboffices. He soon found out that the Kandy manager had misappropriated about 1,000 rupees by selling stock and then disappearing. Patell referred the matter to the police, aiding their work with photographs he had secured of each and every manager with their signatures on the back.[54] After visiting Kandy, Patell used also informal networks—the elderly mother of the defaulter—to try to recover the losses. "The old woman came to my hotel at about 10 pm at night with her relatives and begged forgiveness." He announced a reward of 100 rupees for any information. Finally, his mother brought the culprit to Patell, who was able to go though the books with him. He found that 988 rupees were missing and that the first installment payment on eight machines hired had been misappropriated.[55] The New York office encouraged Patell to be inflexible:

> We are naturally glad when we can avoid resorting to extreme legal measures, but in the case of dishonesty, if we are to protect our interests we believe that the only course we can pursue is to press the prosecution of the offender as a warning against any attempt at similar speculations.[56]

In 1888, however, Mitchell's report on the state of the company's affairs in India advocated a more centralized system with Bombay occupying a pivotal place:

> The subs have in fact in many cases more resembled district offices for the influence exercised over them by the office under which they were nominally working has been almost nil, and in the case of Rawalpindi in the North and Colombo in the South there is reason to believe that their results would have been at least as good if their reports had been sent direct to Bombay, instead of passing through Lahore and Madras respectively.[57]

The absence of any written communication between the Singer Colombo office and the Madras district office seems to suggest that there were virtually no relations between the two. Was there reluctance on the part of Madras staff to intervene in Lanka, a territory ruled separately as a crown colony, or did cultural and language divides between the Hindu Tamil-speaking south India and the Buddhist Sinhala-speaking southern Lanka preclude any close ties? For whatever reason, the flexible boundaries that prevailed in the business world did not apply, and Colombo continued to function in a quasi-autonomous fashion. In spite of having mapped Lanka/Ceylon and Rawalpindi in Punjab as parts of a subcontinental market empire, the company seems to have given these fringe territories separated by natural borders a deliberate space of freedom.

CIRCUITS OF COMMUNICATION

Advertisements fashioned desire in the colony for new objects such as the sewing machine. The large literate population of Lanka avidly read advertisements in the fledgling press, just as much as they consumed news accounts relating to countries where those products originated. One cannot imagine that new objects such as the gramophone and the sewing machine would have entered the homes of the people of Lanka if their worldview had not been shaped by the press of the day. The terrain for the acceptance of the foreign object in their home was prepared by a gradual awareness of the rest of the world. Literacy was an important factor that made possible changes in worldviews. The development of schools had led to a significant increase in the literate population. In 1911 there were five times as many literate females and twice as many literate males as there had been thirty years before. Approximately 40 percent of males and 10 percent of females enumerated in the census of 1911 were able to read and write. It may be supposed that many people who could not read were read to at the workplace or after the workday was over. These people too would have been touched by the new ideas contained in the press of the time. One of the features of the period 1870–1920 was the revolution in communications throughout the British Empire. From 1900 to 1910 the number of letters, newspapers, books, and pamphlets handled by the Colombo post office more than doubled.[58]

The outside world was there in the newspapers and the books that were read in English and in translation. Thanks to the new telegraph lines the reader was now in touch with the news from all parts of the world. The *Lanka Observer* contained the latest telegraphic news by the Indo-European line and the Singapore and Australian lines, as well as news from India. It was the first Indian journal on the Reuters list and had correspondents in different parts of the world.[59]

Among the literate classes of the Sinhalese there was certainly an awareness of the outside world that came from reading the foreign news section in the local newspapers. Other countries in the British Empire, especially South Africa, India, and Burma, figured prominently in local papers like *Lakmini Pahana*. In 1900, Sinhalese readers could follow all the details of the war in the Transvaal that pitted Britain against the Boers. They would also hear about the drought in India and railway construction in Russia. Another event that was well covered in those years was the Boxer Rebellion in China known as the Chinese War. There was also some interest in trivia: the number of women in the postal service or the amount of money earned by the Greek king.[60] In those nondemocratic days, kings, queens, and royal families in the empire and outside—mention was made of the passing away of royals such as the Italian king—made the news, rather than the happenings in the lives of common people.[61] The twenty-second birthday of the Prince of Wales in 1886 was reported in a Sinhalese-language newspaper as an event of some importance.[62]

Through their engagement with an international market, ordinary peoples in colonial Lanka, be they shopkeepers, farmers, or workers, lived different kinds of existence in different temporalities at the same time. They were sometimes "ignorant and hopelessly conservative," and as Leonard Woolf despaired, "They positively hated anything new."[63] But they were also consumers of goods from all parts of the world—not only European goods as E. B. Denham had asserted—and readers of Sinhala newspapers, which created an imaginary encompassing the Boer War, the Boxer Rebellion, the Japanese victory over Russia in 1905, and the exemplary life of Harry Holst, a Dutch Buddhist in Chicago.[64]

These newspaper items literally and figuratively mapped imperial aspirations. They also organized time and space in ways that welded the national and imperial interest, while effacing the crueler aspects of empire, colonialism, and trade.

No more than today, colonial Lankan readers were not passive. Every reading modifies its object. If one accepts with Michel de Certeau that the reader is a poacher, then one can imagine a range of associations and emphases from similar collections of material. If some readers read the foreign news through a mercantilist worldview in which trade and the accumulation of wealth appeared as the highest national good, others may have viewed the news as a way of belonging to empire or to the transnational Buddhist world, and for still others it might have made manifest the somber realities of great power politics. Indeed the idea of a community formed in homogenous time is utopian. The cognitive space of the outside world, as scholars such as Partha Chatterjee have spelled out, can be characterized only by heterogeneity. The consumer of newspaper advertisements and buyer of sewing machines should be placed in heterogeneous practices of reading.

SINGER, "RACE," AND THE CIVILIZING MISSION?

What did the average consumer in Lanka read about the Singer machine? What did Singer consider persuasive advertising? Scholarly analyses of Singer advertisements and business strategies have relied on a close reading of the visual message in trade cards. For example, Mona Domosh's work, which is based on five American international companies including Singer, has relied solely on one particular type of material, the trade card.

FIGURE 5.3: Oil painting of Hemaka Amarasuriya, former chairman of Singer Company, Sri Lanka. Reproduction of a show card used by Singer Sewing machine salesmen in Ceylon in the early part of the 20th century. From the personal collection of Hemaka Amarasuriya Chairman, Singer, Sri Lanka.

The trade card was the result of a new technology called chromolithography, which replaced the wood and copper engraving illustration used in the early nineteenth century. It could provide an almost limitless supply of the same prints from one set of prepared stones. Just like the sewing machine that it advertised, the trade cards, produced and distributed out of large northeastern lithography firms in New York, Boston, Cincinnati, and Philadelphia, were a product of the modern global predilection for replicable serials.[65] During the presidency of Frederick Gilbert Bourne (1889–1905), the Singer Company (figures 5.3 and 5.4) invested in a new advertising department that introduced materials to circulate the Singer brand . Singer calendars, handouts, posters, thimbles, and tape measures bearing the trademark red "S" were widely distributed in all its North American markets. National trade cards were introduced at this moment along with these objects. The cards, according to the Singer Company, did not carry the message on its own. Rather they served two purposes: they provided the salesmen with "talking points" with prospective customers, and they provided an educational service by furnishing "something of a high order that shall appeal to the best element in the Homes."[66] From these trade cards, Domosh infers that there were rep-

FIGURE 5.4: Singer trade card, Ceylon, 1892. Author's private collection.

resentational differences between "civilizing" through colonization and civilizing through the sale of commodities.[67] Relying entirely on a textual analysis of the Singer trading cards, she argues that America's companies "produced a temporally fluid view of culture and place, a narrative of progress, within which all peoples were potential consumers and all nations potentially modern."[68]

What is noteworthy is that consumers in Lanka had little if any access to trade cards, which were essentially aimed at American consumers and collectors in the United States. What Lankans did read were local advertisements produced by the company and published in local newspapers, a genre of literature that Domosh did not consult. The near obsessive urge to understand how the native was "represented" gives us only part of the story, however compelling it might be. I would like to argue that what the local consumer received and was more directly touched by was a different message, one that was mediated by local knowledge producers who were embedded in a known cultural and political background.

The content of advertisements insofar as they are formulated to interact with a background constituted of tacit knowledge, intersubjective meanings, and a form of life sheds light on the worldview of the potential buyer. Advertisements for Singer sewing machines can be found in the English press in Lanka and less frequently in the Sinhalese-language press, a fact that belies the assumption that because Singer invested so heavily worldwide in a selling organization it had no need to make investments in advertising, the "official art of capitalism."

But in fact, as the business archive shows in countries such as India and Lanka, the usual canvasser-collector system selling method had not worked. The Singer Company had to use various other methods and strategies to sell its products in India, Burma, and Lanka. Foremost among these was the production of the "Singer Guide to India Ceylon and Burmah." A total of 20,000 guides were printed in 1901: 19,000 paperbound and 1,000 clothbound. The guide contained the complete illustrated catalogue with prices and the history of the sewing machine. Patell planned to sell the book "through book sellers, or at the book stalls on railway stations or some good firms like Messrs. Thomas Cook and Sons."[69] Advertising was the main strategy to reach potential clients. In the English press, advertisements, unlike trade cards, did not draw on issues of race or civilization, although there was a clear appeal to women as users of the product.

> If you wish to reduce your tailoring expenses
> If you wish to save your time
> If you wish to see your family neatly dressed
> If you wish to see your ladies engaged in useful and intelligent work at home[70]

The appeal was clearly to the housewife as consumer and displayed a conventional perception of what constituted a useful occupation for the women of the country. However, the native retailer and buyer were positioned as male, as the term "your ladies" indicates. Indeed at that time, urban upper-middle-class women were becoming involved in Victorian leisure activities—such as piano playing—which were not considered useful by many nationalist critics. The sewing machine reinscribed putative Victorian templates of female respectability—such as confinement to the home and caring for and looking after husband and children—and reproductive labor in the private sphere of the lower middle classes.

More often, however, and in both Sinhala and English, it was the efficiency of the machine that was proclaimed. For instance, one advertisement claimed that the Singer products had won fifty-four first awards at the World's Fair, the largest number of awards obtained by any single manufacturer and more than double the number of all the other sewing machine companies.[71] An advertisement in the Sinhala paper *Lakmina* warned against imitations and stressed available after-purchase servicing as well as the easy payment scheme.[72] The language was one of business, not of culture. Advertisements were informative; they indicated the name and address of the shops where machines could be purchased, and sometimes information was given on the different purchasing options, either cash or on hire, and on after-purchase service: the availability of repairs and duplicate parts and reminders that accessories like needles, oils, and cottons were always in stock.[73] But the dryness of the language was clear. Singer's main competitor, the German company Pfaff, whose agent was P.

F. Goonesekere, a Sinhalese merchant, advertised in widely read Sinhala newspapers such as the *Sinhala Bauddhaya* and appealed quite openly to the cultural values and traits of its readers.[74] Perhaps Singer, advertised as "under European management," as it was, was less immersed in the cultural idiosyncrasies of the natives.[75] It was business as usual. Thus the Singer Corporation through its local advertisements was not trying to project a certain idea of progress or civilization to a "backward" people; it was treating them as universal consumers. Whereas in North America Singer advertisements sold the idea of civilizational difference, in Lanka it beckoned the buyer into the aura of universal bourgeois consumption. This invitation to consume as part of the world inadvertently gave them a type of liberty, which can be defined as the freedom of making a rational choice. It was made available to a much larger section of the population than those who by 1904 had the right to vote under colonial Ceylon's limited representation structures. You could consume even if you could not vote.[76]

BALANCING PAST AND PRESENT: MARKET MAKING AND NATIONALISM

The market imaginary shaped by the world of advertising was also cultural nationalism. For although the materials that encased the Singer machine beckoned the Lankan into a universal world of consumption, the entry into the world of consumption in this case had to be mediated only through culture. A market imaginary was also fashioned by Sinhalese nationalists who argued that machines could bring nature and the past into balance with the present.

Sinhala intellectuals' attempts to define Lanka's identity and its position in the world at the turn of the century led to the creation of competing tropes. The city, on the one hand, came to represent a colony integrated in the world economy and pursuing a Western-style path toward modernization. The rural village, on the other hand, came to be perceived as the locus of a pristine Sinhalese identity uncontaminated by Western cultural influences, such as alcohol, beef eating, and European forms of dress and attire. In the context of these divisions, in the early twentieth century a new generation of Sinhala literati devised an idea of modernity that departed from both these visions.

The words that are used today in Sinhala to describe the idea of modern, *nutana* and *navina*, both words from Sanskrit, came to common parlance after the 1930s. Martin Wickramasinghe, the most reputed Sri Lankan novelist of the twentieth century, author of a seminal work *Gamperaliya* (The Changing Village), used the term in his editorial columns in two Sinhalese daily newspapers, the *Dinamina* and the *Silumina*, in the 1920s and 1930s and also in his other critical works. But in the late nineteenth century these words were not common. Most Sinhalese writers used the term *abhinava* or *nava* to denote the period, which literally means "new." Some writers used the term *varthamana* (the present, the now) to describe their time. For example, John de Silva's play *Sinhala Parabhavaya Natakaya* (1902), a satire of the upper classes, uses the term *varthamana kalika*, literally the "present times," in the introduction.[77] If an essential part of being modern is thinking you are modern, modernity was understood as an aspiration to be with the times.[78] The term we use today (*nuthanathvaya*) to translate "modernity" was not used in the early twentieth century. Being with the times, I suggest, was practiced by ordinary people through acts of consumption—such as buying a sewing machine—that spawned changes in their everyday life.

In the modern Asian avowedly Buddhist world that vernacular elites sought to align themselves with and foreground for their readers and listeners in Lanka, the machine became central to the Buddhist nationalist imaginary that was fashioned through discrete tropes such as Japan, the rising Asian power, and Colonel Olcott's fashioning of modern practices for the Buddhist peoples. What these elites sought were exemplars from outside the circle of colonial powers, Japan and America.

THE IMAGINED AMERICA AND JAPAN AS AN ASIAN BEACON

Writing about the onset of modernity in Japan, Harootunian claimed that "no figure throughout the industrializing world was more empowering than 'Americanism' which referred to both hegemony of technological production . . . and greater commodification in everyday life."[79] In Lanka as well, the idea of change was expressed through the optic of Americanism and Japanism. Whether as hazy ideas, precise notions, or material objects, America and Japan were present at the turn of the century in the minds of the peoples of Lanka. Ideas varied from person to person depending largely on the fund of prior knowledge about these countries and the accessibility of American or Japanese goods produced and sold in the marketplace to colonized consumers. Objects that entered homes and fields from distant lands, large machines to harvest or sewing machines that hailed from America, and watches or paintings from Japan were constant reminders of the existence of a desired other, far away. Among the educated elites of Lanka, as in most of the colonized world, America was admired as the country that had won its independence from Britain, established a democratic society, and, since President Wilson's declaration, appeared to support self-determination—even if it was not for the "darker races."

The idea of America as the antithesis of Britain was not totally ill founded and was in a way reinforced by Britain's early hostile attitude toward Americans. After America's freedom of war against Britain, British officials in Lanka had become very suspicious of American intervention or influence of any sort in their colonies. In 1802, under new Crown colony legislation, it was specified that no American would be permitted to reside in the British territories in Lanka "unless he was in the service of the English East India Company or had obtained a license to reside."[80] But perhaps more than an elite view of America as a land of freedom, the perception of America by the majority of Sinhalese people living in the south of the island was related to the part played by certain individuals in the emergence of a renewed and reformed Buddhism from the late nineteenth century. In Lanka America was best known and admired as the land that had given birth to an exceptional being, Colonel Olcott, an American theosophist who spent years in Lanka, publicly converted to Buddhism, and became a hero of the Buddhist cause. Olcott embodied American good will, ingenuity, and harmony between East and West sought by the nationalists. It is through him that America entered into the Lankan imaginary.

Now as far as the Americans were concerned, most business undertakings between the United States and Lanka had emerged from relations with India, which explains the Singer Corporation's perception of Lanka as being part of the south Indian region. There was for instance a thriving export of ice from Boston in New England to the port cities of Colombo and Galle. The ice trade was initiated in 1806 by Frederic Tudor, a scion of a well-to-do Boston family.[81] In the 1890s the United States imported from Lanka items such as coconut, pearls and precious stones, plumbago, seeds and plants, whiskey, talc, tea, coffee, and copra and exported to the island a variety of items such as salted beef and pork, casks, earthenware, glass and glassware, tins, kerosene, medicine, and citronella. In 1926 U.S. exports to Lanka were larger than Australia's and only a little smaller than those of British India.[82] If the Singer sewing machine and the Thomas clock were the most famous American exports to Lanka, graphite and plumbago were the most significant imports.[83] Lanka graphite was used in the American Civil War and later for lead pencils. In 1903 the United States was the largest importer of plumbago, with Britain as second until 1903, when Germany took second place, and an American firm in Lanka was the principal agent for Lanka graphite.[84] In 1922, 80 percent of Lanka graphite was imported by America.[85]

Perhaps even more important than the exchanges of goods between the United States and Lanka was the idea that the peoples of Lanka had about America. There was in a sense an imagined America, a land of technically advanced people who were immensely supportive of Buddhism and ready to adopt the ways of the Dharma. This perception came from the publicity given in the local papers to the 1893 World Council of Religions in Chicago and the too often exaggerated accounts of the success Anagarika Dharmapala had encountered in convincing Americans of the importance of Buddhist teachings.[86] Readers of the Maha Bodhi and Sinhala Bauddhaya in Lanka were familiar with the personas of the theosophists Olcott and Madame Blavatsky. The letter they had written offering to help the Buddhists of Lanka had been translated into Sinhala and widely circulated. Apart from Olcott, other American nationals promoted Buddhism in Lanka. Mary Musaeus Higgins, the German widow of an American officer, was instrumental in founding a modern Buddhist school for girls in Colombo in 1895. The less well known Mary de Souza Canavarro converted to Buddhism in a ceremony in New York with Dharmapala officiating and spent three years in Lanka running an orphanage, a school for girls, and a Buddhist convent.[87] In short, through the repeated accounts of Americans converting to Buddhism, and the actual largesse of many American philanthropists toward Buddhist schools and orphanages, America acquired in the public eye an aura that no other non-Asian country had at that time.

Dharmapala, who had significant influence among the ordinary folk from his writing and preaching, epitomized the approach the educated Sinhalese took vis-à-vis Western countries. He visited England four times (1893, 1897, 1904, and 1925–26) and the United States five times (1893, 1896, 1897, 1902–4, 1913–14). Following the dichotomy between East and West inscribed by Hegel and others, he wrote, for instance,

> Europe is progressive. Her religion is kept in the background . . . used for one day in the week, and for six days her people are following the dictates of modern science. Sanitation, aesthetic arts, electricity, etc. . . . are what made the Europeans and American people great. Asia is full of opium eaters, ganja smokers, degenerating sensualists, superstitious, and religious fanatics—Gods and priests keep the people in ignorance.[88]

According to Dharmapala, nature's domination of Asian and especially the Sinhalese people's way of life and thinking were the main obstacles to progress. In his view, however, unlike in the political thought of a contemporary political theorist such as Maruyama Masao, nature and the past needed to be transcended only partially. It was not an either-or situation.

By the mid-nineteenth century Japan was a controller and exemplar of modernity. Japan's victory over Russia in 1905 made it the beacon for Asia. Dharmapala visited Japan in 1889 (a four-month tour), 1893, 1902, and 1913. As a Buddhist country, Japan was present materially and spiritually in Lanka. The headquarters of the Maha Bodi Society in Colombo had a free reading room, a library, and, interestingly, an industrial museum of Japanese goods. There was considerable exchange during this period between the two countries. Japanese students visited Lanka to study Pali at the Vidyodaya Pirivena, the prominent Buddhist seminary. Sinhalese students were sent to Japan to study Japanese technical industries, financed by Colombo's lay Buddhist associations. In 1911 the Rajagiriya Weaving School was created under U. B. Dolaphillai, a Sinhalese graduate of a textile course offered by the Higher Technological School of Tokyo.

While Sinhala Buddhist nativists of the more ardent sort were virulently opposed to all things Westernized that were responsible for the alleged decline of their customs,[89] Dharmapala supported Bhikkus (Buddhist monks) learning English, industrial education, and manual training schools. Science, education, and technology would be emulated and habits modernized, but at the same time cultural authenticity would be protected. The idea was for the Sinhalese to stand up for themselves as financially scrupulous, clean, courteous, pure, indigenized, industrious, and enterprising beings. His message was a fusion of modern technology and economic methods with traditional Buddhist values. The new age was not conceived as the antithesis of tradition but as a rediscovery of the true essence of nature and its reintegration in national life.[90] It was seen as a temporal trajectory to freedom that did not entail a complete rejection of the past, but a syncretic reinvention of past values in accordance to the times.

CONSUMERS AND USERS OF THE SEWING MACHINE

The Singer machine market was a composite part of the conspicuous use and consumption of foreign goods by a diverse group of people in Lanka. There are no statistics on these consumers except from the business papers of companies such as Singer. The growth of new modes of consumption, however, can be linked to wider developments. From 1870 the opening of the Suez Canal made Colombo an international port. As a consequence, the capital city was changing and growing into a more metropolitan space. Massive demographic changes followed. People migrated from the countryside to the city looking for employment and greater economic opportunities, and in so doing were confronted with new, worldly, "cultural" offerings. From 1901 to 1911 the rate of population increase in Colombo was more than double that of the islands as a whole.[91] With urbanization, "modernity" found a privileged terrain.

An important feature of the capital city was its cosmopolitanism. Between the years 1891 and 1921, its Sinhalese inhabitants made up less than half of the population. The rest of the peoples were distributed among Tamils, Europeans, Muslims, Burghers, and Malays.[92] L.J.B. Turner, a colonial administrator of the 1920s, has described the changes that took place in the cities quite predictably in the language of progress and development.

> Of the towns of Ceylon, the most important and progressive is the capital Colombo. It is the main business centre of the island, the seat of the government and its principal officials and the headquarters of the chief mercantile firms. It is consequently the most westernized of all the towns and possesses most of the refinements of modern civilisation, up to date hotels, electric lights, fans and tramways an excellent water supply, an up to date system of water borne drainage, an extensive emporia of goods of all kinds.[93]

Changes in the landscape of the city were not always easily accepted. We do not know the tensions that accompanied people accepting the sewing machine in their home, but the reaction to other everyday technologies may shed some light on people's encounters with modern machines. When trams were introduced in Colombo in January 1899, police officers had to travel in them to protect the new machines against angry people throwing stones. There were also reports of boys placing stones on the tracks in hopes of derailing the trams, and until slower vehicles such as bullock carts and rickshaws were used to their pace, there were a number of accidents in the city. The first motor vehicle that appeared on the roads belonged to the General Post Office, a van that was utilized for collecting mail. In March 1899 this single motor vehicle in the streets of Colombo collided with a tram car and was badly damaged. As a pastiche of the colonial state's urge to police and order public spaces, the Municipal Council took immediate measures to pass a bylaw for the control of motor cars, even though only one car traveled the streets of Colombo![94]

Colombo was the "the center for symbolic capital—the site where new commoditized trappings of prestige were displayed both by the British colonial elites and the indigenous elite who absorbed them."[95] It was essentially in the city that the economy engulfed everyday existence. The conspicuous and public consumption of things like gramophones, fancy clothing, automobiles, and expensive toiletries challenged white ownership of high fashion. An urban-centered bourgeoisie struggled to assume the characteristic "look" of white society and focused on a small number of highly symbolic, visible, public, and relatively affordable commodities.[96] Aspirations for higher status were defined by an assemblage of "modern" objects. Objects consumed became part of a culture in the making where they played an important part in mediating social and spatial relationships. Consumption generated an active mode of relations, not only with other goods but also with the domestic collectivity and empire to which the domestic collectively notionally "belonged."[97] But changes were also taking place among less privileged trade groups through their adoption of new everyday technologies and adaptability to new needs.

NEW TRADES IN THE CITY AND VILLAGE: TAILORS, SEAMSTRESSES

The introduction of the sewing machine led to a number of changes in the gender and ethnic valorization of the art of sewing. It feminized and gentrified tailoring with the birth of seamstresses in the city and also drew ethnic minority communities into the tailoring profession, rather than the Sinhalese who were less likely to possess the available cash to invest in machines. With the conquest of the sewing machine, the tailor too became modernized. This spelled the end of the *Hannalis*, the caste of Sinhalese tailors who worked mainly in the courts of the kings, described by Davy as being "very few" in the early nineteenth century.[98] It led to the growth of a profession more widely distributed across caste, ethnic, and gender lines.

Early census data on tailors allow us to chart the changes that took place in the late nineteenth and early twentieth centuries. The Census of Lanka of 1871 indicates that there were 3,256 tailors and seamstresses across the entire island. Tailoring was clearly an urban occupation, and it is notable that women engaged in this activity as well, unlike in India.[99] The 1891 census gives some very interesting information on the gender distribution of tailors and seamstresses. In the Negombo district there were 153 male tailors and 520 seamstresses. Of the women, 176 were under the age of fourteen years. The ethnic distribution too is fascinating. No European tailors were listed in 1891. The majority of tailors and seamstresses were Sinhalese (86 males and 338 females), then came the Moors or Muslims (8 males and 89 females), the Burghers and Eurasians (33 males and 53 females), and the Tamils (26 men and 40 females).[100] From these figures, it appears that the profession of sewing and mending clothes was undertaken by both sexes, with a predominance of women especially among the Sinhalese community. Did the introduction of the sewing machine in the 1880s and 1890s lead to more men taking up this occupation? What is clear is a gradual change in the ethnic distribution of tailors and seamstresses. One can surmise that buying a sewing machine demanded a certain capital that Muslims and Burghers who were engaged in nonagricultural professions were more likely to be able to harness in the early twentieth century.

Ferguson's Directories of the early twentieth century provide the historian with information on tailors. When we compare the tailoring establishments in 1903, 1914–15, and 1925 in Colombo, Galle, and Kandy, certain trends can be discerned. First, there is clearly ethnic specialization: tailors are distributed among Sinhalese, Muslims, and Burghers, with a clear domination of the latter two groups. Second, from 1915 onward larger establishments owned by British interests such as Cargill's Ltd, Smith Campbell and Co Ltd, Miller and Co Ltd, Grand Central Stores, and Modern Drapery Stores moved into the lucrative tailoring business. Some tailoring establishments such as Whiteaway Laidlaw & Co, Drapers and Outfitters, advertised themselves as users of sewing machines—an added proof of quality tailoring in 1918. The era of the street tailor was retreating while larger business groups were now offering services that were once the preserve of the individual tailor.[101]

Another development in the 1920s was a new occupational category of dressmakers—of thirty-one listed, fifteen were women holding names such as Madame Aimee or Miss Clara de Silva in response to the embourgeoisement of the middle classes in Lanka.[102] Mrs. Clarence, dressmaker in Kollupitiya, Colombo, provides us with some information on the type of clothing generally ordered: men's shirts, with and without collars, white coats, nightgowns (ladies), chemises, petticoats, flannel gowns, Oxford shirts, colored calico skirts, pajamas, and trousers.[103] Her clientele was clearly the British residents or the Westernized Lankanese of the capital. Some tailors were more specialized, as Alfred Martin and Co Ltd, Civil and Military Tailors, who sold broad cloth, Venetians, and cashmeres as well as Bedford cords for riding breeches and who advertised tweed suiting and trousers and materials "in all textures suitable for wearing in any part of Lanka and England."[104]

One of the tailors mentioned in the 1926 *Ferguson's Directory* has left traces of his life and business that I was able to retrieve by chance. The principal document is "the humble petition of Francis Pieterz of St Monica, Demátagoda, Colombo" dated March 19, 1926, to the Police Magistrate Colombo. He introduces himself as a master tailor who started a business in March 1923 at 100 Main Street Colombo under the "name and style of F. Pieterz, gent's tailor." In September 1923 he employed a person called Joseph Mariam Britto of Pettah, Colombo, as a "working partner," and the firm was thereafter registered as Britto, Pieterz and Co. The petitioner claims that he supplied "all the capital and furniture and sewing machines and the stock in trade necessary for the working of this business." At some point he resolved that he would have to dissolve the "so-called partnership as he could not agree with the said Britto on matters connected with the business, especially" as he found out "that the said Britto was attempting to make himself the sole owner of the establishment." Following the departure of Britto to India on February 22, 1926, Pieterz took the opportunity "upon the advice of a lawyer" to assert his claim as sole proprietor of the business. He locked the doors of the shop and placed a watchman to guard it. At midnight of the same day fifteen men belonging to the party of Britto arrived on the spot, threatened the watchmen, and "forcibly" placed two locks of their own on the doors. After he made a complaint to the Pettah police station, Pieterz had those locks broken and replaced the watchman. The next day the doors had once again been relocked! Pieterz then asked for police protection against Britto and his gang. The petition also includes an inventory of the clothes that were being made in the shop: among them were a tweed full suit, a satin dress, a blazer coat, and many other items. The tailor was a ubiquitous part of the everyday life of the city folk. E.F.C. Ludowyk's memoir provides insight into the personalized style of the tailor and his role in the community: the shoemaker, like the tailor, came to his home in Galle to measure and fit his clothes. The tailor who cut his clothes later blossomed into a maker of hoods for motorcars. The trousers he provided were, it seems, ill cut and frayed his thighs![105]

Because durables were expensive, consumers needed to derive maximum and multiple utilities from a product. This led to the development of numerous other skills, mostly self-taught, for the recycling and repair of goods such as sewing machines, bicycles, and radios. The social life of machines was long and varied with use, resale, reuse, and repair. Even in death a machine had a life in a symbolic sense. Old machines were sold for cannibalization, and toys were built of old machines. In Lanka new trades grew out of new needs. Repair shops for bicycles were listed for the first time in 1926 in the Ferguson trade list.[106] Other new trades had sprung up in the cities: watch repairers, music teachers, and motorcar hirers. The consumption of foreign goods crossed class divides. What differed was the nature of the relationship of the consumer with the commodity. While the anglicized bourgeoisie virtually lost themselves in the foreignness of the goods becoming part of their world, more episodic and less privileged consumers transformed their newly acquired possessions into local products.[107]

WOMEN AND THE MACHINE IN THE HOME: EMANCIPATION OR CHAINS?

The Haitian poet René Depestre, born in the 1930s, wrote a beautiful poem about the Singer sewing machine he remembered as a child. His experience is common to all homes in the developing world, Arab, Indian, Malay, Chinese, or Annamite. In the poem the Singer machine is likened to a god that helped them through hard days of hunger and thirst. It acquired a fantastic power to tame tigers and serpents and brave natural elements. The machine had a family, the members of which lived in other similar homes. And the noise the machine made was similar to a wild and ferocious animal that made all objects in the house tremble and move to its rhythms. Most importantly, it was operated by a Third World fairy (*une fée sous-développée*).[108]

The Singer sewing machine was the first machine to enter the space of the home. It was certainly not the first foreign object: early-twentieth-century house inventories give lists of a variety of products from other countries, from German silver trays and Chinese matting on the floor to Japanese pictures painted on glass.[109] It was often an eclectic ensemble of objects, but the entry of foreign objects conveyed familiarity with the outer world. The entry of the machine and its wide-scale acceptance by Sinhalese society must be understood with reference to the transforming of taste in clothing styles. The development of the textile industry in Britain through the expansion of markets for imported thread and machine-manufactured cloth within the empire and beyond the empire contributed to shaping domesticity and offering a terrain for the machine to flourish.

The importance of dress in the acceptance of the sewing machine by Sinhalese people must also be stressed. There was a wide-scale adoption of European fashion by low-country Sinhala women and men. After nationalist outcries against Westernized dress, many urbanized bourgeois women adopted the sari or osariya, but these were worn with a blouse that needed to be sewn. In villages most women continued to wear the cloth and blouse—with long sleeves—inherited from the Dutch presence in the maritime provinces.

The machine played a role quite different from that of other foreign goods. It was not only a consumable item, it was a production system. Unlike most luxury goods, it was a purely functional object that the women of the house used to produce clothes and other items for the household or to sell. In working-class homes, the machine occupied the center of the house, defined the house as it were. Reference was made with a certain amount of deference, for instance, to *mahana gederas* (sewing houses) in villages. As in nineteenth-century Britain or France, the wealth that the poorer classes accumulated was stored not as money in banks but as things in the house. The sewing machine was one such object. It was treated with respect and often covered with a cloth, a domestic practice common to many poor households.[110]

For women who worked in the paddy fields, as artisans or as shopkeepers, the machine was a great labor saver: clothes for the entire family could be mended and remade with ease, and sewing orders could be taken to supplement the family income. If novels reflect to a certain extent people's perception, the petite bourgeoisie did not consider sewing a very respectable profession. This is apparent, for instance, in Piyadasa Sirisena's *Maha Wiyawula* (The Great Confusion), published in 1938, in which the poor but virtuous female character is compelled to live in the slums of Slave Island and sew clothes.

However, there was a need for this new technology on the part of women. The times had clearly changed. In Martin Wickramasinghe's short story *Narak wu piti baduna*, a miserly Sinhala merchant sighs about the fact that young women want scissors and a sewing machine while in "our time" women cut their clothes with the *mannaya*, the large knife used in the kitchen to cut vegetables and fish.[111] But there was no real opposition to the sewing machine on the part of the Sinhala literati of the day. Indeed the sewing machine contributed to strengthening and disseminating the familiar tropes of nineteenth-century domesticity founded on the contrast between the public and the private, industry and home, male and female. The colonial construction of domesticity and its engagement with native ideas of the role of women in the family provided many of the "prior meanings" that shaped the consumption of sewing machines by middle-class women. In this new household, domestic tasks—sewing was one of them—were increasingly seen as the sole and inherent province of women.[112]

The work of Partha Chatterjee on the creation of a "new woman" in Bengal has shown that the nationalist project was not so much a dismissal of modernity as an attempt to "make modernity consistent with the nationalist project."[113] Chatterjee has furthermore argued that it is through the fixing of her "essential femininity" in terms of culturally visible "spiritual" qualities that were manifest through her dress, habits, social demeanor, and religious behavior that the colonized bourgeois Bengali woman could traverse the public sphere.[114] His categorization of bourgeois womanhood as "spiritual" as opposed to the "material" qualities embodied in man has been sharply critiqued by feminist scholars writing on Sri Lanka, although not for the reasons I would propose. Malathi de Alwis has analyzed the new woman in colonized Lanka using the concept of "respectability." Her work has shown how native girls were disciplined and molded in missionary schools through "daily routines and drills, rules of behavior, the regulation of attire" that sought to produce "respectable" ladies who were both pious and industrious, restrained and gentle.[115] Both Chatterjee and de Alwis, by focusing on bourgeois women in Bengal and Lanka, do not underscore working-class women's encounter with machines that embody the material world. The appropriation of the machine by the working class as well as women in Lanka basically disturbs Chatterjee's reading of an appropriation of the machine as the sign of the new women. In Lanka the working-class home became a site of production, thus challenging any interpretation through a clear material/spiritual template and questioning the virtue of "nationalism" alone as a driver of change.

The skill of sewing was part of the qualities that needed to be acquired by all women. For poorer women it would bring employment opportunities; for bourgeois women it was a marker of domesticity. For bourgeois women it embodied the Christian virtues of piety, industry, and docility. It was linked in many ways to the missionary project of transforming heathen bodies into respectable ones.[116] The Singer shop in Colombo conducted sewing classes especially for women at a sewing school in Wellawatte and promoted sewing in three girls' schools. "The girls," said the principal of one of the schools, "have spent their time very profitably."[117]

The Sinhala literati promoted a lifestyle of simplicity and modesty, thus constructing a new kind of "moral economy" for women. The perception of respectability was mobilized by Sinhala Buddhist nationalists to ridicule Sinhala women who were perceived to be too Christian and modern. Certain activities were coded as unrespectable: this included going to movies and parties, playing the piano, tennis, and cards, pursuing athletics, drinking alcohol, smoking, riding horses and bicycles, driving cars, and so on. Interestingly, the sewing machine does not appear in these lists, as it belonged to the world of labor rather than leisure. Indigenous and Christian notions of morality worked together to produce the idea of propriety around the sewing machine. Unlike the bicycle, about which there was an implicit discourse suggesting that it had a sexual effect of stimulating women, the image of automated femininity at a sewing machine did not appear threatening to the Sinhalese man or carry sexual associations. Thus in the early twentieth century a family's social identity was beginning to be constituted through the goods contained in the home rather than purely through caste and landed wealth. New class differentiations, gender, and national consciousness were, however, manifest not only through consumption patterns but also through the use of goods, as in the case of the sewing machine, which acquired different meanings in the urban bourgeois home and in the working-class or village home. A marker of authenticity, respectability, and thrift in the former, it became a marker of status, upward mobility, and worldliness in the latter.

The perception of the machine by Sinhala literati helps us understand the contours of modernity as it was lived: modernity was the new, the technologically advanced world that was emerging in spite of the lack of investment by the British colonial government in the field of technological education. This new vision attempted to debunk the idea that Western-style progress was the only path and constructed tropes of a superior Sinhala/Aryan social system that contained the seeds to realize a better version of modernity than had emerged in the West.[118] Unlike the elite anglicized man who had adopted each and every habit of the British, the Sinhala-speaking modern man wanted to keep some of his cultural traits: his clothes, his language, his religion. Unlike his Bengali counterpart, he opened his house to technology, emulating Japan and the United States. His modernity was prescient in many ways and characterized by an integration of certain elements of Western material culture into everyday practice. Clearly Sinhala nationalism felt the sewing machine was an ally in its casting of the ideal woman as home based, virtuous, modest, and diligent. But many working-class women used the machine to free themselves from these imposed bourgeois structures by earning money through their labor. Thus consumption was also a form of production as the consumer worked with objects to make or do something and in so doing evaded or ignored the cage of the colonial state.

CONCLUSION

This essay has attempted to make apparent the manner in which a market was created through the story of an eponymous object, the Singer sewing machine, while pointing toward the importance of inserting the colony within a wider history of circulation.

When Partha Chatterjee used the term "heterogeneous time" to describe the experience of native peoples at the turn of the twentieth century, he was clearly referring to Walter Benjamin's critique of a concept of history based upon linearity, succession, and homogeneity. Benjamin attempted to elaborate an alternative concept of history and temporality that he called the *Jetzzeit* or Now-Time.[119] Building on this idea, Chatterjee suggested that the same historical period can be lived very differently by diverse actors, anchored in modernity or remaining in a premodern time nevertheless shaped by modernity.[120] His insights are useful in understanding the quality of nonsynchronism that reflects the differentiated and fragmented nature of the category "colonized" in Lanka during the late nineteenth and early twentieth centuries. Including consumption, even though we have only a few traces to follow, in an exploration of the modern can help us rethink the demarcation of tradition and modernity, culture and material objects, culture and economy. To be modern in Lanka seemed to suggest having a split subjectivity that allowed people to consume technology, appreciate machines, and change while being Buddhist and Sinhalese in other ways, through food, religion, dress, and language. It was not the clear-cut division between material/male/modern/public spheres and spiritual/female/authentic/home spheres that Chatterjee described in Bengal. In Lanka the machine had invaded the home and the female domain. Multiple times were coeval in Lanka's modernity. But it was through the tangible and visible changes to their material world that ordinary peoples in Lanka fashioned their idea of the modern.

CHAPTER 6

Speed Metal, Slow Tropics, Cold War

ALCOA IN THE CARIBBEAN

Mimi Sheller

INTRODUCTION: LIGHT MODERNITY

Aluminum played a crucial part in creating our contemporary world both in the material sense of enabling all of the new technologies that we associate with mobile modernity, and in the ideological sense of underwriting a world vision (and creative visualization) that privileges speed, lightness, and mobility.[1] The material culture of aluminum deeply influenced the ideas, practices, and meanings attached to movement in the twentieth century.[2] Aluminum put the world in motion, and the performance of mobility generated symbolic economies revolving around the aesthetics of aerodynamic speed, accelerated mobility, and modernist technological futurism. The built environment that has grown up to support modern mobilities is based on the lightness of aluminum—the engines and bodies of cars, trains, airplanes and rockets; the high-power ACSR (aluminum cable steel reinforced) electricity lines that make up the power grid; the aluminum-clad skyscrapers that gleam in the centers of metropolitan power, starting with the spandrels and window frames of New York's Empire State Building (built at an astonishing speed of twenty-five weeks in 1930), and reaching a tragic apogee in the aluminum curtain walls of the World Trade Towers that so spectacularly collapsed on September 11, 2001, when struck by the aluminum airplanes turned into unexpected aerial weapons with devastating effect.

Many technologies of mobility and speed depend on the special material qualities of aluminum, but they also depend on the *visions of mobility* that industry, artists, and advertisers put into motion: a visual semiotics for the technological sublime epitomized by the latest, fastest vehicles and streamlined objects that keep the world moving. The aluminum industry's design and publicity departments played a crucial part in circulating both visual images of mobility and material objects for mobility, instigating a wider culture of mobility and instilling a positive valuation of lightness and speed. As Florence Hachez-Leroy argues, the market for aluminum was initially nonexistent, and promotion and publicity played a huge part in aesthetically enhancing the appeal of the curious new metal in the 1920s to 1930s, thus requiring the "invention of a market."[3] Yet the design of a material culture of fast, light, streamlined modernism in the United States also generated specific spatial geometries that were not merely representational, but were productive of the political subordination and economic appropriation of places conceived of as nonmodern and peoples conceived of as racialized primitives. Advertising was a productive force, more than simply an act of representation, or even of legitimation. Advertising and industrial design meshed together becoming generative forces of capital and of global political economies in motion.[4]

The very circuits of cultural production that were necessary for the fantasy of aluminum to take flight also excluded other spaces, imagined (and imaged) as "slow," regions where people outside modernity can only aspire to modernization, while supplying its raw materials. In particular, this chapter examines how the Caribbean—a key location of both U.S. bauxite mining and tourism in the twentieth century—was imagined, represented, and materially constructed as a place apart, one that lacks the shine of aluminum.[5] There was an implicit connection between the production of the material culture and visual image of modernity in the United States in the Age of Aluminum and the parallel consumption of the Caribbean's raw materials, labor, and visual images of its tropical backwardness. While the aluminum industry took off by promoting a gleaming aerodynamic modernism and supermobility in its primary consumer markets in the United States, it simultaneously benefited from and reproduced a very different image of an as yet unachieved modernization in the "colorful" Caribbean, often depicted as a colonial remnant where cultural change happened more slowly.

In W. W. Rostow's classic treatise on modernization, *The Stages of Economic Growth: A Non-Communist Manifesto*, first published in 1960, he describes economic development as a series of stages toward technological maturity that begin with a "takeoff" toward sustained growth.[6] The metaphor of modernization as "takeoff" drew on the power of aviation, which is based on the discovery of hardened aluminum, as described below, but also references aluminum's role in the emergence of new consumer markets based on speedier transport, light packaging, and durable goods. Each society must meet certain preconditions of social structure, political system, and techniques of production in order to take off toward modernity. Modernization was premised on motion—rural to urban, old world to new, sea power to air power—and only with mobility is takeoff achieved into a high-flying era of mass-consumption of durable consumer goods and general welfare. Rostow's influential thesis was that communist societies were unable to create the preconditions for such a takeoff, but that the noncommunist "developing" societies would eventually get there and join the leaders (Europe and the United States). The very mobility offered by the aluminum industry was both a condition for producing modernity and a metaphor for modernization. Yet Rostow ignored how the takeoff to modernity was premised less on the invisible hand of the market than on the heavy hand of the state and the monopolistic control of primary commodity markets by powerful multinational corporations. To a large extent it was state intervention and business protection that enabled the industrial takeoff of the United States, including the use of patents, cartels, international trade regimes, corporate monopolies, occasional state ownership, and the benefits of military power to ensure access to raw materials in the "developing" world.

During the Cold War, Caribbean states especially suffered from U.S. efforts to quash communism, which also encompassed the suppression of labor unions, social democracies, and independence movements. American dreams of aluminum-based air power and supermodernity occurred at the very time when Caribbean states were attempting to negotiate labor rights, political rights, and national sovereignty, and to negotiate resource sovereignty with multinational aluminum corporations backed by the U.S. government. Aluminum production tends toward an uncompetitive industrial structure. On a continuum of raw material extractive industries, the aluminum industry falls toward the extreme end of relative scarcity, concentration of resources, technology entry barriers (protected by patents and sunk costs), and inelastic demand, encouraging a highly monopolistic or oligopolistic structure. While these structural features do not determine outcomes, they certainly set tight conditions on the possibilities for resource-rich states to bargain with resource extractors.[7] But rather than focus on this kind of purely economic history, my aim here is to contextualize the actions of industrialists and states within a cultural history of mobility, with an emphasis on material culture, advertising, and imagined modernities.

The industry's celebration of its own contributions to technological advancement and to modernization actually masks the behind-the-scenes work that enabled it to lock in immobilities (of technologies, capital, and people), which were often grounded in global economic inequalities that *prevented* development elsewhere by simply extracting raw materials without any inward investment or societal capacity building. To tell the story of aluminum's role in modernization—and to write a transnational history of the Americas contra Rostow—one must recombine the North American world of mobility, speed, and flight, with the heavier, slower Caribbean world of bauxite mining, racialized labor relations, and resource extraction. It was, ironically, precisely this juxtaposition of cultural velocities that simultaneously created a market for international tourism, the other great pillar of contemporary Caribbean economies, which also arguably promotes mobility regimes that benefit foreign tourists while demobilizing Caribbean nationals.[8]

Just as anthropologist Sidney Mintz argued in *Sweetness and Power* (1986) that the modern Atlantic world was built upon sugar consumption in the age of slavery, we could say that aluminum offers a successor to that story: a late modernity built upon consumption of aluminum and all that it enabled, including speed and mobility itself. The emergence of aluminum reworks the asymmetric material relations and visual circulations between metropolitan centers of consumption and the peripheries of modernity where resource extraction and labor exploitation take place, while just as effectively erasing the modernity and humanity of the workers who produce modernity's aluminum dreams. This is therefore a transnational story that like other recent commodity histories embeds the United States "in larger circuits of people, ideas, and resources," rather than stopping at "the water's edge," as Robert Vitalis puts it in his study of American multinationals on the Saudi Arabian oil frontier.[9]

Another version of this transnational history would begin from within the Caribbean, looking outward from the point of view of Surinamers or Guyanese, Jamaicans or Trinidadians; however, given the limitations of space, this chapter only briefly touches upon the West Indian nationalists, internationalists, and labor leaders who struggled to gain control over their own resources, and cannot fully address the desire of Caribbean people to participate in modernization and to possess the new technologies and goods that modernization promised to bring. Aluminum, bauxite, cruise ships, airplanes, and multinational corporations are all social and technological assemblages that transit through a Caribbean that is not frictionless, but highly animated by resistance, by anticolonial and nationalist politics, by islands bristling with literal and symbolic ports for mooring as well as morasses for becoming bogged down. Only by understanding the complex constellations of mobility and immobility that structure transnational American relations can we begin to rethink the cultural motions of Caribbean modernity, and those constellations begin with the emergence of U.S. air power in the early twentieth century.

AIR POWER IN THE AGE OF ALUMINUM

> We have often said: just like the nineteenth century was the century of iron, heavy metals, and carbon, so the twentieth century should be the century of light metals, electricity, and petroleum.
>
> —Arnaldo Mussolini, 1932[10]

The rise of an aluminum material culture occurred through a combination of new technologies, new aesthetics, and new practices of mobility. Light metal is what set the twentieth century apart from past eras, and in many ways bequeaths to us today the distinctive look and feel of "late modern" material culture based on aeriality, speed, and lightness, including the mundanely mobile objects of modern household life.[11] Built on advances in chemistry and understandings of the forces of electrical current at the atomic level over the course of the nineteenth century, a technological revolution occurred in 1886 with the invention of the electrolytic process that could liberate molecules of pure aluminum from its tightly bonded oxide form. One of the great triumphs of modern chemistry, the dramatic race to invent and secure a patent for making aluminum electrochemically, was achieved simultaneously by a twenty-three-year-old American, Charles Martin Hall, a chemistry graduate of Oberlin College, and a twenty-three-year-old Frenchman, Paul Louis-Toussaint Héroult.[12] The combination of electricity and electrochemical production of metals has been called the second industrialization, replacing the iconic canals, water power, coal, iron, and steam of the first industrial revolution. We might think of this as a shift from heavy to light modernity. Within a few decades the "speed metal" played a crucial part in the development of lighter vehicles and airplanes, lightweight objects and packaging, and national public infrastructures for transportation and electricity. Aluminum consumption growth rates exceeded those of all major metals in the twentieth century.[13]

While still having to overcome difficulties in the production process due to the unique qualities of aluminum, including huge requirements for electricity and the need to develop various alloys and anodized surfaces, applied engineers gradually recognized aluminum as an unusual material that was light yet strong, flexible and easily workable, quick to assemble and disassemble, easy to maintain, and reusable and recyclable. The weight of aluminum is about one-third of an equivalent volume of steel (with a specific gravity of 2.70 versus steel's 7.85), so engineers can use it to achieve dramatic weight reductions.[14] This made it especially attractive in the aviation and transport industries; it could contribute to weight, labor, cost, and time savings. But beyond these practical properties, it also became a significant marker of modernity as a visual symbol of streamlined aerodynamic speed, clean gleaming lines, and the imaginative design of a futuristic world, as seen in early advertising campaigns by the Aluminum Corporation of America (Alcoa) (Figure 6.1).

This was not the first time a new material had transformed the world. Walter Benjamin has written eloquently about the cultural impact of cast iron, which contributed new materials and visions for the transformation of Paris in the 1820s to 1850s into a glittering city of arcades, grand boulevards, and exciting railways. In his *Arcades Project* he spins out a web of cultural connections from the cast iron structures of the gas-lit arcades to the new department stores and the cavernous railway stations, into an

Peer into the Future . . . Alcoa Aluminum is revealed a
shining symbol of strength . . . light weight . . . enduring beauty

Even as we look, the present passes. A decade slips by and the desire for the stimulating contacts of city life has increased our urban population twice as fast as the country at large.

Crowded metropolitan space demands expansion—but how? Probably through buildings rising tier upon tier, overhead traffic lanes, roof space for aeroplane landings, aerial sidewalks, terraced parks—buildings mounting ever upward.

Peer into the future and Alcoa Aluminum is revealed. Weighing only one-third as much as metals now commonly used, Alcoa Aluminum is destined to play a prominent part in future building development.

Alcoa Aluminum resists corrosion. It need not be painted. It will not streak adjoining surfaces. It can be cast, forged, drawn, extruded,

welded and riveted. On the exteriors of buildings its beauty is already seen—its light weight and strength utilized. For the interior trim and furnishings of office buildings, stores, and residences its decorative charm is employed. Providing the architect with a metal that lends itself readily to design and fine detail, that insures permanence, that saves handling of unnecessary dead-weight, and that cuts cost of erection, Alcoa Aluminum will find ever-increasing use.

In each of our offices we have competent representatives who are familiar with the decorative and structural uses of each of the special Alcoa Aluminum alloys. The services of these representatives are available to architects. ALUMINUM COMPANY of AMERICA, 2401 Oliver Building, PITTSBURGH, PENNSYLVANIA.

ALCOA ALUMINUM

Figure 6.1: Alcoa aluminum ad, "Peer Into the Future," *Fortune*, ca. 1931.
Author's private collection.

entire world of capitalist spectacle and new modern attitudes.[15] This was the beginning of a movement toward modernity, and a fascination with the speed of the galloping stagecoach and soon the steaming locomotive thundering on its iron rails, with the instantaneity of daily newspapers and the fascination with kinetoscopes and moving pictures.[16] Combined with steel, and later with plastics, aluminum would open whole new vistas in the quest for speed, and a new material culture of soaring urban heights and glass curtain walls. It would truly bring the apotheosis of speed and the new architectures of luminosity that nineteenth-century writers dreamed of, thrilled at, and feared. Aluminum eventually enabled the flights to the moon first envisioned by Jules Verne, the science fiction writer who recognized aluminum's potential in his 1865 novel *From the*

Earth to the Moon, when this mysterious light element was still a rare and expensive precious metal.

The discovery of aluminum smelting emerged from the 1850s to 1880s, the same period as the invention of cinema. Fast-motion photography was built upon photochemistry and electric triggers, which made instantaneous photographs possible, just as chemistry and electricity together make aluminum possible.[17] Rebecca Solnit has observed that it was the railroad baron Leland Stanford who supported the experiments of photographer Eadweard Muybridge while he carried out his famous motion studies of racehorses. The railroad and the instantaneous photograph became the progenitors of mechanized moving pictures on perforated celluloid strips, as well as the violent means by which Native Americans were pushed off their lands (as the railroad expanded European settlement across the continent), only to be preserved as shadow figures in the Wild West shows and the Hollywood westerns.[18] Aluminum technology plays a similar role in the invention of the Tropical South: its advancement was paradoxically the means of both intensifying U.S. occupation and use of Caribbean land, while also reproducing romanticized visual representations of exoticized storybook lands as the basis for new forms of appropriation via tourism—both thanks to Alcoa, which grew out of the Pittsburgh Reduction Company that was founded upon Hall's and Héroult's combined patented smelting process.

Alcoa's expansion into the Caribbean was closely linked to wartime military needs. Duralumin is an extremely strong heat-treated alloy of aluminum with small percentages of copper, magnesium, and manganese, developed by German metallurgical engineer Alfred Wilm in 1909. It became the basis for the building of Zeppelin airships during Word War I, instigating a race between Britain and the United States to try to develop their own airships.[19] In the end it was the war itself that enabled Alcoa to expand its bauxite mining operations into Suriname, and to gain access to the exact details of the Duralumin patent via the U.S. Alien Property Administrator and "industrial espionage from English and German companies," according to Margaret Graham. After the war U.S. technical missions from the Bureau of Construction and Repair gained access to the German state aluminum works at Staaken and entered plants in England and France. "The result," says Graham, "was Alcoa's 17S, an alloy almost identical in composition to Duralumin."[20] With this "effectively stolen technology" Alcoa drove ahead in its pursuit of new strong alloys, and eventually came up with a thin sheet metal known as Alclad—with a strong alloy core and surface layers of corrosion-resistant pure aluminum integrally bonded to the core—which was indispensable in the development of military and civil aircraft.

Early military uses were crucial to the development of new markets for the metal, including its use in aeronautical engines, aircraft, bombs, explosives, fuses, flares, hand grenades, heavy ammunition, identification tags, machinery, mess kits, motor cars, naval ships, rifle cartridges, trucks, tanks, utensils, and water bottles. Military and later civilian aviation became the most important industry in the widespread use of aluminum, beginning with frames, instruments, and propellers, and extending into many other parts of the aircraft. In May 1927 Charles Lindbergh made the first successful solo nonstop transatlantic flight in his single-seat, single-engine Ryan NYP, the *Spirit of St. Louis*, which had a Wright Whirlwind J-5C engine containing a substantial amount of Alcoa aluminum. His success contributed further to aluminum becoming firmly entrenched in the U.S. aviation industry. During the First World War about 90 percent of all aluminum produced was consumed by the military, whose requirements for 1917 and 1918 totaled 128,867 tons, while in the Second World War, some 304,000 airplanes were produced by the United States alone, using 1,537,590 tons of metal.[21] Flight also brought new technologies of visualization (such as aerial photography and eventually satellite visualization), which were often first exercised in the conquest of colonial empires, along with aerial bombardment.[22]

Aluminum is one of the most abundant minerals on earth, and the most commonly occurring metal, but it is economically recoverable only in limited forms and limited locations. One of those locations is the Caribbean. The successful expansion of the market for aluminum in the 1930s and 1940s, and even more so into the 1950s, required a steady supply of high-quality bauxite. Suriname, where Alcoa first opened mines in 1916, became a key supplier, while its Canadian sister company Alcan sourced its bauxite in British Guiana. But the threats posed by German U-boats to trans-Caribbean shipping during World War II prompted an interest in securing steady supplies closer to the U.S. mainland, including Jamaica, where bauxite ore was discovered only in the 1940s. The increased demand for aluminum during the Second World War, the emergence of the United States as the world's largest aluminum producer, and the dangers of wartime shipping all led to the emergence of Jamaica as the primary supplier of bauxite to the U.S. aluminum companies.[23] The system of Allied collaboration known as "Lend-Lease," along with the September 1940 destroyers-for-bases agreement, also enabled the United States to provide aluminum to British wartime industries (whose European sources of bauxite and power had been seized by Germany) in exchange for air bases in British colonies, including Jamaica, Trinidad, and British Guiana.[24]

These new military bases embodied the waning of Britain's power in the region and gave the United States a valuable military foothold just as

U.S. multinationals were engaging in bargaining over access to resources, preferential tariffs, and deals for low taxation.[25] Bauxite mining underpins a crucial connection between the production of the material culture and visual image of modernity in the United States and the parallel consumption of raw materials and visual images of tropical backwardness in the Caribbean. Surprisingly, the material circulation of mining and light metals is also intimately linked with the embodied practices of tourism that connect the Caribbean and the United States. The aluminum industry interlaced military mobilization and modern economic development in North America, on the basis of control over Caribbean resources, with leisure travel and its visual imagery. A West Indies lacking the luster of metallic modernity was represented as a backward region beckoning American enterprise and adventure. The following sections juxtapose promotions of aluminum as a "speed metal" in the U.S. market with a striking series of luxury magazine advertisements promoting the Caribbean tourist cruises of the Alcoa Steamship Company from 1948 to 1958. This is the period in which Alcoa became the biggest producer of aluminum in the world and depended to a large extent on bauxite mined in Jamaica and Suriname, the two largest exporters of bauxite in the world. In the midst of corporate transnational expansion, aluminum became a significant marker of *national* modernity, a symbol of streamlined aerodynamic speed, whose curvaceous gleaming lines linked it to the imaginative design of a future world, but one from which the Caribbean was excluded.

THE SPEED METAL

> When our boys come flying home from victory, they'll fly straight into a new Age of Aluminum . . . a plentiful supply of the miracle metal that *does so many things so much better*.
> —Reynolds Aluminum ad, 1943

Aluminum moves around the world, changing shape as it moves. It also shapes infrastructures and remakes the "spatiotemporal fix" that locks in certain kinds of mobilities and immobilities. Aluminum became crucial not simply as a new material out of which to make particular objects, but because it contributed to an entire shift in the style of "stuff": the styling of vehicles, buildings, infrastructure, and all around design of the objects of everyday life. Its cultural currency eventually spanned high culture and low culture, city and suburb, indoor intimate objects and outdoor monumental structures, high tech and homey, all linked to a national project of modernization through mobility. Its fluid forms together reshaped the places and networks that enabled its own movements and the movements of others. While it is somewhat fluid, it nevertheless also locks in certain systems, technologies, and infrastructures, which then become difficult to undo. Aluminum can ultimately be thought of not just as a metal, but as a complex network of actors and the connections between them; all such networks are heterogeneous, partial, and only to some degree stable, thus it is crucial to understand how they are stabilized, and how they may also be destabilized through "situated actions."[26]

The qualities of aluminum were an important aspect in the construction of what David Nye calls the "American technological sublime," which could be found in spectacular electrical displays, giant infrastructural projects, or impressive displays of machinic dynamism and speed.[27] Quixotic Italian Futurists like F. T. Marinetti embraced mechanized speed, metallic lightness, and ultimately air power, proclaiming in his *Futurist Manifesto* (1909), "we create a new god, speed, and a new evil, slowness. . . . If prayer means communicating with the divine, racing at high speeds is a prayer." Alcoa's advertising of the 1930s already makes clear the revolution that aluminum had sparked in transportation and mobility. A 1930 ad from the *Saturday Evening Post* declares that "Soon— nearly all Trucks and Buses will have Aluminum Bodies," and describes how "truck and bus bodies that are 1,000 to 6,600 lbs. lighter now speed over the highways." While detailing the savings made in various transport businesses, the ad also highlights other benefits: "Today you may ride in an aluminum train, for several railroads operate trains with cars built largely of Alcoa Aluminum Alloys. All-aluminum planes carrying passengers, merchandise, and mail, reduce coast-to-coast trips to 48 hours. Aluminum trolley cars operate on regular schedules in city and suburbs."

Alcoa's fiftieth anniversary message, printed in *Fortune* magazine in May 1936, gives a good feel for the novel sense of great lightness and increased mobility that aluminum afforded to the transportation sector:

> Aluminum was ready to answer the call for lightness in all moving things: the automobile engine piston, the bus body, the truck body, all moving parts, all mass-in-motion, and finally, the streamlined railroad trains. . . .
>
> For the day of lightness is here. The swan song of needless weight is being sung. Aluminum has become the *speed metal* of a new and faster age. Side by side with older metals it is giving you faster transportation, with greater safety and economy.

Lightness and speed enable efficiency and economy. Lightness combined with strength made aluminum the perfect substance for the new transportation system, and through this quality it came to be associated with speed and a "new and faster age" as the ad puts it. The rise of aluminum occurred through a combination of new technologies and research and development, but also through stylish marketing and the popularization of new modernist aesthetics whose counterpoint was the slower pace and naturalism of tropicalized island spaces and races.

In the United States, companies like Alcoa, Bohn, Reynolds, and Kaiser played an important part in promoting innovation in the use of aluminum and imagining the light modernity of the future. A new vision of an aluminum-based modernism was further shaped by maverick inventors, designers, and dreamers like William Bushnell Stout, a pioneering aircraft designer, whose 1936 aluminum-bodied Stout Scarab was a minivan-like vehicle with a folding table and swivel seats. Stout's motto was "Simplicate and add lightness."[28] Wally Byam, the travel enthusiast who created the Airstream trailer, led the international caravan club that made the trailers world famous by journeying in them across Africa, Latin America, and Asia.[29] Even more influential was R. Buckminster Fuller, the eccentric inventor who designed the all-aluminum Dymaxion house in the 1930s, the aluminum-bodied Dymaxion car in 1933, and eventually the geodesic dome that achieved world fame as the centerpiece of the U.S. Information Agency's American National Exhibition in Moscow in 1959. The streamline aesthetic was also advanced by designer Norman Bel Geddes, whose Motor Car Number 8 sported a teardrop-shaped body. Geddes was the creator of the 1934 "Century of Progress" exhibition at the Chicago World's Fair and the General Motors Pavilion "Futurama" exhibit at the 1939 New York World's Fair (whose theme was "The World of Tomorrow"), which brought viewers riding on moving chairs equipped with sound into a futuristic 1960s world of fantastical skyscrapers, seven-lane highways, and raised walkways, "proposing an infinite network of superhighways and vast suburbs."[30] These future visualizations and simulations shaped the actual material cultures of later decades, as they were realized in material form by the industrial designers, architects, and engineers of modernity.

Above all, the aerial superiority of aluminum over all previous metals made possible what cultural theorist Caren Kaplan calls "the cosmic view" of militarized air power. "Mobility is at the heart of modern warfare," writes Kaplan, and "modern war engages the theories and practices of mobility to a great extent."[31] It is lightweight aluminum-clad bombers that made such a change in military practice possible, later joined by guided missiles, satellites, and rockets. Weaponization of the air expanded through Major Alexander De Seversky's famous book *Victory Through Air Power* (1942), which was also made into a Walt Disney animated feature film of the same name. In the aftermath of Pearl Harbor, wide distribution of the book and the film are said to have influenced both Winston Churchill and Franklin Roosevelt and to have changed national military strategy forever. Wartime air power was supported by the government's massive investment in aluminum production, which was transferred over to civilian capacity after the war's end in part through the breakup of Alcoa and transfer of its assets over to Reynolds and Kaiser. U.S. government investment drove aluminum production to grow by more than 600 percent between 1939 and 1943, outpacing the increase in all other crucial metals.[32] During the war the United States produced 304,000 military airplanes in total, using 3.5 billion pounds of aluminum, claiming more than 85 percent of Alcoa's output.[33] So important was its role in winning the war, some have even called it "the metal of victory."[34] At war's end the government had $672 million invested in fifty wholly state-owned aluminum production and fabrication plants, which were disposed of after the war through the Surplus Property Act.[35]

The striking advertising imagery created in the early 1940s by the Detroit-based Bohn Aluminum and Brass Corporation—which specialized in design and fabrication of aluminum, magnesium, and brass—exemplifies how a wartime technology was transformed into a vision of futuristic modernism that was exploited to make the economic transition from military to civilian applications of aluminum. Bohn designers envisioned a world populated by new futuristic machines made of aluminum and glass—everything from cars, trains, buses, and planes to lawn mowers, tractors, helicopters, and combine harvesters. Ads from the 1940s make explicit the push to unleash the potential of aluminum research and design to transform the mechanized world and remake the built environment, showing how lightness, mobility, and speed were consciously injected into the U.S. landscape: "Today America's manufacturing processes are concentrated solidly on war materials for Victory. From this gigantic effort will spring many new developments of vast economic consequence to the entire universe. The City of the Future will be born—startling new architectural designs will be an every day occurrence!" A metallic glass-fronted streamlined railcar pulls away from a city of modern skyscrapers: "Here's a railway observation car of the future, (figure 6.2) from which you may one day watch the wonders of the world of tomorrow unfold, as you spin by in this super-streamliner. And many things you see will likely be made of Bohn aluminum or magnesium. For these metals possess that matchless combination for the industrial world—strength with lightness".

Even more fanciful departures from existing designs include oversized farm and industrial machinery described as Tomorrow's Power Shovel, a Future Cotton Picker, a Possible Tractor of Tomorrow, and a rocket-powered transoceanic "Dreamliner." The series is attributable to the well-known futurist graphic artist Arthur Radebaugh, who worked in Detroit where the company was also based. Radebaugh was known for his lumi-

FIGURE 6.2: Bohn ad, *Fortune*, ca. 1943. Author's private collection.

nous airbrush illustrations of futuristic vehicles and cities, especially for MoTor Magazine and the Detroit automobile industry, and he deeply influenced the streamline aesthetic and later science fiction illustrators. Radebaugh's "imagineering" depicted a futuristic world of human conveyor belts, glass-domed Futuramas, elevated expressways, amphibious cars, and moveable sidewalks. Harvey Molotch argues that art "radiates visions that span across actors and industrial segments. Art brings enrollment," as inventors, investors, power sources, patents, producers, promoters, and consumers are all enrolled into making and using something new in the world.[36] Radebaugh's art in the Bohn ads does precisely that. His fantastical images of soaring metropolises with high-speed levitating trains, personal helicopters, zeppelin mooring masts, and so on drew on the capacities of aluminum to make possible a new lightweight and malleable architecture of the future.

Thus from a wartime resource of national strategic importance, the aluminum industry mutated into a multifaceted industry that not only produced goods, but produced the capacity to consume more electricity, to transport more goods, and to keep the economy on the move more quickly. Design historian Dennis Doordan argues that the "Age of

Aluminum did not just happen; it was designed to happen, consciously designed by industrial designers working within the framework of the aluminum industry to provide technical information and to promote a climate conducive to creative engagement with aluminum."[37] Aluminum companies "worked to stimulate a climate of creative engagement with aluminum on the part of independent designers" with industry publications including "essays on themes such as creativity, innovation, and the phenomenon of change."[38] Doordan argues that the design departments at Alcoa, Reynolds, and Kaiser Aluminum were in the business of placing knowledge and facilities at the disposal of other designers and fabricators, through a creative collaboration. They were not simply designing objects, but also *information*.

For example, in 1952 Alcoa hired the advertising agency Ketchum, Macleod, and Grove, who produced a marketing campaign that they called FORECAST. They announced that the campaign's "principal objective is not to increase the amount of aluminum used today for specific applications, but to inspire and stimulate the mind of men." They devised a multifaceted marketing campaign with weekly magazine advertisements, the publication of a periodical called *Design Forecast*, and commissions for twenty-two well-known designers to create products using Alcoa aluminum. The practice of forecasting and scenario building employed in this advertising campaign built on the practices of the RAND Corporation, a major player in research and development for the military-industrial complex.[39] They were spreading the news of aluminum's possibilities, stoking dreams of its future potential, and assisting designers and fabricators in turning it into new products.

If corporations were in the business of designing information as much as objects, then their advertising tells us a great deal about what information they wished to circulate and what they wished to keep quiet. Rather than reading the thrilling images of futuristic modern mobility from within a hermetically sealed U.S. national context, it is necessary to follow the silvery thread of aluminum back on its journey out of the ground of Jamaica, Guyana, and Suriname, and into the hopes, dreams, and images it set in motion around the Caribbean, where the majority of the bauxite for the North American smelters originated and where the aluminum companies promoted tourist cruises. What information about the Caribbean was designed into industry publicity? And what alternative meanings of mobility did Caribbean actors attempt to bring to bear on the shaping of mobile modernity? The following section turns to Alcoa Steamship Company advertising campaigns that are situated in this context of the promotion of speed and lightness in American consumer culture; but behind it lies the tough bargaining between multinational corporations with strong financial (and ultimately military) backing from the U.S. government and weak British Caribbean states under pressure from economic stress, colonial social mobilizations, and independence movements.

CRUISING THE CARIBBEAN

> Behind Caribbean romance lurks an export market.
> SURINAME—Thousands of East Indians contribute an Arabian Nights touch to this equatorial land. They also are part of a thriving Caribbean market that needs razors, sewing machines, autos, machinery and other products manufactured here in the U.S.A.
> —ALCOA Steamship Company Ad, *Fortune*, ca. 1948

The Caribbean has long served as a site of tropical semimodernity, set apart from the modern West through forms of colonial exploitation and imperialist exotification of its "colorful" people, "vivid" nature, and "dream-like" landscapes.[40] The cool space-age futurism of aluminum modernity had to be constructed via its contrast with a backward, slow world that happened to lie next door: the American fascination with the steamy jungles of the tropics, the hybrid races of the Caribbean, and the image of "the islands" as primitive, backward neighbors. This grammar of difference helped to construct what anthropologist Michel-Rolph Trouillot calls "the Savage Slot,"[41] yet it depended on making *invisible* the power of U.S. corporations to control and monopolize the mining and processing industries that make modern technology possible, and the military power that it enabled and required. It also hid the emerging modernities of the Caribbean itself, especially its political modernity, which was subsumed beneath the romantic naturalism of tourism and at best acknowledged as a potential market for American-made goods as in the epigraph opening this section. This was a representation challenged by actors within the region, including labor leaders, consumers, and political economists.

The Alcoa Steamship Company played a special role in the Caribbean, not only shipping bauxite and refined alumina to the United States, but also carrying cruise ship passengers, commissioning artists to depict Caribbean scenery, and even recording Caribbean music and sponsoring the Caribbean Arts Prize in the 1950s. The company operated three "modern, air-conditioned ships," each carrying sixty-five passengers, which departed every Saturday from New Orleans on a sixteen-day cruise, making stops in Jamaica, Trinidad, Venezuela, Curaçao, and the Dominican Republic.[42] These ships became not simply a conduit connecting different modernities, but were precisely one of the means by which divergent North Atlantic and Caribbean modernities were produced. David Lambert and Alan Lester argue that the "travel of ideas that allowed for the mutual constitution of colonial and metropolitan culture was intimately bound up with the movement of capital, people and texts between these sites, all dependent in the last resort on the passage of ships."[43] The mobility and increasing speed of ships as steam replaced sail in the nineteenth century reconfigured the space of the Atlantic world as "a particular zone of exchange, interchange, circulation and transmission," suggests David Armitage.[44] And as Anyaa Anim-Addo elaborates in her work on the Royal Mail Steam Packet Company in the Caribbean, "The RMSPC's ships offered an alternative modernity to the railway but also, as mobile places, provided a shifting experiential modernity at various points along the ship's routes."[45] It was precisely in riding onboard ships such as Alcoa's cruise liners, and in consuming their touristic visual grammars, that divergent mobile modernities were constituted, lived, and materialized.

The ship en route was a space of travel and mobility between allegedly separate worlds—one fast and modern, the other traditional and romantically slow—yet ironically those worlds were connected by the material potentialities of aluminum that arose directly out of the ground of the Caribbean. Alcoa's three new ships, built by the Oregon Shipbuilding Co. in 1946, were test beds for Alcoa's new magnesium-silicide alloy 6061, thus becoming a doubly material and symbolic realization of mobility on display:

> These liners, the S.S. *Alcoa Cavalier*, *Clipper*, and *Corsair* used alloy 6061 for deckhouses, bridges, smokestack enclosures, lifeboats, davits, accommodation ladders, hatch covers, awnings, weather dodgers and storm railings, all connected with 6053 rivets. Other alloys, both wrought and cast, were used for doors, windows, furniture, electrical fittings, décor and for miscellaneous applications in the machinery space.[46]

The ships themselves, with their extensive aluminum fixtures and fittings, advanced technology, and modernist design, were at once floating promotions for potential investors, displays of the material culture of aluminum's light modernity, and a means of consuming mobility as touristic practice. Passengers on the three ships were given pamphlets including "Let's Talk about Cruise Clothes," "Taking Pictures in the Caribbean," and "Your Ship: Alcoa Clipper," which described the extensive use of the light metal in the ship, from the superstructure to the staterooms: "Almost anywhere you happen to be on Your Ship you will find some use of aluminum."[47] Thus the ships combined industrial mobilization of commodities, multisensory touristic mobilization of a mobile gaze, and subtle symbolic mobilization of the signs and icons of mobile modernity.

The same economic, political, and spatial arrangements that locked in huge market advantages for transnational mining corporations simultaneously opened up Jamaica and other Caribbean destinations for tourism mobilities. Tourism then instigated the circulation of new visual representations and material means of movement through the Caribbean. While Alcoa promoted novel products, modern skyscrapers, and metallurgical research and development in the United States, the company promoted the Caribbean as a source of bauxite, positioned it as a potential market for "superior" American products, and envisioned it as a timeless destination for tourists traveling on its modern ships to safely step back into the colorful history, exotic flora, and quaint folkways of diverse Caribbean destinations. While these modes of both imaging and moving are not surprising (and continue in other ways today), what is striking is the degree to which the Caribbean produced here diverges from the futuristic images of supermodernity that were simultaneously being promulgated in the U.S. consumer market for aluminum products. Appearing in the luxury publication *Holiday* magazine, the advertising images seamlessly meld together tourism, business travel, bauxite shipment, and cultural consumption, yet carefully detach these Caribbean mobilities from the light, sleek modernity being envisioned and promoted at home in the United States, in magazines such as *Fortune*, and onboard the ships themselves.

The ads also strikingly ignore or erase the presence of modern technology in the Caribbean, including U.S. military bases and the emerging infrastructure of modern ports, urban electrification, and eventually airports. As Krista Thompson has shown in her study *An Eye for the Tropics*, photographic images of the Caribbean produced for tourist markets in the early twentieth century tropicalized nature by emphasizing lush and unusual plants, exoticized local people by showing them in rustic and primitive settings, and erased signs of modernity such as electric power lines or newer urban areas. It is American tourists and modern North American ships that seem to move, while the Caribbean islands and people are pinned down like butterflies to be collected, catalogued, and made known. Here I focus on three moments of the erasure of Caribbean modernity, showing how the motions of the Alcoa ships produce the spatial disjunctures of divergent modernities through their representational practices and cultures in motion.

Tourists, Primitives, and Modern Workers, 1948–52

The first series of ads, which ran from 1948 to 1949, was created and signed by the graphic artist Boris Artzybasheff. A Russian émigré to the United States, Artzybasheff was most well known for his cover portraits for *Time* magazine, his colorful series of Shell Oil ads, and his surreal

FIGURE 6.3: Boris Artzybasheff, Alcoa Steamship Co. ad, *Holiday*, February 1948. (Author's private collection.)

drawings of anthropomorphic machines. For the Alcoa Steamship Company he produced an unusual series of portraits of Caribbean people. A Carib mother and child, for example, are depicted as timeless primitives, holding up fruit and peering out from dark eyes and exotically painted faces (Figure 6.3), in a region described as "rich in the turbulent history of the Carib Indians, Spanish Conquistadors and bloody buccaneers." Afro-Creole women appear in typical poses such as "[d]ark-eyed senoritas, descended of conquistadores of old" or a stereotypical "Creole belle," wearing a madras head tie and gold jewelry. Each image represents an example of racial blending or distinctiveness, portraying a male or female racialized persona in typical costume, including Carib Indians, various types of Afro-Caribbean "blends," East Indian Hindu and Muslim, and even various types of Creole "whites" of Spanish, Dutch, or Anglo-Caribbean origin. Although the images appear at first to promote cultural encounter and ethnological curiosity within touristic contact zones, such typifying images circulate within a long lineage of tropicalizing representations of Caribbean islands and people.[48]

Setting apart the modern U.S. consumer/tourist from the ersatz primitive populations of the tropics, the text of this series emphasizes the swashbuckling colonial history of the Caribbean, which marked the region with diversity: "[I]f you look carefully you'll see how the distinctive architecture, languages and races of this area have been blended by centuries into interesting new patterns." This kind of typifying imagery relates to earlier colonial racial typologies and Spanish *castas* paintings, which attempted to portray all of the racial "types" found through mixtures of different kinds. Each image includes a distinctive flower, colorful foliage, and often a typical bird or butterfly, suggesting a kind of natural history that conjoins island people and wildlife, naturalizing races through attachment to profusely tropical places. This is a mode of visualization that solidifies Caribbean difference as a material, natural, textural distinction that sets "the blue Caribbean" apart from the mainland world inhabited by allegedly modern subjects. Above all, this "tourist gaze" produces a visual grammar of difference.[49]

While suggestive of the complex global mobilities of people and cultures, these historically anchored images fix the Caribbean in time as a series of romantic remnants that exist for the edification and consumption of the modern, mobile traveler. Hindus and Muslims appear in unusual hats in front of their exotic temples, suggesting the mobility of cultures into the colonial Caribbean (see Figure 6.4). A Dominican sugarcane cutter appears as noble worker in one image, with the tools of his trade in hand. Yet the images simultaneously paper over the ethnic, class, and color hierarchies that fanned political unrest throughout the postwar Caribbean; they offer not only a visually flattened perspective, but also a historically and socially flattened one. Left-wing Guyanese labor leader Cheddi Jagan noted in 1945 that wages for workers were "only one-third to one-quarter of comparative wages in bauxite and smelting operations in the United States and Canada," and he dreamed of an independent nation with its own aluminum industry.[50] Ironically, in this very period Alcan's DEMBA mine in British Guiana (part of Alcoa when built) was using racial and ethnic divisions of labor to reinforce the occupational and political divisions between Guyanese of African and East Indian descent, and class hierarchies between black and white.[51] The DEMBA workers engaged in a sixty-four-day strike in 1947, but struggled to form an effective union in the face of company paternalism and tight discipline.

The Caribbean claims one of the most mobile working classes in the world, but it was foreign corporations that governed the patterns of labor migration—whether to work on the sugar plantations of other islands or the banana plantations of Central America or in the building of a transisthmus railway and the Panama Canal. This mobile working class was at times highly politicized, cosmopolitan, and critical of the world eco-

FIGURE 6.4: Boris Artzybasheff, Alcoa Steamship Co. ad, *Holiday*, August 1948. (Author's private collection.)

nomic system. Ideologies such as Garveyism, pan-Africanism, socialism, and communism circulated among them, and between the Caribbean and its U.S. outposts in places like Harlem.[52] The most organized workers in the region were the stevedores and other port workers who, along with sugar plantation workers, led major strikes including the "labor rebellion" of 1937–38.[53] Both Guyanese and Jamaicans in the labor movement struggled to shift the terms of their enrolment in the world economy and transform the ways in which their natural resources (and labor) were being mobilized for the benefit of others.[54] Only a Venezuelan worker placed in front of what is described as a "forest of picturesque oil wells," holding a sturdy wrench among some delicate pink flowers, hints at a modern industrial economy taking shape in the Caribbean, but one that is described as "*hungry* for American-made products—and all that their superiority represents." The feminization of the worker and naturalization of the industrial landscape suggest an awkward attempt to fit indus-

FIGURE 6.5: Harriet and Bernard Pertchik, Alcoa Steamship Co. ad, *Holiday*, April 1951. (Author's private collection.)

trialization into older tropes of Caribbean island paradise. A postcard titled "Alcoa bauxite," for example, captions its image from Trinidad, "The delicate pink blush on the Tembladora Transfer Station is from raw bauxite ore from which Aluminum is made."

The protean Caribbean appears here as a series of renaturalized yet traditional places, outside of modernity yet accessible to the mobile tourist, a "paradise for travelers, export opportunity for businessmen." Special editions of some of the images, suitable for framing, could also be ordered by mail, creating a Caribbean souvenir to take home. A second related series of ads, published in 1951–52, depicts botanical paintings of tropical flowering trees (figure 6.5) by the respected botanical illustrators Harriet and Bernard Pertchik. These images tap into a long tradition of botanical collection and illustration of tropical plants by colonial naturalists, who collected material in the Caribbean and incorporated it into systems of plant classification and medical knowledge.[55] Natural beauty is valued here in a visual economy of touristic consumption, even though the modern light mobility of the American tourist is predicated on clearing and strip mining Caribbean forests for the precious red bauxite ore below them. Tourists themselves are depicted in the corner of each ad, frolicking on the modern space of the ship in motion. The same corporation that transports bauxite out of the Caribbean on its freighters not only carries tourists in, but also through its advertising incites the consumption of new modern products in the U.S. consumer market while the cruise experience itself produces the mobile modern subjects who will consume such products. This constellation of modern mobile subjectivity is explicitly contrasted against the slow, backward, romantic tropics; yet the market relations and power relations that produce these conjoined uneven modernities (including U.S. military bases) are like photographic negative and positive, each a condition for the other.

Bauxite, Folk Dance, and Vernacular Styles in Motion, 1954–59

As Jamaica adopted universal enfranchisement in the 1940s and moved toward self-government in the 1950s, there was "an increasing sense of nationalism and concern for the protection of national resources," especially among the labor parties of the left.[56] Out of the labor movement arose a generation of nationalist leaders who pushed the British West Indies toward independence, and toward democratic socialism. In October 1953 the British government, with U.S. support, forcibly suspended the constitution of Guyana and deposed Jagan's labor-left government, elected by a majority under universal adult suffrage, when he threatened to take back mineral resources and move the colony toward independence.[57] Coming just as the government was in the process of passing a Labor Relations Bill that would have protected unions and labor rights, the coup nipped in the bud Jagan's longer-term plans to create forward linkages through locally based aluminum smelters and fabrication plants using the country's significant potential for hydropower. Bolland argues that the "consequences of the suspension of Guyana's constitution and subsequent British actions were devastating for the development of politics in the colony," leading to a deep racial split within the People's Progressive Party, and long-lasting racial polarization between Afro-Guyanese and Indo-Guyanese.[58] These events make evident the external control over labor movements in the region, and the degree to which they would not be allowed to assert resource sovereignty.

It is in this historical context that we can read the third Alcoa Steamship series, which ran from 1954 to 1955, a striking set of folkloric portrayals of musical performances, parades, or dances, both religious and

FIGURE 6.6: James R. Bingham, Alcoa Steamship Co. ad, *Holiday*, August 1955. (Author's private collection.)

secular, by the graphic illustrator James R. Bingham. Readers are encouraged to write in to purchase 45 rpm recordings of the music that accompanies some of the dances, including the sensationalized Banda dance of Haiti, associated with foreign misrepresentations of "Voodoo" (Figure 6.6), the Joropo of Venezuela, the Merengue of the Dominican Republic, and the Beguine of the French West Indies.

Other ads represent the Pajaro Guarandol "folk dance of the Venezuelan Indians," the steel pan and "stick dance" of Trinidad, the "Simadon" harvest festival of Curacao, the folk dance of the Jibaros of Puerto Rico, and the John Canoe dancers of Jamaica (figure 6.7) whose costumes date back to the eighteenth century and possibly to West Africa. This series connects touristic consumption of musical performances from across the

See the exciting Caribbean
the relaxing Alcoa cruise way

You'll find the Caribbean a colorful, merry-go-round of memories—from these John Canoe dancers in Jamaica to the Calypso singers of Trinidad. You'll find, also, that an Alcoa cruise is the really enjoyable way of seeing the Caribbean's wonderful sights. For 16 days your de luxe, air-conditioned Alcoa ship roams this romantic region calling at six exciting ports in Jamaica, Venezuela, Trinidad and Curacao or the Dominican Republic. Between visits you relax in luxurious comfort, enjoying the ship's outdoor pool, its superb cuisine, its many pleasant and unregimented activities. And all the way you travel in a congenial, yacht-like atmosphere, for Alcoa cruise ships carry an average of only 65 passengers. There's a sailing every Saturday from New Orleans. Or you may prefer one of Alcoa's more modest and leisurely 12-passenger freighter cruises from New York, Montreal or New Orleans. For details see your travel agent; or write for literature "H".

es-minded executives find a thriving market in the ... lly, nearby Caribbean. It is ... le Sam's second best export ...mer, and still growing. To ...ate it for your products, write ... our company letterhead for the ... edition of our "Export Market ...ortunities" book.

ALCOA *serves the Caribbean*
WITH PASSENGER AND FREIGHT SERVICE TO 59 PORTS

:OA STEAMSHIP COMPANY, INC., 17 BATTERY PLACE, NEW YORK 4, N. Y. or ONE CANAL STREET, NEW ORLEANS 12, LA.
HOLIDAY/MAY

FIGURE 6.7: James R. Bingham, Alcoa Steamship Co. ad, *Holiday*, May 1955. (Author's private collection.)

Caribbean with an almost ethnographic project of investigation of traditional cultures and people who persist outside of modernity, a remnant of the past available for modern cruise tourists to visit, but also, as the ads note, "Uncle Sam's biggest export customer, and still growing. To appraise it for your products, write on your company letterhead for the 1955 edition of our 'Export Market Opportunities' book."

Folkloric music was played by costumed performers for the benefit of tourists. Caribbean national elites had an interest in furthering these projects of self-exotification for the tourist market, just as they had an interest in encouraging foreign investment, whether in agriculture or mining. They tried to keep their towns looking quaint and not too modern in order to encourage tourism. When modern buildings such as a new Hilton Hotel were built in the 1950s or 1960s, they became enclaves of modernity for visiting tourists from which the local populace was excluded except as service workers. Yet seldom has the direct connection between the two industries been noted: the mining of bauxite made possible the mobilities of tourism, while the touristic visualization of the Caribbean supported the materialities of dependent development that kept the Caribbean "backward" and hence picturesque.[59] So in a sense the *absence* of aluminum architecture, vehicles, power lines, and designer objects came to define Caribbean material culture, which in contrast came to be associated with the rustic, quaint, vernacular, handmade island tradition, using natural materials and folk processes.

However, the people of the Caribbean were at the same time contesting such images, insisting on their own modernity. Independence movements in the postwar period began to call for self-rule, while migrants to London, New York, and other metropoles, along with the radio, carried styles of modern urban cultural consumption back to the Caribbean; and Caribbean styles of modernity were themselves carried into the metropole, "colonization in reverse" as Jamaican performance poet Louise Bennett called it. The potential circuits of travel of the musical recordings and dance styles hint at the powerful cultural currents emanating out of Caribbean popular cultures and circulating into U.S. urban culture via Caribbean diasporas. Despite the appearance of frozen tradition in Bingham's portrayal of these folk dances, the vivid forms of dance and music also attest to a kind of cultural vitality that could quite literally *move* people in unexpected (and possibly dangerous) ways.[60] Writers, musicians, intellectuals, and artists grappled with the meanings of Caribbean modernity, and produced their own visualizations of the Caribbean past, present, and future.

In 1956 changes in the internal and external political situation led into a new conjuncture for bargaining between the Jamaican state and the transnational corporations. A major renegotiation of the terms of bauxite royalty payments and taxes was undertaken by People's National Party Chief Minister Norman Washington Manley (one of the founding fathers of Jamaican independence) in 1956–57, based on the principle that "[c]ountries in the early stages of economic development ought to derive the largest possible benefits from their natural resources. They ought not to be regarded merely as sources of cheap raw materials for metropolitan enterprises."[61] In October 1957 the Soviet Union launched the first Sputnik satellite, a small aluminum orb that triggered the Space Race with the United States. This, along with the Korean War, made aluminum an even more crucial "strategic material." Jamaica moved from supplying about one-quarter of all U.S. bauxite imports in 1953 to over one-half in 1959, with 40 percent of total shipments of crude bauxite and alumina between 1956 and 1959 going into the U.S. government stockpile.[62] Following tough negotiations, the 1957 agreement reset the royalty paid on ore, which led to a substantial increase in revenues to the Jamaican government. Bauxite royalties contributed more than 45 percent of the country's export earnings by 1959.[63]

Caribbean Modernity in Motion, 1962–75

Ironically, in 1960 the Alcoa Steamship Company was forced to decommission its three beautiful passenger ships, due to high costs, union struggles, and a cost-saving shift to Liberian flags of convenience.[64] A confidential internal memo at the time noted that the company would shift to chartered foreign flag freighters: "Taking advantage of the lower foreign flag operating costs, we will be able to save an estimated $2,077,000 per year immediately and $2,296,000 per year after the passenger ships are sold. . . . This will eliminate jobs for American seamen and there is never a good time to do this particularly when foreign seamen will benefit."[65] The memo goes on to note, "The passenger vessels have undoubtedly been our best form of public relations. However, the Steamship Company, by itself, can no longer justify this costly form of public relations." They would also have to cancel the cruises booked by twenty-six couples, many of whom were "customers of the Aluminum Company of America" and "prominent people." The most serious problem, however, was that the workers on the ships were primarily Trinidadian and "some smattering of Surinamers," who belonged to the Seamen and Waterfront Workers' Union in Trinidad, which at the time was trying to organize with the Seamen's International Union to strike against the cost-saving move. Alcoa executives noted that with the help of the powerful United Fruit Company they would be able to challenge the legality of such strikes, and force the workers out of their jobs before new labor contract negotiations took place.[66]

Jamaica achieved independence in 1962 when it "was the world's largest producer of bauxite" according to historical sociologists Evelyn Huber Stephens and John Stephens. "In 1965, the country supplied 28 percent of the bauxite used in the market economies of the world . . . [and] bauxite along with tourism fueled post-war Jamaican development and the two provided the country with most of her gross foreign exchange earnings."[67] Newly independent Caribbean countries took pride in their mining industry. The $10 note from the Bank of Guyana carries an image of bauxite mining workers on the left, and of a glistening alumina reduction plant on the right. A 2 shilling stamp from Jamaica depicts modern machinery engaged in gathering the deep red ore of a bauxite mine. In the same year of Jamaica's independence, the fifty-foot antenna of the American Telstar satellite, which used 80,000 pounds of aluminum, beamed the first satellite television pictures back to a transmission station in Maine, ushering in the dawning of satellite telecommunications and new dreams of the gravity-defying lightness of the Space Age. Caribbean leaders also desired to escape their colonial past in order to embrace exactly the kind of modernity that U.S. technology promised. They shared the dreams of the Space Age, the prosperity that mining and alumina reduction promised, and the light modernity that aluminum could bring.

Yet the demise of the cruise ships indicates how multinational corporations were evolving into global transnational corporations. American workers would also suffer the consequences as industrial production began its shift to other parts of the world, and containerization undercut the bargaining power of port workers' unions. This was accompanied by another shift in modernization strategies, from sea power to aerial power. Ships were no longer suitable publicity machines for the company, as attention shifted to the new civilian aircraft that were coming into use. In 1965 Alcoa created the "FORECAST Jet," a kind of "flying showcase" that displayed the company's products and services. Described as "an aeronautical ambassador of aluminum," the DC-7CF could be expanded on the ground into a reception area formed by "a semi-circular screen of aluminum beads," with aluminum spiral stairs rising up to an interior conference lounge furnished with woven-aluminum panels, aluminum-fabric upholstery, aluminum sand-casted lighting fixtures, and artworks in aluminum. The jet "functioned both as a sign and signifier of its product as well as a metaphor for the new postwar corporation . . . the aluminum airplane—*the* war machine of World War II—transformed into a sleek communication machine in the Cold War marketplace."[68] Like the Alcoa Steamships, these "communication machines" suggest the close relationship among material objects, semiotic meanings, advertising, and the advance of industry as intertwined actors.

Caribbean cultures were also in motion, promulgating their own communication machines. The New World Group of economists at the University of the West Indies began to publish scathing critiques of foreign capital and the economic underdevelopment of Jamaica and began to call for the nationalization of the Jamaican bauxite industry in the early 1970s. The socialist government of newly independent Guyana nationalized the Demerara Bauxite Company in 1970 and took a 51 percent stake in Alcan's DEMBA subsidiary. In 1973 Prime Minister Michael Manley's People's National Party government "opened negotiations with the aluminum TNCs on acquisition of 51 percent equity in their bauxite mining operations, . . . acquisition of all the land owned by the companies in order to gain control over the bauxite reserves, and a bauxite levy tied to the price of aluminum ingot on the U.S. market."[69] In March 1974, inspired by the success of OPEC, a bauxite producer's cartel known as the International Bauxite Association (IBA) was set up and was quickly able to double the price of bauxite on world markets.

However, Manley's socialist rhetoric, friendship with Fidel Castro, and support for African liberation movements such as the MPLA (Movimento Popular de Libertação de Angola) in Angola did not endear him to the United States, or to the multinationals. In response, American aluminum companies "doubled their bauxite imports from Guinea in 1975, [and] they reduced their Jamaican imports by 30 per cent. . . . Jamaica's share of the world market for bauxite plummeted."[70] The corporate powers that controlled the global aluminum industry would never allow "Third World" countries, especially socialist ones, to wrest control over their own resources. The bauxite taken from the Caribbean allowed the United States to build a material culture of light aluminum, unquestionable military air power, and space-age mobility. At the same time, the terms of oligopolistic international trade and market governance that allowed this transfer of resources to take place helped to lock in place structures of global inequality that prevented Caribbean countries from exercising true sovereignty or benefiting from their own resources—for them Rostow's "takeoff" never came.[71] Instead, the Caribbean remained a tourist mecca, frozen in folkloric performances of the colorful past embellished with tropical foliage, for mass market tourists who now arrived on jets built with Alcoa aluminum. Some countries turned toward offshore banking, a different strategy for leveraging the high-speed mobilities of finance capital, while other actors resorted to the underground movement of drugs and weapons as part of the hidden but vast "narcoeconomy."

CONCLUSION

The emergence of aluminum-based practices of mobility, alongside modern ideologies and representations of that mobility, pivoted on the coproduction of other regions of the world as backward, slow, and relatively immobile—"bauxite-bearing" regions that would be mined by multinational corporations for the benefit of those who could make use of the "magical metal." Such relative mobilizations and demobilizations are constitutive of the connections and disconnections between North America and the Caribbean, with patents, tariffs, tax regimes, and military power locking in the spatial formations that allow disjunctive modernities to exist side by side. The airy lightness of aluminum and its associated visualizations of metallic modernity were wrenched out of the tropical earth of specific places, subjected to modern forms of domination and associated pollution.[72] Toxic red mud from bauxite mining, water and air pollution from alumina refining, excessive energy use for aluminum smelting, and negative health effects on workers and nearby populations are as much a product of the Age of Aluminum as are elegant MacBook Air notebook computers with their "featherlight aluminum design" and promise of mobile connectivity at our fingertips. Advertising and alluring objects continue to enroll us in the fantasy of mobile modernity, while tourist mobilities hide the global rifts on which easy circulation is premised.

By closely examining the aluminum industry's material objects of lightweight modernity alongside its visual representations of its bauxite mining lands in the Caribbean as tourist destinations, this chapter has tried to reconnect the valuation of modern U.S. American mobility with the practices of transnational heavy industry, warfare, tropical dispossession, and economic inequalities upon which it depended. These dichotomies are in truth the two inseparable sides of the same coin. The colonial mobilities of the Caribbean held it in a kind of slow motion, while the postcolonial struggles for democratic socialism and resource sovereignty locked the region into conflicts that were geared to spur the fast-forward motion of the United States while indefinitely delaying the Caribbean takeoff toward the promise of modernity.

It seems fitting that in March 2008 the first European Space Agency Automated Transfer Vehicle, which docked successfully with the International Space Station, was launched on an aluminum Ariane 5 rocket from Kourou, French Guiana. The vehicle is appropriately named "Jules Verne." Gazing toward the heavens, an observer of the historic launch might not have noticed the displaced Saamaka Maroons living as non-national migrants on the fringes of the neighboring French territory of Guyane, a former penal colony known for its brutal and deadly prisons, but where the capital Cayenne is now the location of the European Space Programme.[73] These descendants of runaway slaves who gained treaty rights to an independent territory in the jungle interior of neighboring Dutch Guiana in the eighteenth century lost a huge portion of their homeland in 1966–67 when Alcoa built the Afobaka hydroelectric dam and an artificial lake to power their aluminum smelter at Paranam, displacing thousands of Maroon villagers.[74] The modernizing society of Guyane "is trying so hard to replace its image as a penal colony with that of gleaming Ariane rockets," writes Price, but here again two modernities jarringly converge at a crossroads of sharp contrasts between the traditions of the Maroon past and the gleaming outer-space future.[75] These Caribbean footnotes to the metropolitan world's technological achievements ought to draw our attention back down to the ground of Suriname, Guyana, and Jamaica, where an analysis of the mobile *and* immobile material cultures afforded by aluminum can elucidate not only the cultural history of technology, design, and popular culture, but also the broader currents of global political economy, mobile modernity, and its sites of contestation.

PART III

Translations

FIGURE 7.1: *California Chinese Chatter*, by Albert Dressler (1927).

CHAPTER 7

The True Story of Ah Jake

LANGUAGE, LABOR, AND JUSTICE IN
LATE-NINETEENTH-CENTURY SIERRA COUNTY, CALIFORNIA

Mae M. Ngai

MYRIAD CIRCUITS OF TRADE AND MIGRATION composed the Pacific world in the nineteenth century, connecting East Asia, Southeast Asia, Australasia, and the Americas, and creating throughout this world contact zones, new settlements, and cultural borderlands.[1] This essay is a microhistory that finds in a strange and unusual case—a murder trial of a Chinese gold miner in California—larger social and cultural patterns of colonial and race relations. Specifically it finds in the transpacific circulations of language and diasporic labor organization problems of legibility and translation that are immanent of cultural mixing and collision.

My interest in this case was sparked by the transcript of the Sierra County court's hearing in October 1887, on whether to bring the charge of murder against Ah Jake,[2] an unemployed Chinese gold miner, for the killing of another miner, Wah Chuck. The transcript, as we will see, is remarkable because much of the hearing took place in neither English nor Chinese, but in pidgin, or Chinglish. Throughout the hearing the judge, the district attorney, the defendant, and the Chinese interpreter all spoke in pidgin. For example, the judge asked the defendant if he had any witnesses to call: "You want some man swear?"

Pidgin is a contact language, a language of borderlands—typically colonial or trading borderlands—in this case, California's racial borderlands. Researchers often speak of following the people, or the money, or the "thing" in order to track social processes across time and space. Here, I follow the language to pursue greater historical understanding of ethno-race relations in the borderlands of the eastern Pacific world. At another level, Ah Jake's trial transcripts allude to deeper histories of Chinese-diasporic social formation in the nineteenth century. The present case offers evidence of the circulation of not only linguistic forms but also labor and social organization among the Chinese in the Pacific world. Drawing from common sources in southern China, these formations assumed local variation within the political and cultural economies of Southeast Asia, Australia, and North America. In this essay I hope to show that diasporic and comparative methodologies may afford a richer understanding of social relations in particular sites, in this case, the nineteenth-century California interior.

Although it is unremarkable to note that Chinese miners in California lived at the margins of white society, the use of pidgin in a county courtroom suggests, rather than a simple marginalization, the existence of a contact zone. What was the nature of that contact zone and the social relations it produced? Comparing the characteristics and uses of pidgin in California to that of pidgin in the colonial trading ports of Guangzhou (Canton) and Hong Kong reveals the former to be much less robust than the latter. The differences, I argue, index the relations of power between pidgin-speaking Chinese and Euro-Americans in California and China, respectively. I argue further that the story of Ah Jake offers a more nuanced portrait of Chinese-white relations than those in conventional narratives about the exclusion and driving-out campaigns that swept the North American Pacific coast in the 1880s. Ethno-race relations were not altogether negative and, moreover, could serve to include Chinese, however precariously, within the conventional norms of American justice.

The murder victim in this case, Wah Chuck, does not, of course, speak at trial; nevertheless, court records suggest that he belonged to a secret brotherhood society and a small mining cooperative. These social formations, which traversed the Pacific world in the late nineteenth century, were nearly invisible to contemporary white observers. They have remained largely so to later historians of the United States owing in part to a scarcity of sources, but also to problems of historiography. Disjunctive research agendas and scant exchange characterize the fields of Chinese American history and U.S. labor history, a surprising disjuncture in light of a history of cross-fertilization of immigration and labor histories.[3] With regard to the issues under examination here, Chinese American scholarship has focused mostly on social organization and politics with little attention to the organization of labor in the nineteenth century.[4] Meanwhile, labor and economic historians have persisted in the view that Chinese labor in the nineteenth-century United States was unfree, on the mistaken grounds that Chinese clan and district associations held Chinese workers in bondage through labor contracts and debt peonage.[5] A close reading of the trial records of this case with attention to the broader context of the Pacific world opens up new grounds for understanding the contours of diasporic Chinese social history and the "Chinese question" in Euro-American racial politics.

Let us turn to the story of Ah Jake and how he came to stand trial for murder. We do not know when Ah Jake first came to the United States, but it was probably some time in the late 1860s or early 1870s.[6] Like the overwhelming majority of Chinese migrants in California at the time, he hailed from the *siyi* (four counties), an impoverished region of Guangdong province in southern China. He lived at Texas Bar, near the "joss house" (temple) built by Chinese miners on the bank of Goodyears Creek, not far from where the creek flowed into the North Yuba River. The river and its many little tributaries had yielded a lot of gold in the early 1850s—thousands of prospectors descended upon the area, including many Chinese, and stories abounded about miners finding gold nuggets weighing twenty pounds and more. Goodyears Bar, the main settlement at the junction of Goodyears Creek and the North Yuba, was a thriving gold rush town that included a sawmill, which provided lumber for mining infrastructures, and a large Chinese settlement at the northeast side of town.[7]

In the 1880s several hundred Chinese still lived in towns and small settlements near the sites of old gold claims in the vicinity of North Yuba River. Their housing comprised cabins roughly hewn from logs or rocks, or sometimes bark dugouts, alongside the hand-stacked rock walls and old raceways they had built for their sluice boxes in the 1850s and 1860s.[8] Ah Jake still did a little mining along the creek with his uncle, but, as he explained at trial, "just now no mine now."[9]

On the morning of October 20, 1887, Ah Jake set off for Downieville, the county seat about four miles away, to "buy grub" for himself and his "partner," Ah Chung, and to repair a pair of the latter's boots. In one pocket he had $4.65 and, in another, in a "little carpet sack," two gold pieces worth $30. He carried a pistol and a dirk (a small knife), which was his practice when he traveled with money on his person. When walking on the main stage road that connected Downieville and Sierra City, he ran into two acquaintances, Wah Chuck and Ah Ting. Ah Jake and Wah Chuck quarreled over a $20 loan that Ah Jake had made to Wah Chuck in July of that year. In Ah Jake's telling of the encounter, he told Wah Chuck that the loan had come due, but Wah Chuck refused to pay him and in turn accused Ah Jake of stealing from him a pair of boots and a sack of rice. In the ensuing argument and altercation, Ah Jake shot and fatally wounded Wah Chuck. Ah Jake fled the scene and managed to hide out for two days in attic of a cabin of Chinese miners near Forest City, some ten miles away, before he was apprehended.[10]

A hearing on whether to bring the charge of murder against Ah Jake was held before F. D. Soward, the magistrate judge of Sierra County. Lo Kay, a Downieville grocer, was sworn in as an interpreter to assist with the examination of Ah Ting, Wah Chuck's traveling companion and the only witness to the alleged murder.[11] Lo Kay's knowledge of English and his contact with the local power structure likely derived from his customer base among white residents. However, Lo Kay did not speak English well; instead, he spoke pidgin. More interesting perhaps is that the district attorney and judge also spoke in pidgin when addressing the witness and interpreter. Consider the following:

Q (Smith, the district attorney): When Ah Jake shoot Wah Chuck, what Wah Chuck do?
A (Lo Kay, translating for the witness, Ah Ting): You mean Ah Jake shoot, what Wah Chuck do?
Q: Yes.
A: No say anything at all.
Q: What he do after he get shot? After he get shot what he do?
A: You mean Wah Chuck?
Q: Yes.
A: He say he fell down; no do nothing; no do anything.
Q: He bleed any? . . . Did he got back to where Wah Chuck was?
A: No. . . .
Q: Did he see him dead afterwards?
A: He see him down here, no see him dead that place. . . . He say he see him Funk Kee store; outside door; take him down buggy; see him that time.
DEFENDANT: He no see him dead; he lie.[12]

Ah Jake had already interrupted Ah Ting's testimony twice, interjecting in Chinese (Lo Kay: "He say he don't know what he say") before resorting to Chinglish to challenge the witness, but the judge ordered Lo Kay and Ah Ting to ignore him.[13] However, because Ah Jake did not have legal counsel, the judge accorded him the opportunity to cross-examine the witness:

CORT. TO DEFENDANT. Q: You want to ask him some questions?
DEFENDANT: Me askum him.
COURT: You want to ask him some questions?
DEFENDANT: He lie; he lie too much.
COURT: You don't want to ask him any questions?
DEFENDANT: Wah Chuck give him my money—
COURT: You don't want to ask him any questions? You like to ask him some questions this man. You don't want to ask any question this man.

MR. SMITH: That is all I want to question this witness.

DEFENDANT: He talk lie.[14]

Ah Jake did conduct a spirited cross-examination of the next witness, S. C. Stewart, the sheriff, and put forth his own case that he shot Wah Chuck in self-defense. He spoke directly to the court in pidgin rather than risk having his words mediated by the interpreter, whom he seemed to believe was complicit with Ah Ting's lying. The reader will forgive the lengthy excerpt:

DEFENDANT: You see up here hole me fall? You see hole that stage road?

STEWART: I see two places.

DEFENDANT: One place down river; one place down river; up road; two places, one place down river me fall down; you no see that time; you see up here two time?

STEWART: There were two places; two marks in the road—

DEFENDANT (ILLUSTRATING ON FLOOR): He lay me down that way; he hold my queue that way; me tell him let me up; he no let me up. (Witness lays on floor making motion, etc., many of his remarks being unintelligible.) . . .

STEWART: All I know about it there were two marks in the road there.

DEFENDANT: One mark in the road down side river; one mark down side; one mark up side—I catch him that side; he catch me that side. He shoot me I no know—I burn my coat—I no see him; he fight me back side; he catch my queue that way . . . he make me scare—I no kill him, he kill me; he strong me. . . .

COURT: You want to ask him some question. . . . You got any witness. You want some man swear?

DEFENDANT: I no got man swear. Everybody help him. He talk lie (pointing to Ah Ting). He talk lie; he no say take my queue; put on floor; he no talk. . . . He no hold my foot I no fall down at all; first time he take my bag money; catch my money put him pocket . . . he [Wah Chuck] say he kill me; I get scare. . . . He no rob my money I no shoot him. . . . He say killum me; make me scare. . . . I think make him scare let me up; he say "You shoot me I no care G—d—s—b—."[15]

We may safely assume that Ah Jake and Wah Chuck spoke to each other in their native Chinese, in this case, in *siyi*, a subdialect of Cantonese. An interesting question arises as to whether Wah Chuck uttered "You shoot me I no care G—d—s—b" just as it appears in the transcript, that is, in Chinglish or if he spoke in Chinese but swore "G—d—s—b" in English (what linguists call code switching),[16] or if he spoke entirely in Chinese and Ah Jake translated his Chinese swearing into the common

American-English epithet. Each possibility suggests a different kind of language translation or hybridization, in which speakers mixed Chinese with English phrases or translated idioms not literally but through cultural common knowledge.

Before analyzing the transcript further, we might pause to consider the reliability of the document as historical evidence. The court reporter was Adolph Meroux, a twenty-two-year-old French American, who ordinarily worked as a clerk in his father's grocery store in Downieville. Meroux probably used shorthand to record testimony (machine stenography had just been introduced in the early 1880s) and then later transcribed it with a typewriter. Meroux may have had some familiarity with pidgin (perhaps being spoken with Chinese customers in his father's store). Otherwise he would have had some difficulty recording pidgin testimony with shorthand, which relies upon both phonetic symbols and preset styles for common words and phrases in English. The complexities inherent to language communication—the processes of "translation" that link cognition, speech, reception, and cognition—are made more difficult in transcription and more difficult still when recording an unfamiliar dialect. No court transcript can be considered a verbatim documentation of a proceeding, including Meroux's. At the same time, Meroux's transcript shows an *absence* of correction that contemporary transcribers sometimes made to eliminate traces of vernacular speech and other marks deemed unsuitable for official records. Meroux also honestly recorded where he failed to comprehend the speaker ("many of his remarks being unintelligible"), rather than, for sake of pride or efficiency, elide gaps in his understanding. In the case of Ah Jake's hearing, Meroux's transcript can be considered a fairly reliable representation of the proceedings, at least insofar as we can rely on any text as historical evidence.[17]

What else can we learn about language and translation from the exchanges in the transcripts? At one level, it is tempting to read the judge and district attorney's use of pidgin as an infantilization of their speech, a condescension toward Ah Jake and Lo Kay. Did Ah Jake understand "Have you got lawyer man?" but not "Do you have a lawyer?" It is possible that the court's officers believed Ah Jake's ignorance of English indexed a general condition of ignorance, a common presumption held by Americans about those of non-European and non-English-speaking origins. This analysis of the transcript follows our experience with pidgin on the printed page, used by white writers to represent the speech of racialized subjects. The modern reader cringes when presented with dialogue written in dialect. But the courtroom is an arena of the spoken word, which is highly contingent and functions in real time. In that context the judge and district attorney's use of pidgin appears less as mocking and more as a sincere effort to communicate with the defendant.

They reached for the language they used when they engaged with local Chinese, a house servant, perhaps, or the garden farmer.

In any case, it can be argued that pidgin was the lingua franca of the proceeding. This pidgin derived from Chinese English Pidgin (also called Canton Jargon by contemporaries), the contact language of Guangzhou, Macao, and Hong Kong that developed during the colonial China trade. "Pidgin" is a corruption of the word "business" (itself shortened from "pidginess"): "pidgin English" means "business English." Chinese Pidgin English is characterized by reduced grammatical structure (lack of copulas, plurals, verb tense, definite articles, etc.) and certain phonological inventions (replacement of [r] with [l], e.g., "tomollow"; and insertion of vowels [i] or [u] to word endings, e.g., "lookee"). Its vocabulary draws from English, Portuguese, Hindi, and Cantonese: A *Mandarin*, a government official, comes from the Portuguese verb "mandar" (to command); *joss* derives from "deös." *Lac* is from the Hindi number for one hundred thousand. A *chop*, from the Hindi "chhap," for seal, or stamp, is a document of any kind—an invoice, an imperial edict, a receipt, a bill of lading (the latter a *chop boat*). A servant sent on an urgent errand is told to go "chop chop"—a clever combination that uses the likely object of the errand (fetching or delivering a document) with the Chinese syntax of repetition, recalling *kuai kuai* (lit. fast fast), or hurry. Chinese Pidgin English, in service of European-Chinese business in the exchange of tea, silks, opium, hemp, and silver that was the stuff of the early colonial China trade, was linguistically creative and vigorous.[18]

Outside of the trading house, however, pidgin had limited uses. It was spoken in the colonial household with servants but did not carry over to judicial or diplomatic venues, where precision and nuance in language carried a high premium. Under the colonial convention of extraterritoriality, Europeans living in China's treaty ports were not subject to Chinese law, but when they had occasion to appear in a Chinese court as plaintiffs or as witnesses, interpreters were used. In diplomacy and treaty writing, the British were scrupulous about controlling language. Their diplomats spoke only through their own interpreters, and they wrote into the Treaty of Tianjin (1858, following the Second Opium War) a provision that the English-language version, and not the Chinese, would determine the final meaning of official communications.[19]

The pidgin spoken by Chinese migrants in California was similar to that used in Guangzhou and Hong Kong, but there seem to have been important differences. While the syntax was similar, not surprisingly American English and American social practices shaped Chinese-American pidgin. There were local word forms and importations from other ethno-racial vernaculars, like "askum" and "sarvie" (savvy).[20] More important, nineteenth-century American-Chinese pidgin seems much less robust than its colonial antecedent. It did not evolve from sustained interactions between Chinese and whites as it had in China, but was mainly the product of Chinese migrants' efforts to engage with their new environment, by learning, as one observer described, the "few necessary words and sentences, to assist in mining, traveling, bartering, marketing, and procuring various kinds of employment."[21]

White Americans engaged with Chinese occasionally but not regularly or in sustained engagement, as in China's treaty ports, and may have acquired just a passing familiarity with pidgin. At Ah Jake's trial, the judge and district attorney speak pidgin awkwardly. They mimic imperfectly its syntax, do not use pidgin's novel vocabulary or phonology ("killum"), and resort to clumsy repetition: "You don't want to ask him any questions? You like to ask him some questions this man. You don't want to ask any question this man."[22] Arguably they are not speaking pidgin at all. Linguists contend that pidgin, like any language, must be learned and "cannot be produced by an ad-hoc simplification of his or her own language."[23]

The pidgin of late-nineteenth-century Sierra County denotes the social location of Chinese as a group of ethnic outsiders with regular but limited contact with the mainstream of society. It is a contact language at the very margins of society and not, as in Guangzhou and Hong Kong, a central constituent of a vibrant market where parties met, if not as equals, as contenders. The limitations of Chinese-American pidgin English are manifest in the California courtroom: it simply does not have the depth to express complex ideas or to address the contingencies of a trial court examination. At Ah Jake's hearing, linguistic confusion and misunderstanding at times overwhelmed the parties' ability to communicate. If the British deemed pidgin inadequate for legal proceedings in China, its appearance in a Sierra County court of law suggests the extreme marginality of its Chinese residents.

Insofar as the court did provide an interpreter—the pidgin-speaking Lo Kay—the transcript does not record the primary testimonies given orally in Chinese, only the interpreter's translation into pidgin. Those voices are forever lost, unavailable to an appeals court and, beyond, to history. Here we come upon an important difference between the translation of written texts and that of oral testimonies. In either case, a "good" translation, that is, one that is faithful to the original, is not a mere transfer or substitution of words from one language into another. Translation is not a replication but the production of yet another, wholly different text, in which the meaning of the original is expressed anew. But, whereas the fidelity of a translation of a written text may be judged by comparing it to the original, in oral accounts and testimonies the original vanishes as soon as it is uttered. The written original retains its status as the original and hence its authority; in oral interpreting the translation usurps the authority of the original utterance. No wonder, then, that the monolingual migrant often feels himself or herself to be at the mercy of the court interpreter.[24]

Ah Jake, whose English/Chinglish was comparable to Lo Kay's, realized that he would gain nothing from Lo Kay's interpreting, so he spoke for himself. But Ah Jake's limited knowledge of English was compounded by his lack of proficiency in yet another language: law, the language of the court. He attempted to show how Wah Chuck and Ah Ting assaulted and robbed him, but he did not know how to make his case through the conventions of a criminal proceeding. He declined the opportunity to cross-examine Ah Ting, dismissing him as a liar and not understanding the necessity of revealing his lying through cross-examination.

Perhaps because of Lo Kay's linguistic limitations and owing to the gravity of the charge against Ah Jake, the court hired the services of a professional interpreter for the trial. The interpreter was Jerome Millard, a Euro-American who worked for the criminal court in San Francisco.[25] Millard had come to California during the gold rush, traveling from Michigan by oxcart on the "early road." He befriended and worked with Chinese miners, favoring them over whites, he said, because they did not drink alcohol, and learned Chinese. In the 1860s he supervised the first Chinese labor gangs hired by Charles Crocker and Company for building the transcontinental railroad. By the 1880s he was working full-time as a translator for the criminal court in San Francisco, one of some twenty-odd professional foreign-language interpreters (French, German, Russian, Japanese) employed in the city's courts and customs house. Millard welcomed occasional assignments to "the country" to translate for "important case[s]."[26]

Millard, who was nearly six feet tall and wore a large handlebar mustache, must have cut an imposing figure in the courtroom. Witnesses testifying through the interpreter Millard speak in standard English and, possibly, assume some of his bodily authority. Ah Jake appears to be a different person than the Chinglish speaker in the previous examination transcript: "I have worked at cooking for whites whenever I could get work, and other times I have worked at mining." "He pulled me down by the cue on the ground, as I have here shown [showing] and struck me again. I then got up and he struck me again and it hurt me and I fell in the road. . . . I was then very mad and says I: 'You got my money and won't pay me and strike me' and he says: 'I like to strike you.'"[27]

Ah Jake also had legal representation: two lawyers, A. J. Howe, a local retired judge, appointed by the court, and Bert Schlessinger, a young attorney new to Downieville, hired by Ah Jake's clan association. They contended that the defendant, overwhelmed, assaulted, and robbed by two men, acted in self-defense. Unfortunately the only eyewitness to the event, Ah Ting, did not support that account. The prosecution argued that Ah Jake had robbed and killed Wah Chuck and then returned to the scene of the crime, where he created marks in the road to give the appearance that a scuffle had taken place. As evidence of this theory the district attorney produced two white witnesses, who testified that they had seen Ah Jake shortly after the incident and that he did not have dust on his clothes or in his hair or face, and also that he was pretending to cry.[28]

The jury convicted Ah Jake of murder in the first degree, apparently finding the testimony of the defendant unpersuasive in light of contradicting testimony by Ah Ting and the two white witnesses. The jurors also seem to have heeded the judge's instructions that the "will, deliberation and premeditation" required for a first-degree conviction applied even if only a few seconds lapsed between thought and action.[29] The court sentenced Ah Jake to death by hanging; a motion for a new trial was denied.[30] It would appear that Ah Jake fared no better with the aid of professional translation and legal counsel than he did representing himself in pidgin. The conviction and sentence strike us as an unsurprising outcome of a trial in which Ah Jake had only a "Chinaman's chance."

As it turned out, though, Ah Jake was not hanged. Prominent white citizens of Downieville appealed to Governor Robert Waterman to commute the sentence to life imprisonment. They included Jerome A. Vaughn, editor of the *Mountain Messenger* and a county supervisor, and Charles Kirkbride, the Methodist minister, who wrote letters; some fifty others signed two petitions, citing "grave doubt" as to the guilt of Ah Jake, including among them the town's elites and middling citizens: merchants, lawyers, the superintendent of schools, a notary, miners, a cabinet maker, a jeweler, a surveyor, the telegraph and express agent, and the court reporter. Six of the jurors, including the foreman, asked that the sentence be commuted. Two local citizens who had been at the crime scene shortly after the incident and testified at trial as witnesses for the prosecution wrote the governor to say that they believed a scuffle between Ah Jake and Wah Chuck had taken place there.[31]

Of greatest consequence was an affidavit submitted by Sheriff S. C. Stewart. That document offered a detailed explanation of his examination of the crime scene and his opinion that the marks in the road showed not only that there had been a fight but also that Ah Jake's footprints (he was barefoot after his assailants took his boots) did not track back to the scene of the crime. Judge Soward wrote a letter in support of the sheriff and stated that Ah Jake's lawyers did not mount a proper defense, as they did not elicit full testimony from the sheriff at trial and, moreover, argued with each other in open court.[32]

What accounts for this outpouring of support and the sudden appearance of evidence not adduced at trial? Many of the petitioners stated that they did not know Ah Jake personally but that they were moved to speak out because a grave injustice had been committed. Although Ah Jake was surely not the first Chinese miner in Sierra County to be wrongfully convicted of a crime, the case did give a strong appearance of self-defense. Still, someone had to mobilize the community to produce the petitions, letters, and affidavits. I believe that person was Stewart, the sheriff, aided by Vaughn, the newspaper editor.

Sheriff Stewart was a longtime resident of Goodyears Bar. He was a former lumberman at the sawmill there, and he testified at trial that he had known Ah Jake for some number of years. He may have regretted that his testimony about the track marks on the Downieville stage road was not fully elaborated when, after the conviction and sentencing, the judge issued a death warrant that "command[ed] and require[d] [Stewart] to execute the said Judgment . . . by hanging the said Ah Jake by the neck until he is dead."[33] Only four people had ever been officially executed in the history of Sierra County—three in the 1850s (including an Indian named Pijo who had killed two Chinese miners) and the last in 1885, James O'Neill, as punishment for murdering his employer. As sheriff, Stewart was committed to enforcing the law, and he had in fact hanged O'Neill.[34] But Ah Jake's case seems different: Stewart knew Ah Jake, and he knew Ah Jake was not guilty of first-degree murder. Perhaps the prospect of hanging him was chilling. Stewart brought his concerns to Judge Soward and to Jerome Vaughn, editor of the *Messenger*.[35]

If pidgin was the contact language that marked the space where Chinese and Euro-American social worlds overlapped in Sierra County in late 1880s, that space had been under construction over the course of some thirty years, since the time of the gold rush. Various points of engagement developed and persisted among these "longtime Californ'," both Chinese and white: selling vegetables, buying grub, changing gold dust to coin, cooking and domestic service, missionary work. Such contact did not (and could not) produce among the white people an intimate knowledge of the Chinese around them, but neither did the former regard the latter indiscriminately as anonymous Chinamen. Ah Jake had worked as an occasional cook for white people, including Vaughn, the newspaperman,[36] and his relations with white people seemed to be friendly.[37]

But whereas at least some local white citizens considered Ah Jake to be a good man and spoke in the language of clemency on his behalf, no white people described the dead man, Wah Chuck, as a good man and none demanded justice for him. Wah Chuck was even more marginal to white society than was Ah Jake. Unlike Ah Jake, he did not work for white people. He lived farther out of town, at a small Chinese mining encampment at China Flat, along the South Yuba River, about halfway between Downieville and Sierra City. He came into Downieville occasionally to buy provisions for his "company" and to visit the Chinese gambling house. His patronage there may have prompted the *Mountain Messenger* to declare, "Ah Jake bore an excellent character, whereas that of the deceased was notoriously bad."[38]

Wah Chuck did have powerful Chinese advocates: handsome rewards were offered for Ah Jake's arrest and, later, for his conviction, with the size of the reward pegged to the severity of the conviction. (Indeed, the pidgin interpreter Lo Kay reportedly paid out a $100 reward to Sheriff Hartling, who had arrested Ah Jake in Forest City, although the court apparently did not consider Lo Kay's affiliation with Wah Chuck's people a conflict of interest.) Local whites said that Wah Chuck belonged to a bigger and more powerful native place association than did Ah Jake, but in fact they both were members of same association, the Hop Wo Company (Hehe huiguan), which represented several clans from the siyi region. They even may have been from the same lineage, with "Jake" and "Chuck" being transliterations of the same surname.[39] But Wah Chuck also may have been affiliated with the sworn brotherhood society, the Chee Kong Tong (Zhigongtang). Sworn brotherhoods in China were mutual aid societies found mostly among socially marginal men with weak familial and native place ties. During the early nineteenth century, sworn brotherhoods in Guangdong and Fujian provinces, the Hongmen (lit. flood gate, or vast family) and Tiandihui (heaven and earth society), respectively, were fervent anti-Manchu activists. The Zhigongtang was formed in Southeast Asia, Hawaii, and North America in the 1850s and 1860s by Hongmen and Tiandihui members, who fled China as the Qing suppressed the Taiping Rebellion.[40]

A few bits of evidence suggest Wah Chuck's affiliation with the Zhigongtang. In Downieville, as in other small California towns, the largest and most well-appointed building in the Chinese quarter was the lodge of the Zhigongtang, which likely gave Euro-Americans the impression that it was the most powerful organization among the Chinese.[41] Zhigongtang lodges typically housed an altar for the brotherhood's patron gods and halls for ritual exercise and meeting. In California the secret societies also controlled gambling and other vice industries, and Wah Chuck was an inveterate gambler.[42]

Even more provocatively, Wah Chuck was a partner in a "company" of seven miners that appears to have functioned collectively. One of Wah Chuck's partners, Ah Fock, testified at the trial that as treasurer of the group he had sent Wah Chuck to town on that fateful day to purchase provisions from the butcher and grocer. He clarified that he was not the group's "boss" but "merely" its "treasurer . . . at the time," who "took charge of the [gold] dust as it came out" and kept the groups accounts with local merchants.[43] The company described by Ah Fock bears a canny resemblance to the egalitarian labor organization common among Hakka (an ethnic minority in southern China) in Southeast Asia, especially on the gold fields of West Borneo. Called kongsi (*gongsi*, company), their partners held equal shares and had no boss or headman, but elected officers to serve on a rotating basis. And they were associated with the Hongmen.[44]

There is evidence of small "cooperative ventures for river mining" in California during the 1860s and through the late nineteenth century. Federal census enumerators in 1890 wrote of some one hundred Chinese working at mining along the North Yuba River—in the vicinity of Downieville—"scattered in about a dozen companies" with modest equipment (wing dams, water wheels, rotary pumps, sluices, and the like) and with aggregate net earnings of $10,000 to $20,000 a year (or $200 per man, about $4,500 in current dollars).[45] Wah Chuck must have belonged to one of these companies. More broadly, the state mineralogist reported in 1889 that two-thirds of the 10,000 to 12,000 Chinese miners in the state worked "on their own account [individual prospectors] or for companies composed of their own countrymen," with the balance working for whites.[46]

If, as we know, the Zhigongtang throughout the Pacific world shared identical ritual symbols and practices, its mode of labor organization also seems to have traveled across the diaspora. Chinese mining cooperatives in both Southeast Asia and North America derived from southern China, where itinerant groups of independent miners operated with internal principles that were egalitarian: they drew no wages but shared profits, and were often members of sworn brotherhoods.[47] Chinese miners in California may well have drawn from these traditions, whether from general knowledge or from direct experience.[48]

The small companies noted in the mineralogist's report also drew from antecedents in China. These were typically formed by a local merchant who acted as investor and manager, and which operated either with cash wages or, more likely insofar as yields were meager and sporadic, in shares. A minority of Chinese miners worked for wages for white-owned hydraulic, ditch, and even deep quartz mining companies. Rossiter Raymond, the U.S. Commissioner of Mining Statistics, wrote in 1871 that the charge that Chinese were unfree was born of politics, not fact. "Chinese here are not coolies," he wrote emphatically. "They are quite ready to accept the best wage they can get. They even combine, like other folks, in unions, where that is possible."[49]

If Raymond understood that Chinese were not coolies, his readiness to generalize that they were "like other folks" (i.e., free-white labor) remains invested in the norms of liberal individualism. While I appreciate Raymond's antiracism, I believe we need to think beyond the unfree-free binary to understand the subject positions of nineteenth-century Chinese. Chinese gold miners seem to have combined in their practices and in their thinking elements from non-bourgeois collectivities like the sworn brotherhoods and the modern capitalist-labor market.[50]

* * *

The white support for Ah Jake is particularly remarkable in light of the anti-Chinese "driving out" campaigns that swept the Pacific coast during the middle and late 1880s. Mob violence and threats of mob violence enforcing "sunset" resolutions were ubiquitous in California and other western states, a veritable second wave of extralegal terror that recalled the violence against Chinese in the mining districts in the 1850s and 1860s. In the 1880s campaigns had far broader reach, targeting Chinese laborers brought in on seasonal contracts for mining, lumbering, and fishing, as well as established Chinese communities. During the spring of 1886 anti-Chinese associations in the mining areas of Sierra County agitated for the firing of Chinese from all local establishments and for boycotting those that persisted in employing Chinese. In fact by this time the local quartz mines and sawmills in Sierra County employed Chinese only as cooks or launderers; all the waged production workers were Euro-Americans. But the campaign did succeed in pressuring Downieville hotels to fire Chinese kitchen workers.[51]

Yet there also were white residents who were not antagonistic toward the Chinese because the latter performed useful services at low cost— cooking, laundry, and garden farming. Some thought the anticoolie leagues were "abusive"; others complained they simply could not afford the products or services of white labor.[52] Ah Jake's case reminds us that anti-Chinese agitation was the work of a specific political movement and was not hegemonic among white Californians. It suggests also that even as Chinese labor was driven out of many areas, Chinese remained in towns and counties throughout the California interior, living at the margins of society but nonetheless part of the local fabric, and still engaged with whites as employers, customers, and neighbors.

In November Governor Waterman commuted Ah Jake's sentence to life in prison. Citing evidence not adduced at trial, a lack of competent counsel, and petitions from prominent citizens, the governor concluded that Ah Jake had acted "to a certain element in self-defense" and that there was a "reasonable doubt" as to whether he had committed murder in the first degree. On November 28 Ah Jake was committed to Folsom Prison.[53]

About a year later Lo Kay, the occasional interpreter, told Sheriff Stewart that Ah Ting, the deceased Wah Chuck's traveling companion (who had since returned to China) had given him a different version of the killing than the story he told at the trial. There were also rumors in Downieville that Lo Kay had been promised a large sum of money for Ah Jake's conviction. In light of this information Judge Soward asked the governor to grant Ah Jake a full pardon.[54]

Ah Jake also wrote to the governor directly. His letters were written in formal English in a neat hand, perhaps by a prison scribe or minister. "I was sent to Folsom Prison for defending my Life and Property for life," he wrote. And, "My friend Mr. Spaulding writting [*sic*] from Downieville tells me that all of my papers are in your hands and Dear Sir I do hope that you will let me go as I have borne with as much fortitude my punishment one possible could do." He added that he was in poor health and submitted a letter from the warden attesting to his good behavior.[55]

Finally, on December 30, 1890, a few days before the governor left office, Ah Jake received a full pardon. In his statement, Waterman said that he was "convinced that Ah Jake is an innocent man and should be restored to his liberty." On January 1, 1891, Ah Jake walked out of prison a free man.[56]

Ah Jake was not the only Chinese person in nineteenth-century California to receive an executive pardon.[57] Chinese prisoners received pardons for good behavior,[58] for serious illness,[59] and, most frequently, as Ah Jake's case, when conviction was based on insufficient evidence or perjured testimony.[60] Prosecutors often had little evidence to bring a conviction, and white people in general professed difficulty distinguishing one Chinese person from another, especially when trying to recall the details of a crowded scene. Contemporaries routinely cited language and cultural barriers as the main problems in trying criminal cases involving Chinese. Some local prosecutors dismissed charges against Chinese for want of evidence, while others were determined to "round up the usual suspects" and press for a conviction even when evidence was weak and witnesses lacked credibility. In granting pardons, the governor often referred to "doubt as to his guilt," "a conspiracy on part of Chinese witnesses," "circumstances [that] have come to light which tend to establish his innocence," and the like.[61]

In bringing a motion to dismiss charges against one Ling Ying Toy in 1897, Sacramento district attorney F. D. Ryan stated that "Chinese cases" were the "most difficult to try, because they involve a character of witnesses that . . . makes it almost impossible to get a fair understanding of the testimony, because it necessarily has to come through an interpreter; and it has been my experience in Chinese murder cases, that, usually, it is one society or organization against another. . . . [I]n dealing with this class of people, the crime of murder is committed as a matter of revenge . . . and that the killing of one Chinaman usually results in the killing of another."[62]

Ryan referred to the so-called tong wars that periodically erupted among rival Chinese brotherhoods in the late nineteenth and early twentieth centuries. Although the tong wars practiced the idiom of blood feuds, common to many premodern corporatist cultures, more practically they involved jurisdictional conflicts over control of the vice trades (opium, prostitution, gambling).[63] Although the dispute between Ah Jake and Wah Chuck does not appear to have been related to a tong war, the case did involve a problem of perjured testimony from the witness Ah Ting, as well as an effort by Wah Chuck's people to influence the proceedings by promising a reward to witnesses who helped achieve a conviction. The revelation of Ah Ting's perjury (as Ah Jake had declared, "he talk lie") was one of the key justifications for the governor's pardon.

The practice of granting pardons to convicted Chinese on grounds of perjured testimony is an ironic outcome of broader contemporary judicial opinion that Chinese could not be counted on to tell the truth. During the nineteenth century a body of law evolved in western territories and states that restricted or excluded testimony from Chinese witnesses and defendants in both criminal and civil cases. In California, *People v. Hall* (1854) established testimonial exclusion on simple grounds of racial inferiority—like blacks and Indians, Chinese victims and witnesses could not testify against white defendants.[64] Courts also justified testimonial exclusion, more generally, even when defendant and victim were of the same ethno-racial group, on grounds that Chinese did not understand the sanctity of the Christian oath. In a somewhat mechanistic way, some courts disallowed Chinese testimony because the court could not properly swear in Chinese witnesses. Some judges conceded that Christians were not the only people who valued "truth" and allowed non-Christians to be sworn in according to their own cultural precepts regarding truth telling and lying. But, more often, a proclivity toward lying was deemed to be a racial trait of the Chinese, a critical index of their barbarism. Testimonial exclusion was a pillar of racism against Chinese and Native American Indians in the criminal justice system in nineteenth-century California and other western jurisdictions.[65] That this widespread racist belief should come full circle to vindicate Chinese convicted for capital crimes is a small wonder of history's unintended consequences.

After Ah Jake received his pardon he returned to Goodyears Creek and there he remained for the rest of his days, even after fire destroyed the main Chinese settlement in Goodyears Bar in the 1890s and most Chinese relocated to San Francisco. He continued to mine for gold, scratching out a bare living, going to Downieville once a month to sell what little gold dust he accumulated. He remained dogged by the notoriety of the murder trial, his reprieve from the gallows, and his eventual pardon, but his reputation was surprisingly uneven. In 1927 the town constable John Mason wrote that Ah Jake "always was an all around bad man," citing the time that he robbed the Chinese gambling house in Downieville of $1,700 in coin and pledges. When confronted by Mason, Ah Jake gave himself up immediately and took the constable to an abandoned mine where he had buried "the loot." The constable also recalled that Ah Jake recently had been injured by a large fallen rock and lay pinned for two days until someone found him.[66]

In Mason's telling, Ah Jake seems less like an "all around bad man" than a hapless and pathetic creature with limited and failed acts of agency. Here we might find in Ah Jake a resemblance to Ah Q, the iconic character of the famous short story by Chinese modernist writer Lu Xun. Ah Q was a foolish figure, whose extreme ineptness and rationalizations for his failures symbolized China's flaws during the interwar years.[67] Both Ah Q and Ah Jake stand as a figure for the Chinese "every man." What had been Orientalized as barbarous and backward in the nineteenth century had become, in the twentieth, dangerous only to the Chinese themselves. Indeed, if at Ah Jake's trial in 1887 the judge and district attorney spoke pidgin without irony, by the 1920s white society considered pidgin undignified and parodic, its speakers stupid. After many years of exclusion and marginalization the racial image of Chinese had shifted from that of racial menace to that of racial children, whose use of pidgin—tellingly also called *broken* English—signaled limited intellect and stunted psychic development. At best, stereotyped pidgin conveyed a picturesque exotic. In Hollywood's Charlie Chan movies (1920s–1940s), the detective (played by white actors) sprouted Confucian-like aphorisms in pidgin—"joy in heart more desirable than bullet," "perfect case like perfect donut, has hole."[68]

In a similar vein, Albert Dressler, a German American resident of San Francisco, published in 1927 a little book called *California Chinese Chatter*. The book comprised documents Dressler had found in Sierra County—including the transcript of Ah Jake's court hearing and a cache of telegrams exchanged by Chinese to and from Downieville in 1874. Dressler wrote that although the documents at times appeared "comical," it was not his intention to "lampoon." Rather, he said he wished to show a "heretofore unnoted aspect of California's melting pot." Notwithstanding his proto-multiculturalism, Dressler was clearly taken by the "color abundant and diversified"—that is, the picturesque—in the pidgin documents; an aspiring artist, he also illustrated *Chatter* with cartoonish Chinese figures (Figure 7.1). Framed in this way, the courtroom transcript morphs into racist caricature. Underscoring the sense of the project, the California state librarian acknowledged Dressler's telegrams as the "basis for a series of 'queer queue tales.'"[69] It would not be until the second half of the twentieth century that Asian American writers, notably Louis Chu, Milton Murayama, Maxine Hong Kingston, and Lois Yamanaka,[70] produced a literary Chinglish, weaving it into the dialogue of their novels, rescuing it from its debased status of shame and stereotype and transforming it into a language that, as literary critic Evelyn Chi'en proposes, "refuses ventriloquism and becomes a voice of self-affirmation," that is, a language that is constitutive of ethnic identity.[71]

Ah Jake's fuller voice and life still elude us. We've never heard his voice in his native tongue, in Chinese, only in Chinglish, or through the interpreter Millard and the Folsom Prison scribe, described as a good or bad man by his white neighbors, or, in Dressler's hands, as a stereotype of the West in its "rough and ready days." Today, Ah Jake is remembered on the Internet for being the last Chinese to live in Goodyears Bar. He was "much loved and respected by the local people for his helpfulness," including the time he helped a white lady when she was thrown from her horse into the snow.[72] Such stories of the last Chinese man, imagined as the lonely object of white people's love, befit the websites promoting tourism to the ghost towns of Sierra County.

Through these various mediated voices in the historical record, "Ah Jake" emerges as a series of ethno-racial subjectivities imposed upon him from without. And yet, Ah Jake struggles mightily to be heard above the cacophony of voices that claim to speak for him, even as him, and about him. His agitation in the courtroom—his interjections, his excited speech in Chinglish, and his acting out of the deadly fight with Wah Chuck and Ah Ting on the courtroom floor—reveal his agency, his acts of self-defense on the stage road and before the law. There may not be much more to know about Ah Jake's life and travails or his worldview. But the traces of history apprehended from his trial and pardon, when considered within the frame of transpacific circulations of people, language, and organization, produce new knowledge about social relations in the late-nineteenth-century California interior.

CHAPTER 8

Creative Misunderstandings

CHINESE MEDICINE IN SEVENTEENTH-CENTURY EUROPE

Harold J. Cook

INTRODUCTION

Historians of medicine, no less than others, are facing up to the implications for our subject in light of "global" history. The challenges of thinking about a global history of any kind are very great, but they may be greatest for fields that consider aspects of the history of ideas. Global history is a very important tool for representing connections among people based on the exchange of goods, objects, and specimens, which can flow across cultural borders and be meaningfully reinscribed in new contexts. But while the movement of material things may set the stage for exchanges of knowledge, too, decades of work in cultural studies have taught us that many kinds of knowledge are embedded in practices and languages, remaining meaningful only within the contexts from which they emerge. How "ideas" can move from place to place therefore poses fundamental questions.[1]

In some of my previous historical research and writing, the problem of the mobility of knowledge emerged as something not to be overlooked. In structuring arguments about the development of medicine and science during the Dutch Golden Age, and their connections with commerce, one process that became of most interest was the way in which objects and careful descriptions of them could be easily moved from place to place. The development of the hope for a universal "science" that would apply to all times and places arose in part from processes that gave careful attention to exotic *naturalia*, which were stripped of cultural context when imported to Europe. While the people who interacted with such things in situ endowed them with rich associations, Dutch investigators in the Indies and in the home country, who wrote for an international audience, focused their attention on carefully conveying their materialistic aspects, describing their physical substance and appearance, and medicinal and culinary benefits, and little else. Objects and information about them moved readily, but local discourses about their meanings and associations did not.

For instance, the physician Jacobus Bontius, who resided in the new capital of the Dutch East India Company (VOC), Batavia (now Jakarta), in the late 1620s and early 1630s, wrote several manuscripts on the medicine and natural history of the East Indies that were published posthumously in the 1640s. In these works, he describes plants and animals carefully, often having fine drawings of them made that also appeared in one of them. His investigations relied on local informants for information about their behaviors and uses. He came to admire the people of the region for the enormous fund of knowledge they possessed, even publicly defending them against some compatriots' accusations that they were "barbarians" or worse (and doing so shortly after the virtual extermination of the people of the Banda Islands by the Dutch in the interest of monopolizing the trade in nutmeg). But at the same time, he stripped away what he considered the "superstitions" that his informants associated with the objects of his interest. Nor did Bontius ever comment on the explanations that he must have heard about how various substances worked their healthful effects. Bontius's implicitly materialist information about the objects and substances of the East Indies was easily understood anywhere people had access to his words and pictures, but it conveyed little of their local meanings.[2]

Erasure of some kinds of knowledge in the process of transporting other kinds of knowledge was not the only process at work, however. So, too, were examples of what now look like failed attempts by Dutch authors to understand the views of their interlocutors. An example of this comes from the work of a very well-educated young physician, Willem ten Rhijne, who had been sent by the VOC to Japan in the expectation that he would become a physician to the Shogun. Ten Rhijne resided at Deshima, the Dutch station in Nagasaki, for two years.[3] He had with him at least one Chinese medical text, including authentic diagrams of the channels and points "which," he later wrote, "had long been neglected and ignored through want of an interpreter." Ten Rhijne "made every effort to meet a Japanese physician . . . with a knowledge of Chinese" in order to understand the manuscript. Therefore, in the course of answering many questions about medicine that were put to him by Japanese physicians and officials, he reversed the questioning. One of his interlocutors, Iwanaga Sōko, who had been trained in Chinese medicine, did his best to translate the texts into Japanese, and one of the chief interpreters, Shōdayū Motogi, then did his best to render the result into Dutch. There were no dictionaries for such a process, so they proceeded by discussion, during which there must have been countless frustrations about making sense of one another's words. Ten Rhijne then transformed what he heard into Latin.[4] Consequently, while ten Rhijne gleaned elements of a brief account of the history and practice of medicine in East Asia, given his method of working, and the peculiar Romanization of Chinese names with Japanese pronunciation, he offered far from a transparent translation. Indeed, it is not yet even clear what the original text was from which the "translation" was made.[5]

Thus, some kinds of knowledge, such as information units that point to material things, can move readily, while other kinds are sticky. "Medicine" includes both. Medicinal substances and instructions on their administration can be transported from place to place relatively easily, while the assumptions about well-being, illness, and treatment in one part of the world are not easily transported to another. The latter are framed in words that depend on language, upbringing, repertoire of expression and gesture, ways of life, artifacts, expectations, and even ideas that make up the frameworks we often term "culture." It is notoriously difficult to explain a culture to another person who has not lived in it, even when the person knows something of the language. While it is certainly possible to look for underlying commonalities among peoples and cultures, the main interpretive method in the humanities and ethnographically inspired social sciences during the late twentieth century was to stress differences. The stimulating recent work of Geoffrey Lloyd is a fine example of the kinds of problems raised by contrasting the quest for human similarities (often framed as a shared biology) or our different upbringings (often framed as distinct cultures) that are important in, say, color perception or emotional expression.[6]

The history of cultures approach is also very able in showing how silence, avoidance, subordination, misunderstanding, and negotiation might be as important as conflict and coercion. But it has also accepted that in differences of expression lurks "incommensurability" (to use a word adopted from philosophers of science Thomas Kuhn and Paul Feyerabend).[7] Originally meaning the absence of a common measure that would allow comparison—the absence of the Euclidian proposition that, say, the length of a line can be measured by a series of congruent segments—the term was used to indicate the fundamental difference between one scientific worldview and another: one could not get one set of results from the propositions of the other system, so that the results depend not only on matters such as experimental findings but also on the assumptions of the theories by which they are measured. The application of incommensurability rapidly made its way into many discussions of problems where no common agreement among basic propositions exists. According to some lines of argument, cultures, too, may be incommensurable, making meaningful "translation" between patterns of expression impossible.

An example of an argument for fundamental differences between East Asian and Western European medical practices has been made brilliantly by Shigehisa Kuriyama, in his *The Expressiveness of the Body and the Divergence of Greek and Chinese Medicine* (1999). He examined a practice that seems common to both but turns out to be very different: the "pulse." When Europeans examined Chinese medical methods, they thought they saw practitioners "feel the pulse." This is one among many aspects of "Chinese medicine" that seem to be "just like" classical medicine in Europe before the so-called scientific revolution.[8] But, Kuriyama argues, Europeans who felt the pulse and Chinese who felt the *mo* were experiencing their bodies and their clients' bodies in very different ways. Literate European practitioners understood the body in terms of its solid anatomy, whereas literate Chinese practitioners had a geographical understanding of its changes. The two were therefore attentive to different bodily experiences and oriented toward different interpretative statements of their meanings; consequently they also touched differently. "By the evidence of the eyes, *qiemo*, palpating the *mo*, was unmistakably pulse diagnosis. Chinese writings [however,] testified that the eyes were wrong. The hermeneutics of the *Mojue* were unlike any dialect of the pulse language known in Europe." He goes on to ask, "How can gestures look the same, yet differ entirely in the experience?" Since people had different experiences of embodiment, the explanations they offered for their actions were incompatible. Or, as many Europeans of the time were wont to say, Chinese explanations about their methods—something many people referred to as their "philosophy," as we would now speak of their "theory"—were not simply "mistaken," but were "ridiculous," "phantastical," "chaotic," or "absurd."[9] To Kuriyama, in these differences there is incommensurability: that is, the European and Chinese understandings of the pulse were each necessarily uncomprehending of the other, because the framework of each was based on fundamentally different kinds of evidence and interpretation.

The interconnections among peoples to which global history directs our attention therefore certainly require exploration, but a part of that attentiveness must be given to the variety of kinds of knowledge that are transported or are not. As a working hypothesis we might say that some kinds of knowledge move relatively easily from place to place because it is about objects. The meanings attached to the objects in the places of their origin can be neglected or silenced (although some meanings—such as their "exotic" origin—may move with them despite the silencing). Other kinds of knowledge are stickier, such as when one enters into the process of translation, especially in cases where one or more of the languages is unfamiliar.[10] It may even be that full and transparent interchanges of this kind are impossible because of underlying incommensurabilities. Yet, as with the example of ten Rhijne, people often attempt to overcome the differences despite the difficulties and misunderstandings. The reappropriation of distant knowledge is therefore a creative and meaningful process deserving investigation in its own right. Even when they do not replicate the original in another language, the results can be meaningful and influential. Even misunderstandings have consequences.

My method below takes two main lines of interpretation for exploring such problems. One is to use the "global" as a way to explore many interconnected microhistories. The global history that emerged in the 1990s was distinct from most of the forms of world history that came before, mainly because it took both economic and interactive histories as its focus. It no longer was meant to be a comparative history of civilizations or places, but "connected" history, as Sanjay Subrahmanyam would term it, or *histoire croisée* and similar terms in other languages, in which changes in one place affected changes in another.[11] An early version had been Immanuel Wallerstein's "world-system" approach, which explained the development of Europe's economic domination in terms of its maritime enterprises in interaction with, and sometimes even dependence on, people of the "peripheries."[12] Much of his evidence drew on, and further stimulated, a great number of outstanding studies of European trade around the early modern Indian Ocean.[13] With a rising tide of suspicion about Eurocentrism, however, it became clear that the "center" of such trade was not Europe but the lands around the Indian Ocean and South China Sea, which were of course connected to the rest of the world.[14] The interactive aspects of the economies of different places therefore demanded more and more attention. A consequence was a wider adoption of the view made clear by Arjun Appadurai in *Modernity at Large* (1996): the "global" is made up of many "locals."[15] Then, in the late 1990s, several works gained widespread attention for arguing that the main stimulus for world trade in the early modern period was China: R. Bin Wong's *China Transformed: Historical Change and the Limits of European Experience* (1997), Andre Gunder Frank's *ReOrient: Global Economy in the Asian Age* (1999), and Kenneth Pomeranz's *The Great Divergence: China, Europe, and the Making of the Modern World Economy* (2000).[16] The first two studies sought to demonstrate that Eurocentric social theory of either the Marxist or Weberian kind had failed to understand the ways in which regions such as China functioned, both as imperial realms and as economic systems. In their works, however, "China" is not so much a nation as a region of interconnected trading zones and ethnic groups competing for power, like "Europe," although unlike Europe the empire discouraged armed violence as a method of competition.[17]

In foregrounding the material foundations of large patterns of history, and in shifting attention from the development of European power to a more interactionist model of change, global histories have been both iconoclastic and productive. The new "global" history, therefore, had three legs. It set its face against histories of civilizations and ideological formations, even those that made culture primary, in favor of material interactions as the chief causes of change. It self-consciously treated the nation-state, too, as a political artifact rather than a natural geographical or cultural unit. And, at least for the period before the Industrial Revolution, it placed East Asia at the center of the story rather than Europe. It has been attentive to the eruptive geographies of sea-borne commerce and to the inland "sea" of the Central Asian steppe (the "Silk Road"), rather than to the agricultural lands of long-settled populations. The best examples of the new global histories explicitly reject the kinds of essentialist comparisons that require anyone to group people according civilizations. There are large regions and millions of people in view, but while they may be approached according to one grouping or another, they live in often eclectic mixtures. In each region, there are diverse languages and cultures, rather than single ethnic or ideological totalities. In other words, the examples from the new global histories are mobility and interaction. They do not presume unitary cultures or civilizations, but allow for multiple ones coexisting within the same domain. In all these ways and more, global history has stimulated much rethinking about patterns of historical change, with the small scale as important as the large.

But when one puzzles about interactions among peoples that might be termed ideological or even intellectual, global history poses serious challenges. The vision of a global movement of peoples and goods has plenty of space in it for the exchange of certain kinds of information, but not much for the history of concepts, much less ideologies or even experiences. The exchange of people, practices, information, and goods—and diseases—via merchants, missionaries, soldiers, and the like has clearly been important. The major actors in such transactions were, after all, neither nation-states nor "civilizations," but travelers, intermediaries, and brokers of various kinds.[18] Yet their ability to convey culture-bound "ideas" is far from clear. Analysis must therefore be explored at the level of persons and their interactions as well as at the level of collective processes, and we must expect misinformation and misunderstanding to be as important as transparency.

The second method that I employ below is to explore the process of appropriation of knowledge from afar not by way of a developmental narrative but by a process of excavation. This account begins with the work of an English physician of the early eighteenth century, Sir John Floyer, who is well known to have taken a keen interest in Chinese pulse taking as a part of his own attempts to develop novel methods of diagnosis and treatment. It reports on his work and views, and then explores the sources on which he drew, moving to the seventeenth century in time and to East Asia in place. In so doing, we can see what many others were doing without presuming that history is teleological. Instead, it is enough to assume that people make use of the materials available to them, and even sometimes try to find new materials, in constructing accounts for their own purposes of the moment. They do so not knowing the full story of how those materials came into being nor why, and so borrowing and using words in ways that had not necessarily been intended by the earlier authors. This is a method often employed in comparative literature and other subject areas, and seems especially helpful here as a way to avoid a forward-looking narrative when each step was entangled in a multiplicity of interacting interests and opinions.

So to the problem at hand: in the historical record there are many attempts to obtain a comprehension of other views. It is especially notable in cases where someone in one part of the world sought knowledge of someplace else. Such efforts often presented serious difficulties for the persons attempting mastery of the distant, and may have led to as much or more misinformation and misunderstanding as comprehension. Among such efforts were exchanges between East Asian and European scholars about those aspects of knowledge we term science, technology, and medicine, as well as attempts by still others to draw on the result of such exchanges for their own purposes. The understandings and misunderstandings of such quests have left their legacy in various languages even today. When coining terminology to convey the chemical language of Lavoissier into Japanese, for instance, scholars borrowed words from Buddhist and other kinds of religious and philosophical traditions that brought their own implications.[19] Similarly, as we will see below, when translating Chinese medical terms into European languages, Jesuit authors borrowed from an ancient and medieval language of bodily powers such as the *humidum radicale* (for *yin*) or *calidum innatum* (for *yang*). The results may have been incomplete and even misleading; but they nevertheless sometimes lead to creative responses. If the global approach toward examining connected histories is worth adopting but has only begun to examine the ways in which information and meaning were conveyed from place to place, then having another look at the early modern attempts by Europeans to understand Chinese medical ideas and practices may be illuminating.

SIR JOHN FLOYER AND THE DEFENSE OF CHINESE MEDICINE

A good example of a European response to East Asian medical ideas comes from Sir John Floyer's enthusiastic advocacy for his new method of diagnosing disease from counting the beats of the pulse. At the beginning of the eighteenth century, Floyer was a physician living in Litchfield, in the English midlands north of Birmingham. Samuel Johnson enthusiasts know him as the doctor who, when the young boy was suffering from scrofula, recommended he travel to London to obtain the royal touch from Queen Anne. Like Johnson, he was probably a Tory, having been granted a knighthood in 1684, no doubt due to his support for James during the succession crisis. He was certainly patriotic in arguing that the greatest physician ever had been William Harvey. But during these years of often bitter medical and scientific disputes Floyer was no simple conservative, instead thinking of himself as a major innovator, advocating cold water bathing and new treatments for asthma, for instance. One might imagine that his main aim was to bring the new science of his day, including an interest in both quantitative reasoning and natural history, to the support of individualist and classically oriented medicine. In this way, he was supportive of utilitarian novelties while hoping to build on and preserve what he considered to be the best traditions of his profession.[20]

Floyer is well known for being an advocate for counting the beats of the pulse as a diagnostic method with direct implications for therapy and, in making a case for his new system, for allying himself with concepts and methods from China as well as from classical antiquity.[21] In aligning himself with practices he described as four thousand years old, he was demonstrating how he had found the key to unlocking an almost eternal set of medical truths. In that sense, it does not matter whether his interpretations of Chinese texts on the pulse were correct or authentic, only that he was creating a view of the subject that could help persuade readers of his (English) text. At the same time, Floyer was investing considerable effort in trying to acquire accurate information about Chinese methods of taking the pulse—already made famous by travel writers—and to read and interpret the available Latin texts on the subject, which were in turn translations from Chinese. While Floyer's story is well known for his reformation of pulse taking and genuflection to China and Greece, it is worth another look at his interpretative practices before turning to a further examination of the Latin texts he relied upon. Floyer's methods and interpretations give a revealing picture of how one culture might have effects on another, even when the translation of concepts was not a simple one-to-one movement.

Floyer announced his new method in 1707, in *The Physicians' Pulse-Watch*, which set out both a new method of practice and a new invention.[22] The invention was a watch with a hand that circled the dial in sixty seconds, in effect introducing the second-hand mechanism, which Floyer had commissioned from the London clockmaker Samuel Watson. It had become a necessary adjunct to his new clinical method. Floyer had for some years tried to measure the time during various treatments such as his method of preventative and curative cold bathing (which had already become a subject of some controversy). He also began to measure the number of beats of the pulse per minute. Measuring the time accurately proved to be a challenge. Initially, he had referred to the minute hand on common watches and pendulum clocks in the homes of his patients before hitting on the more accurate "common Sea-Minute Glass" (a kind of hourglass for measuring a half minute when heaving out the log from a ship in order to count the knots).[23] The sea glass was not portable, however, so he "caused a Pulse-Watch to be made which run 60 Seconds, and I placed it in a Box to be more easily carried, and by this I now feel Pulses." (He found that the watch ran a bit faster than his minute glass, so he regulated it by adding five or six to the number of pulse beats counted by the watch.)[24]

The reason Floyer sought to measure the number of beats of the pulse grew from his interest in finding clear and apparent signs of natural changes in the body that would be diagnostic and allow successful remedies for disease. He stood among the many physicians of his day who thought of disease as a falling away from the rightly balanced state of well-being rather than as a thing in itself that needed to be fought off.[25] That is, when it came to understanding illness, he stood in the "physiological" rather than the "ontological" camp.[26] Perhaps his interest in cold water bathing as a method of treatment arose from the contemporary enthusiasm for both drinking and bathing in mineral waters, since in his 1697 book on the subject he comments on his methods for analyzing the waters. There he also briefly described the action of hot and cold baths on the pulse.[27] By 1702, when he published a work strongly advocating the use of cold baths, he had clearly begun to explore the effects of cold, hot, and many other qualities and environmental influences, using the pulse as the chief indicator of the physiological state of the patient.[28] By the time of the *Pulse-Watch*, he was able to provide a series of "tables" indicating the varying number of beats of the pulse per minute according to the degree of latitude, age of the patent, time of day, fasting or full stomach, hot or cold diet, and so on.[29]

Using the pulse as a diagnostic sign was a long-standing tradition in European medicine. Galen had considered the study of the pulse (sphygmology) to be the most important of all diagnostic methods, devoting sixteen books to the subject.[30] At the time of Floyer's youth, it was still important. In a 1662 English partial translation of Jean Fernel's famous oeuvre, taking the pulse remained as fundamental to diagnosis as examining urines. The two "declare diseases what they are, for the Pulse shews the Constitution of the Heart, and Arteries, and the Urine declares the Constitution of the Liver, and the veins, by the administration of which the whol body is governed." By that time, a rich and ambiguous language had accreted for expressing the variety of kinds of pulses. They could be ordinate or inordinate; equal or unequal; recurrent or intercurrent; soft or hard; robust and vehement, or weak and faint; small or full; "often" or infrequent; stretched, wave-like, vibrant, trembling, serrant, or convulsive; or formicant (ant-like), vermiculant (worm-like), myurus (mouse-tailed), or caprizant (uneven)—and many other things as well.[31] One of Floyer's chief concerns was to clarify the enormously complex qualitative language of the pulse used around him by applying a quantitative measure.[32] Using his pulse watch to count the number of beats per minute, Floyer reclassified pulses into three basic kinds, rapid (hot), slow (cold), and irregular ("cacochymic"), with only a few further subdivisions. As he later boasted, "The Art of feeling the Pulse, which I have propos'd . . . 'tis short, easie, and more certain than the Galenical or Chinese Art, because it requires no more than counting of the Pulse, and observing the time by the Pulse-Watch; this will shew the Disease of the Fluids, that is, of the Blood and Spirits; and the Method to raise or sink the Pulse."[33]

Contained in that last phrase about his "Method to raise or sink the Pulse" was what Floyer considered to be the most important part of his discovery: it was no mere diagnostic technique but a means to accurate treatment. In this sense Floyer thought of himself as imitating the Chinese, who were reputed to use the pulse in treatment as well as diagnosis. The rapidity of the pulse indicated the state of a person's circulation, which was for Floyer, as a Harveian, the seat of all physiological processes. Therefore, once the state of a person's physiology had been found, any underlying problems could be treated by prescribing a regimen that would work by contraries to bring the patient's physiology back to a golden mean.[34] He even imagined that "Dr. [William] Harvey did design a Tract about the Pulse, as he intimates, which if he had done he would have pursu'd his Scheme, and drawn it into Practice" along the lines that Floyer had discovered.[35] Accordingly, "the exceeding Pulses will require the cool Tastes, and the deficient Pulses indicate the hot Tastes." But, he also recognized, "by this Method we shall imitate the Chinese Practice."[36] It was in the close bond between feeling the pulse and treating diseases that Floyer thought he was imitating the Chinese. "The Greeks used their ars sphugmon for Prognostications chiefly, and also a part of the Semiotica; but the Chinese also have made that a part of their Therapeutics, as well as of the other; for from the Pulse they take their Indications for cure, in which they excell'd the Greeks." Put another way, by counting the pulse Floyer believed he had made a great advance on the classical systems of pulse taking, but when he tied his new method of semiotics to therapeutics, and "reflected on what I had done, I found my Notions hit with the *Chinese* Practice."[37]

At first, he had little material about Chinese medicine to hand. But he had enough to draw his conclusions. He wrote the *Pulse-Watch* in three parts: the first corrected the Galenic method of "feeling the pulse" in light of his method of counting the beats; the second explained his "mechanical" method of treating diseases according to measuring the indications of the pulse; and the last described "The Chinese Art of Feeling the Pulse" and recommended practicing in imitation of their methods. To compose the third section, "I consulted many Printed Travels."[38] He reported, for instance, that "Samedo the Portugueze commends them for their Skill," while "Farther [*sic*] le Counte says, That a Chinese Emperor writ about the Pulse 4292 Years ago, since which the Chinese have been Famous for Pulses."[39] It is surprising that he does not mention one of the most widely read works on China, the book of Athanasius Kircher best known by its short title, *China Illustrata* (1667)—who summarizes the views of Semedo—but perhaps at the time, with the Catholic "Pretender" posing a real threat to the British government, Floyer was hiding his reliance on a Jesuit source.[40] He made much more of information he drew from the 1669 English translation of Jan Nieuhof's very influential and lavishly illustrated Dutch book on China, *An Embassy from the East India Company of the United Provinces to the Grand Tartar Cham Emperor of China* (1665).[41] Nieuhof provided information on many aspects of Chinese society, including medicine. They are "very skilful in discovering by the [pulse] the inward distempers of the Body," he explained. Practitioners "take notice of six different beatings" of the pulse in each wrist. "And therefore that they may with the greater constancy and judgment deliver their opinions, they are at least half an hour in feeling the Pulse of the Sick." Once the pulse has revealed the illness, "then for the Curing of the Sick, they apply and make use of several Simples and Roots; to say the truth, they are generally very well experienced in the knowledge of the several Vertues of all kinds of Herbs growing amongst them."[42] While it is not clear that any of these sources explicitly state that the Chinese attentiveness to taking the pulse was directly tied to their therapeutics, Nieuhof implied it, and no doubt so did other travel writers.

In such medical examples we can begin to glimpse the more general interest in China taken by many Europeans of the late seventeenth and eighteenth centuries. Historians have long remarked on the popularity of Asian matters in various aspects of European life at the time, especially for their effects on food, fashion, architecture, and garden design.[43] We might also include medicine, especially with the growing popularity of tea drinking. As Floyer himself suggested, "I suppose my Readers will be pleas'd to Practice according to the Chinese Mode, as well as to adorn their Houses with their curious Manufactures, and to use their Diet of

Thea."[44] While the fashion for so-called Chinoiserie included influences from throughout maritime Asia, from Persia to today's India, Southeast Asia, and Japan, China figured most heavily in European accounts of Asia. Because it was especially esteemed for its ancient textual heritage and its apparently peaceful and stable government, China became of special interest to those debating various kinds of philosophical and natural knowledge. As early as 1642 (in his *Vertu des payens*), François La Mothe le Vayer praised the natural religion of China as even better than that of Rome, Greece, and Egypt, and included Confucius (along with Socrates and Plato) among the virtuous pagans he refused to condemn to the fires of hell.[45] He and others came to rely mainly on evidence produced for a European audience by the Jesuit mission in China begun by Matteo Ricci, in works such as Nicholas Trigault's 1615 book on China.[46] By the 1660s a growing body of work about China was becoming available in Latin and in the vernacular.[47] Fragments of learned Chinese texts themselves also appeared including the *Sapientia Sinica* in 1662 and *Sinarum scientia politico-moralis* in 1667–69 (the latter was given a French translation by Melchisédec Thévenot in his *Relations de divers voyages curieux* in 1672).[48] In 1687 access to a Latin version of the main "philosophical" sources for the learning of the mandarins became possible with the publication by the Jesuits (under the patronage of Louis XIV) of a luxurious folio edition of the "Confucian" "Four Books." This, the *Confucius Sinarum Philosophus*, affirmed the Jesuit view of Confucius as one of the *prisci theologii*, or one of the earliest teachers of God's revealed moral, theological, and natural laws, long prior to His coming in the form of Christ.[49] This edition of Confucius's works was in turn soon translated into several vernacular European languages.[50]

Indeed, given the richness of the sources on the views of the Chinese literati and the verifiable antiquity of Chinese texts, many European savants came to take a keen interest in "China," with fierce debates soon raging, in particular about the extent to which Chinese learning might represent a modern vestige of almost Adamic antiquity, about the possibility that it represented the pinnacle of knowledge gained according to natural reason, and about the goodness of the apparent philosopher's kingdom.[51] It was from having an impression of such sources (although he does not quote from them directly) that Floyer was able to spend many pages on "A Short Account of the Chinese Phylosophy" in the third part of his book. He explained that "In the beginning they say the World was produc'd out of a Universal Substance, which they call Chaos or Vacuum, and that they call Li; out of this arose an Air call'd Kie [modern *qi*], which by Motion, Heat and Rarification, or Cold, Rest and Condensation, produc'd five Elements. . . . This Phylosophy makes Matter eternal, as the Greeks; and that the World was produc'd by Chance, and govern'd by Fate; and that at first all Things were produc'd out of Matter, and are reducible into the same, so that all Things are one. . . . Since this Philosophy is like that of the Epicureans, our Western Philosophers do not exceed the Chinese Literati, who went as far as Reason could lead them in the Production of the World" without access to revelation.[52] In explaining all this and more Floyer was repeating the general consensus that had grown up in Europe.[53]

Initially, Floyer's best evidence about Chinese medicine per se came from William Wotton, surprisingly enough. Wotton had looked into the topic in order to refute Sir William Temple's admiration for Chinese philosophy, as stated in his essay *Of Heroic Virtue* (1690). There Temple had repeated the view that Chinese "physicians excel in the knowledge of the pulse, and of all simple medicines," although they went "little further; but in the first [they] are so skilful, as they pretend not only to tell by it, how many hours or days a sick man can last, but how many years a man in perfect seeming health may live, in case of no accident or violence. And by simples they pretend to relieve all diseases that nature will allow to be cured. They never let blood."[54] Wotton, however, had nothing but contempt for such opinions, and his *Reflections upon Ancient and Modern Learning* (1694) trumpeted the superiority of modern European thought. If Chinese learning was so outstanding, why were Jesuits held in high regard for teaching the emperor and other learned men astronomy and other things they should have known? But Wotton was particularly scathing about the silliness of Chinese medical theory and its methods of taking the pulse, giving long quotations from Chinese medical texts as evidence of their confusion. To do so, he quoted passages from Andreas Cleyer's *Specimen Medicinae Sinicae, sive Opuscula Medica ad Mentem Sinensium* (The Pattern of Chinese Medicine, or Medical Work According to Chinese Thought) of 1682, which had printed some translations and commentaries. "It would be tedious to dwell any longer upon such Notions as these [that] every Page in Cleyer's Book is full of," he concluded. Clearly, Wotton considered that no truth was contained in the Chinese texts, only fancies, for "The Anatomical Figures annexed to the Tracts, which also were sent out of China, are so very whimsical, that a Man would almost believe the whole to be a Banter, if these Theories were not agreeable to the occasional Hints that may be found in the Travels of the Missionaries."[55] How could they be taken seriously?

Floyer jumped to the defense of Chinese medicine. He began when he had only the quotations from Cleyer's *Specimen* that were published in Wotton's book. Being already well disposed to the reputation of Chinese physicians for their knowledge of the pulse, Floyer ingeniously contradicted Wotton by explaining what bodily phenomena their words must have been intended to indicate. Floyer compared them to the ancients.

He found "as much natural Philosophy in their Writings, as was in *Hippocrates*, in *Plato's* and *Aristotle's* Time, and their Anatomy was not more Exact that the *Chinese*. In this discourse quoted from *Cleyer*, I find good Sense, tho' express'd in the *Asiatic* way, whose Words are sorts of Hieroglyphicks, as well as their Characters; and their Expressions are fitter for Poetry and Oratory, than Phylosophy; the *Asiatics* have a gay luxurious Imagination, but the *Europeans* excel in reasoning and Judgment, and clearness of Expression." From Wotton's quotations, then, he extracted an interpretation of the three "high" pulses, which were related to various organs. The first, for example, described the liver, from which "the Sanguine Temper is described, and the Spirits of the Liver or Blood move the Nerves, and make a full and great pulse."[56] Then he gave a rationale for the three "low" pulses, and so on. From such a reinterpretation, he drew the conclusion that for Chinese physicians all diseases were due to a too rapid or too languid circulation of the blood, with the same for the animal spirits, and from this understanding of the pulse they had therefore developed their cures.[57]

He could not, however, lay his hands on a copy of the book from which Wotton had quoted, Cleyer's *Specimen Medicinae Sinicae*, "till these Papers were Printing ."[58] What he was searching out was the best known of the three books then available in Europe containing translations of Chinese medical texts. According to a note on the flyleaf of the copy Floyer later gave to Queen's College, Oxford, he finally obtained it on January 16, 1703, as a gift from "the Honourable Charles Hatton," a collector of works on the natural history of Asia, among other topics.[59] Presuming the date and comment about the printing of the *Pulse-Watch* are correct, Floyer must have made a serious attempt to master Chinese views of the pulse, stopping the press for about three years while he attempted to make medical sense in his own terms of the material in Cleyer's book. In the final version of his book an appendix in the form of a one-hundred-page letter to Hatton (dated January 1, 1706) reflected these efforts—an addition of comparable length to other sections of the work. Floyer's letter summarized the treatises on the pulse contained in the *Specimen* that had been used by Wotton, with an English translation of some excerpts from it.[60] In it, he boiled down his interpretations to six topics: "1. The Chinese Directions for feeling the Pulse. 2. The Mistakes of the Chinese in this Art. 3. The differences of the Pulse observ'd by the Chinese. 4. The Alterations of the Pulse by the Non-Naturals, and Diseases. 5. The prognostications by the Pulse. 6. The Cure of the Preternatural Pulses by simple Medicines."[61] While he had earlier attributed problems of interpretation to the "Hieroglyphick" manner of expression in Chinese and their "gay luxurious Imagination," after working closely over Cleyer's texts he now attributed the problem to the incomprehension of the translators. But, he concluded, "the Antiquity of this Art of feeling the Pulse . . . seems to be deriv'd from Noah, because the Chinese derive it from their first Kings, 2600 years before our Saviour; they have this Art by Tradition, as well as the Notion of the Circulation, because their Books give no other account of it, nor reason for it, but that they received them from their Predecessors." "All Arts are grounded on a long Experience," he concluded, "and the Chinese have had above 4000 Years Knowledge in this Art," which is why they had become so skilled in it.[62] Floyer continued to work on incorporating what he knew of Chinese sources into an interpretation of the pulse. In the second volume of the *Pulse-Watch*, published three years later, he expanded his views about how diseases are caused by problems of the circulation that can be identified by taking the pulse, concluding with his own synthesis of Greek and Chinese methods.[63]

In other words, one of the important innovations in European medicine of the early eighteenth century—the counting of the beats of the pulse as a diagnostic tool[64]—was seen by its chief advocate as a revision of a medical method that powerfully linked diagnosis and treatment, and which had previously been best practiced by the Chinese, who were representatives of the earliest natural philosophy, and so even had a knowledge of the circulation of the blood coming down almost from the beginnings of human existence.[65] It was a view that Floyer had adopted from the Jesuits.

ACQUIRING KNOWLEDGE OF CHINESE MEDICINE

Floyer had been well disposed to taking a favorable view of Chinese medicine from his earlier general reading, and from his further interpretations derived from Cleyer's work containing direct translation, the *Specimen Medicinae Sinicae*. Not surprisingly, both kinds of sources were heavily influenced by the interpretative program of the Society of Jesus, although other figures were also involved in the efforts to convey Chinese medicine to a European audience. For instance Cleyer's *Specimen* identified its author as a German then in Batavia (now Jakarta), while indicating that many of its parts were by an "erudite European." Nevertheless, as we shall see, the fundamental translations and commentaries originated with Jesuit missionaries in China, although they were assembled and edited by Dutch hands. The *Specimen* was the first and best known of two Latin works on Chinese medicine published in the seventeenth century. The other, the *Clavis Medica ad Chinarum Doctrinam de Pulsibus* (Medical Key to the Chinese Doctrine on the Pulse), was printed in 1686 in the series of the Academia Naturae Curiosorum (later the "Leopoldina"), a "scientific" society founded in 1652 and composed almost entirely of physicians living in the Holy Roman Empire.[66] Its title page correctly identified the author as Michel Boym of the Society of Jesus, who had been a missionary in China. The work had been twenty years in the making, distancing it from Boym's day-to-day experiences and acquisitions in China. The text was largely assembled from fragments by Cleyer with the help of the procurator of the Society of Jesus's China mission, R. P. Philippe Couplet. A third work, *Les secrets de la medecine des Chinois, Consistent en le parfaite connoissance du Pouls* (1671), was not identified with the name of an author or editor, only indicating that it was sent out of China by a French person of "great merit"; but it also contained an "Avis au Lecteur" dated October 21, 1668, from one of the Jesuit missionaries then under house arrest in Canton (Guangzhou).[67] In other words, knowledge of Chinese medicine in a form that could be read in Europe emerged from a program of study within the Jesuit China mission, being assisted at times by members of the VOC and the German scientific community. Much more study of these works is deserved, especially for seeing what kind of information can be found about the necessary collaborations between the Jesuits and their Chinese colleagues.[68] Until such examinations are undertaken, the composition of these works and the language choices made by the translators and commentators will not be well understood. But as a starting point, they can be read in light of the outlook of the Jesuit mission and its need to persuade Europeans to support their efforts to bring China into the Christian fold. Floyer seems to have had no problem with accepting their implicit views about Chinese medicine as one aspect of Chinese natural philosophy.[69]

By the time the Jesuits turned their collective attention to medicine, their policy of "accommodationism," intended to bring China into the Christian orbit, was well developed. All missionaries of course needed to know local languages in order to communicate with those they were trying to convert. In their attempts to bring East Asians into the Christian fold from the first period of Portuguese settlement in Japan and China, Dominican, Franciscan, and Jesuit missionaries, among others, struggled to master new and difficult languages, which were neither perfectly understood nor necessarily capable of carrying meanings transparently back and forth. Inevitably, these linguistic struggles had effects on how the Christian message was spoken and heard.[70] But from the last decade of the sixteenth century, the Jesuits set themselves the additional task of mastering the canon of Chinese literature so as to make themselves equal to the learned mandarins who staffed the offices of government, which they did with the help of well-educated Chinese colleagues, often learned converts. Those efforts enabled the policy of accommodationism, which was, first, an attempt to adapt Christian teachings to the language and customs of China in order to make them unobjectionable to the literati and, second, a philosophically syncretic approach to find the essential commonalities between the various classical texts that formed the basis of the Chinese *ru*, or true learning, and their own Christian religion. Their engagement with Chinese learning involved them in intellectual exchanges and discussions with the literati, and even the imperial court, which in turn opened opportunities to persuade some of the highest-ranking members of the government of the truth of Christianity. At the same time, however, these efforts led both to dangerous accusations from rivals at the imperial court and to charges from within the Catholic Church that in their willingness to adapt Christian doctrine to local orientations they were altering essential tenets of the true faith. At the end of the seventeenth century this "rites" controversy would cause a break with the emperor of China and threaten the very existence of the order.[71]

In the meantime, the philosophical orientation of accommodationism can be noted in the Jesuits' reliance on both Thomistic views of natural reason and widespread assumptions at the time of a *prisca theologia*.[72] They took the general view that the Chinese lacked only God's revelations and the teaching of Christ and his apostles to see the full truth of things. (Floyer echoed this sentiment in his comment that Chinese literati "went as far as Reason could lead them in the Production of the World, 'tis only Revelation, which can discover the true Philosophy of the Creation, and the Nature of the God who made all Things," that was superior.)[73] The Jesuits identified the ancient teacher of the true natural philosophy as a figure from the beginning of Chinese history, Kongzi, whose name they Latinized as "Confutius" or Confucius, arguing that all the other texts, authors, and commentators took their principles from his original insights, just as in Europe it was argued that the Egyptian Hermes Trismegistus, sometimes identified with Moses, had been the first lawgiver, philosopher, and priest, from whom all learning had descended. As the Jesuit polymath Athanasius Kircher would put it, "The most ancient and indigenous Chinese sect is the literati, which rules this kingdom, has many books, and is more praised than the others. They acknowledge Confucius as the author or chief of philosophers, just as the Egyptians do Thoyt [Thoth], whom the Greeks call Hermes Trismegistos."[74] The Jesuits also applied their philological expertise to Chinese literary history, making persuasive arguments about how missing texts could be reconstructed and others re-edited to bring out the essential meaning of *ru*, shaping what was arguably a multitudinous textual tradition into a single harmonious system. In other words, the Jesuits assembled a kind of "Confucian monotheism," which they tried to enrich by adding Christian teaching to it.[75]

The Jesuit mission was in turn deliberative in their conveyance of European learning into Chinese.[76] Because of their mastery of both European mathematical sciences and classical Chinese, they famously managed to gain a place in the office that annually established the calendar, which was fundamental to the sacerdotal functions of the emperor, and which provided a framework of hope for conversion at the very top. But while the Jesuits are understandably best known for their work in astronomy and mathematics, they also took an interest in medicine.[77] For instance, Johann Schreck, known as Terrentius, who joined the Jesuit order in 1611 and soon the China mission, had studied medicine in Paris, Montpellier, Bologna, and Rome, and had been a member of the Italian scientific academy, the Lincei, for whom he worked on an edition of the natural history of New Spain. While in China he began to gather a botanical compilation of over five hundred plants previously unknown in Europe and, working in Hangzhou with Li Chih Tsao, composed a work in Chinese on human anatomy inspired by his friend, Caspar Bauhin.[78]

While efforts to translate their own knowledge into Chinese occupied the Jesuits almost from the first, they began to publish Chinese works in Latin only in the later seventeenth century.[79] In this effort, medical knowledge played a large part. Michel Boym (who appeared on the *Clavis*'s title page) took a lead in this effort, although his efforts were bound up with a tragic story. Originally from Lwów, he shipped out to the Far East in 1642 on Portuguese trading routs, stopping at Mozambique on the way, and, after mastering spoken and written Chinese in Macao, was the chief Jesuit envoy for Tongkin and Hainan, in the south.[80] The region destined him for a difficult road. When the Manchus took over Beijing in 1644, establishing the Qing (or Ch'ing) dynasty, the remnants of the Ming government (including several high-ranking Christian converts), persisted in the southern Chinese provinces, and even reconquered Canton and other areas in 1648. Boym was asked to carry letters to Rome asking for assistance, effectively serving as an ambassador from the Ming court to the pope. Shortly after Boym and two converts set out for Rome in late 1650, however, the Qing recaptured Canton and soon drove the last of the Ming forces into the southwest, making an ambassador from the old regime unwelcome to Portuguese officials in Asia. Finding his way frequently obstructed, it took Boym's group two years of travel by sea and land to get to the Levant, from where Boym continued on to Venice, from where he slipped into Rome with Venetian and French help. He spent 1652 to 1655 cooling his heels while various officials and councils considered how the pope should respond to the letters he delivered. His return journey proved no smoother. Boym set out in 1656 for Lisbon and then Goa along with several young recruits to the Jesuit mission who would later also engage in translations—especially Philip Couplet and Prospero Intorcetta—then, because of a Dutch blockade, the party proceeded overland for the Bay of Bengal, and on to Siam (which he reached at the beginning of 1658). Since he carried letters for the Ming and so remained unwelcome by Portuguese officials, it took him some months further to find a ship to Tonkin, from where he at last found a way to travel to the Ming court in southwest China. He found the passes of Guangxi blocked by Manchus, however, and while trying to find a way around, he fell ill and died, in August 1659.

But while working in the southern Chinese provinces in the 1640s, Boym had also occupied himself with acquiring a knowledge of Chinese natural history and medicine. When in Rome he and his Chinese companion, Andreas Zheng, were instrumental in helping the famous Jesuit polymath Athanasius Kircher to acquire information about east Asia, which later resulted in a remarkable book known as Kircher's *China Illustrata* (1667). It included a section on the discovery of a Christian Nestorian monument from the eighth century CE in "Hsi-an Fu" (modern Xian or Xi'an), which was brought to the attention of the Jesuits in the 1620s: it was this early Christian connection that first motivated Kircher's study of China.[81] One of the authors cited by Floyer, Father Semedo, was the first to see and describe the stele, and he was quoted by Kircher, but Boym and Zheng brought Kircher a more detailed description of the monument, and possibly the rubbing of the Syriac and Chinese texts on it that was later displayed in Kircher's museum.[82] Boym and Zheng worked up a transcription of the Chinese text in numbered columns, providing a Romanization and translation of it in word-for-word order, as well as a more fluent interpretation, which Kircher published in his book and which in the imagination of many European scholars became a kind of Rosetta Stone, the "clavis Sinica" to unlock the meanings contained in Chinese characters.[83]

But while in Rome Boym also completed a work of his own on the natural history of China, the *Flora Sinensis* (1656), and was working on several other projects, including one on medicine.[84] In 1654, he published an account of his embassy, to which he attached an appendix outlining seven studies he was readying for the press, including the *Flora Sinensis*.[85] The maps of China and the Latin account of the China mission that he promised have been identified, the latter of which included his opinion that the Chinese could not only diagnose but predict the course of a disease according to the pulse and that they also had many herbs and herbal medicines unknown to Europeans.[86] He also had in hand an account of the moral philosophy of the Chinese (*Moralis Philosophia Sinarum*), which was most likely a version of the work later published in 1662 as *Sapientia Sinica* (with Ignatius da Costa and Prospero Intorcetta named as editors) and modified in 1667 as *Sinarum scientia politico-*

moralis (with Intorcetta as editor). Perhaps not surprisingly for the son of a physician, he was also preparing a work on Chinese medicine with special attention to their ability not only to diagnose disease but to treat by touching the pulse—the program that had excited Floyer's imagination.[87] Like the work on moral philosophy, however, Boym took it along with him for further study and consultation when he returned to China. On that journey he was accompanied by a new recruit, Intorcetta, who, after Boym's death, became the editor of one of the projects; another of his companions on the return journey, Phillippe Couplet, would be named as an editor of Boym's book on the pulse. Both works no doubt underwent further work by members of the China mission after Boym's death before they were finally ready for the press.

The story of how two medical works originating with Boym returned to Europe is also full of incident.[88] The first, the *Clavis*, was actually published second. On their separate travels from Goa to China, Couplet and Boym met briefly in Siam during 1658, during which time another one of the young missionaries, Ignatius Hartogvelt, died; via the Dutch VOC, Couplet sent some of Hartogvelt's things back home, and at the same time, he also included some of Boym's materials on Chinese pulse methods in the package directed to VOC officials in Batavia. According to a letter of 1687 from Couplet, Boym intended them to be published, but because the VOC blamed the Jesuits for their failure to secure trading rights in China, they were not sent on to Europe.[89] They ended up in the hands of the VOC's chief medical officer, Cleyer. But then from the end of 1681 to early 1683 Couplet himself stopped in Batavia on his return to Europe (as procurator to gather renewed support for the mission), and spent time with Cleyer; he apparently came across Boym's papers again. With Cleyer's support—the latter was by then a member of the Academia Naturae Curiosorum, which printed them—they appeared in 1686 as the *Clavis*. That book contained three letters about Chinese medicine from Boym, dated Siam, 1658, two other prefaces (probably also by Boym), a seventeen-chapter treatise on the pulse in Chinese medicine, and six woodcut illustrations.[90] There seems no reason to doubt that, as the title page says, this latter work is Boym's work as collected by Cleyer and revised by Couplet.

But the *Specimen*, which Floyer and many others drew on, had an even more tangled origin. Boym was, of course, not the only Jesuit to take an interest in Chinese medicine. Couplet's own "passion" to translate a Chinese medical work into Latin was noted in a contemporary Portuguese account referring to 1659 or 1661. Moreover, when Couplet or his colleague, François de Rougemont, fell ill, they entrusted themselves to Chinese physicians, two of whom were mentioned by name: *Vam C*u lai* (modern Wang Tzu-lai) and *Cham Chun poi*.[91] From 1665 to 1671, when all the Jesuit missionaries spent a period together under house arrest in Canton, and could not proselytize, they conducted further work translating and commenting on classic works. For instance, the massive translation of four Confucian works that Couplet later published in Europe, the *Confucius Sinarum Philosophus* of 1687, was completed during the period in Canton.[92] Apparently *Les Secrets de la Medicine* was also polished for publication shortly before October 1668, when its preface was composed.

At the same time, a working relationship between the Jesuits and the VOC had been established. Cleyer and Couplet may have met in 1662, when a VOC delegation was in China to seek trading privileges and Couplet assisted it; we know that in 1666 a letter from Couplet singled out Cleyer as one of his "special friends." Cleyer had by then started to engage in medical practice in Batavia, and within a couple of years had become the senior medical officer in the East Indies, organizing an effort to obtain effective local medicines from places throughout Asia. When another VOC delegation was in Canton from September 1668 to March 1669, Cleyer received yet further messages from Couplet, and responded warmly. (It may be this route by which *Les Secrets de la Medicine* was conveyed to Europe.) Cleyer received a Chinese herbarium from the Jesuits, while he in turn sent them newspapers and medicines, and 300 gilders—they were greatly in need of money—along with a request to send him more medical works from China, asking in particular for "the translation of a work dealing with Chinese 'pulse-method,' if possible with illustrations."[93] The relationship between Couplet and Cleyer developed into a regular "Holland-connection" that allowed the Jesuits to send packages of their letters to Cleyer, who posted them on to Amsterdam, from where they would be sent to their local destinations in Europe, often via Antwerp.[94] It is almost certain, then, that the four letters published in Cleyer's *Specimen* from an anonymous "erudit" sent to Cleyer from Canton and dated February 12 and October 20, 1669, and November 5 and 15, 1670, which concern pulse diagnosis and the circulation, and are followed by nine diagrams and tables, are from Couplet. In Batavia, Cleyer collected further manuscripts and illustrations and in 1676 apparently sent an early version of what became the *Specimen* to Amsterdam for publication, although a more complete version, or a more complete version of one of the Chinese texts intended for it, followed in 1681.[95]

But it may well have been the presence of the physician Willem ten Rhijne, whom we met at the beginning of this essay, who urged Cleyer to think of publishing the works he was collecting, just as ten Rhijne stimulated a Batavian clergyman to publish a book on a local treatment for gout, moxibustion.[96] Ten Rhijne resided at Deshima, the Dutch station in Nagasaki, for two years, where, as we saw, he immersed himself in an effort to translate a Chinese medical text into Dutch and Latin via Japanese intermediaries.[97] After his hopes of becoming a physician to the Shogun were dashed, ten Rhijne returned to Batavia in 1676 without further instructions. While the government of the VOC was slowly making up its mind how to make use of him, he made good use of his time by writing a number of treatises about his medical experiences. These included the first long tract in a European language on acupuncture and moxibustion, which in turn included the remarks on Chinese medicine he had gleaned from his Japanese colleagues and four charts of the acupuncture points. At the same time, he also assisted Hendrik van Reede with the editing of his huge and impressive work on the botany of the Malabar coast.[98] He also agreed to help Cleyer sort and edit the texts that went into the *Specimen*; perhaps he had even initiated this by persuading Cleyer to think of publishing what he had been collecting. The two later had a falling out, but if a letter from Cleyer is correct, a version of the *Specimen* was sent to Amsterdam in 1676 intended for publication;[99] if we can trust ten Rhijne, further supplementary material was sent to Europe for publication in 1681.[100]

The *Specimen*, which finally appeared in 1682, is therefore, and self-evidently, a compilation of various kinds of texts, translations, tables, and illustrations, assembled in Batavia. Because it was made up of several different, independently paginated sections, copies I have examined have the contents bound in different order, some missing sections present in others. The copy used by Floyer has all the parts found in any other copy, and ordered similarly to the manuscript meant for the printer, so we will take that as our example.[101] Following the title page, a dedication by Cleyer to the governors of the VOC, and a Latin poem in praise of Cleyer's achievement, the first main text was a fifty-four page translation of a four-part treatise on the different pulses and their indications, mainly taken from "Vám Xó Hó." This is probably, in modern Romanization of the name, Wang Chou Houo, the third-century CE author of the *Mo Tsing*, or "Treatise of the Pulses," which describes and graphically depicts the twenty-eight forms of the pulse.[102] A few of its parts are said in the titles "not" to be from "Hoâm tý," or Huangdi, the famous Yellow Emperor of classical Chinese medicine. Whether the Jesuits were working from a medical compilation of their own time, or one they put together with advice, or whether the final version of the text was assembled by ten Rhijne after his consultations in Japan, this section was stitched together from at least two very early textual sources. A second section of 108 consecutive pages was titled "Treatise on the Pulse as Collected by an Erudite European." This also contained various parts, opening with a treatise on the pulse said to be taken from an ancient work on medical philosophy, "Nuy kim," probably the *Nei Jing* (or Inner Canon of the Yellow Emperor, Huangdi) of the second century CE. (Kajdański believed that this material must also have come from Boym, but it could as well have come from ten Rhijne or Couplet, or other learned Europeans.)[103] Other parts in this section include chapters 17 through 21 of a work on East Asian medicine written by an erudite European; excerpts from anonymous letters dated February 2, 1669, October 20, 1669, November 5, 1670, and November 15, 1670 (no doubt letters from Couplet to Cleyer); charts and tables assembling information about what feeling the pulses could explain; and anatomical tables showing channels and points on the body for acupuncture and moxibustion. A third section on treatment, in fifty-four consecutive pages, again from Wang Chou Houo, gives recipes to counteract various problems identified from the seven exterior pulses and the eight interior pulses, followed by a list and brief description of 289 simples (perhaps the "herbarium" sent to Cleyer in 1668–69). The fourth and final section consists of a treatise on tongue diagnosis (with diagrammatic illustrations) in sixteen pages. Three final remarks indicate that much of the information came from a learned Christian convert who was also a doctor.[104] At the end, twenty-six woodcut illustrations pertaining to the previous materials are attached.

In other words, the *Specimen* was an assemblage of various Chinese medical treatises translated into Latin, mainly but not exclusively devoted to the pulse, together with several learned commentaries on them, and recommendations for treatment, along with lists of medicines, summary tables, diagrams, and illustrations. Its publishing history shows that it was not under the editorial control of the Jesuits, but of a more eclectic VOC physician in Batavia with input from various other people, probably with the intention of collecting something like "information" about Chinese medicine, especially the methods of diagnosis by pulse and tongue, and of treatment. At the same time, however, in the commentaries of those Europeans who understood Chinese, and even in the Latin words chosen for translation—such as *humidum radicale* for *yin, calidum innatum* or *calorem primigenium* for *yang, chaos seu materiam incompositam* for *kie* (*qi*), or *spirituum os* for *ki keu*—the editors and translators drew on Latin terms derived from medieval and classical sources rather than the post-Cartesian medicine of their contemporaries.[105] In other words, despite the fragmentation of the work, it gave many of its readers the impression that Chinese medicine was a unified whole, of great antiquity, and in keeping with a universal and holistic natural philosophy originating with the *prisci philosophi* and therefore containing extraordinary hints of the first principles behind health and disease—a mythology about Chinese medicine that persists to this day.[106]

CONCLUSION

For Floyer, the excitement of reading a work like the *Specimen* was that it confirmed in him something to which he was already committed: making the pulse a fundamental part of medicine, not only for diagnosis but for treatment. In "Chinese medicine" as read through the lens of the *Specimen*, he saw sources of ancient wisdom that could be clarified and improved by the application of modern mechanical principles. In building on a solid philosophy confirmed by thousands of years of experience, Floyer could see himself bringing a timeless universal method to the attention of all humankind. In that sense, he did not have to understand the classical texts of Chinese medicine perfectly. As a matter of fact, the passages from the *Specimen* that Wotton had attacked in print, and which Floyer chose to translate and reinterpret in a favorable light, were actually not from a distant Chinese medical philosopher at all, but can instead be matched up with pages 85 to 87 of the second part of the *Specimen*, which happens to be an excerpt of a letter dated November 5, 1670, probably from Couplet to Cleyer.[107] The substance of the debate between Wotton and Floyer was therefore not about an ancient text but about how a Jesuit had summarized a portion of what he considered to be a canon.

At first glance, then, it would appear that Floyer worked away without an authentic understanding of what Chinese practitioners did and wrote, relying on representations of exotic knowledge and practice. The terms of the debate were set by more than one interpretation of and commentary on Chinese texts; these in turn were framed by various parties with deep interests in European debates about the foundations of knowledge—including but not limited to medicine—who recruited appropriate representations of Chinese knowledge to strengthen their cases. In these terms, it matters little whether the Jesuits chose medical texts that were "representative" of Chinese medicine as practiced in their day or in antiquity (although to their credit they touched many of the same sources as modern historians of medicine). Nor does it matter whether they translated and summarized the originals in ways that we would consider accurate according to our own standards (although it must be noted that making such translations remains very difficult). What the Jesuits were doing was transmitting a view of Chinese medicine that was in keeping with the themes of their accommodationist policy; their words were reassembled and edited in turn in Dutch-speaking Batavia; and when the fragmented results were published in Germany, some of the European audience sought syncretic views that would allow the construction of universal knowledge systems, while others wished to build on other foundations, making "Chinese medicine" a point of controversy.

And yet, Floyer's interest in finding out about Chinese pulse methods was not simply to confirm what he already thought. Kuriyama is no doubt correct to show that taking the pulse and feeling the *mo* are incommensurable activities. Yet many people labored for decades—as they still do—to bridge the differences, at least in part because they hoped to glimpse worlds that had not been visible before, or not as clearly. It might therefore be significant that the most debated and quoted work was the *Specimen* rather than the *Clavis*, probably because in the former Cleyer was attempting to transmit information about methods and practices as well as explanations, while in the latter Boym was giving a more formal exposition of medical philosophy. Floyer's excitement, for instance, was in the "real" effects that could be elicited from practitioners touching patients.[108] It was the imaginary contact with bodily practice invoked by the words that excited him and on which his own interpretations could be constructed.

In other words, Floyer's enthusiasm was generated not by the interpretative medical philosophy of East Asia per se but by a vision of Chinese practitioners touching something in other bodies that could be articulated and shared: they were literally putting their fingers on the beating heart of life using methods that others could not only learn from but improve upon. Floyer did not necessarily want to imitate their practices, but he did want to note the real effects drawn from them and to draw lessons for his own practice. His hopes for healthful change in his patients, emergent from counting the beats of the pulse, not self-enlightenment, moved him. The Jesuits may have begun their project in hope of a universal human conversation with shared truth as the foundation; Floyer thought he could build on that by finding a universal practice in a simplified method of noting physical ("mechanical") realities. Floyer's response to Chinese medicine may have been based on misunderstandings, but it was profoundly creative. It was so because he was not content with the representations alone: he struggled to find the sources of authentic physical truths in the bodies he touched.

What moved relatively easily between China and Europe, then, were tangible things. Lists of medicines, rules of practice, and indications of how to touch all dealt with objects or the related "objective" aspects of people and the rest of nature. What moved less easily were the assumptions and expectations that were expressed in words alone, the things we often refer to as theories or concepts. In that sense, global history is helpful for understanding only a part of the historical connections between people. Modeled on economic history, it is very good at conveying the ways in which people interacted with one another when dealing with material objects and the words associated with those things and their properties, and with processes of production, accumulation, and exchange. We might say that the more materialistic the practice, the more easily it moved—which may well be why certain kinds of knowledge practice, now called science, are relatively easily shared. Other kinds of knowledge are less easily moved. Some parts of even the largest incommensurable lumps, however, moved from one "civilization" or another. The bridges of understanding between distant ways of life and language might be shaky, incapable of conveying all the weight placed upon them and prone to collapse. But imperfect as they may be, even figures like Floyer were grateful for their existence and risked ridicule by traveling across them from time to time. As many of his contemporaries argued, it was from sociability and attention to the real that any hope of human flourishing might emerge from an imperfect world. Communication takes shape not from words and gestures alone, but from touch as well.

CHAPTER 9

Transnational Feminism

EVENT, TEMPORALITY, AND PERFORMANCE AT THE 1975
INTERNATIONAL WOMEN'S YEAR CONFERENCE

Jocelyn Olcott

IN MID-JUNE 1975, thousands of people converged on Mexico City for the United Nations World Conference marking International Women's Year (IWY). Billed as the "world's largest consciousness-raising session," the conference opened with fanfare and ceremony, drawing some twelve hundred delegates to the intergovernmental conference and an estimated six thousand more to a parallel nongovernmental organization (NGO) tribune.[1] As demonstrators outside protested against human rights abuses in Chile and the exclusion of poor women from the festivities, an all-star cast of prominent women intellectuals, activists, and political leaders from around the world paraded into the inaugural celebration at Juan de la Barrera Gymnasium—the U.S. feminist Betty Friedan and her Australian alter ego Germaine Greer; international icons such as the Soviet cosmonaut Valentina Tereshkova and the Iranian Shah's twin sister, Princess Ashraf Pahlavi; first ladies, including Egypt's Jehan Sadat and her Israeli counterpart Leah Rabin; and prominent stateswomen, including Sri Lankan prime minister Sirimavo Bandaranaike and the U.S. congresswoman Bella Abzug. Reporters and participants alike remarked on the visual novelty as the auditorium filled with a sea of women in saris, kaftans, huipiles, and European-style suits—an image that signaled both the unprecedented diversity of attendees and the unusual topical focus on women's status.

These twin aspects of the IWY conference—its novelty and diversity—defined its dynamics and legacies. Although the cast assembled in Mexico City was homogeneous compared to the diversification that occurred over the subsequent UN women's conferences in Copenhagen (1980), Nairobi (1985), and Beijing (1995), participants in these later gatherings formed their expectations in large part from the preceding conferences. In 1975, however, the Mexico City conference was sui generis. Although hardly the first international women's conference—the nineteenth-century abolition and suffragist meetings and the early-twentieth-century Pan-

American Union congresses stand as notable precursors—it witnessed a radical expansion, achieving a more global reach in terms both of regions represented and of social sectors involved.[2] It also was among the first of the thematic UN conferences to have a parallel NGO tribune, a fact that would powerfully shape both the conference itself and subsequent activism.[3] Indeed, these conferences contributed to the dramatic rise of NGOs during the 1970s.[4]

As the first major international women's organizing effort since the near-universal granting of women's political rights, the IWY events not only drew a motley bunch but also included many women who had received political educations either formally or through their labor unions and community organizations. The NGO tribune organizers had conscientiously reached out to participants from all over the world and from different sectors of women's advocacy, and they had secured funding from the Ford and Rockefeller Foundations to cover expenses for participants from poor countries.[5]

The moment many people—activists and scholars alike—describe most vividly from the IWY conference was when the Bolivian tin miner's wife Barrios de Chungara confronted the Betty Friedan. "Domitila Barrios de Chungara and the women she spoke for," recounts historian Francesca Miller,

> dismissed as irrelevant the concerns of feminists over reproductive rights, political and economic equity with men, the subordinate position of women within the family. Betty Friedan led the attempt to explain and defend the feminist position and the need to include their platform in the World Plan of Action. The result was a clash between Barrios de Chungara and Friedan.[6]

Sociologist Göran Therborn similarly explains, "[A]bove all, the Tribune witnessed a confrontation between North American feminism, well represented by Betty Friedan, and Third World feminine Leftism, eloquently voiced by Domitila Barrios."[7] Such depictions of this showdown gave lie to fantasies of global sisterhood by spotlighting a gaping divide that put First World, liberal, and white on one side and Third World, Marxist, and nonwhite on the other.[8] The challenge for forging a transnational feminism, many observers believed, would be to close this divide, teaching Western feminists to listen to women like Barrios de Chungara. As the economist Bina Agarwal explains, "In Mexico, grassroots Southern women, such as the Bolivian worker Domitila Barrios, had to protest persistently against the hijacking of the conference agenda by Northern women and assert: 'Let me speak.' In Huairou [the Beijing NGO forum] the tables had turned."[9] Lest Agarwal's Hegelianism seem too oblique, the political scientist Carolyn Stephenson puts it even more starkly:

Differences in perspective between First and Third World feminism eventually led to synthesis into an international movement. Each brand of feminism was affected by the other. Women went home from Mexico City with an awareness that there was more to this business of feminism than they had experienced in their own country.[10]

What occurred in Mexico City in the summer of 1975, however, was far more interesting than a head-on collision between two ideologies or two geopolitical realities, and what ensued was far more complicated and creative than a dialectical synthesis between anything that might be imagined as First World and Third World feminism.[11] The encounter in Mexico City in this sense resembles the World Social Forum (WSF) meetings, which, as the sociologist Boaventura de Sousa Santos explains, demand a "wide exercise in translation to expand reciprocal intelligibility without destroying the identity of the partners of translation."[12] Such spaces form a "contact zone" where "disparate cultures meet, clash, and grapple with each other, in highly asymmetrical relations of domination and subordination."[13] In other words, the efforts to foster coherence and solidarity through translation never escape the power relations within which they emerge. Efforts at cultural and political translation in such circumstances are always mistranslations—creating imperfect equivalences, fixing meanings that are fluid, and reflecting anticipated understandings. As Santos explains, the translations at the WSF—much like at the IWY, but with far more experience—involved the decoding and recoding of knowledges and actions as much as discourses, and the translations reflect emotions and dynamics particular to a given context. The unpredictability that has made for the most significant exchanges at both the IWY and the WSF has always exceeded the capacities of translation but reveals a liminal space between that resists fixing—what the anthropologist Diane Nelson dubs fluidarity in lieu of solidarity—but nonetheless opens the most generative transnational exchanges.[14] The IWY offered an unprecedented encounter among a radically diverse array of participants—overwhelmingly women—who brought with them experiences and conceptions of cultural change and social justice that far exceeded what could be captured in the dyad invoked by the Friedan–Barrios de Chungara conflict.

Barrios de Chungara, the radical leader of the tin mining union's Housewives Committee, did not make it to Mexico City in time to witness the pomp and protest of the inauguration. Bolivia's Ministry of the Interior had repeatedly delayed granting her an exit visa until the combined impact of her brandishing the official UN-issued invitation and the union's threatening a walkout finally resulted in begrudging permission to leave the country. According to her memoire, as she prepared to board the plane, a woman from the ministry wished her a good trip and reminded her that, if she wanted to return to Bolivia and see her children again, she should be careful what she discussed in Mexico City.[15] Had she arrived for the inaugural ceremonies, however, it is easy to imagine that Barrios de Chungara would have remained outside, shaking her fist at the enactments of authority taking place within—a lifetime of militancy, after all, had left her deeply distrustful of all things official. By the end of the IWY conference, and certainly in the years to follow, Barrios de Chungara came to stand in for all the diversity both inside the gymnasium and clamoring outside its walls, while Friedan symbolized a played-out feminism best left behind.[16]

Tellingly, however, no direct confrontation actually occurred between the two women; the story is apocryphal. Both the women's memoirs and the contemporary documentation describe each of them having different sets of conflicts. Although Barrios de Chungara's *testimonio* mentions a "conversation" with Friedan, the real confrontation she and others describe occurred between her and the *Mexican* feminist Esperanza Brito de Martí, arguably Friedan's analog as the leader of the mainstream Movimiento Nacional de Mujeres (National Women's Movement). The issue at stake in this particular confrontation was not Friedan's feminist views or even the authority Friedan had arrogated to herself to represent the tribune to the intergovernmental conference but rather the legitimacy of calls for unity and equality at the IWY tribune. Amid accusations that she was fascist, reactionary, and imperialist, Brito chastened her hecklers, "The only image that we are giving is that we cannot unite ourselves. Come on, Latin American sisters, let's fight for equality of women and men."[17] Barrios de Chungara seethed, "We can't speak about equality between games of canasta. Women can't be equals any more than poor and rich countries are equals."[18]

Brito's emphasis on unity pointed to mounting anxieties that "politics" would eclipse "women's issues." Indicating that a clear division existed between these two distinct realms and that reasonable people would agree on where the boundary lay, participants imagined that if they could simply peel away all the layers of politics, they would reach an authentic ideal that the intergovernmental conference dubbed consensus and the tribune imagined as unity. Throughout the IWY meetings, participants expressed mounting frustration at the elusiveness of such concurrence, lamenting that the entire opportunity would be squandered should they fail to reach this Shangri-la. The aspiration is understandable, particularly at this conjuncture. Countless labor battles, civil rights movements, and national liberation struggles had conveyed the lesson that victory depended upon setting aside differences for the sake of solidarity. Another lesson, however—and one that women had learned time and again—was that solidarity and unity implied exclusions and reifications. Françoise Giroud, the French Secretary of State for Women's Affairs, lamented the myriad instances when women had offered solidarity in revolutionary and social justice movements only to find themselves relegated to cooking and making coffee. "If that happens again," she told reporters, "International Women's Year will be yet another deceit."[19]

The repeated calls for consensus and unity at the IWY meetings, after all, begged the question of their contents. The notion of unadulterated "women's issues" depended, in turn, upon a shared understanding of womanhood—of some combination of experiences and biology that defined a set of concerns that pertained primarily to women. "To establish a normative foundation for settling the question of what ought properly to be included in the description of women," the feminist theorist Judith Butler reminds us, however,

> would be only and always to produce a new site of political contest. That foundation would settle nothing, but would of necessity founder on its own authoritarian ruse. . . . To refuse the contest is to sacrifice the radical democratic impetus of feminist politics. That the category is unconstrained, even that it comes to serve antifeminist purposes, will be part of the risk of the procedure.[20]

Indeed, the contestation was continuous and generative, if also immensely frustrating to many participants who perceived "antifeminist purposes" in every challenge to their own priorities. Given the uncertain future of transnational women's activism, participants hurried to get on the table the concerns they saw as the most compelling, but one person's core issue was another's political distraction. Equal pay legislation and educational opportunities seemed superfluous in settings where women faced annihilation by disease, starvation, or political repression. Insistence on lambasting economic injustice or human rights violations, however, seemed to many participants to fall outside the purview of IWY. When delegates from Australia and New Zealand argued at the intergovernmental conference for the inclusion of "sexism" in the World Plan of Action's list of obstacles to women's emancipation (along with racism, imperialism, and economic inequality), they were voted down on the grounds that the term was a "nasty North American neologism."[21]

Amid this frustration, the story about a Friedan–Barrios de Chungara face-off persists for several reasons. First, it reflects the anticipated geopolitical fault lines going into the IWY meetings. Before the opening session, journalists predicted conflicts between "Third World women," focusing on structural problems of economic inequality, and "Western feminists," concentrating on sex-specific issues such as reproductive freedom, wage equity, and women's educational and professional opportunities. The

New York Times, covering the inaugural festivities in the newspaper's "Family/Style" section, noted, "Observers agree that the major goal set out by the organizers—improving the status of women—is not going to be an easy one in light of the political arguments that are expected to erupt between delegates of the industrialized countries and the third world."[22] More pointedly, Pacifica Radio titled its interview with Friedan, *Betty Friedan versus the Third World.*[23] Second, the story imposes a kind of coherence and legibility on a set of encounters and disputes that proved far more unsettling than these forecasts would allow. It implies a predictable, recipe-like model of diversity that calls for the right array of ingredients in the correct proportions to achieve a satisfactory outcome. Finally, the synthetic narrative implies a teleological progression in which all the disputes and miscommunications and misidentifications resolve into a coherent transnational feminism with clean edges and knowable contents.

To understand what happened at the 1975 IWY meeting, however, we need to see beyond the media depiction of a clash between two caricatured types to consider not only the range of experiences and ideas that participants brought with them—different understandings of political gestures, competing conceptions of the dynamics and time frames of social change, and diverse perceptions of the most significant obstacles to women's "emancipation"—but also the unforeseeable implications of this heterogeneity. As perceptions, expectations, and convictions all collided in the spaces of the IWY meetings, they combusted to generate both tremendous anxiety and tremendous political energy and creativity, the heat and fire that would propel transnational women's activism for the ensuing decades. Indeed, the intensely fraught and emotional exchanges that occurred at the IWY gatherings attest to the extent to which these encounters unsettled participants' commonsense understandings and deeply held convictions about women and their place in the world.

Although contemporary and retrospective accounts have endeavored to distill these collisions into a more easily legible shorthand such as the imagined Friedan–Barrios de Chungara confrontation, appreciating the accomplishments and the unintended consequences of the IWY meetings requires attending to a more complex heterogeneity and the interactions it produced. The payoff of such an approach is not simply a finer-grained, more detailed picture of what happened at the IWY conference. Rather, it offers a more dynamic, moving image that shows how different parts articulated with one another and informed each other's actions and how the ruptures and explosions induced by misarticulations, the crossed signals, and the unpredictable interactions transformed the structures and cultures of transnational women's advocacy.

Historian William Sewell argues that historians could most productively move beyond these typologies and road maps through a return to narrative that attends to what he dubs the "logics of history—fatefulness, contingency, complexity, eventfulness, and causal heterogeneity."[24] Such narratives would not offer a tidy recounting of events, much less provide a stage for history's "great men" (or even "great women"), nor simply serve an antiquarian or journalistic curiosity about eccentric or exceptional figures from the past. Rather, Sewell calls for using narrative devices—including development of complex characters, recognition of dramatic tensions and emotional expressions, attention to temporality and the ordering of events, and attention to what Wittgenstein dubs "language games"—to explore the simultaneous and interrelated importance of structures and agency, culture and contingency, power and affect. Such narratives consider not simply histories as they played out but also the many possibilities present in histories as they developed as well as how such stories shape an event's meaning. Piecing together a narrative about the IWY conference—a narrative that addresses broader historical implications rather than simply engaging anecdotes—demands investigation of three interrelated elements that played particularly critical roles in its unfolding history: how the conference came to be imagined as an event, the role of temporality in structuring that imagination, and how questions of representation and identification informed participants' conduct.

UNITY AND CONJUNCTURE: MAKING AN EVENT OF THE INTERNATIONAL WOMEN'S YEAR CONFERENCE

It may seem obvious why the Mexico City conference would be considered an event—it was, after all, created as such. Conceptualizing an event for the sake of historical inquiry, however, centers on two elements in particular: how a set of episodes becomes linked as a unified, coherent set designated as a single event—in other words how we describe both its boundaries and its contents—and how a given event comes to be considered a pivotal historical moment or a conjuncture that changes its surrounding world in a significant way. An "eventful" narrative, as Sewell terms it, will demonstrate the contingencies and contestation over both these aspects—bearing in mind not only how the event unfolded but also the roads not taken, the ideas and actors excluded, and the surrounding developments that make an event into a turning point. However, the IWY departs from Sewell's paradigmatic example of the storming of the Bastille. While it shares with the Bastille event the quality of having gained importance in retrospect, particularly as the subsequent UN women's conferences grew in size and influence, it operated as a catalyzing event, however, in a quite opposite fashion—rather than consolidating around a coherent political subject, the IWY highlighted the impossibility of that coherence and the necessity of cultivating a decentered and multivalent political practice. While the Bastille acted as a centripetal force amid the chaos of revolution, Mexico City had a centrifugal effect on the effort to consolidate a global women's movement.

Theorists from Marshall Sahlins to Alain Badiou have stressed the importance of examining how a collection of linked episodes becomes unified as a set, or as the mathematically minded Badiou puts it, as a one.[25] Sewell reminds us of the need to historicize this process—both to locate a particular event formation within its specific context and to show the progression of actions and significations through which incidents become bound together into a single event. What we learn from a closer examination of the IWY event is that this unity, this oneness, was not a convergence or a dialectical synthesis of either female subjectivity or core women's political issues—however much organizers aspired to such outcomes—but rather a contestation and a destabilization.[26] In other words, the fragmentation of an episode designated a priori as a unified event was not simply a stage along the way to consolidation but rather was the event itself. Contemporary and subsequent narrations have reinscribed anticipated fault lines, but such accounts obscure the most consequential aspect of what occurred in Mexico City: the unforeseen and unpredictable encounters that fostered a reimagination of women as political actors.

Despite the hyperbolic claims of its organizers, the fact that the Mexico City conference occurred was largely an accident of politics and fate. It was only through what Sahlins dubs the "structure of the conjuncture"—the shaping of contingent events through control over resources—that the Mexico City conference even took place at all, much less that it gained status as a founding moment of a transnational feminism. The UN Committee on the Status of Women (CSW), established in 1946, had called repeatedly for an international women's conference. In 1972, the communist bloc NGO Women's International Democratic Federation (WIDF) convinced the Romanian delegate to propose a UN Year of the Woman to assess the CSW's progress in improving women's status. In December 1972, the UN General Assembly designated 1975 as International Women's Year, and Warsaw Pact countries began planning a conference in East Berlin for October 1975. At the beginning of 1974, when it appeared that the main IWY event would take place behind the Iron Curtain, the U.S. representative to the CSW, Patricia Hutar, began to advocate for an official UN conference that would take place in a noncommunist country. The CSW began planning for an intergovernmental conference in Bogotá that later moved to Mexico City amid political uncertainty in

Colombia. Through the spring of 1974, the East Berlin and Bogotá conferences seemed to maintain equal stature, with indications that East Berlin might host an NGO gathering, while the Bogotá conference would consist solely of government representatives. Through a series of Cold War–inflected actions and decisions, these two events were separated and the Mexico City (*née* Bogotá) conference gained status as the principal IWY event. The East Berlin conference still took place—albeit with even fewer resources than were dedicated to the Mexico City conference—but it remains largely forgotten.

Even after the Mexico City conference emerged as the IWY focal point, the conference itself consisted of many parts that might have emerged as a series of episodes rather than a singular event. Before the conference inauguration, two mini-conferences took place that helped define the tenor of the official proceedings: a seminar on women and development, organized by the American Association for the Advancement of Science, and a journalists' "encounter," sponsored by the UN's Centre for Economic and Social Information. The conference itself consisted of two parallel but related gatherings—the intergovernmental conference of instructed delegations from UN member states and an NGO tribune of activists of different stripes. These two events themselves disintegrated in telling ways that demonstrate the structures of conjuncture, the institutional and material factors that shaped the conference.

The intergovernmental conference split most dramatically and predictably between the industrialized countries and the Group of 77 (G77), a bloc of Third World countries, including the more radical nonaligned group that prioritized the creation of a New International Economic Order and vocally condemned Zionism as a form of racist imperialism. As recently decolonized nations finally took control of the General Assembly in 1974, the GA had made the struggle against racism and imperialism a top priority on the UN's agenda, and Arab and African nations consistently formed a bloc to challenge industrialized countries on everything from trade to communications. In the end, the G77 would issue a separate conference report, the Declaration of Mexico, which differed markedly in tone and content from the more technocratic World Plan of Action drafted by a consultative committee to the UN secretariat. The conference would approve both documents—as would the GA—but only the World Plan of Action gained legitimacy as a policy document. How the IWY conference became, over the long run, the event that sanctioned the World Plan of Action rather than the event that sanctioned the Declaration of Mexico forms a critical part of the IWY history.

The NGO tribune witnessed deep divisions that mirrored those of the intergovernmental conference. Whereas the conference reflected the growing divide between poorer countries—particularly those that had gained independence after World War II—and wealthier ones, the tribune revealed the ongoing debates over democratic process. The tribune had been organized by professionalized women who ran established NGOs that enjoyed consultative status with the UN's ECOSOC—organizations such as International Planned Parenthood Federation and the Young Women's Christian Association.[27] In fact, the main organizers and staff arrived fresh from having staged a similar NGO forum during the 1974 UN Population Conference in Bucharest, where they had succeeded in getting the issue of women's status into the official document. This experience not only forged strong bonds within this particular group of women but also schooled them in yet another language that allowed for only inadequate translation—what NGO tribune organizer Mildred Persinger dubbed UN-ese, the bureaucratic language of international politics.[28] They originally had planned a three-day preconference (akin to those for journalists and development specialists) that would include only representatives of consultative-status NGOs. In January 1975, when the Mexican government offered the auditorium and meeting rooms of the National Medical Center as well as translation services, the tribune organizers significantly revised their plans, arranging instead for an NGO tribune to run parallel to the conference. They set about putting together panels and events featuring "experts" who would address the conference themes of equality, development, and peace, often with a didactic tenor meant to educate activists about suitable and effective modes of advocacy. NGOs were particularly encouraged to send representatives, but anyone could attend the conference as long as they registered in advance—and even the registration requirement was abandoned a few days into the conference.

This dramatic expansion of the tribune—from a three-day conference of consultative NGOs to a full-scale parallel event open to anyone who showed up—meant that participation mushroomed much like the GA membership had, and participants arrived with radically diverse expectations of what the tribune might accomplish and how its daily business would proceed. Much like the intergovernmental conference, the tribune splintered into factions, and the parallel play of spontaneous, participant-initiated exchanges soon eclipsed the carefully choreographed scheduled sessions. Indeed, Persinger echoes a belief held by many U.S. participants that the Mexican government imported several thousand Latin American women to "overwhelm the US women at the tribune."[29] If the organizers envisioned orderly panels following parliamentary procedures and UN protocols that modeled women's capacity for global citizenship, the activists who arrived by borrowed jalopies, donated plane tickets, and sweaty, livestock-laden busses anticipated an adventure in participatory democracy. Participants began to organize "global speak-outs," interest-based consciousness-raising groups, and informal forums that soon over-shadowed the formal tribune agenda, transforming the tribune into what the *New York Times* described as "the scene of much shouting, scheming, plotting, and general hell-raising."[30] Animated by all the optimism and intensity of their convictions, activists at the tribune slammed headlong into the soul-crushing bureaucracy and political machinations of the UN. For many participants, their experiences at the tribune precipitated a sort of political crisis as they found themselves galled that the tribune would have no say in the conference deliberations, alienated from the stiff-ness and formality of the tribune agenda, and confused by encountering women activists with such starkly different objectives from their own. In other words, the NGO tribune not only functioned as an event within an event but also functioned differently as a pivotal moment for its varied participants.

If how we interpret an event depends upon where we imagine its bound-aries, it depends just as surely on the people and ideas that fall within those boundaries. The women who populated the planning committees for the IWY meetings had a powerful—although not dispositive—say in who and what made their way onto the official programs in Mexico City. Those with agenda-setting authority could not entirely exclude pressing questions, but their power to sanction certain issues over others under-scores the importance of investigating how they attained such power. Correspondence with private foundations reveals a shared emphasis on maintaining order and avoiding political disruptions from either Third World nationalists or "women's libbers."[31] In June 1973, Shahnaz Alami, the WIDF's representative to the CSW and chair of the CSW's subcom-mittee on human rights, had written to Margaret Bruce, then assistant director of the Human Rights Division and head of the Status of Women section, to inform her that a special NGO committee on human rights had begun planning the IWY event in East Berlin. Alami, an Iranian exile living in East Berlin since 1953 and a seasoned activist in human rights and women's rights, seemed a promising choice to organize the NGO forum. In March 1974, Niall MacDermot, the head of the Geneva NGO Committee on Human Rights, wrote to UN Secretary-General Kurt Waldheim to stress the importance of involving Alami in any NGO activities for IWY. By then, however, a group of professionalized NGO activists in New York City—led by Rosalind Harris, who had organized the NGO forum at the UN Population Conference—had assumed for itself the role of planning the IWY tribune. Harris sent MacDermot a curt note assuring him that her committee included NGO representatives from all but three of those on the CSW and that he should not confuse matters by making individual appeals to the secretary-general.[32] Nota-bly, the WIDF, which had initially proposed IWY, was among the three excluded from the New York committee, and the ensuing documentation shows the New York group anxiously keeping the WIDF—and Alami in particular—at arm's length. The WIDF had long been considered a Cold War rival for U.S.-based NGOs. In March 1953, the United States had refused a visa to the WIDF representative to attend CSW meetings at UN headquarters in New York, arguing that she posed a "security threat."[33] The following year, the United States allowed a visa for the WIDF to travel in the "immediate vicinity" of the UN headquarters, but orchestrated the WIDF's suspension from the CSW during that session. The WIDF's consultative status was not reinstated until 1967. As Francisca de Haan has shown, the U.S. activists (and later historians) consistently presented the WIDF as a deeply ideological organization, while liberal organizations such as the International Alliance of Women and the International Council of Women were seen as apolitical and above ideological skirmishes.[34] Given the compressed planning schedule, limited budget, and relative proximity of New York to Mexico City, the New York group quickly claimed exclusive control over the tribune program. Clearly "politics" had informed "women's issues" at every turn, not least in deciding which organizations were considered too political.

If the New York committee constrained Alami's participation in the NGO tribune, planning developments for the intergovernmental conference seem to complete her marginalization, exemplifying Sahlins's notion of structures of conjuncture. The UN's weak financial commitment to IWY—particularly compared with its generous support for the 1974 population and food conferences—created an opportunity for those willing to help cover the expenses of the IWY meetings.[35] In December 1974, Princess Ashraf Pahlavi presented Waldheim with a Declaration on International Women's Year, signed by sixty-three heads of state, along with a pledge of $1 million to support the IWY events. By February, Pahlavi had been named as chair of the Secretariat's twenty-three-member IWY consultative committee, the body charged with formulating the draft World Plan of Action—the policy recommendations that would emerge nearly unchanged from the IWY conference. Questions of human rights, which Alami had seen as the centerpiece for improving women's status, went unmentioned in both the draft World Plan of Action and the tribune program.[36] Only through a series of vocal and well-attended protests would human rights command attention in Mexico City.

Despite efforts to control the IWY meetings' content, official delegates, NGO volunteers, and grassroots activists arrived in Mexico City ready to do battle over a broad range of issues that affected women's lives, including not only the conference's official themes of equality, development, and peace but also concerns such as human rights; women's labor burdens; sexuality, public health, and reproductive rights; and the role of education and the "mass communications media" in shaping perceptions of women and appropriate sex roles. These issues fragmented, however, even as they proliferated. The Soviet cosmonaut Valentina Tereshkova invoked the theme of peace, for example, to call for an end to nuclear proliferation, while a group of Ukrainian hunger strikers appealed to the same theme to call for the release of political prisoners held by the Soviet government. Israeli first lady Leah Rabin asserted that women's political participation would naturally yield a more peaceful society, while the South Vietnamese delegate Ma Thi Chu highlighted the importance of women's participation in Vietnam's armed struggle for national liberation.[37]

Deliberations over reproductive labor—the subsistence efforts including feeding, cleaning, and caring—precipitated similarly divergent understandings of the central problems. Many women sought either the redistribution or socialization of their reproductive labors by delinking them from sex roles, while other women adamantly favored a model of gender complementarity, albeit one in which reproductive labors earned more recognition. Some participants favored the commodification of reproductive labor—through models such as wages for housework—and others staunchly resisted the further encroachment of commodification into their everyday lives. Even in this most naturalized and biologized realm, politics and women's issues remained inseparable.[38] Although some issues highlighted difference more than others, even matters that organizers had seen as uncontroversial might raise troubling questions and reveal unseen assumptions. The strong emphasis on literacy programs, for example, implied a privileging of some forms of knowledge production and dissemination over others. The aggressive promotion of training programs to incorporate women into the "productive life" of the labor market indicated that women's uncommodified labor was unproductive and that labor commodification offered the only sure path to development. The central conference theme of equality set in relief the contemporary debates about how equality related to sexual difference.[39] In short, every effort to establish common ground seemed only to till the terrain of diversity, churning up more and starker differences among participants.

It is precisely because of the discussions and ruptures generated by these differences that the IWY conference fulfilled the other expectation that distinguishes a historical event from an interesting episode: it played a game-changing role in transforming the surrounding resource structures and cultural practices. Indeed, the IWY conference occupies an iconic place in the history of transnational feminism. It transformed the culture of transnational women's activism by launching the "NGO-ization" of women's advocacy, creating a prominent role for NGOs that would continue to grow over the following three decades.[40] The proliferation and diversification of NGOs introduced new political actors and new languages and practices around women's advocacy, emphatically turning away from states and toward a reimagined civil society. The Nobel laureate Wangari Maathai, explaining thirty years later how she launched Kenya's Green Belt movement, described a process that took place in many parts of the world:

> It was around the mid-1970s, and many women will remember that was the year when women of the world met in Mexico during the very first United Nations conference on women. It was that conference, by the way, that declared the first women's decade, and we were preparing in Kenya for us to go and participate at that meeting. And it was during that preparation that I listened to the women from the rural areas, and as they articulated their issues, their agendas, their concerns, I noticed that they were talking about the need for fire wood, the need for energy, the need for clean drinking water, the need for food, and the need for income, and all of these connected very closely to the environment.[41]

The creation of the Women's World Bank and UNIFEM planted the seeds of what has become the microfinance orientation of development programs.[42] International attention induced many governments to pass legislation that promised important improvements in women's status. The material resources made available from the UN, donor governments, and private foundations sponsored the creation of centers for women's advocacy and education that otherwise would have remained very low priorities for home governments. These programs made an important difference in women's lives, and women's histories from around the world either explicitly or implicitly periodize around 1975 as a watershed in women's rights.[43] And Mexico City was the point of embarkation for the rocky but often exhilarating journey that took many women activists to Copenhagen and Nairobi on the way to Beijing.

TIME AFTER TIME: TEMPORALITY AND SIGNIFICATION

The IWY's status as a conjunctural event—as a watershed in transnational women's activism—depends in part upon the meaning-making role of temporality. Considerations of temporality necessarily include not only the world-historical context of the Cold War, decolonization movements, and the growing influence of feminist thought but also the local and national contexts of the IWY participants, the imagined arcs of historical time that they carried with them, the microconjunctures that occurred at the IWY meetings themselves as issues and encounters layered on top of one another over the two-week period, and the temporal allusions that reminded participants of other historical moments. None of these temporalities operated in uniform or predictable ways. Temporal allusions that resonated powerfully with some participants remained meaningless to others. Participants in the IWY gatherings saw themselves as actors in a wide array of historical metanarratives and understood history itself to be moving at different paces and toward distinct horizons. While participants involved in reform-oriented movements and development politics spoke of long-term processes and interim benchmarks, for example, those who arrived from recently victorious national-liberation movements had experienced a compressed historical time of rapid and extraordinary change. As the feminist theorist Elizabeth Grosz implores us to recognize, "[Q]uestions about culture and representation, concepts of subjectivity, sexuality, and identity, as well as concepts of political struggle and transformation all make assumptions about the relevance of history, the place of the present, and the forward-moving impetus directing us to the future."[44]

Dramatic, world-historical developments combined to create the impression that a new age had dawned at the United Nations and perhaps in global politics more generally. On the broadest scale, events such as the recent wave of decolonization movements and the 1973 Arab-Israeli War conspicuously informed political maneuvers within the UN and, by extension, at the conference. A voting practice that the U.S. State Department branded logrolling and the nonaligned countries viewed as Third World solidarity had, by the end of 1974, led to the suspension of South Africa's credentials at the General Assembly. The attacks on Zionism at the IWY conference clearly formed part of a larger strategy to paint Israel with the same brush in order to suspend its credentials as well. Furthermore, the 1973 oil shock contributed to economic dislocations that heightened demands for economic justice and strengthened incentives for Third World nations to make common cause with oil-producing countries, creating an affinity between anti-Zionism and calls for the New International Economic Order.[45] By the summer of 1975, the momentum seemed entirely on the side of the allied forces of decolonization and anti-Zionism as oil-producing Arab countries exercised outsized economic power and national liberation movements gained victories around the world. The United States had finally withdrawn from Vietnam at the end of April, Angolan independence fighters were on the verge of triumph, and Mozambique won independence even as the IWY conference was under way, precipitating a hasty invitation to the new nation to join the proceedings.

Other, more geographically contained developments informed debates at the IWY as well. Two of the world's three female heads of state—India's Indira Gandhi and Argentina's Isabel Perón—were prevented from attending the conference because of mounting political unrest at home. In the context of conference discussions about efforts to bring more women into leadership positions, their absence seemed like a major setback. During the course of the conference, India would declare a state of emergency that would last nearly two years. By the spring of 1976, a military junta had overthrown Perón, launching a terror regime that would endure until 1983. The imbrication of the IWY deliberations with all these far-flung events was evidenced on the front pages of Mexico City newspapers, where daily conference updates were interspersed with headlines about Israel's permanent claim to Gaza Strip and the Golan Heights, Pinochet's declaration that Chile would not hold elections during his lifetime, and the Organization of American States' demand for laws to govern transnational corporations—the "corsairs of economic interdependence."[46] This widespread instability—and its magnification through mass media—underscored the sense of both uncertainty and opportunity created by the global flux.

Particularly in UN-sanctioned spaces, where the voices of new nations increasingly drowned out the great powers, the force of historical change seemed to push toward a revolution in global power structures and a shift toward revolutionary time. Indeed, the language of revolution and decolonization had become infectious by the mid-1970s and appropriated even by those who did not align themselves with revolutionary nationalism. Betty Friedan, for example, referred to herself as a revolutionary and repeatedly called for the decolonization of women's minds.[47] In 1975, the insurgent "majority caucus" within the U.S. National Organization for Women (NOW) took over the organization under the slogan "out of the mainstream and into the revolution." The Australian lesbian rights activist Laurie Bebbington referred to heterosexuality as a form of cultural imperialism.[48] Writing in the African American newspaper *Chicago Defender*, journalist Ethel Payne likened the Mexico City conference to another pivotal historical moment, the 1955 Bandung Conference, which was later credited with consolidating the Non-Aligned Movement. "It is safe to venture that after Mexico City, the world will not be the same," Payne explained. "The rising tide of expectations has gone past evolution to revolution."[49] By contrast, Jennifer Seymour Whitaker, writing in *Foreign Affairs*, described as counterrevolutionary—to the "women's revolution"—those "delegates from the developing countries [who were] so intent on the redistribution of resources between rich and poor."[50]

The setting of a UN conference highlighted the roles that states might play in determining the pace of social transformation. More authoritarian regimes, particularly those with a revolutionary ethos, had made efforts to impose changes from above. International Women's Year had started, as the *Economist* tastelessly reported, "with a bang."[51] On January 11, 1975, Somalia's Supreme Revolutionary Council, under the leadership of the modernizing socialist Siad Barre, issued a decree to abolish all forms a sexual discrimination. "In the name of Islam," according to the *Economist*, "a number of outraged traditionalists went into the city's mosques and harangued the faithful about the iniquity of the new decree." President Siad had the protesters arrested, insisting the decree enjoyed the imprimatur of Somalia's Muslim leadership. On January 23, ten of the protesters were executed by firing squad.

Other state-led efforts to expedite social transformations were mercifully less violent and arguably more significant, if less likely to draw media attention. In July 1974, the Cuban Women's Federation began deliberations about legislation to address the so-called second shift. On March 8, 1975—International Women's Day of International Women's Year—the Cuban government enacted the new Family Code, mandating the equal redistribution of domestic labor burdens among men and women.[52] The Mexican government, soon after the IWY conference was relocated from Bogotá to Mexico City, pushed through a constitutional amendment declaring men and women equal before the law—a development that highlighted the floundering of the Equal Rights Amendment in the United States. Valentina Tereshkova, meanwhile, insisted that Soviet women had already achieved complete equality with the 1917 revolution. All these efforts and assertions of course begged the question of whether they made any difference in social practice, but the rapid creation of new states confronting long-standing social injustices—as well as the destabilization of old states confronting new crises—drew particular attention to how states would figure into what appeared at the time as an emergent political order.

These global developments informed the ways that IWY participants interpreted the central issues under discussion in Mexico City. For example, for women who had struggled for the right to limit the number of children they had—including the many IWY organizers who had gained UN experience at the 1974 Population Conference—the prominence accorded abortion and contraception rights felt like a positive step in their progress toward emancipation from domestic life. For the many more women who had been targeted by population-control programs, including involuntary sterilizations, these discussions exemplified yet another way in which states and development agencies policed their bodies.[53] Indeed, when USAID administrator Daniel Parker (who would co-head the U.S. delegation at the IWY conference) proposed to Secretary of State Henry Kissinger that the United States link food aid to population-control benchmarks, National Academy of Sciences president Philip Handler responded, "How do you do that internationally without appearing racist? You have to convince the [less developed countries] that population control is in their interest not ours."[54] Radical women's organizations both within the United States and abroad lambasted this eugenicist approach, tagging family-planning policies as genocidal rather than liberatory, sparking accusations against the "population control establishment" and charges of "indiscriminate birth control" in lieu of policies to mitigate starvation wages and the uneven distribution of resources.[55] One columnist in the Mexican daily *Excélsior* lamented the implications of the IWY's "population bomb" sloganeering, which discouraged poor women from having children who consume "food, goods, and space that rightfully belong to others" and implied they posed an obstacle to women who wanted to "liberate themselves, to work and to study."[56]

In other words, the significance of the IWY debates about family planning might have fit into competing temporal orderings, drawing distinct trajectories of causality. For those anxious to draw attention to the global "problem" of population growth, the IWY discussions strengthened the link between population control and women's status.[57] For those who understood women's liberation as emancipation from the domestic realm and unfettered entrance into the commodified labor market, the ability to control fertility seemed like an unqualified accomplishment. For dependency theorists who argued that First World prosperity and ever-increasing consumption depended upon Third World poverty and exploitation, the emphasis on population control seemed like the next step in a *reductio ad absurdum* in which poorer populations would be annihilated to conserve "food, goods, and space that rightfully belong to others." The meanings of the entire issue of family planning fit into all of these larger arcs of historical developments.

The relationship between temporality and the signification of the event extended to the intentional and even unintentional gestures at the IWY meetings. The intergovernmental conference occupied two spaces that conjured Mexico's own political conjuncture of 1968. The inauguration venue Gimnasio Juan de la Barrera, named after a young lieutenant who died during the 1847 U.S. occupation of Mexico City, had served as an important site of the 1968 Olympics, and the conference itself took place at the Ministry of Foreign Relations at Tlatelolco Plaza, most remembered as the site of the infamous 1968 student massacre.[58] On the one hand, the selection of these locales was largely logistical—the Olympic-size gym had the largest capacity of any indoor facility in Mexico City, and it certainly made sense to hold the diplomatic conference at the Ministry of Foreign Relations. On the other, for Mexicans and anyone who had paid attention to recent Mexican history, these two locales recalled both Mexico's aspirations to global prominence and the violent authoritarianism that accompanied those aspirations.

While such gestures were particularly conspicuous—indeed, monumental—the IWY gatherings were replete with smaller gestures that the performance theorist Diana Taylor would describe as repertoire, the ephemeral and embodied acts that transmit knowledges through the performance of meanings and identities.[59] The significance of performances such as those at the IWY tribune hinges upon their attendant *scenarios*, the "meaning-making paradigms that structure social environments, behaviors, and potential outcomes."[60] Building on the more familiar historical concept of *context*, the scenario—the costumes and sets and locales that surround the acting—informs expectations by gesturing to well-known plots and story lines. "The scenario makes visible, yet again, what is already there: the ghosts, the images, the stereotypes," Taylor explains. "The scenario structures our understanding. It also haunts our present, a form of hauntology that resuscitates and reactivates old dramas. We've seen it all before. The framework allows for occlusions; by positioning our perspective, it promotes certain world views while helping to disappear others."[61]

REPRESENTING WOMEN: ACTORS, PERFORMANCE, AND AUTHENTICITY

The IWY conference and tribune each had scenarios of their own and were composed of participants who came with their own hauntologies— their own dramas and histories that might be reactivated in surprising ways. Scenarios materially informed the ways that participants perceived and participated in not only the IWY meetings but also the protests, festivities, and late-night rap sessions. In countless settings, participants engaged in elaborate performances not only of political identities but also of womanhood itself.[62] These performances, ranging from the sartorial to the ideological, were not feigned or fraudulent—although some aspects of them clearly were more self-conscious than others—but rather inhabitations of particular political roles. Barrios de Chungara performed her subjectivity as a union militant just as Sirimavo Bandaranaike performed hers as prime minister or Ashraf Pahlavi performed hers as a feminist modernizer and international powerbroker. Participants' speech, dress, and actions were informed by both their own understandings of suitable comportment as well as the expectations or perceived expectations of their audiences. During the course of interactions in Mexico City, these performances adapted—sometimes temporarily and sometimes more durably—as participants developed new understandings of their roles at the IWY meetings and beyond.

Bodies served as sites to express politics, nationalism, ideology, and ethnic identity, and observers offered constant commentary on women as embodied political subjects, including not only remarks upon women's dress, adornment, and hairstyles but also discussions about the comparative beauty and relative "femininity" of first ladies Leah Rabin and Jehan Sadat or U.S. feminists Gloria Steinem and Kate Millett. Reporters noted that Ashraf Pahlavi arrived in an elegant European-style suit but with no jewelry and only a small retinue and that the "iron butterfly" Filipina first lady Imelda Marcos "was embraced by three Chinese women delegates in sober, dark-gray trouser suits."[63]

Once under way, the events quickly became stages for political performances directed not only at an international audience but also at audiences in participants' home countries and communities, resulting in a cacophony of mingling performances rooted in different contexts and intended not only for fellow tribune participants but, perhaps more importantly, for an array of allies and rivals not present. Deracinated from the scenarios that generated them, inserted into a newly fabricated scenario, and communicating with multiple audiences at once, the performances at the IWY gatherings produced a confusion of meanings. As Barrios de Chungara noted, "We spoke very different languages, no?"[64] Sewell reminds us, however, that it is precisely amid this Geertzian "confusion of tongues" that "social encounters contest cultural meanings or render them uncertain."[65] It was this uncertainty, in turn, that most animated the IWY meetings and that renders them exceptional spaces for seeing both the diversity of gendered performances and the ways those performances articulated. As Sewell observes, the "imperfections or slippages in the articulations" between practices of language and performance more generally function as "important sources of changes in the overall shape of the [language] games in question—which is to say, of social life."[66]

The social life at the IWY gatherings centered on two practices that functioned both in tandem and in tension: representation and identification.[67] When Barrios de Chungara later described her anticipation of the IWY tribune, she recalled thinking there would be two groups: elite women in Tlatelolco Plaza "making fancy statements" and, at the tribune, "people like me . . . people with similar problems, you know, poor people."[68] Like many tribune participants, Barrios de Chungara arrived in Mexico City with low expectations for representation and high expectations for identification. She was, to put it mildly, disappointed. Instead she met women whom she imagined spent their days playing canasta and living comfortable lives. "They couldn't see the suffering of my people," she explained. "They couldn't see how our *compañeros* are vomiting their lungs up bit by bit, in pools of blood. They didn't see how underfed our children are. And, of course, they didn't know, as we do, what it's like to get up at four in the morning and go to bed at eleven or twelve at night, just to be able to get all the housework done, because of the lousy conditions we live in."[69]

The problem of representation posed a challenge from the earliest planning stages of the IWY. Disputes over who would control and populate the planning committees were compounded by intense confrontations over the composition of official delegations. U.S. feminists protested loudly, for example, when USAID director Daniel Parker was chosen to lead the U.S. delegation. (He eventually served as co-head with Patricia Hutar, and the State Department claimed the whole kerfuffle had resulted from a misunderstanding.) They protested again when the intergovernmental conference elected Mexican attorney general Pedro Ojeda Paullada to preside over the proceedings. Their objections, which hinged entirely on Ojeda Paullada's sex and made no mention of his role in a repressive political regime, conjured their own hauntologies as security officials envisioned Friedan leading thousands of women in a protest march down Mexico City's equivalent of Fifth Avenue. In a particularly heated confrontation at the U.S. embassy, a group of Congress of Racial Equality (CORE) activists insisted that delegation member Jewel Lafontant—herself a founding member of CORE, an officer of the NAACP's Chicago chapter, and a veteran of Chicago's lunch-counter sit-ins—could not sufficiently represent the interests of African American women. The question of representation seemed to be, as the saying goes, turtles all the way down; there was no firm foundation upon which representational claims might comfortably rest.

The tribune organizers demonstrated awareness of this difficulty from the outset, and the tribune enjoyed more freedom than the conference to sidestep the thorny question of representation. When they opened participation to anyone interested in attending, they diminished claims that the participants might represent larger groups and insisted that the tribune would not produce any official minutes or reports and that nobody was authorized to represent the tribune to the press or to the intergovernmental conference. Friedan attempted to assume this role, organizing a "feminist caucus" and then presenting its recommended amendments to the IWY secretary-general Helvi Sipïla, but her efforts earned her only disapprobation at the tribune. The Latin American women split between a group that loosely aligned with Friedan's caucus and the more militant and Marxist "group of 200" that adopted Barrios de Chungara as its standard-bearer, with the fault line running not between the First and Third World but rather along ideological and political lines—or what the cultural geographer Cindi Katz has fruitfully dubbed "contour lines"—that did not respect geopolitical boundaries.[70]

Barrios de Chungara's immediate experience of both poverty and repression set her apart from most participants and probably goes some distance toward explaining why she became such an iconic figure. Although very few extremely poor women attended the conference, concerns about rural poverty and malnutrition had gained international attention as they increasingly seemed to threaten geopolitical and environmental security. The two preceding UN conferences—on population and food production—had highlighted the perceived threat posed by the growing legions of rural poor who increasingly populated insurgent movements, migrated to cities and settled in squatter communities, or remained in their home communities as stark reminders of the limitations of modernization projects. These concerns arrived at the IWY conference via dozens of background papers and mediated by development specialists living in impoverished regions or by privileged sectors of those regions. The concerns of sub-Saharan African women, for example, were expressed by Margaret Snyder, a development specialist with the UN's Economic Commission for Africa; the Ghanaian supreme court justice Annie Jiagge; the Nigerian health minister Victoria Mojekwu; or the Kenyan legal scholar Opinya Okoth-Ogendo. While this marked a dramatic expansion of perspectives from previous international women's conferences, the discussion still rarely included the voices of those who saw rural poverty not as a distant problem in need of containment but rather as a personal daily struggle. "These conferences are global theater," Gayatri Spivak has written about the 1995 Beijing UN Women's Conference, which achieved exponentially greater levels of socioeconomic diversity. "People going to these conferences may be struck by the global radical aura. But if you hang out at the other end, participating day-to-day in the (largely imposed) politics of how delegations and NGO groups are put together . . . you would attest that what is left out is the poorest women of the South as self-conscious critical agents."[71] What Barrios de Chungara seemed to personify, then, was unmediated authenticity, although what she "authentically" represented was projected upon her. Even as she claimed to speak for herself —she titled her memoir *Let Me Speak!*, after all—she also became an unwitting ventriloquist for those seeking, to invoke Spivak again, to make the subaltern speak.[72]

Aspirations for identification were widespread but generally disappointed. Chicanas imagined a return to the motherland to "share a common sisterhood" with Mexican feminists but found no such affinity. "We though, oh, yeah, we're Mexican Americans," recalled Chicana activist Sandra Serrano Sewell, "we're going to find all [these] natural connections, you know, and sort of like a romantic view that was quickly dispelled."[73] "Third World women" from the United States hoped to develop bonds of solidarity with women from the geopolitical Third World but found little common ground. Friedan describes Sudha Acharya of the All-India Women's Conference "shaking with rage" at the protests by U.S. Third World women. "We all know there is racial discrimination in the United States," she reportedly fumed, "but black or white, you are better off than we are. In my country, women and their families must live on a per capita income of six dollars a month."[74] For her part, Friedan maneuvered between reflecting pools and Olmec sculptures during an official dinner at the National Anthropology Museum in order to approach the delegates from the People's Republic of China. Noting the PRC women's embodied indicators of oppression—they wore "blue uniforms and no make-up; the head of the delegation had square-cut black hair; a younger one had light-haired pigtails"—Friedan spoke to them through an interpreter, declaiming the accomplishments of the U.S. feminist movement. Suddenly, the Chinese ambassador "barked out something that sounded authoritative," and the women withdrew from the conversation. Undaunted by either the obvious language barriers or the ambassador who, "like blocking a tackle in a football game," tried to prevent further contact, Friedan persisted. "[S]he was a woman. I didn't accept the impossibility of talking to her. Maybe if I could sit next to her, some woman-to-woman things would get across."[75]

Arguably no question of identification proved more unsettling than the lesbians' interventions at the tribune.[76] Women's sexuality, apart from oblique discussions around family planning questions, had been left off the scheduled program and received only limited attention even in informal sessions. Nonetheless, lesbians' very presence at the tribune seemed to provoke such intense anxiety that they disrupted the possibilities of identification more than any other group. In Barrios de Chungara's *testimonio*, she points to back-to-back encounters with lesbians and prostitutes as the moment of her alienation from the IWY meetings.[77] Certainly the insistence by some lesbian participants that women should choose lesbianism as a way of opting out of patriarchy posed a powerful challenge to the maternalist feminism based in gender complementarity that prevailed in most of Latin America. Mexican newspaper columnists insisted that lesbians should not even be allowed to enter the tribune.[78] The Marxist left set up a zero-sum game between recognizing lesbian rights and opposing the Pinochet regime in Chile.[79] Mexico's most prominent lesbian, the theater director Nancy Cárdenas, attempted to suture this ruptured identification. Cárdenas recalled her dismay at hearing that her comrades had walked out on a session when the question of lesbianism arose. "They told me that the Communists, my own *compañeras* from earlier in the party, abandoned the conference hall when an Australian girl said 'I'm a lesbian feminist,'" she recalled later in an interview. "They said, 'Throw out the sickos, we're out of here' and abandoned the hall. That seemed to me to give an incomplete image of Mexico, because I was also a leftist militant, was a lesbian, and I had another position and raised my finger."[80] Cárdenas's efforts were futile, at least in the short term; her public proclamation of Mexico's first lesbian manifesto, while it stands as a turning point in Mexican lesbian history, provoked only more intense vitriol from the Catholic right and the Marxist left.

All these missed connections generated an overwhelming sense of frustration as participants sought identification with and recognition from other participants. Throughout her *testimonio*, Barrios de Chungara identifies "people like me" exclusively by class, hoping to meet working and peasant women at the IWY tribune. However, during the tribune—and even more in the years since—people imagined that she might have ended that sentence differently: "people like me . . . indigenous people" or "people like me . . . Latin Americans" or "people like me . . . Marxists." The dissatisfaction with these incomplete or failed identifications fostered claims to authenticity paired with accusations of manipulation. Friedan aggressively insisted that any women who prioritized economic rights over women's rights were subject to manipulations by communists, the CIA, or the "far right." Barrios de Chungara insisted that both feminism and machismo were inventions of U.S. imperialism intended to divide men and women who should be joined in class struggle.

The frustration that many participants experienced stemmed, to a large extent, from the expectations they carried with them to Mexico City. Many women hoped, like Betty Friedan, that "woman-to-woman things would get across" at the IWY, only to discover the impossibility of a normative conception of womanhood. The tensions between those expectations and the developments at the conference and tribune mounted from day to day, exploding into heated confrontations as each forum tried to distill the tumult of conflicts and encounters into unified statements of purpose. The elusiveness of unity precipitated hand-wringing and accusations all around as participants and organizers perceived they had failed in one of their principal objectives. What they could not have seen, however, is that the IWY meetings—precisely because of this failed unification—contributed to what have become some of the most important interventions of feminist thought in the subsequent decades: radical heterogeneity and challenges to normativity, an appreciation for the ways that political performances constitute political subjects, and an unsettling and decentering of dominant historical narratives.

The IWY gatherings were hardly the first attempt to use an international conference to distill solidarity out of heterogeneity, but they offer important historical lessons about the nature of transnational social movements. Perhaps the closest historical analog, as the journalist Ethel Payne pointed out, would be the 1955 Bandung Conference, which launched what the international relations specialist Mark T. Berger has dubbed the Bandung Era (1955–75).[81] As the historian Christopher Lee puts it, Bandung "generated what has often been taken as self-evident: the idea of a Third World."[82] As with the IWY conference, participants and observers have debated Bandung's meanings and legacies.[83] Critics have pointed out the many ways in which the participants fell short of the economic and even nonaggression promises of the conference's final communiqué, invoking arguments that presaged IWY efforts to parse politics from women's issues. The historian Roland Burke describes Bandung as the "subject of determined reinvention by the ideologues of Afro-Asian solidarity and non-alignment. Their imagined Bandung, more legend than fact, has become the dominant perspective on the conference, despite the collapse of any meaningful Afro-Asian movement over four decades ago."[84] Bandung's boosters, meanwhile, highlight the ways in which the "Bandung Spirit" signified, as Vijay Prashad puts it, "that the colonized world had now emerged to claim its space in world affairs, not just as an adjunct of the First or Second Worlds, but as a player in its own right." As a "refusal of both economic subordination and cultural suppression," he explains, "The audacity of Bandung produced its own image."[85]

Both Mexico City and Bandung produced enduring movements despite the fact that both at the conferences and in their aftermaths participants continued to disagree about even the most critical issues—nonaggression, for example, or reproductive labor. The explosive diversity of their founding moments—and the necessity of accommodating this diversity—gave both these movements their staying power. Much like the IWY conference, Bandung generated a document that simultaneously fell short of its signatories' aspirations and exceeded their capacities for implementation; it drew a roster of participants who were relative newcomers to international politics and who understood their roles as both agitators and lawmakers; and it emerged as a signifier elastic enough—a "spirit"—that rendered it durable as a historical watershed.

The IWY exhibited similar elasticity—occasionally tipping into revisionism—that allowed participants to reimagine rivals as allies. In a 2006 interview, the New York-based IWY tribune organizer Mildred Persinger described the interventions by the "fiery" Bolivian tin miner's wife who was "something of a revolutionary."[86] In a moving description about the uncertainty surrounding Barrios de Chungara's arrival in Mexico City and her emotional entrance at the tribune, Persinger describes Barrios de Chungara as having "started a project among the women to bake a special kind of biscuit that is very popular in Latin America and sell them." In place of Barrios de Chungara's militancy and radicalism—which had involved hunger strikes and hostage taking and long stretches in prison getting beaten to a pulp, even when eight months pregnant, but very little biscuit making—appears the kind of entrepreneurship that has become the zeitgeist of the microfinance age. In the twenty-first-century rendition of IWY, the militant revolutionary apparently will be played by an enterprising young woman with a business plan and a microloan.

Such representations reveal not only the challenge of translations at the IWY events but also its promise. Women arrived with experiences that were not simply incommensurate; they often were unimaginable. While her glancing encounters with the U.S. civil rights movement might have given Persinger the faintest whiff of what Barrios de Chungara had confronted, she had no personal experiences that would allow her adequately to translate the violence and deprivation endured by a militant tin miner's wife. Nonetheless, the contact zone created in Mexico City—much like those in Bandung or at the World Social Forum—opened the possibility of developing a common language of transnational feminism, however power laden and fraught. To the extent that the series of UN women's conferences have brought about real changes in women's status and greater awareness of the failure to achieve many other changes, those accomplishments reflect the increasingly shared lexicon of performances and experiences that have made diverse feminisms intelligible and fostered the creation of a new language of transnational feminism.

Itinerancy and Power

Bhavani Raman

THIS VOLUME OF ESSAYS is a collective effort to write peripatetic histories. Its contributors attend to itinerancy rather than place, and journeys rather than destinations. The journey is the story and the trajectory of things, practices, and concepts; it is the very object of scholarly attention. The idea of motion in these essays is not dissimilar to Aristotle's notion of *kinêsis*. To Aristotle kinêsis was potentiality actualized. In his conception, potentiality was distinct from outcomes, something that he explained in the *Metaphysics* as the difference between house building and the result, the house. Both house building and the finished object are different actualizations of the same potentiality of a set of materials—bricks and mortar—that is buildable into a house.[1]

The essays of this volume attend to motion in this sense of house building, and in that spirit, they take the conceptual vocabulary that is often associated with intercultural encounter and fashion from it analytical frames that emphasize the contingent quality and multiple trajectories of exchange. The agility of concepts revealed in motion helps our contributors break from imprisoning dualisms of local and universal. Rather than look for resolution or synthesis in a point of convergence or in radical incommensurability, these essays retain the spaces in between, the moment of transit or suspension, as the spaces where things happen and meanings matter.

Centering itinerancy as concept and method enables a reconsideration of scale in the historian's craft. The essays all follow itinerant matter and practices (music and musicians, body movements, pidgin, gifting, aluminum), and in their own narrative journeys scale up and scale out, traversing vast spaces—oceans, regions—or centuries, or both at the same time. The volume does not seek to redefine or demarcate region or space; it does not echo the *longue durée* temporality of Fernand Braudel's celebrated study of the Mediterranean. Attending to motion, instead, opens up a field of perspectives that reveals how inconsequential quotidian acts like taking the pulse bear the imprint of past collisions, a deep history. Very little of this traffic has left a material trace in writing, anecdote, or memory. However, when carefully recuperated through the lens of itinerancy, this traffic is reconstituted in the historian's eye and promises to reconceive afresh the fractured pasts of our globalized present. Itinerancy thus opens up other paths, other histories of possibility. As many of the essays demonstrate, it allows the historian to recuperate ways of life and transactions occluded by contemporary discourses of self, racial, and national ascription.

These gains of contingency and scale notwithstanding, itinerant histories produce their own hazards. Attending to cultures in motion always runs the risk of treating cultures as "things" that travel, as opposed to a set of claims about collective or shared sensibility. Furthermore, peripatetic history can be haunted by the exercise of power that its own lens finds difficult to address.[2] In emphasizing the importance of reciprocal exchange in the production of new forms and practices, peripatetic history runs the risk of underplaying the starker and more violent conditions that underwrote those transactions. Histories of early modern science that stress the anonymous, reciprocal processes of blending by which knowledge, meaning, and practice grow have not always taken adequate account of less benign themes: the inextricable linkages between European interest in New World nature and its commercial exploitation. European observation took the form of "asset stripping," disembedding natural objects from their contexts and histories, and incorporating them into European natural history and commerce. In a similar vein, the element of reciprocal exchange between historical actors as radically different in power as Black and Irish challenge dancers in early-nineteenth-century New York should not mask the role of racial subordination and political conquest in creating the conditions that made those processes possible.

The point at issue is not the intentions of the agents. The issue is that such transfers rendered matter, techniques, and objects into a commodity, a substance of exchange value, and thereby, a different entity. Flows and exchange are freighted acts; they are not naturally or essentially cosmopolitan. Itinerant histories, in other words, are burdened by the contradiction between the ecumenical and transcendental hope held out by the making of new entities and the violence of displacement that inevitably underwrote it. So it is that these histories allow us to appreciate contingency. But they also force a careful consideration of the limits of a reciprocity-dominated approach to knowledge and practice.

A critical eye to itinerancy can lead to new ways of understanding the constitution of practices and ideas. Nira Wickramasinghe's essay on the sewing machine, for example, narrates Sri Lankan modernity through the rise of consumers and consumption. As she demonstrates, the mere act of consumption under the weight of colonial rule required a great amount of discursive labor to produce the modernity that was also decidedly Lankan. Wickramasinghe's essay is thus not a syncretic account of the sewing machine where the consumption of goods represents the triumphant participation of the colonial consumer in some happy equalizing global market society. Market modernity in Lanka was simultaneously a project of entering a global or universal time and a project burdened with producing Lankan, culturally marked, consumers who were further differentiated by class and gender. In a similar way, Peter Brown, in his essay on the gift in late antiquity, identifies the history of gifting not as a journey from the world of civic reciprocity to Christian philanthropy, but as the emergence of a new set of dispositions to wealth that owe a simultaneous debt to both sets of norms. The practice of gifting is not a stable concept moving through historical periods. Rather the changing notion of gifting allows the historian to reflect on the nature of historical transition in new ways.

If the older vocabulary of contact zones and hybridity took as its foundation the problem of describing intercultural encounters, then itinerant history holds out the possibility of taking potentiality seriously. Rather than use the market, a silent analogy to rework the colonial genealogies of certain concepts, attending to kinêsis, can allow us to think more critically about how the protocols of market exchange have shaped scholarly perspectives on knowledge and power. The stakes are serious. For as these essays, in their limitations and in their possibilities, suggest, an exchange-driven orientation to historical narrative does not dissolve the violence of displacement. We need critical approaches to the ready cosmopolitanism underlying the aspirations of new global histories. The itinerant histories in this volume offer a beginning.

From Cultures to Cultural Practices and Back Again

Helmut Reimitz

THE AUTHOR OF THIS AFTERWORD must confess at the outset: he is actually an Austrian.[1] The difference may seem trivial to others, but to most people who grew up in Vienna after World War II, as I did, the distinction became immensely important. The determination to set apart an Austrian identity and culture distinct from Germany can hardly be exaggerated. Like every schoolchild, I was given a properly "Austrian" dictionary, though we barely used it, and I cannot remember ever looking up a single word in it once I got a little older. It functioned less as a tool of instruction than as one of several strategies of distinction with which Austrians coped with their national identity crisis after 1945. To transform the notion of a common German culture into a distinctively Austrian culture—language, conversation, cuisine, music, theater, history, and identity—was a pressing national project. The joke ran that the small Austrian nation had succeeded in convincing the world that Hitler, born in what is present-day Austria, was really a German and that Beethoven, born in Bonn, was really an Austrian—a relocation of culture that might amuse even one of its most eminent experts, Homi Bhabha.

One could say that this has little to do with the subject of this volume, *Cultures in Motion*. At first glance my observations may seem to instrumentalize culture by associating it with political strategy. They seem less a matter of culture and more a matter of *Kulturpolitikskultur*—as one of the most important German writers of the twentieth century, the Austrian Robert Musil, ironically called it.[2] Not coincidentally, Musil coined the term in the 1930s to criticize the cultural policy of the Austrofascist regime, in which some of the efforts to demarcate an Austrian culture from a German one had already begun to emerge. In a speech he made at a conference on the "Defense of Culture" in Paris in 1935, he remarked,

> My Austrian homeland more or less expects its poets to be Austrian poets of the homeland, and there are engineers of cultural history (*Kulturgeschichtskonstrukteure*) who make a show of demonstrating

that an Austrian poet had always been something different than a German one.[3]

Musil also knew that these forms of cultural appropriation were evident in other countries, too. Among vastly different political persuasions and nations, according to Musil, "the claims of the most dissimilar fatherlands and of their political and social conviction have overridden the concept of culture."[4] And he uneasily observed not only how single nations appropriated the concept of culture, but also how the very conference he was participating in was guilty of the same thing. He said that he did not know where to begin with the congress title "Defense of Culture," except to defend the individual as culture's source.[5] The Austrian's appeal to establish a political framework that would make individual cultural expression possible was what many might have seen a very un-German solution at the time. But the many concepts, versions, and drafts that Musil sketched for this speech show that he was not entirely satisfied with his proposal.[6] He obviously recognized that the concept, with its enormous potential to be adjusted and appropriated, posed a problem. But in no version of the speech did he call the concept itself into question. As so often in his writings, he solved the problem with irony: Kulturpolitikskultur.

Musil's ironic neologism can also draw our attention to a problem that is closely tied to the subject of this volume. As many of the contributions show, culture is not a set pool of ideas, concepts, and practices. Rather, it arises—as Musil already figured—as a possibility between social realities and their transformation. Most of the essays, and Daniel Rodgers's introduction as well, concentrate on motion in space in order to explore how culture can be observed at the point when cultural practices break loose from their historical bondages, when their mutability becomes visible. But Musil's irony, and its social and political context, might also help us make two additional remarks at the end of this volume. First, one should not forget that cultures in motion are not only movements in space but also movements over time. Second, Musil's Kulturpolitikskultur suggests that the constant motion of complex "amalgams of cultural practices" (Dan Rodgers) can also be affected by the concept of culture itself, when "culture" becomes the focus of social strategies to give order and meaning to the social world. But it also shows that in such reflections, the concept of culture poses a problem of identity which the concept itself cannot solve.

It is hardly a coincidence that this aspect of culture became a particularly pressing issue in the first half of the twentieth century. But the tension between complex amalgams of cultural practices and their conceptualization as culture is much older. As we will see, it goes back to the establishment of the modern concept of culture in the course of the eighteenth century. Since the time of Musil this has been seen not only as a problem but also as an opportunity to explore and analyze cultural practices and processes. In particular William Sewell has suggested studying the tension between the concept of culture and cultural practices with the help of a distinction between "culture" in the singular, as an analytical practice that organizes difference, and cultures in the plural. "Cultural processes" are the result of the dialectic between this "nonpluralized form of culture" and "culture" in the singular. If cultural practices and products move incessantly between sites, as the essays in this volume demonstrate, they also include strategies of stabilization, differentiation, negotiation, and identity formation. As Sewell suggests, the concept of culture in the singular has always been an important instrument for such efforts to define and stabilize cultures. As most of the assembled essays also indicate, these efforts to stabilize and define cultural difference and practices in certain places and times constantly react or even counteract to the disturbing experience of cultures in motion. While the essays mainly focus on how movements of cultural practices constantly undermine the idea of established or dominant cultures, I would like to suggest looking at the concept of culture and its modern use as a blueprint of such processes. Such an analytic perspective on "culture as cultural practice" however challenges us to define the historical specifics of a cultural practice—that is, culture itself—more precisely.

In order to do this, we might turn to the conceptualization of culture that the German philosopher Niklas Luhmann proposed some years ago. Luhmann hardly thought of himself as a culture theorist, and his few experiments with a historical concept of culture should rather be understood in the broader context of his lifelong project to develop a "Theorie der Gesellschaft."[7] This may be one of the reasons why historical scholarship outside of Germany has to date not seriously considered what Luhmann proposed. Another reason could be that his perspective was linked to a conception of modernity that many historians may understandably find suspect. But I hope to be able to show that by translating, displacing, and disembedding Luhmann's ideas we might overcome their limitations and put them to work in a broader historical perspective.

As Günther Burkert has shown, Luhmann devoted only a few sections of his entire oeuvre to the concept of culture.[8] The first was an extensive consideration that appeared three years before his death, in the fourth volume of his *Gesellschaftsstruktur und Semantik.*[9] Here Luhmann begins with the reminder that the term "culture" itself had its own place and time. It originated in Europe in the late eighteenth century, and its emergence marked the beginning of a new mode of comparison in the modern world.[10] In order to study the development of this mode, he resorted to one of the theoretical concepts central to his study of modern societies: the difference between observations of the first and second order.[11] Whereas first-order observations are operations in which things are observed and differentiated, second-order observations are observations of those (first-order) observations. First-order observations create differences without considering the difference itself: the differentiated subjects that result from the observation are assumed to be definitive, without reflecting on the criteria for the distinction in the first place. One can, for instance, enjoy a Mozart concerto in the Viennese Konzerthaus, and appreciate it as a beautiful and well-performed piece of Mozart's music. Second-order observation, however, means not only observing such acts of observation, but also observing *how* observers observe. It means reflecting upon the criteria by which Mozart's music has been understood and evaluated in certain contexts—for instance, as part of the effort to forge an Austrian identity during the Austrofascist period, or after World War II , through a specifically Austrian musical tradition. Culture, Luhmann suggested, should be understood as such a form of second-order observation. In its modern sense, as he saw it, culture was not what you get when the world is divided into different entities or matters (*Gegenstände*). Culture was the very act of observing and reflecting about how these entities and matters were divided and differentiated.[12]

The shift of the concept of culture to second-order observations, however, raises the question of what form second-order observation then takes. To answer this, Luhmann linked the emergence of the modern concept of culture to the new interest in comparison that arose in an increasingly globalized Europe. Comparison introduced a new level of communication in which culture could be treated abstractly as one possible form among many other possible forms. New forms of life, other societies, the foreign, the esoteric, and the exotic could be reintegrated again and again. Comparison itself became a culture-generating operation. Luhmann did not develop a romanticized view in which European society opened itself up to alternative forms of culture through globalization and enlightenment. Instead he saw the thematicization of culture in the eighteenth century as a specifically European or even Eurocentric reaction to an emergent global society. Culture could be anywhere, and through the introduction of the modern concept of culture, it could be located geographically and historically, throughout time and in every part of the world. But reflection on it always had to occur at a specific point in time and in a specific place. And that first reflection took place in modern Europe, which affirmed itself through the very process of drawing comparisons.

As Luhmann remarks, however, there was a latent possibility that both the comparison and the results of the comparison could have gone a different way. That inherent contingency seems to have been what Luhmann found most interesting about the modern concept of culture. It was here that he saw a link to his theory of modern society, which he had studied through its processes of communication and concluded that the attempts to dismantle contingency in communication continually led to new communications and contingency.[13]

The contingency of the concept of culture has also been used in recent decades, independently of Luhmann's ideas, to redefine culture and its use in the humanities. In the process, new approaches were developed that made it easier to analyze culture as a dynamic concept where efforts to manage the inherent contingencies of cultural definitions of the self and the other repeatedly engendered new reactions and new contingencies. Borrowing Luhmann's terminology, one could say that the work of recent decades has shown us new ways to study the ongoing differentiation of social and cultural systems as open-ended processes. But these propositions also make clear that these processes by no means lead to the breakdown of cultural, social, and political differences and barriers. Rather, the second-order processes of observing and articulating culture invariably contribute to the demarcation of cultural difference. Even when contingency is especially visible in "middle grounds," "hybrid cultures," or "zones of cultural friction," these points of contact are not mere byproducts of larger hegemonic demands (whether from mighty Germany or tiny postwar Austria). Rather, they are necessary to designating and affirming a specific amalgam of practices in a state of transformation as a distinctive culture.

Andrew Sartori's work on the global dissemination of the European concept of culture through the case of Bengal makes an important contribution in this regard.[14] But it seems to me that recourse to Luhmann could go in yet a different direction. The focus would not just be on a comparison of possibilities and limits that arise through the appropriation and use of contingency. It would also consider the way in which contingency arose—and with it, culture—when society's gaze shifted to alternative forms and possibilities.[15] In this way, the historical investigation of culture could emancipate itself from its basically "modernist" conception. The question would therefore be less about which processes of communication were a product of attempts to deal with the contingency of the concept of culture, as people sought to manage, control, or use it in different places and times. Instead, the focus would be on the study of that cultural practice that introduces comparison as a level of communication, in which "culture" is treated abstractly and can be discussed as such, in order to determine a specific "amalgam of cultural practices" that makes culture.[16] Second-order observation can itself be studied as the cultural practice of culture. One can, in short, move from cultures to cultural practices and back again.

Perhaps I can illustrate the possibilities I have raised with the help of some of the contributions to this volume. Celia Applegate's essay illustrates the process by which second-order reflection on the cultural practice of culture established itself and what an enormous historical reaction it was capable of launching. Applegate's history of musical movements in Europe begins before the establishment of the culture concept in the eighteenth century—and therefore also before the concept of music as culture in the modern sense. But she follows this history into the "Europe of Nations" of the nineteenth century. One might expect from such a history that musical culture would be increasingly monopolized by a flourishing nationalism. But Applegate draws a different picture. If we follow her history of musicians and their identities and identifications from the sixteenth to the nineteenth centuries, a different relationship between culture and nation seems to present itself. The *idea* of a musical culture loosened its protagonists more and more from their local ties and oriented them to the idea of a common culture; but for practical reasons, their identity could not be derived from music, nor—because of the modern conception of culture as a mode of comparison—from the culture concept itself. To differentiate itself in this comparison, musical culture increasingly resorted to regional and national differences, through which specific cultural practices and phenomena could be combined anew, as Applegate forcefully shows in the history of choral associations in the nineteenth century. What does not arise in her examination is evidence that a national (musical) culture emerged as a kind of by-product of nationalism. It is the modern concept of culture itself that continuously articulated a problem of identity, and in so doing operated as one of the main catalysts of national identity in modern Europe.[17]

Harold Cook's and Pamela Smith's contributions also guide us through the period before the establishment of the modern concept of culture. Both examine the *flow* of "cultural materials and practices" between Europe and Asia, but they arrive at different results. Whereas Smith emphasizes a relatively free cultural flow in Eurasia, Cook observes that some cultural materials overcame the "human boundaries that human communities have constructed" more easily than others. In his exploration of cultural processes of transfer and exchange in early modern medicine, Cook suggests a distinction between "material things that can move readily" and other "more sticky kinds."

At first glance, this seems to fit well with Smith's study of the color red. Through the complex manufacturing of red dye, cultural knowledges seem to have wandered far across Eurasia. But her observations suggest that the color red and its production were also associated, in each of its different contexts, with different social semantics, memories, and belief systems. And so the question arises, when does a material thing stop being a mere material thing? With the help of Luhmann's insights, one might consider not simply differentiating between material things and less tangible objects but also linking such transfers with the different ways in which they were observed. Do cultural materials travel more easily if they are taken as they are, as cultural materials in first-order observations; and do they become "stickier" when they are integrated in a social praxis that objectifies them as part of an amalgam of cultural practices, objectified through second-order observations?

The methodological path, *from cultures to cultural practices and back again*, can also be applied to cultures in motion over time. Peter Brown's contribution underlines this point by illustrating the complex instruments of reflection through which societies were created long before the modern concept of culture emerged. This essay is closely related to his extensive study of fundamental social transformation in which he analyzes the relationship between wealth and Christianity from late Roman to medieval society in the Latin West.[18] He shows how Christian negotiations of property and wealth, and of their meaning and their function for the community, created social and political structures that would characterize Europe and the West for a long time. Beyond this, he also shows how this social transformation was made possible through extensive processes of reflection that developed a sense of a distinctive Christian culture in contrast to other cultures, above all as a counterculture to Roman society. Exegetical practice made it possible for Christian communities to define themselves as a new chosen people and, at the same time, to use this essentially Christian reinterpretation of the culture of biblical Israel to delineate themselves from the Roman world. This presupposes a substantial and complex tradition of social self-reflection and reflection on the other, which could be characterized perfectly as second-order observation.

Brown's study is a striking example of how the mode of second-order observation should by no means be seen as originating in modernity (as Luhmann suggested). More importantly, the essay also shows what far-reaching consequences such processes of reflection about the social and political organization of society can have. Perhaps Brown's essay can then also help the author of these lines to justify the relocation of Luhmann-esque ideas to a premodern age, for it illustrates how new possibilities for the study of culture can be further developed, not just for European societies before the eighteenth century but also for societies beyond Europe that predate the globalization of the modern concept of culture.[19] What forms of second-order observation were developed in different times and different regions of the world as the cultural practice of culture? Since antiquity, historiography might have had a comparable function to the modern concept of culture. One thinks of Plutarch's sharp criticism of the cultural relativity of Herodotus, the father of historiography, or of the extensive reflections and reinterpretations of the Roman and classical world's mythical-historical memories in Augustine's *De civitate Dei*.[20] For the history of both Europe and other parts of the world, new applications of such an approach could lead to a deeper understanding of cultural processes and their role as catalysts of social transformation.

Such reflection of cultural processes extending backward past European modernity also raises new questions about the history of how the modern concept of culture was itself established in Europe. Given the potential diversity of cultural practices of culture, the issue of the concept's historical formation raises questions not only about the convergence and compatibility of these practices, but also about the preconditions or older cultural practices in general that enabled it to be established in Europe in the eighteenth century. Here the student of the late antique and medieval West may observe that Peter Brown's essay is closer to the other contributions than its chronological distance might make it seem at first. Certain institutions that developed in conjunction with the social restructuring of post-Roman Europe had a remarkably long history. Some of the poor houses that were founded in the sixth century were still around in the eighteenth and nineteenth centuries. The house for the poor in Le Mans was in use until 1789, Trier's even to the time of Napoleon.[21] One could also take this as evidence that the cultural practices that made the founding of these institutions possible had an equally far-reaching history into the European future. This again raises the question of to what extent the establishment of the modern concept of culture built on modes of reflection that developed and redeveloped Christian forms of second-order observations over many centuries.

The contributions collected in this volume, however, remind us to be careful with such broad observations. They show what meticulous work and complex differentiations are necessary in thinking about a genealogy of culture in history. Academic formats that encourage experiments, essays, and case studies are all the more important, therefore, precisely because they do not aim for such a synthesis but instead seek to provide new impetus through the critical mass that their variety generates. The multiyear discussion of cultures in motion that this volume reflects is a good example of this. How useful the experiments, case studies, and reflections here are is something the reader must judge. But I hope that they, and this afterword, have made clear that without the numerous conversations, the collective experimentation with concepts, and the mutual exchange of historical contexts that took place in the two years of this project at the Davis Center, they would not have even been imaginable in the first place.

List of Papers

PAPERS PRESENTED TO THE DAVIS SEMINAR
ON CULTURES AND INSTITUTIONS IN MOTION

2008–9

*Celia Applegate, "Musical Itinerancy in the World of Nations: The Case of Germany, Its Music, and Its Musicians"

Sven Beckert, "The Empire of Cotton: A Global History"

*Thomas Bender, "America: A Global History"

Alan Bewell, "Colonial Natures in Translation"

John Carson, "Between Medical Authority and Legal Precedent: Adjudicating 'Unsoundness of Mind' in Nineteenth-Century Anglo-American Jurisprudence"

Linda Colley, "Power, Gender, and Obsession: The World-wide Political Thought of Philip Francis"

Harold J. Cook, "Creating a Medical Movement in the Early Enlightenment: Chinese Medicine, the Jesuits, and the Dutch East India Company"

Frederick Cooper, "Citizenship between Empire and Nation: France and French Africa, 1945–1960"

Molly Greene, "Documents for the Pirates: The Use of Consular Authority in the Early Modern Mediterranean"

Frank Guridy, "Performing Garveyite Culture in Cuba, 1919–1930"

*April Masten, "The Challenge Dance: Transatlantic Exchange in Early American Popular Culture"

Barbara Metcalf, "Nawab Shah Jahan Begum: Dress, Design, and Decorum in Colonial India and England"

*Susan Pennybacker, "Political Exile in Postwar London: The South Africans"

Clifford Rosenberg, "Between France and Algeria: TB and TB Control, c. 1890–1940"

*Mimi Sheller, "Out of the Ground, Into the Sky: How Aluminum Put the World in Motion"

*Robert Stam, "Transmutations of a Trope: The Figure of the Radical Indian"

Sanjay Subrahmanyam, "A Roomful of Mirrors: On the Circulation of Textual and Visual Representations between Early Modern India and Europe"

James Turner, "Altertumswissenschaft in Motion: British Adaptations of German Scholarship in the Nineteenth Century

*David Wasserstein, "Islam and the Making of Medieval Jewry"

Phyllis Whitman Hunter, "Improvising Identity: The Arts of Asia in Early America"

*Nira Wickramasinghe, "Perception, Reception and Reinvention of a Commodity: The Singer Sewing Machine in Colonial Sri Lanka"

Andrés Mario Zervigón, "Modernity Inverted: Looking Closely at Erna Lendvai-Dircksen's Face of the German Race"

2009–10

Cemil Aydin, "Debating the Ottoman Caliphate and the 'Muslim World,' 1839–1924: A Global Intellectual History"

Daniel Botsman, "Freedom Without Slavery? The Case of the Maria Luz and the Meanings of Emancipation in Nineteenth Century Japan"

*Michael David-Fox, "Showcasing the Great Experiment: Cultural Diplomacy and Western Visitors to Soviet Russia, 1921–1941"

Patrick Geary, "The 'Living Dead': Disputing Texts and Claiming Languages in the Nineteenth Century"

*Petra Goedde, "Cold Peace: The International Discourse on Peace during the Cold War"

*Elena Isayev, "Paradoxes of Place: Pausing Motion in Ancient Italy and Now"

Webb Keane, "Materiality, Deep Time, and Cultural Comparison"

*Thomas Lekan, "Green Tourism: Consumption and Conservation in Twentieth-Century Germany"

Ania Loomba, "Re-orienting the English Renaissance"

Elizabeth Mancke, "Spatially Radical Empires: European Expansion and the Making of Modern Geopolitics"

Adam McKeown, "The Movement and Meaning of Mobility 1830–1940"

John McNeill, "Lord Cornwallis vs. Anopheles Quadrimaculatus, 1780–81"

Mae Ngai, "The True Story of Ah Jake: Translation and Justice among Chinese Miners in Nineteenth-Century California"

*Mary Nolan, "Europe and America in the Twentieth Century"

*Dorothy Noyes, "From the Camel's Mouth: The Moving Local of Seventeenth-Century Languedoc"

*Jocelyn Olcott, "The Greatest Consciousness-Raising Event in History: The 1975 International Women's Year Conference and the Challenge of Transnational Feminism"

Steven Shapin, "Eating Good in the Neighborhood: The Medical and Moral History of Dietary Localism"

Julia Smith, "Gathered Together from Everywhere: Mapping Early Medieval Relic Collections, c.700–c.1100"

*Pamela H. Smith, "Knowledge in Motion: A History of Science in the Early Modern World"

Eve Troutt Powell, "Bodies Caught on Film: Photographing Sudanese Slaves in the Early Twentieth Century"

*Davis Center fellow

List of Contributors

EDITORS

Bhavani Raman, associate professor and David Rike University Preceptor at Princeton University, is a historian of South Asian society, politics, and culture. Her recently published book explores the practices of writing, transcription, and translation that undergirded British rule in colonial India (*Document Raj: Writing and Scribes in Early Colonial South India*, 2012).

Helmut Reimitz, assistant professor and Harold Willis Dodds Presidential University Preceptor at Princeton University, is a historian of late antique and early medieval Europe. The editor of several volumes of historical essays, he is completing a study on the history of Frankish identity as a window into the formation of a Western conception of ethnicity in the late antique and early medieval West.

Daniel T. Rodgers is the Henry Charles Lea Professor of History, emeritus, and was director of the Shelby Cullom Davis Center for Historical Studies at Princeton University (2008–12). A historian of American ideas and culture, he is the author of four prize-winning books, including *Atlantic Crossings: Social Politics in a Progressive Age* (1998) and, most recently, *Age of Fracture* (2011).

CHAPTER CONTRIBUTORS

Celia Applegate, William R. Kenan, Jr. Professor of History in the Department of History at Vanderbilt University and past president of the German Studies Association, is a historian of modern German society and culture. Her publications include *A Nation of Provincials: The German Idea of Heimat* (1990) and *Bach in Berlin* (2005). She was a fellow at the Davis Center in 2008–9.

Peter Brown is the Philip and Beulah Rollins Professor of History, emeritus, at Princeton University. He has written a dozen books that, starting with *Augustine of Hippo* (1967), have defined the religious, cultural, and social dimensions of the late antique world. His most recent book is *Through the Eye of a Needle: Wealth, the Fall of Rome, and the Making of Christianity in the West, 350–550 AD* (2012).

Harold J. Cook, the John F. Nickoll Professor of History at Brown University, is a historian of science medicine in the early imperial age. His

Matters of Exchange: Commerce, Medicine, and Science in the Dutch Golden Age (2007) won the Pfizer Prize of the History of Science Society.

April F. Masten, an associate professor of American history at SUNY Stony Brook, is a historian of American culture. Her work explores the interconnections between cultural production and political economies. She is the author of *Art Work: Women Artists and Democracy in Mid-Nineteenth-Century New York* (2008). She was a fellow at the Davis Center in 2008–9.

Mae M. Ngai, the Lung Family Professor of Asian American Studies and professor of history at Columbia University, is a leading historian of Asian American history and the history of immigration. Her work includes *Impossible Subjects: Illegal Aliens and the Making of Modern America* (2005) and *The Lucky Ones: One Family and the Extraordinary Invention of Chinese America* (2010). She is now at work on a study of the Chinese gold miners in the nineteenth-century North American West, Australia, and South Africa.

Jocelyn Olcott, associate professor of history at Duke University, works on feminist history of Mexico. She is the author of *Revolutionary Women in Postrevolutionary Mexico* (2005). She was a fellow at the Davis Center in 2009–10.

Mimi Sheller is professor of sociology and director of the Mobilities Research and Policy Center at Drexel University. She is a founding coeditor of the journal *Mobilities* and her work on politics, citizenship, and consumption in the Caribbean includes the books *Consuming the Caribbean: From Arawaks to Zombies* (2003) and *Citizenship from Below: Erotic Agency and Caribbean Freedom* (2012). Her most recent book is *Aluminum Dreams: The Making of Light Modernity* (2014). She was a fellow at the Davis Center in 2008–9.

Pamela H. Smith, professor of history at Columbia University, is the author of numerous books and articles on science, material culture, and art in early modern Europe. *The Business of Alchemy* (1994) won the Pfizer Prize of the History of Science Society. She was a fellow at the Davis Center in 2009–10.

Nira Wickramasinghe, chair and professor of modern South Asian studies at the University of Leiden, is a scholar of identity, politics, and everyday life in colonial South Asia. Her most recent book is *Sri Lanka in the Modern Age: A History of Contested Identities* (2006). She was a fellow at the Davis Center in 2008–9.

Notes

NOTES TO AN INTRODUCTION

1. James Clifford, *Routes: Travel and Translation in the Late Twentieth Century* (Cambridge, MA: Harvard University Press, 1997), 3; Clifford Geertz, as quoted in Karen J. Winkler, "Anthropologists Urged to Rethink Their Definitions of Culture," *Chronicle of Higher Education*, December 14, 1994, A18; Akhil Gupta and James Ferguson, "Beyond 'Culture': Space, Identity and the Politics of Difference," *Cultural Anthropology* 7, no. 1 (February 1992): 9. See also M. Kearney, "The Local and the Global: The Anthropology of Globalization and Transnationalism," *Annual Review of Anthropology* 24 (1995): 547–63.

For the parallel turn in sociology and geography: Mimi Sheller and John Urry, "The New Mobilities Paradigm," *Environment and Planning A* 38 (2006): 207–26; John Urry, *Sociology beyond Societies: Mobilities for the Twenty-First Century* (New York: Routledge, 2000); Tim Cresswell, *Place: A Short Introduction* (Malden, MA: Blackwell, 2004); David Harvey, "From Space to Place and Back Again: Reflections on the Condition of Postmodernity," in *Mapping the Futures: Local Cultures, Global Change*, ed. Jon Bird et al. (London: Routledge, 1993); Henri Lefebvre, *The Production of Space* (1974; repr., Malden, MA: Blackwell, 1991).

In area studies: Jerry H. Bentley, Renate Bridenthal, and Anand A. Yang, eds., *Interactions: Transregional Perspectives on World History* (Honolulu: University of Hawaii Press, 2005). In comparative literature: Stephen Greenblatt et al., *Cultural Mobility: A Manifesto* (New York: Cambridge University Press, 2010); Wai Chee Dimock, *Through Other Continents: American Literature across Deep Time* (Princeton: Princeton University Press, 2006); Renate Brosch and Rüdiger Kunow, eds., *Transgressions: Cultural Interventions in the Global Manifold* (Trier: Wissenschaftlicher Verlag Trier, 2005); Caren Kaplan, *Questions of Travel: Postmodern Discourses of Displacement* (Durham, NC: Duke University Press, 1996); Mary Louise Pratt, *Imperial Eyes: Travel Writing and Transculturation* (London: Routledge, 1992).

2. Harold J. Cook, *Matters of Exchange: Commerce, Medicine, and Science in the Dutch Golden Age* (New Haven: Yale University Press, 2007); Sanjay Subrahmanyam, "Connected Histories: Notes towards a Reconfiguration of Early Modern Eurasia," *Modern Asian Studies* 31, no. 3 (July 1997): 745.

3. On transnational histories: Akira Iriye and Pierre-Yves Saunier, eds., *The Palgrave Dictionary of Transnational History* (Basingstoke: Palgrave Macmillan, 2009); C. A. Bayly et al., "AHR Conversation on Transnational History," *American Historical Review* 111, no. 5 (December 2006): 1441–64; Thomas Bender, *A Nation among Nations: America's Place in World History* (New York: Hill and Wang, 2006); Gunilla Budde, Sebastian Conrad, and Oliver Janz, eds., *Transna-*

tionale Geschichte: Themen, Tendenzen und Theorien (Göttingen: Vandenhoeck und Ruprecht, 2006); Thomas Bender, ed., *Rethinking American History in a Global Age* (Berkeley: University of California Press, 2002). On global history: Jerry H. Bentley, ed., *The Oxford Handbook of World History* (Oxford: Oxford University Press, 2011); Pamela Kyle Crossley, *What Is Global History?* (Cambridge: Polity, 2008); Jerry H. Bentley, "Myths, Wagers, and Some Moral Implications of World History," *Journal of World History* 16, no. 1 (March 2005): 51–82; Arif Dirlik, "Performing the World: Reality and Representation in the Making of World Histor(ies)," *Journal of World History* 16, no. 4 (December 2005): 391–410; Benedikt Stuchtey and Eckhardt Fuchs, eds., *Writing World History, 1800–2000* (Oxford: Oxford University Press, 2003); Patrick Manning, *Navigating World History: Historians Create a Global Past* (New York: Palgrave Macmillan, 2003); Philip Pomper, Richard J. Elphick, and Richard T. Van, eds., *World History: Ideologies, Structures, and Identities* (Oxford: Blackwell, 1998).

4. Dirk Hoerder, *Cultures in Contact: World Migrations in the Second Millennium* (Durham, NC: Duke University Press, 2002).

5. Jane Burbank and Frederick Cooper, *Empires in World History: Power and the Politics of Difference* (Princeton: Princeton University Press, 2010); James Epstein et al., "AHR Forum: Entangled Empires in the Atlantic World," *American Historical Review* 112, no. 3 (June 2007): 710–99; John Darwin, *After Tamerlane: The Rise and Fall of Global Empires, 1400–2000* (London: Allen Lane, 2007); J. H. Elliott, *Empires of the Atlantic World: Britain and Spain in America, 1492–1830* (New Haven: Yale University Press, 2006); Paul A Kramer, "Power and Connection: Imperial Histories of the United States in the World," *American Historical Review* 116, no. 5 (December 2011): 1348–91; Charles S. Maier, *Among Empires: American Ascendancy and Its Predecessors* (Cambridge, MA: Harvard University Press, 2006).

6. Stephen Howe, ed., *The New Imperial Histories Reader* (London: Routledge, 2009); Catherine Hall and Sonya O. Rose, eds., *At Home with the Empire: Metropolitan Culture and the Imperial World* (Cambridge: Cambridge University Press, 2006); Mrinalini Sinha, *Specters of Mother India: The Global Restructuring of an Empire* (Durham, NC: Duke University Press, 2006); Ann Laura Stoler, ed., *Haunted by Empire: Geographies of Intimacy in North American History* (Durham, NC: Duke University Press, 2006); Paul A. Kramer, *The Blood of Government: Race, Empire, the United States, and the Philippines* (Chapel Hill: University of North Carolina Press, 2006); Antoinette Burton, ed., *After the Imperial Turn: Thinking With and Through the Nation* (Durham, NC: Duke University Press, 2003); Ann Laura Stoler, *Carnal Knowledge and Imperial Power: Race and the Intimate in Colonial Rule* (Berkeley: University of California Press, 2002); Frederick Cooper and Ann Laura Stoler, eds., *Tensions of Empire: Colonial Cultures in a Bourgeois World* (Berkeley: University of California Press, 1997); Nicholas B. Dirks, ed., *Colonialism and Culture* (Ann Arbor: University of Michigan Press, 1992).

7. Simon Schaffer, Lissa Roberts, Kapil Raj, and James Delbourgo, eds., *The Brokered World: Go-Betweens and Global Intelligence, 1770–1820* (Sagamore Beach, MA: Science History Publications, 2009); C. A. Bayly, *Empire and Information: Intelligence Gathering and Social Communication in India, 1780–*

1870 (Cambridge: Cambridge University Press, 1996); James H. Merrell, *Into the American Woods: Negotiators on the Pennsylvania Frontier* (New York: Norton, 1999).

8. Homi K. Bhabha, *The Location of Culture* (London: Routledge, 1994), 9.

9. Peter N. Stearns, *Globalization in World History* (London: Routledge, 2010); Jürgen Osterhammel and Niels P. Peterson, *Globalization: A Short History* (Princeton: Princeton University Press, 2005); A. G. Hopkins, ed., *Globalization in World History* (New York: Norton, 2002).

10. Charles Stewart and Rosalind Shaw, eds., *Syncretism/Anti-Syncretism: The Politics of Religious Synthesis* (London: Routledge, 1994); Corinna R. Unger, "Histories of Development and Modernization: Findings, Reflections, Future Research," *H-Soz-u-Kult*, 09.12.2010, http://hsozkult.geschichte.hu-berlin.de/forum/2010-12-001.

11. Richard White, *The Middle Ground: Indians, Empires, and Republics in the Great Lakes Region, 1650–1815*, 20th anniversary ed. (New York: Cambridge University Press, 2011); Susan Sleeper-Smith et al., "Forum: The Middle Ground Revisited," *William and Mary Quarterly*, 3rd ser., 63, no. 1 (January 2006): 3–93; Jeremy Adelman and Stephen Aron, "From Borderlands to Borders: Empires, Nation-States and the Peoples In-Between in North American History," *American Historical Review* 104, no. 3 (June 1999): 814–41.

12. Rudyard Kipling, *Kim* (1901; repr., Oxford: Oxford University Press, 1998), 239; John McBratney, *Imperial Subjects, Imperial Space: Rudyard Kipling's Fiction of the Native-Born* (Columbus: Ohio State University Press, 2002).

13. Bhabha, *Location of Culture*, especially "Signs Taken for Wonders: Questions of Ambivalence and Authority under a Tree Outside Delhi" and "Of Mimicry and Man: The Ambivalence of Colonial Discourse." The quotations are on 115, 89, 112.

14. Robert J. C. Young, *Colonial Desire: Hybridity in Theory, Culture, and Race* (London: Routledge, 1995), 25. See also Pnina Werbner and Tariq Modood, eds., *Debating Cultural Hybridity: Multi-Cultural Identities and the Politics of Anti-Racism* (London: Zed Books, 1997); Charles Stewart, "Syncretism and Its Synonyms: Reflections on Cultural Mixture," *Diacritics* 29, no. 3 (Autumn 1999): 40–62; Avtar Brah and Annie E. Coombes, eds., *Hybridity and Its Discontents: Politics, Science, Culture* (London: Routledge, 2000).

15. David Harvey, *The Condition of Postmodernity: An Enquiry into the Origins of Cultural Change* (Oxford: Blackwell, 1989); Manuel Castells, *The Rise of the Network Society* (Cambridge, MA: Blackwell, 1996), chaps. 6–7; Arjun Appadurai, "Disjunction and Difference in the Global Cultural Economy," *Public Culture* 2, no. 2 (Spring 1990): 1–24; Arjun Appadurai, *Modernity at Large: Cultural Dimensions of Globalization* (Minneapolis: University of Minnesota Press, 1996); Zygmunt Bauman, *Liquid Modernity* (Cambridge: Polity, 2000); John Tomlinson, *Globalization and Culture* (Chicago: University of Chicago Press, 1999).

16. Frederick Cooper, "What Is the Concept of Globalization Good For? An African Historian's Perspective," in his *Colonialism in Question: Theory, Knowledge, History* (Berkeley: University of California Press, 2005), 94, 91. In the same vein: James Ferguson, *Global Shadows: Africa in the Neoliberal World Order* (Durham, NC: Duke University Press, 2006).

17. Peter Schöttler and Michael Werner, "Transferts, Voyages, Transactions," introduction to a special issue of *Genéses* 14 (January 1994): 2–3; Johannes Paulmann, "Internationaler Vergleich und interkultureller Transfer: Zwei Forschungsansätze zur europäischen Geschichte des 18. bis 20. Jahrhunderts," *Historische Zeitschrift* 267, no. 3 (December 1998): 649–85; Hartmut Kaelble, "Herausforderungen an die Transfergeschichte," *Comparativ* 16, no. 3 (2006): 7–12; Hartmut Kaelble, "Die Debatte über Vergleich und Transfer und was jetzt?," *H-Soz-u-Kult*, 08.02.2005, http://hsozkult.geschichte.hu-berlin.de/forum/id=574&type=artikel.

18. Michael Werner and Bénédicte Zimmermann, "Beyond Comparison: *Histoire croisée* and the Challenge of Reflexivity," *History and Theory* 45, no. 1 (February 2006): 30–50.

19. W. Jeffrey Bolster, "Putting the Ocean in Atlantic History: Maritime Communities and Marine Ecology in the Northwest Atlantic, 1500–1800," *American Historical Review* 113, no. 1 (February 2008): 19–47; Kären Wigen et al., "Oceans of History," *American Historical Review* 111, no. 3 (June 2006): 717–80; Suguta Bose, *A Hundred Horizons: The Indian Ocean in the Age of Global Empire* (Cambridge, MA: Harvard University Press, 2006); K. N. Chaudhuri, *Asia before Europe: Economy and Civilisation of the Indian Ocean from the Rise of Islam to 1750* (Cambridge: Cambridge University Press, 1990); Jack P. Greene and Philip D. Morgan, eds., *Atlantic History: A Critical Appraisal* (New York: Oxford University Press, 2008); Subrahmanyam, "Connected Histories"; Alfred W. Crosby, Jr., *The Columbian Exchange: Biological and Cultural Consequences of 1492* (Westport, CT: Greenwood, 1972); Charles C. Mann, *1493: Uncovering the New World Columbus Created* (New York: Knopf, 2011).

20. Anna Lowenhaupt Tsing, *Friction: An Ethnography of Global Connection* (Princeton: Princeton University Press, 2005), xi, 4.

21. On goods: Sidney W. Mintz, *Sweetness and Power: The Place of Sugar in Modern History* (New York: Viking, 1985); Kristin L. Hoganson, *Consumers' Imperium: The Global Production of American Domesticity, 1865–1920* (Chapel Hill: University of North Carolina Press, 2007). On sacred rituals: Erik R. Seeman, *Death in the New World: Cross-Cultural Encounters, 1492–1800* (Philadelphia: University of Pennsylvania Press, 2010); Inga Clendinnen, *Ambivalent Conquests: Maya and Spaniard in Yucatan, 1517–1570*, 2nd ed. (New York: Cambridge University Press, 2003). On political cultures: Thomas Munck, *The Enlightenment: A Comparative Social History, 1721–1794* (New York: Oxford University Press, 2000); David Armitage, *The Declaration of Independence: A Global History* (Cambridge, MA: Harvard University Press, 2007); Jeremy Suri et al., "AHR Forum: The International 1968," *American Historical Review* 114, no. 1 (February 2009): 42–135 and 114, no. 2 (April 2009): 329–404; Sidney Tarrow, *The New Transnational Activism* (New York: Cambridge University Press, 2005).

22. Julia M. H. Smith, "Portable Christianity: Relics in the Medieval West (c. 700–c.1200)," *Proceedings of the British Academy* 181 (2012): 143–67; Pamela H. Smith, *The Business of Alchemy: Science and Culture in the Holy Roman Empire* (Princeton: Princeton University Press, 1994).

23. Alan Bewell, "Colonial Natures in Translation" (Davis Seminar paper, Princeton University, November 14, 2008); Londa Schiebinger, *Plants and Empire: Colonial Bioprospecting in the Atlantic World* (Cambridge, MA: Harvard University Press, 2007); Sanjay Subrahmanyam, "A Roomful of Mirrors: The Artful Embrace of Mughals and Franks, 1550–1700," *Ars Orientalis* 39 (March 2011): 39–83; Nira Wickramasinghe, "Fashioning a Market: The Singer Sewing Machine in Colonial Lanka" (this volume). Anthony Giddens, *The Consequences of Modernity* (Stanford: Stanford University Press, 1990), who helped set the term "disembedding" into circulation, used it in a more restricted way than I have here.

24. Benedict Anderson, *Imagined Communities: Reflections on the Origin and Spread of Nationalism* (London: Verso, 1983), 4.

25. Celia Applegate, "Musical Itinerancy in a World of Nations: Germany, Its Music, and Its Musicians" (this volume); Sidney Tarrow, *Power in Movement: Social Movements, Collective Action, and Politics* (New York: Cambridge University Press, 1994). Judith A. Carney, *Black Rice: The African Origins of Rice Cultivation in the Americas* (Cambridge, MA: Harvard University Press, 2001); James H. Sweet, *Recreating Africa: Culture, Kinship, and Religion in the African-Portuguese World, 1441–1770* (Chapel Hill: University of North Carolina Press, 2003); Jerry H. Bentley, *Old World Encounters: Cross-Cultural Contacts and Exchanges in Pre-Modern Times* (New York: Oxford University Press, 1993).

26. Brooke L. Blower, *Becoming Americans in Paris: Transatlantic Politics and Culture between the World Wars* (New York: Oxford University Press, 2011); Susan D. Pennybacker, *From Scottsboro to Munich: Race and Political Culture in 1930s Britain* (Princeton: Princeton University Press, 2009).

27. Margaret D. Jacobs, *White Mother to a Dark Race: Settler Colonialism, Maternalism, and the Removal of Indigenous Children in the American West and Australia, 1880–1940* (Lincoln: University of Nebraska Press, 2009); Kenneth Mills, *Idolatry and Its Enemies: Colonial Religion and Extirpation, 1640–1750* (Princeton: Princeton University Press, 1997); Jean Comaroff and John L. Comaroff, *Of Revelation and Revolution*, 2 vols. (Chicago: University of Chicago Press, 1991–97).

28. Partha Chatterjee, *Nationalist Thought and the Colonial World: A Derivative Discourse* (Minneapolis: University Minnesota Press, 1993); Partha Chatterjee, *The Nation and Its Fragments: Colonial and Postcolonial Histories* (Princeton: Princeton University Press, 1993).

29. Peter Brown, "*From Patriae Amator to Amator Pauperum* and Back Again: Social Imagination and Social Change in the West between Late Antiquity and the Early Middle Ages, ca. 300–600" (this volume); Victoria de Grazia, *Irresistible Empire: America's Advance through Twentieth-Century Europe* (Cambridge, MA: Harvard University Press, 2005); Mary Nolan, *The Transatlantic Century: Europe and America, 1890–2010* (New York: Cambridge University Press, 2012).

30. April F. Masten, "The Challenge Dance: Black-Irish Exchange in Antebellum America" (this volume); Kathy Peiss, *Zoot Suit: The Enigmatic Career of an Extreme Style* (Philadelphia: University of Pennsylvania Press, 2011); Luis

Alvarez, *The Power of the Zoot: Youth Culture and Resistance during World War II* (Berkeley: University of California Press, 2008); Jonathan Friedman, "The Political Economy of Elegance: An African Cult of Beauty," *Culture and History* 7 (1990): 101–25; Eric Zolov, *Refried Elvis: The Rise of the Mexican Counterculture* (Berkeley: University of California Press, 1999).

31. Douglas R. Howland, *Translating the West: Language and Political Reason in Nineteenth-Century Japan* (Honolulu: University of Hawaii Press, 2002); Mae M. Ngai, "The True Story of Ah Jake: Language, Labor, and Justice in Late-Nineteenth-Century Sierra County, California" (this volume); Carol Gluck and Anna Lowenhaupt Tsing, eds., *Words in Motion: Toward a Global Lexicon* (Durham, NC: Duke University Press, 2009); Lydia H. Liu, ed., *Tokens of Exchange: The Problem of Translation in Global Circulations* (Durham, NC: Duke University Press, 1999); Peter Howlett and Mary S. Morgan, eds., *How Well Do Facts Travel? The Dissemination of Reliable Knowledge* (Cambridge: Cambridge University Press, 2011).

32. William H. Sewell Jr., *Logics of History: Social Theory and Social Transformation* (Chicago: University of Chicago Press, 2005), chap. 8; Jocelyn Olcott, "Transnational Feminism: Event, Temporality, and Performance at the 1975 International Women's Year Conference" (this volume).

33. Sven Beckert, "Emancipation and Empire: Reconstructing the Worldwide Web of Cotton Production in the Age of the American Civil War," *American Historical Review* 109, no. 5 (December 2004): 1405–38; Andrew Zimmerman, *Alabama in Africa: Booker T. Washington, the German Empire, and the Globalization of the New South* (Princeton: Princeton University Press, 2010); Mimi Sheller, "Speed Metal, Slow Tropics, Cold War: Alcoa in the Caribbean" (this volume); Sheller and Urry, "New Mobilities Paradigm"; Zygmunt Bauman, *Globalization: The Human Consequences* (Cambridge: Polity, 1998).

CHAPTER I

THE CHALLENGE DANCE:

BLACK-IRISH EXCHANGE IN ANTEBELLUM AMERICA

1. Thank you Dan Rodgers and my Davis Center colleagues Robert Stam, David Wasserstein, Celia Applegate, Tom Bender, and Nira Wickramasinghe for your ideas and encouragement. For advice, insights, references, and editing, thank you Nicholas Carolan and librarians at the Irish Traditional Music Archive; Betty Falsey and the librarians at the Harvard Theatre Collection; Jackie Penny, Elizabeth Pope and librarians at the American Antiquarian Society; Pat Cline Cohen, Robin Cohen, Jay Cook, Daniel Dawson, Gail Day, T. J. Desch Obi, Cara M. DiGirolamo, Vincent DiGirolamo, Colin Dunne, Steve Edwards, Mary Friel, Louis Gerteis, Angela Gleason, William Glenn, Bill Jordan, Ned Landsman, Library Company of Philadelphia, William J. Mahar, Mick Maloney, Timothy Meagher, Kerby Miller, Bríd Ní Heslín, Patrick O'Sullivan, Monique Patenaude, Gill Redfearn, Alan Rice, Donna Rilling, Elena Schneider, John Waters, Sean Wilentz, Tom Woodhouse, and participants at the "Celtic Identity in the New Millennium" research symposium, Monroe College, Rochester, NY; "Contesting

Culture: Battling Genres in the African Diaspora" conference, Baruch College, New York; "Transatlantic Exchange: African Americans and the Celtic Nations" conference, University of Wales, Swansea; AHRC/CRONEM Conference 2009, University of Surrey; In-Dialogue: "Currents of Transatlantic Exchange: Medicine, Music, Dance," Humanities Institute, Stony Brook University and "Close to the Floor" conference, Glucksman Ireland House, New York University. For time and financial assistance I also recognize the Shelby Cullom Davis Center for Historical Studies, Princeton University; SUNY Stony Brook Department of History and NYS/United University Professions; Kate B. & Hall J. Peterson Fellowship, American Antiquarian Society; John Hope Franklin Research Grant for travel to Ireland, American Philosophical Society; and John M. Ward Fellowship in Dance and Music for the Theatre, Houghton Library, Harvard University.

2. William Carleton, *Traits and Stories of the Irish Peasantry* (Dublin: William Curry, Jun. and Co., 1843), 5.

3. Carleton, *Traits and Stories* (Dublin: W.F. Wakeman, 1833), 43, 55.

4. Stan Hugill, *Shanties and Sailors' Songs* (New York: Praeger, 1969), 35; W. Jeffrey Bolster, *Black Jacks: African American Seamen in the Age of Sail* (Cambridge, MA: Harvard University Press, 1997), 217; Peter Linebaugh and Marcus Rediker, *The Many-Headed Hydra: Sailors, Slaves, Commoners, and the Hidden History of the Revolutionary Atlantic* (Boston: Beacon, 2000), 321.

5. Jane Robins, *The Trial of Queen Caroline* (New York: Free Press, 2006), 182, 213–14, 256; "The Queen's Trial," *Freeman's Journal*, October 14, 1820, 2; "Royal Hibernian Theatre," *Freeman's Journal*, November 28, 1809, 1.

6. J. Rosamond Johnson, "Why They Call American Music Ragtime," *Colored American Magazine* 15 (January 1909): 636.

7. Jacqui Malone, *Steppin' on the Blues: The Visible Rhythms of African American Dance* (Urbana: University of Illinois Press, 1996), 52–54; Shane White and Graham J. White, *Stylin': African American Expressive Culture from Its Beginnings to the Zoot Suit* (Ithaca, NY: Cornell University Press, 1998), 79; Hans Nathan, *Dan Emmett and the Rise of Early Negro Minstrelsy* (Norman: University of Oklahoma Press, 1977), 61; Eric Lott, *Love and Theft: Blackface Minstrelsy and the American Working Class* (New York: Oxford University Press, 1993), 112–13; Mark Knowles, *Tap Roots: The Early History of Tap Dancing* (Jefferson, NC: McFarland, 2002), 86, 92; Robert C. Toll, *Blacking Up: The Minstrel Show in Nineteenth-Century America* (New York: Oxford University Press, 1974), 43.

8. Lynne Fauley Emery, *Black Dance from 1619 to Today* (Princeton: Princeton Book Co., 1988), 87–101; Marshall Stearns and Jean Stearns, *Jazz Dance: The Story of American Vernacular Dance* (New York: Macmillan, 1968), 45.

9. Hazel V. Carby, "What Is This 'Black' in Irish Popular Culture?," *European Journal of Cultural Studies* 4 (August 2001): 326.

10. Shane White, *Somewhat More Independent: The End of Slavery in New York City, 1779–1810* (Athens: University of Georgia Press, 1991), 153–55; R. F. Foster, *Modern Ireland 1600–1972* (London: Penguin, 1989), 345.

11. Many of these texts were written for a readership of "literate sporting men" interested in the leisure activities of the lower classes. Patricia Cline Cohen et al., *The Flash Press: Sporting Male Weeklies in 1840s New York* (Chicago: University of Chicago Press, 2008), 1, 186–89.

12. Ira Berlin, "From Creole to African: Atlantic Creoles and the Origins of African American Society in Mainland North America," *William and Mary Quarterly* 53 (April 1996): 253; Linebaugh and Rediker, *Many-Headed Hydra*, 126, 321.

13. George G. Foster, *New York in Slices* (New York: WF Burgess, 1849), 110, 113–14 and *New York by Gas-Light and Other Urban Sketches*, ed. Stuart M. Blumin (Berkeley: University of California Press, 1990), 149, 164, 167; "Sue Shannon's Ball," *Whip and Satirist*, April 2, 1842, 3; "The Devil Recruits in Staten Island," *New York Flash*, October 31, 1841, 3.

14. Robin Cohen, "Creolization and Cultural Globalization: The Soft Sounds of Fugitive Power," *Globalizations* 4, no. 3 (September 2007): 370.

15. Malone, *Steppin' on the Blues*, 10.

16. Carleton, *Traits and Stories*, 7; Peggy Harper, "Dance," in *Encyclopedia of Africa: South of the Sahara*, ed. John Middleton (New York: Scribner, 1997), 1:396.

17. Lenwood Sloan (unpublished lecture, Close to the Floor: Conference on Percussive Dance, Glucksman Ireland House, New York, April 29, 2005); Harper, "Dance," 397; Pearl Primus, "African Dance," Esilokun Kinni-Olusanyin, "A Panoply of African Dance Dynamics," and Doris Green, "Traditional Dance in Africa," in *African Dance: An Artistic, Historical and Philosophical Inquiry*, ed. Kariamu Welsh Asante (1996; repr., Trenton, NJ: Africa World Press, 1998), 6–8, 32, 15; Malone, *Steppin' on the Blues*, 32–34, 15; Brendán Breathnach, *Folk Music and Dances of Ireland* (1977; repr., London: Ossian, 1996), 52–53.

18. These are not ultimate origins. After all, Portuguese traders were in Africa and English and Scottish settlers had occupied Ireland by the 1600s.

19. Dance scholars usually trace competitive jubas to the Haitian word *giouba(e)*, a general term for African sacred and secular stepping dances. But the name may be a corruption of the Kikongo word *nzuba* or *zuba*, which means "to only dance (a man) with his partner" or "to strike a blow with," knock, hit, or batter. Marion Hannah Winter, "Juba and American Minstrelsy," in *Chronicles of the American Dance*, ed. Paul Magriel (New York: Henry Holt, 1948), 40; *Dictionnaire Kikongo et Kituba—Français: Vocabulaire Comparé des Langages Kongo Traditionnels et Véhiculaires* (Bandundu: Ceeba, 1973), 2:521, 805; W. Holman Bentley, *Dictionary and Grammar of the Kongo Language* (London: Baptist Missionary Society, 1887), 481.

20. F. W. Wurdemann quoted in Emery, *Black Dance*, 27.

21. *A Concise Historical Account of All the British Colonies in North-America, Comprehending Their Rise, Progress, and Modern State . . .* (London: J. Bew, 1775), 183.

22. Charles J. Kickham, *Knocknagow, Or the Homes of Tipperary* (Dublin: A.M. Sullivan or J. Duffy, 1879), 36–37; Mary Friel, *Dancing as a Social Pastime in the South-East of Ireland, 1800–1897* (Dublin: Four Courts Press, 2004), 40–41; R. Shelton Mackenzie, *Bits of Blarney* (New York: Redfield, 1854), 299.

23. Helen Brennan, *The Story of Irish Dance* (Lanham, MD: Roberts Rinehart, 2001), 28, 136; John F. Szwed and Morton Marks, "The Afro-American Transformation of European Set Dances and Dance Suites," *Dance Research Journal* 20, no. 1 (Summer 1988): 29; William Carleton, "The Country Dancing-Master,

an Irish Sketch," *Irish Penny Journal*, August 29, 1840, 69–71; Primus, "African Dance," 7; Breathnach, *Folk Music*, 59.

24. Sterling Stuckey, *Slave Culture: Nationalist Theory and the Foundation of Black America* (Oxford: Oxford University Press, 1988), 21; Barton Atkins, *Modern Antiquities: Comprising Sketches of Early Buffalo and the Great Lakes . . .* (Buffalo, NY: Courier Company, 1898), 44; "Dancing for Eels," *Flash*, November 12, 1842, 1.

25. Primus, "African Dance," 8; John Argyle, "Dance as Social Statement," in *Encyclopedia of Africa: South of the Sahara*, ed. John Middleton (New York: Scribner's, 1997), 1:400; Ivor Miller, "Battling in Ekpe Education" (unpublished paper, Contesting Culture: Battling Genres in the African Diaspora conference, Baruch College, New York, May 2, 2008).

26. Breathnach, *Folk Music*, 50, 53; Kickham, *Knocknagow*, 45; Patrick Logan, *Fair Day: The Story of Irish Fairs and Markets* (Belfast: Appletree, 1986), 102–3; Carleton, "Country Dancing-Master," 70; Breandán Breathnach, *Ceol agus rince Na hÉireann* (Dublin: An Gúm, 1989), 178–79.

27. Harper, "Dance," 395; T. J. Desch Obi, *Fighting for Honor: The History of African Martial Art Traditions in the Atlantic World* (Columbia: University of South Carolina Press, 2008), 59, 358.

28. Breathnach, *Folk Music*, 51; John W. Hurley, *Shillelagh: The Irish Fighting Stick* (Pipersville, PA: Caravat Press, 2007), 62; Carleton, "Country Dancing-Master," 69–70; Desch Obi, *Fighting for Honor*, 32–33.

29. Carleton, *Traits and Stories*, 43–44; "A Glorious Ball," *Whip and Satirist*, February 5, 1842, 1; Emery, *Black Dance*, 92.

30. Green, "Traditional Dance in Africa," 18; Primus, "African Dance," 8; Argyle, "Dance as Social Statement," 400–401; Miller, "Battling in Ekpe Education."

31. "The Cake Dance," *Béaloideas: The Journal of the Folklore of Ireland Society* 11, nos. 1–11 (1941): 126–28, 131, 137; Emery, *Black Dance*, 91–92.

32. Miller, "Battling in Ekpe Education"; Ken Bilby, "Playful Insults in Aluku: Guianese Maroon Variations on an African Diasporic Theme," and comments by C. Daniel Dawson (Contesting Culture conference); Breathnach, *Folk Music*, 52; Carleton, *Traits and Stories*, 42; "Cake Dance," 127.

33. Catherine Esther Foley, "Irish Traditional Step-Dancing in North Kerry, A Contextual and Structural Analysis" (PhD diss., University of London, 1988), 9; Friel, *Dancing as a Social Pastime*, 41; Kinni-Olusanyin, "Panoply of African Dance Dynamics," 32; Harold D. Langley, "The Negro in the Navy and Merchant Service, 1789–1860," *Journal of Negro History* 52, no. 4 (October 1967): 277; Emery, *Black Dance*, 127; James Thomas, *From Tennessee Slave to St. Louis Entrepreneur: The Autobiography of James Thomas*, ed. Loren Schweninger (Columbia: University of Missouri Press, 1984), 42, 69–70.

34. *Compact Edition of the Oxford English Dictionary* (Oxford: Oxford University Press, 1971), 269; J. S. Bratton, "Dancing a Hornpipe in Fetters," *Folk Music Journal* 6, no. 1 (1990): 69; Foley, "Irish Traditional Step-Dancing," 27.

35. *Dancing between Two Worlds: Kongo-Angola Culture and the Americas*, ed. Robert Farris Thompson and C. Daniel Dawson (New York: Caribbean Cultural Center, 1991), 8.

36. "New Brunswick," *Flash*, November 6, 1841, 3.

37. Carleton, "Country Dancing-Master," 69.

38. Charles Dickens, *American Notes for General Circulation* (London: Chapman and Hall, 1842), 102.

39. *Silvia Dubois, A Biografy of the Slav Who Whipt Her Mistres and Gand Her Fredom*, ed. C. W. Larison (Ringoes, NJ: CW Larison, 1883), 67, 84.

40. David R. Roediger, *The Wages of Whiteness* (London: Verso, 1991), 100–103.

41. Thomas F. De Voe, *The Market Book* . . . (New York: printed for the author, 1862), 1:344; John Fanning Watson, *Annals of Philadelphia* . . . (Philadelphia: Uriah Hunt, 1830), 224; "Dancing for Eels," 1.

42. De Voe, *Market Book*, 344; Atkins, *Modern Antiquities*, 43–44.

43. De Voe, *Market Book*, 344–45.

44. Mackenzie, *Bits of Blarney*, 296; "Buried in Sweets," *Rhode-Island Republican*, August 8, 1838, 3.

45. De Voe, *Market Book*, 322, 345.

46. *Silvia Dubois*, 93, 60; Breathnach, *Folk Music*, 53; Brennan, *Story of Irish Dance*, 167; Mackenzie, *Bits of Blarney*, 295.

47. Emery, *Black Dance*, 98; "Dancing for Eels," 1; Stearns and Stearns, *Jazz Dance*, 14–15.

48. De Voe, *Market Book*, 345; "Negro Minstrels and Their Dances," *New York Herald*, August 11, 1895, sec. 4, (Undigested) Clippings folder, box 1, Playbills—Subjects, Harvard Theatre Collection (HTC); "The Nomenclature of the West," *Liberator*, September 13, 1834.

49. "Dancing for Eels," 1.

50. T. Allston Brown, "Early History of Negro Minstrelsy: Its Rise and Progress in the United States," *New York Clipper*, February 24, 1912, 5; "Negro Minstrels and Their Dances."

51. Kerby A. Miller, *Ireland and Irish America: Culture, Class, and Transatlantic Migration* (Dublin: Field Day, in association with the Keough-Naughton Institute for Irish Studies at the University of Notre Dame, 2008), 152; Mary C. Waters, "Optional Ethnicities: For Whites Only?," in *Rereading America: Cultural Contexts for Critical Thinking and Writing*, ed. Gary Colombo et al. (Boston: Bedford Books, 2001), 643; Dale Cockrell, *Demons of Disorder: Early Blackface Minstrels and Their World* (Cambridge: Cambridge University Press, 1997), 85–86; Graham Hodges, "'Desirable Companions and Lovers': Irish and African Americans in the Sixth Ward, 1830–1870," in *The New York Irish*, ed. Ronald H. Bayor and Timothy J. Meagher (Baltimore: Johns Hopkins University Press, 1996), 123.

52. *Ins and Outs of Circus Life or Forty-Two Years Travel of John H. Glenroy, Bareback Rider*, comp. Stephen Stanley Stanford (Boston: MM Wing, 1885), 27–28.

53. Diamond/Dimond is an old Ulster surname. Patrick Woulfe, *Irish Names and Surnames* (Dublin: MH Gill, 1923), 496; "Early History," February 24, 1912, 5; P. T. Barnum to Francis Courtney Wemyss, January 21, 1840, and February 27, 1841, in A. H. Saxon, *Selected Letters of P.T. Barnum* (New York: Columbia University Press, 1983), 9–10.

54. Watson, *Annals of Philadelphia*, 244; John Thomas Scharf and Thompson Westcott, *History of Philadelphia, 1609–1884* (Philadelphia: L.H. Everts and Co., 1884), 2:1012.

55. "Broadway Circus," *New York Herald*, January 20, 1840, 2; National Theatre playbill, Boston, June 9, 1840, Diamond Minstrels and Master Diamond folder, box 5 (Co-Du), HTC; "Philadelphia," *New York Herald*, January 27, 1845, 4; Knowles, *Tap Roots*, 86; "Early History," February 24, 1912, 5.

56. Thomas, *Tennessee Slave*, 48–49; James Logan, *Notes of a Journey through Canada, the United States of America, and the West Indies* (Edinburgh: Fraser and Co., 1838), 113; Frederick Law Olmsted, *The Cotton Kingdom: A Traveller's Observations on Cotton and Slavery in the American Slave States* (New York: Mason Brothers, 1862), 2:287.

57. Patrick Kennedy, *The Banks of the Boro* (1867), quoted in Friel, *Dancing as a Social Pastime*, 39.

58. Thomas, *Tennessee Slave*, 49.

59. Frank Dumont, "The Golden Days of Minstrelsy," *New York Clipper*, December 19, 1914; "Broadway Circus," 2; "Early History," October 19, 1912, 3; P. T. Barnum, *Struggles and Triumphs* (Hartford: J.B. Burr, 1869), 91.

60. *From Slavery to Affluence: Memoirs of Robert Anderson, Ex-Slave*, ed. Daisy Anderson (1927; repr., Steamboat Springs, CO: Steamboat Pilot, 1967), 30–31.

61. "Pioneers of Minstrelsy," *Negro Minstrelsy in New York*, vol. 2, Clippings, Extra-Illustrated Volumes, HTC; Bratton, "Dancing a Hornpipe in Fetters," 68, 70–71; Mackenzie, *Bits of Blarney*, 294–95.

62. Bratton, "Dancing a Hornpipe in Fetters," 66, 68.

63. National Theatre playbill, June 9, 1840, HTC.

64. Louis S. Gerteis, "Blackface Minstrelsy and the Construction of Race in Nineteenth-Century America," in *Union & Emancipation: Essays on Politics and Race in the Civil War*, ed. David W. Blight and Brooks D. Simpson (Kent, OH: Kent State University Press, 1997), 101–2; Lawrence W. Levine, *Highbrow/Lowbrow: The Emergence of Cultural Hierarchy in America* (Cambridge, MA: Harvard University Press, 1988), 24; Nathaniel Hawthorne, *The American Notebooks* (Columbus: Ohio State University Press, 1972), 501–4.

65. Edward Ingle, *The Negro in the District of Columbia* (Baltimore: Johns Hopkins University Press, 1893), 47; New Theatre playbill, Mobile, February 22, 1841, New Theatre folder, OS Posters box, HTC; "Bowery Amphitheatre," *New York Herald*, February 1, 1843, 3; Arthur Herman Wilson, *A History of the Philadelphia Theatre, 1835 to 1855* (1935; repr., New York: Greenwood, 1968), 25, 35.

66. "The Drama," *Whip*, December 24, 1842, 3; "Master Diamond at Mobile," *Weekly Picayune*, March 1, 1841, 10.

67. "Master Diamond," *New Orleans Times Picayune*, January 3, 1841, 2; "Negro Dancers," *Whip*, January 21, 1843, 2; Thomas L. Nichols, *Forty Years of American Life* (London: J. Maxwell and Co., 1864), 229; Noah Miller Ludlow, *Dramatic Life as I Found It* (St. Louis: GI Jones and Co., 1880), 533.

68. "Franklin," *Whip*, January 21, 1843, 3.

69. "Chatham Theatre," *New York Herald*, February 8, 10, and 13, 1840, 3; "Things Theatrical. *The Chatham*," *Spirit of the Times*, February 15, 1840, 600.

70. "The Negro Minstrels of the Nights Gone By . . . The Great Match-Dance— Barnum's Museum Against Pete Williams' Dance-House" [ca. 1875], Clips Pers (Bryant, Dan), HTC.

71. Barnum to "Messrs. Fogg & Stickney, Ludlow & Smith," Mobile, February 27, 1841, in Saxon, *Selected Letters*, 12.

72. "Negro Dancers," 2.

73. Ann Fabian, *Card Sharps, Dream Books, & Bucket Shops: Gambling in 19th-Century America* (Ithaca, NY: Cornell University Press, 1990), 40–41; Jackson Lears, *Something for Nothing: Luck in America* (New York: Viking, 2003), 4.

74. "Negro Minstrels of the Nights Gone By"; "Excitement among the Sporting Community—Match between John Diamond and Juba," *New York Sporting Whip*, January 28, 1843, 4.

75. "Negro Minstrels of the Nights Gone By."

76. Olmsted, *Cotton Kingdom*, 48–49; Cockrell, *Demons of Disorder*, 86.

77. James W. Cook, "Dancing across the Color Line," *Common-Place* 4 (October 2003), www.common-place.org.

78. "Meanness," *Whip and Satirist*, July 2, 1842, 2.

79. "Free-and-Easy," *Whip*, Nov. 19, 1842, p. 3; *Whip and Satirist of New York and Brooklyn*, April 23, 1842, p. 3.

80. "Pioneers of Minstrelsy"; *Ins and Outs of Circus Life*, 24; Brantz Mayer, *Baltimore: Past and Present* (Baltimore: Richardson and Bennett, 1871), 91; "Dancing," *New York Clipper*, March 28, 1857, 387.

81. "Negro Minstrels of the Nights Gone By"; "Our Eleventh Walk about Town," *Whip*, December 31, 1842, 2.

82. *Evening Tattler*, January 25, 1840, quoted in Cockrell, *Demons of Disorder*, 86.

83. "Our Eleventh Walk about Town," p. 2; "Negro Minstrels and Their Dances"; Eric Homberger, *Mrs. Astor's New York* (New Haven: Yale University Press, 2004), 187; Nathaniel P. Willis, *Complete Works* (New York: J.S. Redfield, 1846), 582; Tyler Anbinder, *Five Points* (New York: Free Press, 2002), 26, 33–34; Carol Groneman Pernicone, "The 'Bloody Ould Sixth': A Social Analysis of a New York City Working-Class Community in the Mid-Nineteenth Century, (PhD diss., University of Rochester, 1973), 197–98.

84. Roy Rosensweig, "The Rise of the Saloon," in *Rethinking Popular Culture*, ed. Chandra Mukerji and Michael Schudson (Berkeley: University of California Press, 1991), 143, 147; Fabian, *Card Sharps*, 41.

85. "Cake Dance," 131.

86. "Negro Minstrels of the Nights Gone By."

87. Elliott J. Gorn, *The Manly Art: Bare-Knuckle Prize Fighting in America* (Ithaca, NY: Cornell University Press, 1986), 46, 85, 137.

88. Denis Brailsford, *Bareknuckles: A Social History of Prize-Fighting* (Cambridge: Lutterworth, 1988), 140–44.

89. The playbill that scholars (e.g., Lott, *Love and Theft*, 115) cite as evidence that Diamond only challenged whites to dance against him (figure 1.14) actually reads, "MASTER DIAMOND, who delineates the Ethiopian character superior to

any other *white* person, hereby challenges any person in the world to a trial of skill at Negro Dancing."

90. Kevin R. Smith, *Black Genesis: The History of the Black Prizefighter 1760–1870* (New York: iUniverse, 2003), 19, 30.

91. "Negro Minstrels and Their Dances"; "Negro Minstrels of the Nights Gone By."

92. Robert Farris Thompson, *African Art in Motion* (Berkeley: University of California Press, 1979), 16.

93. Emma Jones Lapsansky, "'Since They Got Those Separate Churches': Afro-Americans and Racism in Jacksonian Philadelphia," *American Quarterly* 32 (Spring 1980), 65; Logan, *Notes of a Journey*, 113; Dumont, "Golden Days of Minstrelsy."

94. "The colloquial term still used in Irish for a session of step dance, *babhta rince*—a bout of dance—indicates the element of challenge which was never far from the surface." Brennan, *Story of Irish Dance*, 42.

95. "Negro Minstrels of the Nights Gone By"; Susan Eike Spalding, "Aesthetic Standards in Old Time Dancing in Southwest Virginia: African American and European-American Threads" (EdD diss., Temple University, 1993), 73.

96. "Negro Minstrels of the Nights Gone By"; "Georgia Champions" playbill, Portland, June 19 [1845], Juba—Mins folder, box 7 (H-K), HTC.

97. "Negro Minstrels of the Nights Gone By."

98. "Great Public Contest," *New York Herald*, July 4, 1844, reprinted in "Black Musicians and Ethiopian Minstrels," *The Black Perspective in Music* 3.1 (Spring, 1975):82.

CHAPTER 2
MUSICAL ITINERANCY IN A WORLD OF NATIONS:
GERMANY, ITS MUSIC, AND ITS MUSICIANS

1. Brahms to Clara Schumann, November 18, 1862, in *Johannes Brahms: Life and Letters*, ed. Styra Avins, trans. Styra Avins and Josef Eisinger (New York: Oxford University Press, 2001), 258; Jan Swafford, *Johannes Brahms: A Biography* (New York: Vintage Books, 1999), 496.

2. See, for instance, Jeffrey Richards, *Imperialism and Music: Britain 1876–1953* (Manchester: Manchester University Press, 2001).

3. James Clifford, *Routes: Travel and Translation in the Late Twentieth Century* (Cambridge, MA: Harvard University Press, 1997), 17.

4. Ibid., 2–3.

5. William Weber, *The Great Transformation of Musical Taste: Concert Programming from Haydn to Brahms* (New York: Cambridge University Press, 2008), 21.

6. On the musicological subject of "exoticism" in music, see Jonathan Bellman, *The Exotic in Western Music* (Boston: Northeastern University Press, 1998); and Ralph Locke, *Musical Exoticism: Images and Reflections* (New York: Cambridge University Press, 2009).

7. The term and the mapping metaphor come from Fernand Braudel, *The Mediterranean and the Mediterranean World in the Era of Philip II*, trans. Siân

Reynolds (Berkeley: University of California Press, 1998), 835. On "mapping" literary culture, see Franco Moretti, *Atlas of the European Novel, 1800–1900* (London: Verso, 1998) and *Graphs, Maps, Trees: Abstract Models for a Literary History* (London: Verso, 2005).

8. Akira Iriye's Albert Shaw Memorial Lectures at Johns Hopkins University in 1988, subsequently published as *Cultural Internationalism and World Order* (Baltimore: Johns Hopkins University Press, 1997), 2.

9. Prasenjit Duara, *Rescuing History from the Nation: Questioning Narratives of Modern China* (Chicago: University of Chicago Press, 1997), 65.

10. Nate Schweber, "For Two Jazzmen, Work Meant Life on the Road," *New York Times*, February 15, 2009.

11. Heinrich W. Schwab, "The Social Status of the Town Musician," in *The Social Status of the Professional Musician from the Middle Ages to the 19th Century*, ed. Walter Salmen, trans. Herbert Kaufman and Barbara Reisner (New York: Pendragon Press, 1983), 33–59.

12. Johann Beer, *Teutsche Winternächte*, in *Sämtliche Werke*, ed. Ferdinand van Ingen and Hans-Gert Roloff (Bern: Peter Lang, 2005), 7:117–19.

13. To name but a few: see Werner Danckert, *Unehrliche Leute: die Verfemten Berufe* (Bern: Francke Verlag, 1963). Danckert, trained as a concert pianist and then as a musicologist, subjected his richly original mind to the dreary predictability of racial science in the 1930s, eventually joining the Nazi Party and the cultural bureaucracy of Hans Rosenberg. After the war, he wrote many works of what we would now call ethnomusicology. See also Kathy Stuart, *Defiled Trades and Social Outcasts: Honor and Ritual Pollution in Early Modern Germany* (Cambridge: Cambridge University Press, 1999), and Carsten Küther, *Menschen auf der Strasse* (Göttingen: Vandenhoeck & Ruprecht, 1993), and Küther, *Räuber und Gauner in Deutschland*, 2nd ed. (Göttingen: Vandenhoeck & Ruprecht, 1998).

14. The definitive study is Walter Salmen, *Der fahrende Musiker im europäischen Mittelalter* (Kassel: Johann Philipp Hinnenthal, 1960).

15. The most famous example of this was, of course, the Bach family, of whom more than fifty members were professional musicians, for the most part in Thuringia.

16. Dieter Krickeberg, "The Folk Musician in the 17th and 18th Centuries," in Salmen, *Social Status*, 101.

17. Henry Raynor, *A Social History of Music, from the Middle Ages to Beethoven* (New York: Schocken Books, 1972), 68.

18. Martin Wolschke, *Von der Stadtpfeiferei zu Lehrlingskapelle und Sinfonieorchester* (Regensburg: Gustav Bosse Verlag, 1981), 33–36.

19. Ralf Gehler, "Dorf und Stadtmusikanten im ländlichen Raum Mecklenburgs, zwischen 1650 und 1700," in *Historical Studies on Folk and Traditional Music*, ed. Doris Stockman (Copenhagen: Tusculanum Press, 1997), 47–58.

20. Steven Rose, "The Musician-Novels of the German Baroque: New Light on Bach's World," *Understanding Bach* 3 (Bach Network, 2008): 63–64, http://www.bachnetwork.co.uk/ub3/ROSE.pdf.

21. James Sheehan, *German History 1770–1866* (New York: Oxford University Press, 1990), 153.

22. These novels were quite popular in their day but were rediscovered only in the twentieth century, though not uncritically. Hans Menck said of Beer's *Jan Rebhu* that he expressed "only the unique and historically bounded experiences of the musician's condition in his time," not the nature of a true artist (*Der Musiker im Roman* [Heidelberg: Carl Winters Universitätsbuchhandlung, 1931], 28). See also Richard Alewyn, *Johann Beer: Studien zum Roman des 17. Jahrhundert* (Leipzig: Mayer & Müller, 1932), and George Schoolfield, *The Figure of the Musician in German Literature* (Chapel Hill: University of North Carolina Press, 1956). Stephen Rose's *The Musician in Literature in the Age of Bach* (Cambridge: Cambridge University Press, 2011) is now the starting point for exploring this literature.

23. James Hardin, *Johann Beer* (Boston: Twayne, 1983), 27. See also Gordon J. Burgess, *"Die Wahrheit mit lachendem Munde": Comedy and Humor in the Novels of Christian Weise* (Bern: Peter Lang, 1990).

24. Alan Menhennet, *Grimmelhausen the Storyteller: A Study of the "Simplician" Novels* (Columbia, SC: Camden House, 1997), 13.

25. On the limitations of *Simplicissimus* as a guide to the life of Grimmelshausen or the sufferings of the Germans, see Robert Ergang, *The Myth of the All-Destructive Fury of the Thirty Years' War* (Pocono Pines, PA: The Craftsmen, 1956); see also Geoffrey Parker, ed., *The Thirty Years' War*, 2nd ed. (London: Routledge, 1997), 210–16.

26. Suspicion of music in Western Christianity constitutes a very long strand of thought and practice that predates the Reformation, and despite Martin Luther's ringing endorsement of music as the greatest gift of God after salvation, some Pietist sects tried to do away with service music altogether.

27. His musical tracts included *Ursus Murmurat* (The Bear Growling), *Ursus Vulpinatur* (The Bear Scheming), *Bellum Musicum* (The Musical War), *Musicalische Discurse* (*Musical Discourses*), and *Schola Phonologica* (*The School of Phonology*), the latter a work of instruction in music theory and harmonization that remained unpublished in his lifetime. All are now available in modern printed editions: Vol. 12 of Beer, *Sämtliche Werke*. See also Michael Heinemann, "Stil und Polemik: Zur Musikanschauung von Johann Beer," in *Beer 1655–1700, Hofmusiker, Satiriker, Anonymus: eine Karriere zwischen Bürgertum und Hof*, ed. Andreas Brandtner and Wolfgang Neuber (Vienna: Turia & Kant, 2000), 117–46.

28. Beer placed Printz in a madhouse cell in his satirical novel *Narrenspital* (Fools' Asylum).

29. See Andreas Angler, "'Ich bin kein Spiel-mann': die Verteidigung des bürgerlichen Status und das künstlerische Selbstbewusstsein der Hauptfiguren in den Musiker-romanen von Wolfgang Caspar Printz," *Daphnis: Zeitschrift für mittlere Deutsche Literatur* 30, no. 1 (2001): 333–54.

30. Joseph Kerman and Gary Tomlinson, *Listen*, 6th ed. (New York: Bedford/St. Martin's, 2008), 100.

31. Erich Reimer, *Die Hofmusik in Deutschland, 1500–1800: Wandlungen einer Institution* (Wilhelmshaven: Florian Noetzel Verlag, 1991), 16–17.

32. On musical life especially, see Tanya Kevorkian, *Baroque Piety: Religion, Society, and Music in Leipzig, 1650–1750* (Aldershot: Ashgate, 2007). For a com-

parison, see Gerald Lyman Soliday, *A Community in Conflict: Frankfurt Society in the Seventeenth and Early Eighteenth Centuries* (Hanover, NH: University Press of New England, 1974). In Frankfurt, the struggles between the aristocracy and the burgher-citizens impeded the development of its cultural life until later in the century.

33. See Christoph Wolff, *Johann Sebastian Bach: The Learned Musician* (New York: Norton, 2000), 1–11, 305–39; for his immersion in the politics of the Dresden court, see Ulrich Siegele, "Bach and the Domestic Politics of Electoral Saxony," in *The Cambridge Companion to Bach*, ed. John Butt (Cambridge: Cambridge University Press, 1997), 17–34.

34. Mack Walker, *German Home Towns: Community, State, and General Estate* (Ithaca, NY: Cornell University Press, 1971), 130; Hardin, *Johann Beer*, 38.

35. Quotations from Wolff, *Johann Sebastian Bach*, 179, 2, 237–38.

36. Walker, *German Home Towns*, 2–3.

37. Hans Leo Hassler (1564–1612) traveled to Venice at age twenty and brought back the new polychoral style of the early baroque.

38. Cited in Klaus Hortschansky, "The Musician as Music Dealer in the Second Half of the 18th Century," in Salmen, *Social Status*, 217.

39. J. F. Reichardt, "An junge Künstler," *Musikalisches Kunstmagazin* 1 (1782): 5.

40. Reimer, *Hofmusik*, 125–41.

41. This is one of the more famous of the genre and one of only two that have been translated into English, thanks to the work of James Hardin and the Camden House press. See Kuhnau, *The Musical Charlatan*, trans. John R. Russell, intro. James Hardin (Columbia, SC: Camden House, 1997).

42. Ibid., 1–2.

43. Ibid., 4.

44. Collegia musicum participated in the transnational movement of German musical institutions. The Moravian Brethren emigrants to North America established collegia musicum in many of their communities, in Pennsylvania and North Carolina.

45. Kuhnau, *Charlatan*, 4.

46. Ibid., 4, 7–8, 20–21.

47. He even briefly (1713–14) published his own version of the English taste-making weeklies the *Tatler* and the *Spectator*.

48. Otto Dann, *Nation und Nationalismus in Deutschland 1770–1990* (Munich: Beck, 1993), 39.

49. Johann Mattheson, *Das Neu-eröffnete Orchestre* (1713; repr., Hildesheim: Olms Verlag, 1993), 200–231.

50. He gave it a suitably verbose subtitle, laden down with claims to erudition (which given his polemics against musical pedants may be regarded as ironic)—"searching critiques and assessments of the many opinions, arguments, and objections," designed "to eradicate . . . all vulgar error and to promote a freer growth in the pure science of harmony." It appeared between 1722 and 1726.

51. The title is essentially untranslatable—"complete" is no problem, but no single English term encompasses the functions of organizer, performer, and composer required of the eighteenth-century *Capellmeister*, which is why it is usu-

ally left in German. An English translation does exist: Ernest C. Harriss, *Johann Mattheson's* Der vollkommene Capellmeister: *A Revised Translation with Critical Commentary* (Ann Arbor, MI: UMI Research Press, 1981).

52. On the meaning of "patriot," see the discussion of "Bürger," an even more complicated term, in *Geschichtliche Grundbegriffe: Historisches Lexikon zur politisch-sozialen Sprache in Deutschland*, ed. Otto Brunner, Werner Conze, and Reinhart Koselleck, 8 vols. (Stuttgart: Klett-Cotta, 1987–92), 1:686.

53. This section essentially copied and then expanded on a contemporary French treatise of 1737 called *Discours sur l'harmonie d'un Anonyme*, now known to be the work of the dramatist Jean-Baptiste-Louis Gresset, who is remembered mainly for the comic story *Vert-Vert*, about a foul-talking parrot in a convent. Mattheson was also a great reader of travel literature; his claims about the Chinese, for instance, seem to have derived from his reading of the Jesuit Martino Martini's seventeenth-century *History of the Great and Renowned Monarchy of China*.

54. Koselleck, "Volk, Nation, Nationalismus, Masse," in Brunner, Conze, and Koselleck, *Geschichtliche Grundbegriffe*, 7:305–6.

55. Mattheson, *Neu-eröffnete Orchestre*, 214; Praetorius, in the introduction to his Singspiel libretto *Calypso, oder Sieg der Weissheit Ueber die Liebe*, quoted in Gloria Flaherty, *Opera in the Development of German Critical Thought* (Princeton: Princeton University Press, 1978), 69.

56. William Weber, *The Rise of Musical Classics in Eighteenth-Century England: A Study in Canon, Ritual, and Ideology* (Oxford: Clarendon, 1992), 101.

57. By 1815, the United States had its Handel and Haydn Society in Boston, with many more to follow. France developed its own version of institutionalized mass singing in the form of the Orphéon choral society, founded in Paris in the 1830s as a quasi-educational society for working-class men but soon a mass male-voice choral movement with thousands of local branches.

58. Haydn's *Creation* was an even more transnational piece of music than Handel's oratorios. Its genesis lay in Haydn's trips to England in the 1790s and his exposure to the English Handel performances. An Englishman wrote the libretto for Haydn, and Baron Gottfried van Swieten, a key musical traveler himself, did the translation in Vienna in 1796. *The Creation/Die Schöpfung* may be the first piece of music published in a bilingual edition (1800).

59. Percy A. Scholes, *The Mirror of Music, 1844–1944: A Century of Musical Life in Britain as Reflected in the Pages of the* Musical Times (London: Novello & Company, 1947), 2:642.

60. Weber, *Rise of Musical Classics*, 127–41.

61. Hiller's star is beginning to rise among musicologists; see the recent translation of one of his key pedagogical texts: Johann Adam Hiller, *Treatise on Vocal Performance and Ornamentation*, trans. and ed. Suzanne J. Beicken (Cambridge: Cambridge University Press, 2001).

62. See Cecilia Porter, "The New Public and the Reordering of the Musical Establishment: The Lower Rhine Music Festivals, 1818–1867," *19th-Century Music* 3 (1979–80): 211–24; Porter, *The Rhine as Musical Metaphor: Cultural Identity in German Romantic Music* (Boston: Northeastern University Press, 1996), 169–77.

63. Brian Vick, *Defining Germany: The 1848 Frankfurt Parliamentarians and National Identity* (Cambridge, MA: Harvard University Press, 2002), 16, 22–

23, 205–8. Joachim Whaley's definitive two-volume history of *Germany and the Holy Roman Empire* includes a vigorous dismantling of the notion that a political and a cultural German nation were ever distinct from each other in the minds of the inhabitants of the empire: see *Germany and the Holy Roman Empire*, vol. 2: *From the Peace of Westphalia to the Dissolution of the Reich 1648–1806* (New York: Oxford University Press, 2012), 438–44.

64. Celia Applegate, *Bach in Berlin: Nation and Culture in Mendelssohn's Revival of the* St. Matthew Passion (Ithaca, NY: Cornell University Press, 2005).

65. At the same time, Hans Georg Nägeli in Switzerland embarked on a similar process of musical improvement and historical revival, founding in 1805 the Zürich *Singinstitut*, publishing music for choral performance, and encouraging festival oratorio performances on the scale of the English ones.

66. Karen Ahlquist, "Men and Women of the Chorus: Music, Governance, and Social Models in Nineteenth-Century German-Speaking Europe," in *Chorus and Community*, ed. Karen Ahlquist (Urbana: University of Illinois Press, 2006), 265–93.

67. Dieter Düding, "Nationale Oppositionsfeste der Turner, Sänger und Schützen im 19. Jahrhundert," in *Öffentliche Festkultur: Politische Feste in Deutschland von der Aufklärung bis zum Ersten Weltkrieg*, ed. Dieter Düding, Peter Friedemann, and Paul Münch (Hamburg: Rowolt, 1988), 166–90.

68. Josef Eckhardt, "Arbeiterchöre und der 'Deutsche Arbeiter-Sängerbund,'" in *Musik und Industrie: Beiträge zur Entwicklung der Werkchöre und Werksorchester*, ed. Monica Steegmann (Regensburg: Gustav Bosse Verlag, 1978), 45–106.

69. Jessica Gienow-Hecht cites a representative of the Prussian cultural ministry in the early twentieth century who claimed that the Germans had built their unity out of songs (and gymnastics): Gienow-Hecht, *Sound Diplomacy: Music and Emotions in German-American Relations, 1850–1920* (Chicago: University of Chicago Press, 2009), 34n102.

70. See the illuminating analysis of the German reception of Verdi's *Requiem* in Gundula Kreuzer, *Verdi and the Germans: From Unification to the Third Reich* (New York: Cambridge University Press, 2010), 39–84.

71. Quoted in Porter, *Rhine as Musical Metaphor*, 129.

72. A marvelous exploration of this truth is Louise Erdrich's novel about German immigrants in a small town in South Dakota, *The Master Butchers Singing Club* (New York: HarperCollins, 2003).

73. Carl Friedrich Zelter, *Selbstdarstellung*, ed. Willi Reich (Zurich: Manesse Verlag, 1955), 71–72.

74. E. Valentin, "Chor und Hausmusik," *Jahrbuch des deutschen Sängerbund* 17 (1961): 80.

75. See Annette Friedrich, *Beiträge zur Geschichte des weltlichen Frauenchores im 19. Jahrhundert in Deutschland* (Regensburg: Gustav Bosse Verlag, 1961), 7–9.

76. See, for instance, the *Jahresbericht des Münchener akademischen Gesangvereines: XXVI. und XXVII. Vereins-Semester, November 1873 bis Oktober 1874* (Munich: Münchener Akademischer Sangverein, 1874).

77. Blacking, *How Musical Is Man* (Seattle: University of Washington Press, 1973), 107.

78. Carl Maria von Weber, fragments of a *Tonkünsters Leben*, in *Writings on Music*, ed. John Warrack, trans. Martin Cooper (Cambridge: Cambridge University Press, 1981), 318–19.

CHAPTER 3

FROM *PATRIAE AMATOR* TO *AMATOR PAUPERUM* AND BACK AGAIN: SOCIAL IMAGINATION AND SOCIAL CHANGE IN THE WEST BETWEEN LATE ANTIQUITY AND THE EARLY MIDDLE AGES, CA. 300–600

1. I am particularly grateful to my friend and colleague Philip Rousseau for his pertinent comments, and for the discussion that followed these comments at the seminar of the Davis Center. I discuss at length many of the points that I raise in this essay in my book *Through the Eye of a Needle: Wealth, the Fall of Rome, and the Making of Christianity in the West, 350–550 AD* (Princeton: Princeton University Press, 2012).

2. C. Tedeschi, *Congeries lapidum. Iscrizioni Britanniche dei secoli v-vii*, Scuola Normale Superiore di Pisa: Centro di Cultura Medievale (Pisa: Scuola Normale Superiore, 2005), Gso-7, 117–19, with plate 26.

3. Venantius Fortunatus, *Carmina* 3.5.9 and 38.17, in *Venance Fortunat: Poèmes, Livres I–IV*, ed. M. Reydellet (Paris: Belles Lettres, 1997), 91 and 98; 5.3.5, in Reydellet, *Poèmes, Livres V–VIII* (Paris: Belles Lettres, 1998), 17.

4. J. M. Reynolds and J. B. Ward Perkins, *Inscriptions of Roman Tripolitania* (London: British School at Rome, 1952), 159, no. 603. See also C. Lepelley, *Les cités de l'Afrique romaine au Bas-Empire* (Paris: Études Augustiniennes, 1981), 2:353, 348n63. See esp. A. Giardina, *Amor Civicus. Formule e immagini dell'evergetismo nella tradizione epigrafica, La terza età dell'epigrafia*, ed. A. Donati (Faenza: Fratelli Lega, 1988), 67–87. The term may have had Punic roots.

5. M. Foucault, *Security, Territory, Population* (Basingstoke: Palgrave Macmillan, 2007), 155.

6. Ibid., 129.

7. Ibid., 168.

8. Ibid., 128.

9. Venantius Fortunatus, *Carmina* 4.9.10 and 24, 140–41.

10. P. Brown, *Power and Persuasion: Towards a Christian Empire* (Madison: University of Wisconsin Press, 1992), 151–52; C. Rapp, *Holy Bishops in Late Antiquity: The Nature of Christian Leadership in an Age of Transition* (Berkeley: University of California Press, 2005), 279–89.

11. In general, see C. Wickham, *Framing the Early Middle Ages: Europe and the Mediterranean 400–800 AD* (Oxford: Oxford University Press, 2005), 703–15. The sheer scale and complexity of this undertaking is studied in all its aspects in *Nourrir la plèbe. Acts du colloque à Genève en hommage à D. Van Berchem*, ed. A. Giovannini, Schweizerische Beiträge zur Altertumswissenschaft 22 (Basel:

F. Reinhardt, 1991). On the strictly civic nature of entitlement, by which each citizen-recipient had to show a *tessera*, a leaden token, see C. Virlouvet, *Tessera frumentaria. Les procédés de la distribution du blé public à Rome*, Bibliothèque des écoles françaises d'Athènes et de Rome 296 (Rome: Palais Farnèse, 1995), 243–62. See also J.-M. Carrié, "Les distributions alimentaires dans les cités de l'empire romain tardif," *Mélanges de l'école française de Rome: Antiquité* 87 (1975): 995–1101; D. Vera, "Giustiniano, Procopio e l'approvvigionamento di Costantantinopoli," in *Politica, retorica e simbolismo del primato: Roma e Costantinopoli (secoli iv-vii)*, ed. F. Elia (Catania: Spazio Libri, 2004), 9–44.

12. H. Inglebert, *Histoire de la civilisation romaine*, Nouvelle Clio (Paris: Presses Universitaires de France, 2005), 483.

13. P. Veyne, *Le pain et le cirque* (Paris: Le Seuil, 1976), abridged translation *Bread and Circuses* (Harmondsworth: Allen Lane Penguin, 1990); E. Patlagean, *Pauvreté économique et pauvreté sociale à Byzance: 4e-7e siècles* (Paris: Mouton, 1977). These and other contributions are assessed in P. Brown, *Poverty and Leadership in the Later Roman Empire* (Hanover, New Hampshire: University Press of New England, 2002), 2–9.

14. For my own reservations, see Brown, *Poverty and Leadership*, 9–11. The issue has received pertinent comment from J.-M. Carrié, *Nihil habens praeter quod ipso die vestiebatur. Comment définir le seuil de la pauvreté à Rome? Consuetudinis amor. Fragments d'histoire romaine (iie-vie siècles) offerts à Jean-Pierre Callu*, ed. F. Chausson and E. Wolff (Rome: Bretschneider, 2003), 71–102, at pp. 77–84.

15. R. Finn, *Almsgiving in the Later Roman Empire: Christian Promotion and Practice, 313–450* (Oxford: Oxford University Press, 2006); C. Freu, *Les figures du pauvre dans les sources italiennes de l'Antiquité tardive*, Collection de l'Université Marc Bloch. Études d'archéologie et d'histoire ancienne (Paris: de Boccard, 2007).

16. J. Gernet, *Buddhism in Chinese History: An Economic History from the Fifth to the Tenth Century* (New York: Columbia University Press, 1995), 241.

17. P. Brown, *Body and Society: Men, Women and Sexual Renunciation in Early Christianity*, reprint with Introduction (New York: Columbia University Press, 2008), 341–86.

18. Artemidorus, *Oneirocriticon* 3.53, trans. R. J. White, in *The Interpretation of Dreams* (Park Ridge, NJ: Noyes Press, 1975), 171.

19. Lactantius, *Divine Institutes* 6.11.8.

20. S. Schwartz, *Were the Jews a Mediterranean Society? Reciprocity and Solidarity in Ancient Judaism* (Princeton: Princeton University Press, 2010), 30.

21. On Socrates and Seneca, see esp. M. Hénaff, *Le Prix de la Verité: le don, l'argent et la philosophie* (Paris: Le Seuil, 2002).

22. Schwartz, *Were the Jews a Mediterranean Society?*, 31n19.

23. Ibid., 40.

24. M. Weinfeld, *Social Justice in Israel and in the Ancient Near East* (Jerusalem: Magnes, 1995).

25. Jerome, *Commentary on Isaiah* 2.5: *Patrologia Latina* 24: 79C.

26. See esp. Freu, *Les figures du pauvre*, 257–69.

27. E.g., Leo, *Sermon* 44.2: see now S. Wessel, *Leo the Great and the Spiritual Rebuilding of Universal Rome*, Supplement to Vigiliae Christianae 93 (Leiden: Brill, 2008), 179–207; Brown, *Poverty and Leadership*, 90. See now F. R. Stasolla, "Modi e luoghi dell'assistenza nelle opere di Gregorio Magno," in *L'Orbis Antiquus di Gregorio Magno*, ed. L. Ermini Pani (Rome: Società dell Biblioteca Valicelliana, 2007), 1:223–80, see esp. 249 on "distribuzioni 'para-annonarie.' " See also O. Bucarelli, "La carità del papa. Benefici e beneficiati nelle Epistole di Gregorio Magno and G. Pilaro, La gestione dell'annona civile e militare a Roma durante il pontificato di Gregorio Magno," *L'Orbis Antiquus di Gregorio Magno* 2 (2004): 421–36, 505–629.

28. This lacuna was pointed out in a perceptive review by C. Sotinel in *Antiquité Tardive* 11 (2003): 359–63, 362.

29. Veyne, *Le pain et le cirque*, 44–54, and *Bread and Circuses*, 26–29; Patlagean, *Pauvreté économique et pauvreté sociale*, 181–203.

30. K. Bowes, *Private Worship, Public Values and Religious Change in Late Antiquity* (Cambridge: Cambridge University Press, 2008), 10.

31. A.H.M. Jones, "The Social Background to the Struggle between Christianity and Paganism," in *The Conflict between Paganism and Christianity in the Fourth Century*, ed. A. D. Momigliano (Oxford: Clarendon, 1963), 17–37, 21.

32. For the background to this widespread misconception, see P. Brown, "The Study of Elites in Late Antiquity," in "Elites in Late Antiquity," ed. R. Salzman and C. Rapp, special issue, *Arethusa* 33 (2000): 321–46, 324–26 and 336. The "middling-ness" of the Christian church is most clearly revealed in the personnel of the clergy: see esp. C. Sotinel, "Les évêques italiens dans la société de l'antiquité tardive: l'émergence d'une nouvelle élite?," in *Trasformazioni delle élites in età tardoantica*, ed. R. Lizzi Testa (Rome: Bretschneider, 2006), 377–404, for Italy, is decisive. This article has now been translated into English as "The Bishops of Italy in Late Antique Society: A New Elite?," in C. Sotinel, *Church and Society in Late Antique Italy and Beyond* (Farnham, UK: Ashgate/Variorum, 2010). S. Hübner, *Der Klerus in Gesellschaft des spätantiken Kleinasiens* (Stuttgart: F. Steiner, 2005) has reached similar conclusions.

33. G. Anderson, "Redeem Your Soul by the Giving of Alms: Sin, Debt and the 'Treasury of Merit' in Early Jewish and Christian Tradition," *Letter and Spirit* 3 (2007): 39–69.

34. Freu, *Les figures du pauvre*, 161; J.-M. Carrié, "Pratique et idéologie chrétiennes de l'économie (ive-vie siècle)," *Antiquité Tardive* 14 (2006): 17–26, 19; Schwartz, *Were the Jews a Mediterranean Society?*, 129–45.

35. Augustine, *Erfurt Sermon* 3.3, ed. I. Schiller, D. Weber, and C. Weidmann, "Sechs neue Augustinuspredigten: Teil 2 mit Edition dreier Sermones zum Thema Almosen," *Wiener Studien* 122 (2009): 1–34, 18.

36. C. E. Newlands, *Statius' Silvae and the Poetics of Empire* (Cambridge: Cambridge University Press, 2002), 145n44.

37. M. Bloch and J. Parry, "Introduction," *Money and the Morality of Exchange*, ed. M. Bloch and J. Parry (Cambridge: Cambridge University Press,

1989), 1–32, 2. See also J. Parry, "*The Gift*, the Indian Gift and the 'Indian Gift,' " *Man* n.s. 21 (1986): 453–73, 466.

38. Augustine, *Sermon* 66.5, see Finn, *Almsgiving*, p. 47.

39. Schlumberger, "Monuments numismatiques et spragistiques du moyen-âge," *Revue archéologique* n.s. 40 (1888): 193–212, 205 (commenting on the "dog-tags" of the poor in Byzantium); *Midrash Tehillim: The Midrash on Psalms* 1.10, trans. W. G. Braude (New Haven: Yale University Press, 1959), 13.

40. E. Diehl, *Inscriptiones Latinae Christianae Veteres* (Zurich: Weidemann, 1970), 1:189, no. 997.

41. Ibid., 2:194, no. 3400. See Finn, *Almsgiving*, 198–201.

42. Julianus Pomerius, *de vita contemplativa* 2.9: *Patrologia Latina* 59: 454A.

43. B. Caseau, "A Case Study in the Transformation of Law in Late Antiquity: The Legal Protection of Churches," in *Confrontation in Late Antiquity*, ed. L. Jones Hall (Cambridge: Orchard Academic, 2003), 61–77.

44. II Orléans (549), canons 13 and 16, ed. C. de Clercq, *Concilia Galliae A.511–A.695*, *Corpus Christianorum* 148 A (Turnhout: Brepols, 1963), 152 and 154; I Mâcon (581/585), canon 4, p. 224; Valence (583/585), p. 235; Paris (614), canon 9, p. 277; and Clichy (626/627), canon 24, p. 296.

45. II Tours (567), canon 25, p. 192. Psalm 108 (109): 15.

46. Freu, *Les figures du pauvre*, 73; K. Bosl, "*Potens* und *Pauper*. Studien zur gesellschaftlichen Differenzierung im frühen Mittelalter und zum 'Pauperismus' des Hochmittelalters," in *Frühformen der Gesellschaft im mittelalterlichen Europa*, ed. K. Bosl (Munich: Oldenburg, 1964), 106–34 remains the classic statement for the subsequent medieval evolution of the two terms.

47. This is well seen by A. Firey, "'For I Was Hungry and You Fed Me': Social Justice and Economic Thought in the Latin Patristic and Medieval Traditions," in *Ancient and Medieval Economic Ideas and Concepts of Social Justice*, ed. S. T. Lowry and B. Gordon (Leiden: Brill, 1998), 333–70, 344–45.

48. II Mâcon (585), canon 12, pp. 244–45.

49. S. Esders, *Römische Rechtstradition und merowingisches Königtum. Zum Rechtscharakter politischer Herrschaft in Burgund im 6. und 7. Jahrhundert* (Göttingen: Vandenhouck and Ruprecht, 1997), 319–38.

50. Gernet, *Buddhism in Chinese Society*, 166.

51. Foucault, *Security, Territory, Population*, 129.

52. J. Schopen, *Buddhist Monks and Business Matters: Still More Papers on Monastic Buddhism in India* (Honolulu: University of Hawaii Press, 2004), 28–34.

53. J. M. Pardessus, *Diplomata, cartae, epistulae, leges aliaque instrumenta ad res gallo-francicas spectantes* (repr., Aalen: Scientia Verlag, 1969), no. 273, 2:37.

54. Ibid., no. 241, 1:227.

55. T. Sternberg, *Orientalium more secutus. Räume und Institutionen der Caritas des 5. bis 7. Jhdts*, Jahrbuch für Antike und Christentum. Ergänzungsband 16 (Münster in Westfalen: Aschendorff, 1991), 128 and 137.

56. *Eric the Red's Saga* 4, in Gwyn Jones, *The Norse Atlantic Saga*, 2nd ed. (Oxford: Oxford University Press, 1986), 220.

CHAPTER 4

KNOWLEDGE IN MOTION: FOLLOWING ITINERARIES
OF MATTER IN THE EARLY MODERN WORLD

1. Joseph Needham, Ho Ping-Yü, and Lu Gwei-Djen, *Science and Civilization in China*, vol. 5: *Chemistry and Chemical Technology*, pt. 3 (Cambridge: Cambridge University Press, 1976), 2–3.

2. "Kermes" comes from the Arabic/Persian word for red or carmine, *qirmiz*, derived from the Sanskrit *krimija*, meaning "worm-made," indicating the widespread significance and movement of this color. Most red dye in India and Southeast Asia was produced from the lac beetle. Elena Phipps, "Cochineal Red: The Art History of a Color," *Metropolitan Museum of Art Bulletin* 47, no. 3 (Winter 2009): 1–48, 8–9.

3. Kermes and Cochineal are members of the same superfamily of the Coccoidea beetle. Ibid., 14 and 17.

4. The recipes as well as the last wills of Willem and Katalina were probably copied by their son Pieter, who inherited his father's business in 1691. The Pekstok papers are held in the Amsterdam Gemeente Archiv no. N 90.23, and the description of vermilion making has been published by A.F.E. van Schendel, "Manufacture of Vermilion in 17th-Century Amsterdam, The Pekstok Papers," *Studies in Conservation* 17 (1972): 70–82. Amsterdam was the center of vermilion making in Europe in the seventeenth century; only China produced finer pigment. R. D. Harley, *Artists' Pigments 1600–1835*, 2nd ed. (London: Archetype, 2001), 127. Vermilion had been made in Europe since the early Middle Ages: Daniel V. Thompson, Jr., "Artificial Vermilion in the Middle Ages," *Technical Studies in the Field of the Fine Arts* 2 (1933–34): 62–70. I have published portions of the following analysis of the vernacular science of metalworkers in "Vermilion, Mercury, Blood, and Lizards: Matter and Meaning in Metalworking," in *Materials and Expertise in Early Modern Europe: Between Market and Laboratory*, ed. Ursula Klein and Emma Spary (Chicago: University of Chicago Press, 2010), 29–49.

5. The following description and quotations are from van Schendel's transcription and translation of the process in "Manufacture of Vermilion," 71–82.

6. For the relationship of butter to mercury, see Pamela H. Smith, "From Lived Experience to the Written Word: The Reconstruction of Knowledge in Early Modern Europe" (manuscript in progress).

7. I provide this detailed account of the process because the strenuous bodily labor of making vermilion could easily be overlooked. Here for example is how one modern author describes it: "Synthesizing cinnabar was accomplished by sublimating one part mercury and two parts sulfur [this proportion is surely backwards] in a crock sealed with an iron cover (or in an apparatus made up of two pots sealed together with fireclay) and then recovering the vermilion powder that adhered to the upper part of the inside of the crock." From Joseph Needham and Peter J. Golas, *Science and Civilization in China*, vol. 5, pt. 13, "Mining" (Cambridge: Cambridge University Press, 1999), 145–46.

8. Albertus Magnus, *Book of Minerals*, thirteenth century, trans. Dorothy Wyckoff (Oxford: Clarendon, 1967), 81.

9. Cennino D'Andrea Cennini, *Il libro dell'Arte (The Craftsman's Handbook)*, trans. Daniel V. Thompson, Jr. (New York: Dover, 1960), 95.

10. Christiane Kruse, "Fleisch werden—Fleisch malen: Malerei als 'incarnazione.' Mediale Verfahren des Bildwerdens im Libro dell'Arte von Cennino Cennini," *Zeitschrift für Kunstgeschichte* 63 (2000): 305–25. See also Daniela Bohde and Mechthild Fend, eds., *Weder Haut noch Fleisch: das Inkarnat in der Kunstgeschichte*, Neue Frankfurter Forschungen zur Kunst, vol. 3 (Berlin: Gebr. Mann, 2007).

11. John Gage, "Colour Words in the High Middle Ages," in *Looking through Paintings: The Study of Painting Techniques and Materials in Support of Art Historical Research*, Leids Kunsthistorisch Jaarboek XI, ed. Erma Hermens (Baarn, Netherlands: Uitgeverij de Prom, 1998), 35–48, 39.

12. See Caroline Walker Bynum, *Wonderful Blood: Theology and Practice in Late Medieval Northern Germany and Beyond* (Philadelphia: University of Pennsylvania Press, 2007), esp. chaps. 7 and 8.

13. Theophilus, *The Various Arts. De Diversis Artibus*, ed. and trans. C. R. Dodwell (Oxford: Clarendon, 1986), 189–90. The recipe strives for a tone that would indicate that the practice comes out of experience even when it in fact goes back millennia more or less unchanged at least to Pliny, *Natural History*, book 37 (The Natural History of Precious Stones), chap. 15 (Adamas). Berthold Laufer, *The Diamond: A Study in Chinese and Hellenistic Folk-Lore*, Anthropological Series, vol. 15.1 (Chicago: Field Museum of Natural History, 1915), pub. 184, 16n1, 23–25, recounts the philological evidence for this story passing from Pliny to the Physiologus (second to fourth century CE) to India and from there to Fu-nan and from Fu-nan to China, where it is recorded by the fourth-century Daoist adept Ge Hong (Ibid., 21 and 23).

14. Albertus Magnus, *Libellus de alchimia*, fourteenth century (first printed 1561), trans. Virginia Heines, S.C.N. (Berkeley: University of California Press, 1958), notes on p. 19 that gold stimulates heat and life.

15. Just one example comes from the anonymous "Goldsmith's Storehouse" (ca. 1604), Ms. V. a. 179, Folger Shakespeare Library, Washington, DC, fol. 55r, chap. 25.

16. For examples of pigment recipes in which red and gold are associated, see Spike Bucklow, "Paradigms and Pigment Recipes: Vermilion, Synthetic Yellows and the Nature of Egg," *Zeitschrift für Kunsttechnologie und Konservierung* 13 (1999): 140–49, 145–47.

17. Cennini, *Il libro*, "Mosaic gold," 101–2.

18. Arie Wallert, "Alchemy and Medieval Art Technology," in *Alchemy Revisited*, ed. Z.R.W.M. von Martels (Leiden: Brill, 1990): 154–61, 158–59..

19. Theophilus, *Various Arts*, 119–20. There is a great deal of discussion of this recipe by historians of alchemy. The most recent contribution to this debate is Robert Halleux's view that it is based on Arabic recipes, perhaps part of the Jabirian corpus. Robert Halleux, "The Reception of Arabic Alchemy in the West," in *Encyclopedia of the History of Arabic Science*, ed. Roshdi Rashed (London: Routledge, 1996), 3:886–902, 887–88.

20. Rechter Gebrauch der Alchimei / Mitt vil bisher verborgenen uund lustigen Künstien / Nit allein den fürwitzigen Alchmisten / sonder allen kunsbaren

Werckleutten / in und ausserhalb feurs. Auch sunst aller menglichen inn vil wege zugebrauchen (1531), fol. 13.

21. See Pamela H. Smith, *The Body of the Artisan: Art and Experience in the Scientific Revolution* (Chicago: University of Chicago Press, 2004), 117–23. Modern scientists are still interested in lizards: geckos, which can amputate their own tails at will in order to distract predators, are now being studied for the insight that they give into neurons that make up central pattern generators in the spinal cord: "The Tail of a Gecko Has Life of Its Own," *New York Times*, September 9, 2009. Male South African lizards can prolong their adolescence in order to stay out of the way of mature male lizards by hiding out with the female lizards. "Transvestiten-Eidechsen," *Berliner Morgenpost*, March 5, 2009. The all-female species of whiptail lizards can reproduce without males and maintain a high level of genetic variation, "Puzzle Solved: How a Fatherless Lizard Species Maintains Its Genetic Diversity," *New York Times*, February 23, 2010, D3.

22. See Nitza Behrouzi, *The Hand of Fortune: Khamsas from the Gross Family Collection and the Eretz Israel Museum Collection* (exhibition, Eretz Israel Museum, Tel Aviv, 2002), 25, 70–71. I thank Zohar Jolles for this reference.

23. Such a vernacular science has also been discussed as an "indigenous knowledge system" and a *savoir prolétaire*. For example, David Brokensha, D. M. Warren, and Oswald Werner, eds., *Indigenous Knowledge Systems* (Washington, DC: University Press of America, 1980); Helen Watson-Verran and David Turbull, "Science and Other Indigenous Knowledge Systems," in *Handbook of Science and Technology Studies*, ed. Sheila Jasanoff, Gerald E. Marble, James C. Peterson, and Trevor Pinch (London: Sage, 1995), 115–39; for *savoir prolétaire*, see Florike Egmond, "Natuurlijke historie en savoir prolétaire," in *Komenten, monsters en muilezels. Het veranderende natuurbeeld en de natuurwetenschap in de zeventiende eeuw*, ed. Florike Egmond, Eric Jorink, and Rienk Vermij (Haarlem: Arcadia, 1999), 53–71. See also Clifford Geertz, *Local Knowledge: Further Essays in Interpretative Anthropology* (New York: Basic Books, 1983), chap. 4, "Common Sense as a Cultural System," 73–93, and Steven Shapin, "Proverbial Economies: How an Understanding of Some Linguistic and Social Features of Common Sense Can Throw Light on More Prestigious Bodies of Knowledge, Science for Example," *Social Studies of Science* 31, no. 5 (2001): 731–69.

24. For an excellent discussion of the significance of mercury in alchemical theory, see Karin Figala, "Quecksilber," in *Alchemie. Lexicon einer hermetischen Wissenschaft*, ed. Claus Priesner and Karin Figala (Munich: C. H. Beck, 1998), 295–300.

25. Another translator added a preface to his text, which announced, "[A]s your Latin world does not yet know what alchemy is and what its composition is, I will clarify it in the present text." Halleux, "Reception of Arabic Alchemy in the West," 890–91.

26. Halleux notes that there was no guiding principle except availability: Ibid., 893.

27. For a vivid example of the hurdles faced by Arabic translators in working from the Syriac and Greek texts, see Emilie Savage-Smith, "The Exchange of Medical and Surgical Ideas between Europe and Islam," in *The Diffusion of Greco-Roman Medicine into the Middle East and the Caucasus*, ed. John A. C.

Greppin, Emilie Savage-Smith, and John L. Gueriguian (Delmar, NY: Caravan Books, 1999): 27–55, 30–31.

28. Georges C. Anawati, "Arabic Alchemy," in Rashed, *Encyclopedia of the History of Arabic Science*, 3:853–85, 876, and Halleux, "Reception of Arabic Alchemy in the West," 895.

29. Jābir's identity is not entirely clear, and the enormous corpus of texts ascribed to him was not the work of a single individual. Al-Rāzī's copious writings concentrate on practical processes—he was clearly experimenting with the chemical processing of any materials he could get his hands on.

30. Along with these texts, new instruments such as the astrolabe and distillation apparatus also entered the consciousness of European scholars. Albertus's contemporary Roger Bacon (ca. 1214–92/94) formulated a new method of reasoning in his treatise on *scientia experimentalis* (1266–67), which grew out of his reading of Arabic treatises on perspective and mathematics, his use of the astrolabe, which had entered Europe via Iberia in the tenth or eleventh century, and his experiments with magnets and metals. Anawati, "Arabic Alchemy," 867–69; Seyyed Hossein Nasr, *Science and Civilization in Islam* (Cambridge, MA: Harvard University Press, 1968), 268ff.; and J. Hackett, ed., *Roger Bacon and the Sciences* (Leiden: Brill, 1997).

31. Quoted in Albertus, *Book of Minerals*, xxviii.

32. Ibid., 153.

33. Ibid., 212. Albertus never traveled to the Iberian Peninsula, and his remarks about the extraction of mercury from cinnabar ore (a process he might have observed in the Iberian mines) are not derived from firsthand observation (Ibid., 207–8). In addition, Albertus's ideas about the process of sublimating mercury with "salts" to produce white chlorides or ammonium salts are confused. He sees these as poisonous, which some indeed are, but others were employed as medicines in the Arabic pharmacopeia at the time (and subsequently also in Europe up through the nineteenth century as a cure for scabies and syphilis).

34. A point made by Wallert, "Alchemy and Medieval Art Technology," 155.

35. Albertus Magnus, *The Book of Secrets of Albertus Magnus of the Virtues of Herbs, Stones and Certain Beasts: Also a Book of the Marvels of the World*, late thirteenth century, 1530 English translation, ed. Michael R. Best and Frank H. Brightman (Oxford: Clarendon, 1973), 104.

36. Edgar Thurston, *Omens and Superstitions of Southern India* (New York: McBride, Nast & Co., 1915). My thanks to Robert Goulding for this reference and for allowing me to read his lecture "Snakes in a Flame" (unpublished manuscript).

37. *Jin* is a unit of weight that varies according to time and place. One modern *jin* is 0.5 kg.

38. According to the oldest extant Chinese dictionary, *Erya* (earliest portions compiled third century BCE), *shou gong*, *xi yi*, and *yan yan* are synonyms. My deep thanks to Dorothy Ko for this communication.

39. Marshall G. S. Hodgson, *Rethinking World History*, ed. Edmund Burke (Cambridge: Cambridge University Press, 1993), 17.

40. A how-to manual on horse training for chariot use exists in cuneiform on a clay tablet from the fourteenth century BCE. Joan Aruz, Kim Benzel, and Jean M.

Evans, eds., *Beyond Babylon: Art, Trade, and Diplomacy in the Second Millennium B.C.*, Metropolitan Museum exhibit catalog, November 18, 2008–March 15, 2009 (New Haven: Yale University Press, 2008), 158.

41. Joseph Needham, Ho Ping-Yü, Lu Gwi-Djen, and Wang Ling, *Science and Civilization in China*, vol. 5, pt. 7 (Cambridge: Cambridge University Press, 1986), 17.

42. Arnold Pacey, *Technology in World Civilization: A Thousand-Year History* (Cambridge, MA: MIT Press, 1991), 73.

43. Thomas T. Allsen, *The Royal Hunt in Eurasian History* (Philadelphia: University of Pennsylvania Press, 2006).

44. Alfred W. Crosby, Jr., *The Columbian Exchange: Biological and Cultural Consequences of 1492* (Westport, CT: Greenwood, 1972), 199 (peanut), 200 (sweet potato), and 189 (maize).

45. Robert M. Hartwell, "Foreign Trade, Monetary Policy and Chinese 'Mercantilism,'" in *Collected Studies on Sung History Dedicated to James T. C. Liu in Celebration of His Seventieth Birthday*, ed. Kinugawa Tsuyoshi (Kyoto: Dohosha, 1989), 453–88, 469 and 474. My thanks to Nicola di Cosmo for this reference.

46. Hartwell, ibid., 479, records dragon's blood for this purpose rendered as tribute during the Southern Song; and Schafer states that during the Tang it was used as an astringent drug and prescribed for hemorrhages. Edward H. Schafer, *The Golden Peaches of Samarkand: A Study of T'ang Exotics* (Berkeley: University of California Press, 1963), 211.

47. Schafer, *Golden Peaches of Samarkand*, 219.

48. Hartwell, "Foreign Trade," 458.

49. Tha'ālibī, *The Book of Curious and Entertaining Information: The Latā'if al-ma'ārif of Tha'ālibī*, trans. with intro and notes by C. E. Bosworth (Edinburgh: Edinburgh University Press, 1968), 140. Jonathan Bloom argues persuasively that Tha'ālibī's paper-making genealogy cannot be true because paper had already been employed before 751 in Central Asia, but this does not change the fact that prisoners were regarded as valuable repositories of technique. A single line of diffusion need not be established for this and other techniques. Jonathan Bloom, *Paper Before Print: The History and Impact of Paper in the Islamic World* (New Haven: Yale University Press, 2001), 8–9, 42–43.

50. Quoted in Ahmad Yousif Al-Hassan, "Chemical Technology in Arabic Military Treatises," in *From Deferent to Equant: A Volume of Studies in the History of Science in the Ancient and Medieval Near East in Honor of E.S. Kennedy*, ed. David A. King and George Saliba (New York: New York Academy of Sciences, 1987), 153–66. See also Pacey, *Technology in World Civilization*, 8, for another example.

51. Hartwell, "Foreign Trade," 466–68.

52. Another example of this dynamic occurred around 1500, when racialized hierarchies of caste and *casta* emerged together with truly global linkages and exchange. C. A. Bayly, "'Archaic' and 'Modern' Globalization in the Eurasian and African Arena, ca 1750–1850," in *Globalization in World History*, ed. A. G. Hopkins (New York: Norton, 2002), 46–73, makes this point, 55.

53. From 1937 to 1939, a French expedition to Begram, in the lands of ancient Bactria, unearthed two walled-up storerooms of transit trade goods, probably

seized by the Kushan kings before 250 CE. The stores included Indian ivory objects and Chinese lacquerware going west and bronze and glass vessels of Syria and Alexandria going east. Joseph Needham, Ho Ping-Yü, and Lu Gwei-Djen, *Science and Civilization in China*, vol. 5, pt. 4 (Cambridge: Cambridge University Press, 1980), 414–15 note h.

54. The Indian Ocean was an area of particularly intense exchanges of food and shipbuilding technologies during this period. On the remarkable speed of Indian shipyards in adopting and adapting new technologies, see Pacey, *Technology in World Civilization*, 65–70.

55. The evidence is not such to prove beyond a doubt that Kelly was correct in his assertion about Bessemer: Joseph Needham and Donald B. Wagner, *Science and Civilization in China*, vol. 5, pt. 11, "Metallurgy" (Cambridge: Cambridge University Press, 2008), 361–65. As might be expected, this question is a locus of fierce controversy.

56. Robert Hartwell, "Markets, Technology, and the Structure of Enterprise in the Development of the Eleventh-Century Chinese Iron and Steel Industry," *Journal of Economic History* 26, no. 1 (1966): 29–58. See also Needham and Wagner, *Science and Civilization in China*, vol. 5, pt. 11. Very high quality steel was also being produced from a very early period on the Indian subcontinent and shipped to the lands of Islam for use in making Damascene armor and swords. The relationship, if any, between Chinese and Indian steelmaking techniques is not clear. B. Prakash, "Metallurgy of Iron and Steel Making and Blacksmithy in Ancient India," *Indian Journal of History of Science* 26, no. 4 (1991): 351–71. It might be noted that the use of mercury and tin amalgam for dental fillings, which was first introduced to Europe by M. Taveau in 1826, was already practiced in China from at least the seventh century (Joseph Needham and Lu Gwei-Djen, *Science and Civilization*, vol. 5, pt. 2 [Cambridge: Cambridge University Press, 1974], 243). There is no doubt there are further examples of the European adoption of technical processes originating far to the east at a much earlier date.

57. Bayly, "'Archaic' and 'Modern' Globalization." He calls this "archaic globalization," because the social and economic links beyond each particular locality were influenced by broader ideologies of power, sanctity, and humoral balance (71).

58. Ibid., 50–51.

59. Ibid., 52–53.

60. Joseph Needham and Lu Gwei-Djen, *Science and Civilization in China*, vol. 6, pt. 6: "Medicine," ed. Nathan Sivin (Cambridge: Cambridge University Press, 2000), 38–45. See also Geoffrey Lloyd and Nathan Sivin, *The Way and the Word: Science and Medicine in Early China and Greece* (New Haven: Yale University Press, 2002). Lloyd and Sivin see great differences in basic concepts used to articulate ideas about nature in ancient Greece and China, stating that the Greeks focused on "nature and the elements, the Chinese on *ch'i*, yin-yang, the five phases, and the Way" (6).

61. The trade in precious stones was carried on as far back at the very least as 4000 BCE, when a gem market is recorded in Babylon. India has exported diamonds, sapphires, and rubies at least since 400 BCE. The alluvial deposits of Sri Lanka and Madagascar have also long been a source of precious gems: Webster Anderson, *Gems: Their Sources, Descriptions, and Identification*, 4th ed. (Lon-

don: Butterworths, 1983). Berthold Laufer argues that the view that wonders originated in India emerged out of an aristocratic Arabic-Persian milieu (Laufer, *The Diamond*, 11). Muzaffar Alam and Sanjay Subrahmanyam, *Indo-Persian Travels in the Age of Discoveries, 1400–1800* (Cambridge: Cambridge University Press, 2007), note that medieval travel literature the world over includes "wonders" or *aja'ib*, which are marvels, astonishing things or "mirabilia" (p. 4), most often told in first-person narrative. For the European literature on wonders, see Lorraine Daston and Katherine Park, *Wonders and the Order of Nature, 1150–1750* (New York: Zone Books, 1998), in which they recount that the very first of 129 wonders that Gervase of Tilbury lists in his 1210 *Otia imperialia* is the magnet, "an Indian stone," with the property of attracting iron (21). William of Auvergne (ca. 1180?–1249) wrote that "in parts of India and other adjoining regions, there is a great quantity of things of this sort [i.e., wonders], and on account of this, natural magic particularly flourishes there" (75).

62. Buzurg ibn Shahriyar, *Kitab 'ajayib al-Hind*, Arabic text with French translation by L. Marcel Devic (Leiden: Brill, 1883–86), 47ff. and 120ff.

63. Ibid., 157 and 173.

64. Ibid., 7–8.

65. Ibid., 171. Muḥammad ibn Aḥmad Bīrūnī's (973?–1048) *Kitab al-Hind* (Book of India) has a very different tone than these books of wonders. Although he mentions oddities, such as "in shaking hands they grasp the hand of a man from the convex side," and "they spit out and blow their noses without any respect for the elder ones present, and they crack their lice before them," and "in playing chess they move the elephant straight on" (1:182), and he relates several examples of charms, he concludes that "most of their charms are intended for those who have been bitten by serpents," about which he says, "I, for my part, do not know what I am to say about these things, since I do not believe in them" (1:194). And about the people in India in general, "in all manners and usages they differ from us to such a degree as to frighten their children with us, with our dress, and our ways, and customs, and as to declare us to be devil's breed, and our doings as the very opposite of all that is good and proper. By the bye, we must confess, in order to be just, that a similar depreciation of foreigners not only prevails among us and the Hindus, but is common to all nations towards each other" (1:20). Edward C. Sachau, *Alberuni's India*, 2 vols. (London: Trübner & Co., 1888; repr. Elibron Classics, Adamant Media, 2005).

66. Berthold Laufer's pioneering philological research on folk beliefs, such as *The Diamond*, and "The Story of the Pinna and the Syrian Lamb," *Journal of American Folk-Lore* 28 (1915): 103–28; and "Asbestos and Salamander," *T'oung Pao*, 2nd ser., 16, no. 3 (1915): 299–373 shows just how ancient some of these tales are, as well as tracing the remarkable accretions they acquired as they moved over time and space. The three mentioned here trace "exotic" concepts and objects back to the Hellenistic-Roman East, whence, he argues, they spread throughout Eurasia.

67. This contention necessitates a great deal more research.

68. Needham and Golas, *Science and Civilization*, vol. 5, pt. 13, 139.

69. Needham and Gwei-Djen, *Science and Civilization*, vol. 5, pt. 3, 6.

70. Ibid., vol. 5, pt. 2, 69.

71. Mosaic gold was being made in China at the time Ge Hong wrote; Ibid., vol. 5, pt. 2, 271. Although imitation gold in China and in Europe possessed the same chemical makeup, this does not necessarily imply that they possessed the same meaning and significance in both places. Objects and materials may have the same physical makeup, but they cannot therefore be automatically treated as "the same."

72. Ibid., vol. 5, pt. 2, 67. For this reason, gold might be found below cinnabar deposits.

73. Ibid., vol. 5, pt. 2, fig. 1335, plates.

74. Ibid., vol. 5, pt. 3, 3.

75. Fabrizio Pegadio, *Great Clarity: Daoism and Alchemy in Early Medieval China* (Stanford: Stanford University Press, 2006), 30. He also makes clear that the earliest alchemical texts show that the performance of rites is part of alchemical practices from their earliest recorded mention (31).

76. Needham and Gwei-Djen, *Science and Civilization*, vol. 5, pt. 2, 286.

77. Indeed, in ca. 800, mention is made of mercury and cinnabar being used to fabricate gold vessels, but these are regarded as poisonous. Does this perhaps indicate the influence of Arabic texts about poisons in China? Ibid., vol. 5, pt. 2, 243.

78. Needham and Golas, *Science and Civilization*, vol. 5, pt. 13, 149.

79. Needham and Gwei-Djen, *Science and Civilization*, vol. 5, pt. 2, 128.

80. Needham, Ping-Yü, and Gwei-Djen, *Science and Civilization*, vol. 5, pt. 3, 4–5.

81. Ibid., vol. 5, pt. 4 (Cambridge University Press, 1980), 300–301.

82. Ibid., vol. 5, pt. 3, 126. Pegadio, *Great Clarity*, makes clear that alchemy was never just about producing materials, but always aimed at higher enlightenment through the process of producing these materials.

83. See Needham, Ping-Yü, and Gwei-Djen, *Science and Civilization*, vol. 5, pt. 4, 300–305, for a very interesting example of this.

84. Knowledge of nature—what we would call "science"—possessed myriad meaning and uses. Benjamin Elman's works, including *On Their Own Terms: Science in China 1550–1900* (Cambridge, MA: Harvard University Press, 2005), make clear the variety of approaches to the natural world and natural things that existed over the very long term in China.

85. Emilie Savage-Smith, *Science, Tools and Magic* (Oxford: Nasser D. Khalili Collection of Islamic Art, Nour Foundation and Oxford University Press, 1997), vol. 12, pt. 2, 328–30, notes this trade and discusses the possible vessels in which mercury was carried.

86. Nasr, *Science and Civilization in Islam*, 272.

87. Needham and Golas, *Science and Civilization*, vol. 5, pt. 13, 146.

88. Pacey, *Technology in World Civilization*, emphasizes the importance of stimulus, response, and dialogue in the dynamics of technology "transfer."

89. Halleux, "Reception of Arabic Alchemy in the West," 886.

90. Needham, Ping-Yü, and Gwei-Djen, *Science and Civilization*, vol. 5, pt. 4, 437ff.

91. Emilie Savage-Smith, "Exchange of Medical and Surgical Ideas," 35.

92. Needham, Ping-Yü, and Gwei-Djen, *Science and Civilization*, vol. 5, pt. 4, 452.

93. Needham, Ping-Yü, and Gwei-Djen, ibid., vol. 5, pt. 4, make this point in their section on China and the Arabic world, 388ff.

94. Another example of such an amalgam comes from Chandra Mukerji, "Tacit Knowledge and Classical Technique in Seventeenth-Century France," *Technology and Culture* 47, no. 4 (2006): 713–33, who documents the use of hydraulic mortar (i.e., mortar that can be used under water) on the Canal du Midi. At the time of the canal's building, waterproof mortar was a rural French masons' practice (perhaps dating from Roman times), unknown to the scholarly tradition. In fact, hydraulic mortar had been discussed by the Roman architect Vitriuvius, but the textual knowledge of the technique had fallen out of historical memory, while the practice itself survived. In the eighteenth century, the technique was rediscovered in Vitruvius, which then came to be regarded as the source of the use of waterproof mortar in the building of the canal. In fact, what had happened was that a practice had moved in and out of written tradition. As a practice it had survived, but it was lost and then found again in the written tradition. This example indicates the complexity of the relationship between practice and text, and alerts us to the pitfalls of thinking about them in a hierarchical or binary way.

95. Sanjay Subrahmanyam has suggested "connected histories" as a way to avoid nationalist narratives in "Connected Histories: Notes towards a Reconfiguration of Early Modern Eurasia," *Modern Asian Studies* 31, no. 3 (1997): 735–62. See also Michael Werner and Bénédicte Zimmermann, "Beyond Comparison: *Histoire croisée* and the Challenge of Reflexivity," *History and Theory* 45, no. 1 (2006): 30–50.

96. George Saliba, *Islamic Science and the Making of the European Renaissance* (Cambridge, MA, MIT Press, 2007). Jamil Ragep makes the same point in "Tusi and Copernicus: The Earth's Motion in Context," *Science in Context* 14, nos. 1/2 (2001): 145–63, and "Copernicus and His Islamic Predecessors: Some Historical Remarks," *History of Science* 45 (2007): 65–81. Saliba and Ragep's works lead to the question of whether the revolution in astronomy should be viewed rather as an Arabic-Latinate revolution that took place over a much longer time span than what we now call the Copernican revolution. Richard W. Bulliet performed a similar reconceptualization in a different sphere in *The Case for Islamo-Christian Civilization*, 2nd ed. (New York: Columbia University Press, 2004).

97. Phipps, "Cochineal Red," 18, 22.

98. Ibid., 27ff.

99. Ibid., 26.

100. Ibid., 43–44.

101. For an overview and relevant literature, see Tony Ballantyne, "Empire, Knowledge and Culture: From Proto-Globalization to Modern Globalization," in Hopkins, *Globalization in World History*, 114–40, 120–21. See also Londa Schiebinger, *Plants and Empire: Colonial Bioprospecting in the Atlantic World* (Cambridge, MA: Harvard University Press, 2007).

102. Ballantyne, "Empire, Knowledge and Culture," 138.

103. Ibid., 129. Moreover, cultural forms, such as the pursuit of science, were constructed as superior modes of knowing that distinguished the modernity of the European colonizer from the "primitive" colonized subject. In colonial India, for example, the pursuit of science functioned as a dividing line between colo-

nizer and colonized, as individuals of Indian extraction were not allowed to be members of the Asiatic Society in Mumbai (founded 1830), the premier scientific institution in South Asia. David Arnold, *Science, Technology and Medicine in Colonial India* (Cambridge: Cambridge University Press, 2000), 31.

104. Scrying was an ancient method of divination, practiced at least since the Greeks. See Deborah E. Harkness, *John Dee's Conversations with Angels: Cabala, Alchemy, and the End of Nature* (Cambridge: Cambridge University Press, 1999).

105. Oliver Meslay, "Murillo and 'Smoking Mirrors,'" *Burlington Magazine* 143, no. 1175 (February 2001): 73–79.

106. For Walpole's acquisition of and interest in this stone, see Alicia Weisberg-Roberts, "Singular Objects and Multiple Meanings," in *Horace Walpole's Strawberry Hill*, ed. Michael Snodin, with the assistance of Cynthia Roman (New Haven: Yale University Press, 2009), 87–105, 97, 100. My thanks to Alicia Weisberg-Roberts for directing me to Meslay's article.

107. Meslay, "Murillo and 'Smoking Mirrors,'" 73–74.

108. Schiebinger, *Plants and Empire*; Londa Schiebinger and Claudia Swan, eds., *Colonial Botany: Science, Commerce, and Politics in the Early Modern World* (Philadelphia: University of Pennsylvania Press, 2005); and Antonio Barrera-Osorio, *Experiencing Nature: The Spanish American Empire and the Early Scientific Revolution* (Austin: University of Texas Press, 2006). An exemplary examination of Spanish spice growing in the Americas is Paula de Vos, "The Science of Spices: Empiricism and Economic Botany in the Early Spanish Empire," *Journal of World History* 17, no. 4 (2006): 399–427. See also Jorge Cañizares-Esguerra's *How to Write the History of the New World: Histories, Epistemologies, Identities in the Eighteenth-Century Atlantic World* (Stanford: Stanford University Press, 2001) and *Nature, Empire, and Nation: Explorations of the History of Science in the Iberian World* (Stanford: Stanford University Press, 2006), as well as James Delbourgo and Nicholas Dew, eds., *Science and Empire in the Atlantic World* (New York: Routledge, 2008).

109. Richard Drayton, "The Collaboration of Labor: Slaves, Empires, and Globalizations in the Atlantic World, ca. 1600–1850," in Hopkins, *Globalization in World History*, 106–15, 109.

110. Daniela Bleichmar, "Books, Bodies, and Fields: Sixteenth-Century Transatlantic Encounters with New World," in Schiebinger and Swan, *Colonial Botany*, 83–99, 95, 98–99.

111. Harold J. Cook, *Matters of Exchange: Commerce, Medicine, and Science in the Dutch Golden Age* (New Haven: Yale University Press, 2007).

112. Marcy Norton, "Tasting Empire: Chocolate and the European Internalization of Mesoamerican Aesthetics," *American Historical Review* 111 (2006): 660–91, 691. See also Marcy Norton, *Sacred Gifts, Profane Pleasures: A History of Tobacco and Chocolate in the Atlantic World* (Ithaca, NY: Cornell University Press, 2008). For an overview of some of the work on nineteenth- and twentieth-century Latin America that seeks out these kinds of creolizations, see Barbara Weinstein, "History Without a Cause," *International Review of Social History* 50 (2005): 71–93, 90–91.

113. As Jordan Kellman has recently made clear, in the case of cochineal, it was only input from indigenous cochineal farmers in the 1740s that finally settled the

question of whether the pigment derived from a plant or an insect. Jordan Kellman, "Nature, Networks, and Expert Testimony in the Colonial Atlantic: The Case of Cochineal," *Atlantic Studies* 7 (2010): 373–95. Similarly, Miruna Achim, in "From Rustics to Savants: Indigenous *Materia Medica* in Eighteenth-Century Mexico," *Studies in the History and Philosophy of Biological and Biomedical Sciences* 42 (2011): 275–84, makes clear that in the eighteenth century, Creole elites in Mexico began to claim authority by appealing to an "intimate knowledge of the land and of its people," including knowledge about the healing properties of lizards.

114. In *The Perception of the Environment: Essays in Livelihood, Dwelling and Skill* (London: Routledge, 2000), Tim Ingold makes this point elegantly.

115. Robert K. Merton first pointed out this phenomenon in the 1940s in "Singletons and Multiples in Science," in *The Sociology of Science: Theoretical and Empirical Investigations* (Chicago: University of Chicago Press, 1973), 343–70. In recent years, there have been both scholarly and popular accounts of the collective nature of invention and innovation. For example, see Arnold Pacey, *The Maze of Ingenuity*, 2nd ed. (Cambridge, MA: MIT Press, 1992) and Clifford D. Conner, *A People's History of Science: Miners, Midwives, and "Low Mechanicks"* (New York: Nation Books, 2005).

CHAPTER 5
FASHIONING A MARKET: THE SINGER SEWING MACHINE IN COLONIAL LANKA

1. Sidney W. Mintz, *Sweetness and Power: The Place of Sugar in Modern History* (New York Viking, 1985).

2. I use the term *Lanka*, which was the name given to the island in the Sinhala language, instead of the colonial name *Ceylon*.

3. E. B. Denham, *Ceylon at the Census of 1911* (Colombo: H. Ross Cottle, Government Printer, 1912), 4.

4. Andrew Gordon, in his "Selling the American Way: The Singer Sales System in Japan, 1900–1938," *Business History Review* 82 (Winter 2008): 671–99, deploys an array of sources including a 1922 photograph of salesmen and teachers employed by Singer, a 1903 report filed by Hata Toshiyuki, occupying a managerial post in the Singer Company, and a retrospective account of the life of a salesman—*Osaka tsuhsho sangyokyoku ed Mishin Kogyo* [The Sewing Machine Industry] (Osaka, 1951), cited in Gordon, "Selling the American Way," 676.

5. David Arnold, "The Indian Sewing Machine, 1875–1952," *Journal of Global History* 6 (2011): 407–29.

6. See Jean Taylor, "The Sewing Machine in Colonial Era Photographs: A Record from Dutch Indonesia," *Modern Asian Studies* 46, no. 1 (January 2012): 71–95.

7. Denham, *Ceylon at the Census*, 193.

8. Timothy Burke, *Lifebuoy Men, Lux Women: Commodification, Consumption and Cleanliness in Modern Zimbabwe* (Durham, NC: Duke University Press, 1996), 214.

9. Denham, *Ceylon at the Census*, 173.

10. H. Harootunian, cited in Frederick Cooper, *Colonialism in Question: Theory, Knowledge, History* (Berkeley: University of California Press, 2005), 128.

11. Ann Laura Stoler, ed., *Haunted by Empire: Geographies of Intimacy in North American History* (Durham, NC: Duke University Press, 2006), 27.

12. For a critique of this approach, see John Kelly and Martha Kaplan, *Represented Communities: Fiji and World Decolonization* (Chicago: University of Chicago Press, 2001).

13. Partha Chatterjee, *The Nation and Its Fragments: Colonial and Postcolonial Histories* (Princeton: Princeton University Press, 1993), 5.

14. Harry Harootunian, *History's Disquiet: Modernity, Cultural Practice and the Question of Everyday Life* (New York: Columbia University Press, 2000), 49.

15. David Arnold and Erich de Wald, "Everyday Technology in South and Southeast Asia: An Introduction," *Modern Asian Studies* 46, no. 1 (2012): 1.

16. Andrew Godley, "Selling the Sewing Machine Around the World: Singer's International Marketing Strategies, 1850–1920," *Enterprise and Society* 7, no. 2 (2006): 266–314, 266–67.

17. The history of the firm has been well covered in the following: Mira Wilkins, *The Emergence of Multinational Enterprise: American Business Abroad from the Colonial Era to 1914* (Cambridge, MA: Harvard University Press, 1970); Robert Davies, *Peacefully Working to Conquer the World* (New York: Arno Press, 1976); Ruth Brandon, *A Capitalist Romance: Singer and the Sewing Machine* (Philadelphia: J.B. Lippincott, 1977); Don Bissel, *The First Conglomerate: 145 Years of the Singer Sewing Machine* (Brunswick, ME: Audenreed Press, 1999).

18. See, for instance, Michael Adas, *Machines as the Measure of Men: Science, Technology and Ideologies of Western Dominance* (Ithaca, NY: Cornell University Press, 1989); Caroll Purshell, *The Machine in America: A Social History of Technology*, 2nd ed. (Baltimore: Johns Hopkins University Press, 2007).

19. Robert Davies, "Peacefully Working to Conquer the World: The Singer Manufacturing Company in Foreign Markets, 1854–1889," *Business History Review* 43 (Autumn 1969): 299–346.

20. Krystyn Moon, in *Yellowface: Creating the Chinese in American Popular Music and Performance, 1850–1920s* (New Brunswick, NJ: Rutgers University Press, 2005), examines depictions of Chinese and Chinese Americans across a variety of popular musical and theatrical conventions.

21. Bissel, *First Conglomerate*, 107.

22. Cited in Davies, *Peacefully Working*, 97n116. Singer Sewing Machine Company, *Mechanics of the Sewing Machine*, Monograph 5, National Education Association (New York: Singer Sewing Company, 1914), 42.

23. Andrew Gordon, *Fabricating Consumers: The Sewing Machine in Modern Japan* (Berkeley: University of California Press, 2012). Also see Andrew Gordon, "From Singer to Shinpan: Consumer Credit in Modern Japan," in *The Ambivalent Consumer: Questioning Consumption in East Asia and the West*, ed. Sheldon Garon and Patricia Maclachlan (Ithaca, NY: Cornell University Press, 2006), 114–62.

24. See Davies, *Peacefully Working*, chap. 6.

25. Department of Commerce and Labor Bureau of Manufactures, *Monthly Consular and Trade Reports*, no. 300 (September 1905).

26. Consular Reports, U.S. Bureau of Foreign Commerce, U.S. Department of Commerce and Labor (Washington, DC: Government Printing Office, 1905), 8. For a separate listing on Lanka, see Special Consular Reports, U.S. Bureau of Foreign Commerce, U.S. Department of Commerce and Labor, U.S. Bureau of Manufactures (Washington, DC: Government Printing Office, 1900), 123.

27. Victoria de Grazia, *Irresistible Empire: America's Advance through Twentieth-Century Europe* (Cambridge, MA: Harvard University Press, 2005), 8.

28. Letter from Mitchell to Singer Manufacturing Company Directors, April 20, 1888, Wisconsin Historical Society Archives, Singer Papers, box 89.

29. John Mitchell to Singer Directors in London, Bombay, April 20, 1888, Singer Papers, box 89.

30. List of Offices in India, Burmah, and Lanka, 1904; list of offices in India, Burmah, and Lanka, 1905; both in Singer Papers, box 89, folder 7.

31. *The Ceylon Law Reports—Being Reports of Cases Decided by the Supreme Court of Lanka*, vols. 1–3 (Columbo: Lanka Examiner Press, 1887–97).

32. *Ceylon Independent*, September 2, 1899.

33. Ibid.

34. Directory of shops for the sale of Singer sewing machines throughout the world (revised January 1906), 5, Singer Papers, box 109, 2m3605.

35. *The Amicus Annual* (1915), Sri Lanka National Archives, Colombo.

36. Letter from John Mitchell to Head Office in New York, April 20, 1888, Singer Papers, box 89.

37. *Ferguson's Directory* (1900, 1910, 1926, 1930).

38. Denham, *Ceylon at the Census*, 366.

39. Andrew Godley, "The Global Diffusion of the Sewing Machine, 1850–1914," *Research in Economic History* 20 (2001): 1–45, 22.

40. *Amicus Annual*.

41. *Report of the Proceedings at the Presentation of an Address to N.M. Patell, Esquire JP, Agent for India, Burmah and Ceylon, The Singer Manufacturing Company, on His Retirement* (Washington, DC: Smithsonian Institution Libraries, 1911), 15–16.

42. See Patell's contract, Singer Papers, box 88, folder 8.

43. Parsees were, according to tradition, descendants of Iranian Zoroastrians who emigrated to western India over a thousand years ago.

44. Mitchell to Mr. N. M. Patell, Agent at Bombay, April 17, 1888, Singer Papers, box 89. Parsis were a very small community in Ceylon/Lanka—they numbered 184 in 1911—engaged mainly in trade but also were prominent as philanthropists. See Denham, *Ceylon at the Census*, 241–42; Dosabhai Framji Karaka, *History of the Parsis Including Their Manners, Customs, Religion and Present Position*, 2 vols. (1884; repr., Kila, MT: Kessinger, 2004).

45. Letter from Edward Sang to G.R.M. Mackenzie, August 10, 1883, Singer Papers, box 88, 1992/83.

46. Godley, "Selling the Sewing Machine," 281–85.

47. Letter to G. R. Mackenzie, August 10, 1883, Singer Papers, box 88, 1992/83.

48. Davies, *Peacefully Working*, 184.

49. Ibid., 174.

50. Letter from Edward Sang to Mackenzie, August 10, 1883, Singer Papers, box 88.

51. Ibid.

52. Letter from Edward Sang to Patell, April 17, 1888, Singer Papers, box 88.

53. At the beginning of the British period, Nattukottai Chettiars became an important part of the local banking system by advancing money to European merchants. When European exchange banks established themselves, Chettiars lost that trade but continued to provide credit to Lankan farmers, shopkeepers, coconut millers, arrack producers, and estate owners. They linked the village and the plantation sectors of the economy, supplying planters with rice for their laborers, selling rice to villagers, and often owning paddy land. A credit crisis brought down many Chettiar firms in 1925, forcing many merchants into pawnbroking.

54. Patell to Singer Manufacturing Co., NY, November 7, 1901, Singer Papers, box 89, folder 6.

55. Patell to Singer Manufacturing Co., November 15, 1901, Singer Papers, box 89, folder 5.

56. NY Office to Mr. Patell, December 13, 1901, Singer Papers, box 89, folder 5.

57. Mitchell to Mr. N. M. Patell, Agent at Bombay, April 17, 1888, Singer Papers, box 89.

58. Mark Frost, "'Wider Opportunities': Religious Revival, Nationalist Awakening and the Global Dimension in Colombo, 1870–1920," *Modern Asian Studies* 36, no. 4 (October 2002): 937–67, 940.

59. "Catalogue of Newspapers, Periodicals, Books and Maps," compiled by A. M. and J. Ferguson in *Ferguson's Directory 1895* (Colombo: Lanka Observer Press, 1895), 4–5.

60. *Lakmini Pahana*, July 28, 1900.

61. *Lakmini Pahana*, September 1, 1900.

62. *Dinara Prakasha*, February 6, 1886.

63. Leonard Woolf, *Diaries in Lanka 1908–1911. Records of Colonial Administrator* (Colombo, 1962), 51. Leonard Woolf returned to England in 1911 and a year later married Adeline Virginia Stephen (later known as Virginia Woolf).

64. In 1911, 47.9 percent of low-country Sinhalese males and 36.4 percent of Kandyan (up-country) males were literate in their mother tongue (Sinhala). The figures for females were still very low: 17.4 percent of low-country females and 2.8 percent of Kandyan females. Denham, *Ceylon at the Census*, 401. Sinhala men of the early twentieth century were avid readers of the *Maha Bodhi*, the journal of the Maha Bodhi Society, which regularly featured Buddhist events in America. See Thomas A. Tweed, *The American Encounter with Buddhism 1844–1912: Victorian Culture and the Limits of Dissent* (Bloomington: Indiana University Press, 1992).

65. M. M. Mehaffy, "Advertising Race/Raceing Advertising: The Feminine Consumer(-nation), 1876–1900," *Signs* 23 (1997): 131–74, 137–38.

66. Bissel, *First Conglomerate*, 116, cited in Davies, *Peacefully Working*, 99; S. M. Colema to Agents, July 26, 1892, General Circular No. 33, Singer Papers, box 159.

67. Mona Domosh, *American Companies in an Age of Empire* (New York: Routledge, 2006). On the idea of "civilizing mission" in U.S. foreign policy, see Amy Kaplan and Donald E. Pease, eds., *Cultures of United States Imperialism* (Durham, NC: Duke University Press, 1993); Harald Fisher-Tine and Michael Mann, eds., *Colonialism as Civilizing Mission: Cultural Ideology in British India* (London: Anthem Press, 2004). On the idea of imperial governmentality, see Stoler, *Haunted by Empire*.

68. Mona Domosh, "Selling Civilization: Towards a Cultural Analysis of America's Economic Empire in the Late Nineteenth and Early Twentieth Centuries," *Transactions of the Institute of British Geographers* 29, no. 4 (2004): 453–67, 464. Singer's set of nation cards, all identical in format, all showing people posed around a Singer machine, with similar color schemes, was originally issued as a set of twelve cards, then increased in number to twenty-four in 1892 and thirty-six in 1893. Lanka was one of the thirty-six nations depicted in 1893. The context is important. The cards were issued at the World's Columbian Exposition held in Chicago to celebrate Columbus's "discovery" of America, aptly described by Anne McClintock as the first "commodity spectacle" of American imperialism, the staging for America's move from nation-state to imperial power.

69. Patell to Singer Manufacturing Company New York, October 10, 1901; Patell to Singer Manufacturing Company, New York Executive Office, January 6, 1900; both in Singer Papers, box 29, folder 6.

70. *The Ceylon Independent*, February 6, 1904.

71. Patell to Singer Manufacturing Company New York, October 10, 1901; Patell to Singer Manufacturing Company, New York Executive Office, January 6, 1900; both in Singer Papers, box 29, folder 6.

72. *Lakmina*, January 4, 1896.

73. *The Ceylon Independent*, September 17, 1898, September 2, 1899.

74. *Sinhala Bauddhaya*, May 5, 1936.

75. *Amicus Annual*.

76. In 1904 the voting population was 3,013, as literacy in English was the only recognized qualification for civic rights. In 1921 and 1924, when the constitution recognized literacy in the vernacular, the voting population rose to 54,207 and 189,335, respectively.

77. I owe these insights to Sandagomi Coperahewa, Department of Sinhalese, University of Colombo.

78. C. A. Bayly, *The Birth of the Modern World 1780–1914* (Malden, MA: Blackwell, 2004), 10–12.

79. Harootunian, *History's Disquiet*, 67.

80. P.V.J. Jayasekera, "The American Impact on Sri Lanka: Historical Background," in *The American Impact on Sri Lanka*, ed. C. R. de Silva (Colombo: American Studies Association of Sri Lanka, 1989), 1.

81. David G. Dickson, "The Nineteenth Century Indo-American Ice Trade: An Hyperborean Epic," *Modern Asian Studies* 25, no. 1 (February 1991): 53–89.

82. *Ferguson's Directory 1926*, 358–59.

83. Purshell, *Machine in America*. The American mass-produced clock, originally made of wood but subject to warping, was not sold overseas. Once it was made of metal, it became cheap and met no competition (184).

84. Commerce Reports, U.S. Bureau of Manufactures, Bureau of Foreign and Domestic Commerce (Washington, DC: Bureau of Foreign and Domestic Commerce, U.S. Department of Commerce, 1912), 1302–3.

85. Thomas Edward Thorpe, *A Dictionary of Applied Chemistry* (London: Longmans, Green, 1922).

86. Anagarika Dharmapala was the most celebrated preacher and reformer of the period. He was the son of a furniture dealer who attended a Roman Catholic school, then an Anglican school. He worked as a clerk in the Education Department. Following Colonel Olcott's visit to the island in 1880, he became active in the Theosophical Society for almost twenty years. He established the Maha Bodhi Society as the institutional vehicle to restore the Bodh Gaya site (where the Buddha was enlightened) and deliver its holy ruins to Buddhist hands. He emerged as a fierce critic of Christian beliefs and a leading agitator for Buddhist revival.

87. Tweed, *American Encounter with Buddhism*, 56–57.

88. Cited in Richard F. Gombrich, *Theravada Buddhism: A Social History from Ancient Benares to Modern Colombo* (London: Routledge Kegan Paul, 1988), 193.

89. Michael Roberts, "For Humanity, for the Sinhalese: Dharmapala as Crusading Brosat," *Journal of Asian Studies* 56, no. 4 (1997): 1006–32, 1008.

90. Balkrishna Govind Gokhale, "Anagarika Dharmapala: Toward Modernity through Tradition in Lanka," in *Tradition and Change in Theravada Buddhism: Essays on Lanka and Thailand in the 19th and 20th Centuries*, ed. Bardwell L. Smith (Leiden: E.J. Brill, 1973), 30–39, 39.

91. B. L. Panditaratne, "Trends of Urbanization in Lanka 1901–1953," *Lanka Journal of Historical and Social Studies* 7, no. 2 (July–December 1964): 203–17, 206.

92. The Burghers are a Eurasian ethnic group consisting for the most part of descendants of male Portuguese and Dutch colonists and local women.

93. L.J.B. Turner, *Handbook of Commercial and General Information for Lanka* (Colombo: H. Ross Cottle, Government Printer, 1922), 4.

94. A. C. Dep, *A History of the Lanka Police*, vol. 2: *1866–1913* (Colombo: Police Amenities Fund, 1969), 364–65.

95. Roberts, "For Humanity," 1011.

96. See Kumari Jayawardena, *Nobodies to Somebodies: The Rise of the Colonial Bourgeoisie in Sri Lanka* (Colombo: SSA and Sanjiva Books, 2007).

97. See Jean Baudrillard, *La Societé de Consommation* (Paris: Gallimard, 1968).

98. Cited in Bryce F. Ryan, *Caste in Modern Lanka: The Sinhalese System in Transition* (New Brunswick, NJ: Rutgers University Press, 1953), 113–14.

99. *Census of Ceylon 1871*, 97, table 6; *Census of Lanka 1871*, 97–98, 187, table 7.

100. *Census of Ceylon 1891*, 374–75, table 65.

101. *Ferguson's Directory 1903*, 773; *Ferguson's Directory 1914–15*, 931, 940, 947; *Ferguson's Directory 1925*, 764, Sri Lanka National Archives, Colombo.

102. List of tailors in *Ferguson's Directory 1926*, 843.

103. *Ferguson's Lanka Handbook and Directories*, advertisement on 37.

104. *Ferguson's Directory 1880*, advertisement on xi.

105. E.F.C. Ludowyk, *Those Long Afternoons: Childhood in Colonial Lanka* (Colombo: Lake House Bookshop, 1989), 75.

106. *Ferguson's Directory 1926*, 821.

107. On the social, relational, and active nature of consumption, see Arjun Appadurai, ed., *The Social Life of Things: Commodities in Cultural Perspective* (Cambridge: Cambridge University Press, 1986).

108. René Depestre, *Anthologie personnelle* (Paris: Actes du Sud, Gallimard, 1993), 28–29.

109. Denham, *Ceylon at the Census*, 166.

110. Andrew Skuze, "Enlivened Objects: The Social Life, Death and Rebirth of Radio as Commodity in Afghanistan," *Journal of Material Culture* 10, no. 2 (2005): 123–37, 128.

111. Martin Wickramasinghe, *Narak Wu piti baduna* (Colombo, 1924).

112. See Malathi de Alwis, "Gender, Politics and the Respectable Lady," in *Unmaking the Nation: The Politics of Identity and History in Modern Sri Lanka*, ed. P. Jeganathan and Q. Ismael (Colombo: SSA, 1995).

113. Chatterjee, *Nation and Its Fragments*.

114. Ibid., 130.

115. Malathi de Alwis, "The Production and Embodiment of Respectability: Gendered Demeanours in Colonial Ceylon," in *Sri Lanka: Collective Identities Revisited*, ed. Michael Roberts (Colombo: Marga Institute, 1997), 1:131.

116. Malathi de Alwis, "'Respectability,' 'Modernity' and the Policing of 'Culture' in Colonial Ceylon," in *Gender, Sexuality and Colonial Modernities*, ed. Antoinette Burton (London: Routledge, 1999), 177–92, 178–79.

117. *Red S Review*, Wellawatta Sewing School, September 30 and August 31, 1935.

118. The "West" here refers to an essentialized conceptual category used by the Sinhala literati rather than an objectified unified entity.

119. Walter Benjamin, *Illuminations*, trans. Harry Zohn (New York: Schocken Books, 1979), 261.

120. Partha Chatterjee, "The Nation in Heterogeneous Time," in *The Politics of the Governed: Reflections on Popular Politics in Most of the World* (New Delhi: Permanent Black, 2004).

CHAPTER 6
SPEED METAL, SLOW TROPICS, COLD WAR: ALCOA IN THE CARIBBEAN

1. I would like to thank the Shelby Cullom Davis Center for Historical Studies at Princeton University for supporting my research for this project as a Davis

Fellow in the fall semester of 2008. Special thanks to Dan Rodgers, Jeremy Adelman, and Bhavani Raman for their very helpful comments, as well as to all of the participants in the "Cultures and Institutions in Motion" seminar. This chapter is based on my, *Aluminum Dreams: Lightness, Speed, Modernity* (Cambridge, MA: MIT Press, forthcoming); and draws on Mimi Sheller, "Metallic Modernities in the Space Age: Visualizing the Caribbean, Materializing the Modern," in *Architectures of the Visual: Embodied Materialities, Politics and Place*, ed. Gillian Rose and Divya Tolia-Kelly (Aldershot: Ashgate, 2011), and Mimi Sheller, "Space Age Tropics," in *Surveying the American Tropics: Literary Geographies from New York to Rio*, ed. Maria Cristina Fumagalli, Peter Hulme, Owen Robinson, and Lesley Wylie (Liverpool: Liverpool University Press, 2013).

2. Tim Cresswell, *On the Move: Mobility in the Modern Western World* (New York: Routledge, 2006), describes mobility as consisting of physical movement, meanings and representations of movement, and embodied practices; all three dimensions are involved in my understanding of aluminum.

3. Florence Hachez-Leroy, *L'Aluminium français: L'invention d'un marché, 1911–1983* (Paris: CNRS Editions, avec l'Institut pour l'histoire de l'aluminium, 1999).

4. Thus, although the consumption of aluminum shares many similarities with Jeffrey L. Meikle's account of *American Plastic: A Cultural History* (New Brunswick, NJ: Rutgers University Press, 1997), it differs greatly in its production, which was driven by highly vertically integrated and monopolistic transnational corporations for which any version of an "American" history must be a transnational history that spans the Americas and beyond.

5. I thank editor Bhavani Raman for this suggestive formulation.

6. Thanks to Jeremy Adelman for bringing Rostow to my attention.

7. Bradford Barham, Stephen Bunker, and Dennis O'Hearn, "Raw Material Industries in Resource-Rich Regions," in *States, Firms, and Raw Materials: The World Economy and Ecology of Aluminum*, ed. Barham, Bunker, and O'Hearn (Madison: University of Wisconsin Press, 1994), 29. This profile, they argue, leads to a market structure with a few large corporations, consumer-state involvement to secure stable supplies, and producer-state involvement seeking "rents," in which strategic behavior and bargaining are central to the market structure. See also Evelyn Huber Stephens, "Minerals Strategies and Development: International Political Economy, State, Class, and the Role of the Bauxite/Aluminum and Copper Industries in Jamaica and Peru," *Studies in Comparative International Development* 22, no. 3 (1987): 60–97.

8. For a more detailed analysis of Caribbean mobility regimes in relation to tourism, see Mimi Sheller, "Demobilizing and Remobilizing the Caribbean," in *Tourism Mobilities: Places to Play, Places in Play*, ed. M. Sheller and J. Urry (London: Routledge, 2004), 13–21; Mimi Sheller, "The New Caribbean Complexity: Mobility Systems, Tourism and the Re-scaling of Development," *Singapore Journal of Tropical Geography* 30 (2009): 189–203; Mimi Sheller, "Air Mobilities on the US-Caribbean Border: Open Skies and Closed Gates," *Communication Review* 13, no. 4 (2010): 269–88.

9. Robert Vitalis, *America's Kingdom: Mythmaking on the Saudi Oil Frontier* (Stanford: Stanford University Press, 2007). Thanks to Bradley Simpson for this source.

10. Arnaldo Mussolini, brother of Benito Mussolini, quoted in the preface to the inaugural issue of *Alluminio* 1 (January–February 1932): 1, cited in Jeffrey T. Schnapp, "The Romance of Caffeine and Aluminum," *Critical Inquiry* 28, no. 1 (Autumn 2001): 258n21.

11. Aluminum revolutionized packaging, starting with foil cigarette wrappers and extending into all kinds of foil, lids, linings, and, above all, lightweight aluminum cans, with pull-top and later press-down tabs, all of which enabled great weight reductions and less spoilage in the movement of foods and drink around the world.

12. This simultaneous invention, as well as the larger international unfolding of the aluminum industry, should remind us that "[h]owever often technologies appear to cause changes, technical change itself is frequently the *result* of underlying changes in the availability of raw materials, in the structure of firms, and in social forms and economic conditions" (Thomas J. Misa, *A Nation of Steel: The Making of Modern America 1865–1925* [Baltimore: Johns Hopkins University Press, 1995], xvii). If the United States was a "nation of steel" up until 1925, corporate, government, and military interests also made it a nation of aluminum as military strategy shifted to air power.

13. For good accounts of the development of the U.S. industry, see George David Smith, *From Monopoly to Competition: The Transformation of Alcoa, 1888–1986* (Cambridge: Cambridge University Press, 1988); on Europe, see Hachez-Leroy, *L'Aluminium français*.

14. Aluminum's specific weight is 27 kN/m^3, one-third of the weight of copper or steel. Its melting point is approximately 660 degrees Celsius, and its high conductivity can "replace copper in many applications" (Hugues Wilquin, *Aluminum Architecture: Construction and Details* [Basel: Birkhäuser, 2001], 12–13).

15. Walter Benjamin, *The Arcades Project*, ed. R. Tiedemann, trans. H. Eiland and K. McLaughlin (Cambridge, MA: Belknap, 2002).

16. See also Wolfgang Schivelbusch, *The Railroad Journey: The Industrialization of Time and Space in the Nineteenth Century* (Berkeley: University of California Press, 1986).

17. Aluminum is produced using an electrolytic process in which a high current is passed through dissolved alumina in order to split the aluminum from its chemical bond with oxygen. Today 13,500 kilowatt hours of electricity are needed to produce one ton of aluminum, although the figure was higher in the first half of the twentieth century.

18. Rebecca Solnit, *River of Shadows: Eadweard Muybridge and the Technological Wild West* (New York: Penguin, 1993), 219.

19. Margaret Graham notes, "Because it had no copper, Germany relied more heavily on aluminum than any of the other belligerents" in World War I. Germans were also leaders in chemistry and metallurgical research, including Count Ferdinand von Zeppelin, who "developed new structural concepts for the rigid airship that involved girders made of aluminum parts stamped out from sheet metal

and assembled." Margaret Graham, "R&D and Competition in England and the United States: The Case of the Aluminum Dirigible," *Business History Review* 62, no. 2 (1988): 265.

20. Ibid., 274.

21. Carlton E. Davis, *Jamaica in the World Aluminum Industry, 1838–1973*, vol. 1. (Kingston: Jamaica Bauxite Institute, 1989), 49–50.

22. On the development of aerial vision technologies in the colonial world, see Peter Adey, *Aerial Life: Spaces, Mobilities, Affects* (Oxford: Wiley-Blackwell, 2010).

23. Davis, *Jamaica in the World*.

24. Ibid., 54; also O. Nigel Bolland, *The Politics of Labour in the British Caribbean* (Kingston: Ian Randle, 2001), 443.

25. Following negotiations with the Canadian and U.S. aluminum multinationals, Jamaica's British colonial government enacted the Minerals (Vesting) Act and the Mining Act in 1947, which set a very low royalty payment of only one shilling per ton of bauxite mined, equivalent to about 20 U.S. cents, and also set a very low level of assumed profit on which taxation would be based. Kaiser Aluminum based its new mining operations in Jamaica, and the American mining companies acquired up to 142,000 acres of agricultural land for mining exploration, while Reynolds Metals gained exclusive access to 206,000 acres of Crown land in British Guiana. Gerald Horne, *Cold War in a Hot Zone: The United States Confronts Labor and Independence Struggles in the British West Indies* (Philadelphia: Temple University Press, 2007), 160.

26. This formulation is influenced by actor-network theory and wider science and technology studies, including W. E. Bijker, T. P. Hughes, and T. J. Pinch, eds., *The Social Construction of Technological Systems: New Directions in the Sociology and History of Technology* (Cambridge, MA: MIT Press, 1987); W. E. Bijker and J. Law, eds., *Shaping Technology/Building Society: Studies in Sociotechnical Change* (Cambridge, MA: MIT Press, 1994); Lucy Suchman, *Human-Machine Reconfigurations: Plans and Situated Actions* (Cambridge: Cambridge University Press, 2007).

27. David Nye, *American Technological Sublime* (Cambridge, MA: MIT Press, 1994).

28. Phil Patton, "A Visionary's Minivan Arrived Decades Too Soon," *New York Times*, January 6, 2008, Automotive sec., 6.

29. Bryan Burkhart and David Hunt, *Airstream: The History of the Land Yacht* (San Francisco: Chronicle Books, 2000).

30. Andrew Garn, ed., *Exit to Tomorrow: World's Fair Architecture, Design, Fashion, 1933–2005* (New York: Universe Publishing, 2007), 62.

31. Caren Kaplan, "Mobility and War: The 'Cosmic View' of Air Power," *Environment and Planning A* 38 (2006): 395.

32. Dennis Doordan, "Promoting Aluminum: Designers and the American Aluminum Industry," *Design Issues* 9, no. 2 (Autumn 1993): 46.

33. In total, 18 billion kilowatt hours of electricity were used in 1943 to produce the 920,000 tons of aluminum made in the United States that year (enough electricity to supply half the residents of the country for an entire year).

34. Hachez-Leroy, *L'Aluminium français*, 138.

35. Charles C. Carr, *ALCOA: An American Enterprise* (New York: Rinehart & Co., 1952), 257, 263–64.

36. Harvey Molotch, *Where Stuff Comes From: How Toasters, Toilets, Cars, Computers, and Many Other Things Come to Be as They Are* (New York: Routledge, 2005), 87.

37. Doordan, "Promoting Aluminum," 49.

38. Ibid.

39. Annmarie Brennan, "Forecast," in *Cold War Hothouses: Inventing Postwar Culture, from Cockpit to Playboy*, ed. Beatriz Colomina, Annmarie Brennan, and Jeannie Kim (New York: Princeton Architectural Press, 2004), 71–72.

40. Mimi Sheller, "Iconic Islands," in *Consuming the Caribbean* (London: Routledge, 2003); Krista Thompson, *An Eye for the Tropics* (Durham, NC: Duke University Press, 2006).

41. Michel-Rolph Trouillot, *Global Transformations: Anthropology and the Modern World* (New York: Palgrave Macmillan, 2003).

42. The company also ran several freighters out of New York, Montreal, and New Orleans, which carried twelve passengers and made longer, slower trips delivering bauxite and alumina for Reynolds, Kaiser, and Alcoa.

43. David Lambert and Alan Lester, "Introduction: Imperial Spaces, Imperial Subjects," in *Colonial Lives Across the British Empire: Imperial Careering in the Long Nineteenth Century*, ed. David Lambert and Alan Lester (Cambridge: Cambridge University Press, 2006), 1–31, 10.

44. David Armitage, "Three Concepts of Atlantic History," in *The British Atlantic World, 1500–1800*, ed. David Armitage and Michael J. Braddick (Basingstoke: Palgrave Macmillan, 2002), 11–27, 16.

45. Anyaa Anim-Addo, "Place and Mobilities in the Maritime World: The Royal Mail Steam Packet Company in the Caribbean, c. 1838 to 1914" (PhD thesis, Department of Human Geography, Royal Holloway, University of London, 2011), 137.

46. David Macintyre, "Some Practical Aspects of Aluminum in Shipbuilding" (presented at the Joint Meeting, Portland, Oregon, February 12th, 1959, the Society of Naval Architects and Marine Engineers, Pacific Northwest Section, the Society of Marine Port Engineers, Portland Chapter), 4, Heinz History Center Library and Archives (HHC), MSS 282, box 11, folder 7. The pamphlet notes the "classic use of aluminum" in the superliner *S.S. United States*, which utilized over 2,000 tons of aluminum, and today sits forlornly in the port of Philadelphia awaiting restoration.

47. "Your Ship: Alcoa Clipper," Alcoa Steamship Company, 13, HHC, Shelf Items, G550 A56 1949. The pamphlet also notes, "While sailing in the Caribbean, chances are that you will pass one or more freighters of the Alcoa fleet loaded to the Plimsoll Mark with bauxite, the ore from which aluminum is made. Most of these ships will be en route from Suriname and British Guiana to Gulf ports, where they will discharge the raw ore for processing and manufacturing in the United States" (43).

48. W.J.T. Mitchell, *Landscape and Power*, 2nd ed. (Chicago: University of Chicago Press, 2002); Richard Grove, *Green Imperialism: Colonial Expansion*,

Tropical Island Edens, and the Origins of Environmentalism, 1600–1860 (Cambridge: Cambridge University Press, 1995); Candace Slater, "Amazonia as Edenic Narrative," in *Uncommon Ground: Rethinking the Human Place in Nature*, ed. William Cronon (New York: Norton, 1996); Sheller, *Consuming the Caribbean*; David Arnold, *The Tropics and the Traveling Gaze: India, Landscape and Science, 1800–1856* (Seattle: University of Washington Press, 2006).

49. John Urry, *The Tourist Gaze*, 2nd ed. (London: Sage, 2002); Arnold, *Tropics and the Traveling Gaze*; Sheller, "Iconic Islands."

50. Horne, *Cold War in a Hot Zone*, 160.

51. An interesting account by a former mine worker is provided by Odida T. Quamina, *Mineworkers of Guyana: The Making of a Working Class* (London: Zed Books, 1987); on class and ethnic divisions in Guyana, see Walter Rodney, *A History of the Guyanese Working People, 1881–1905* (Baltimore: Johns Hopkins University Press, 1981); Brackette Williams, *Stains on My Name, War in My Veins: Guyana and the Politics of Cultural Struggle* (Durham, NC: Duke University Press, 1991).

52. Cedric J. Robinson, *Black Marxism: The Making of the Black Radical Tradition* (Chapel Hill: University of North Carolina Press, 2000).

53. Ken Post, *Arise Ye Starvelings: The Jamaican Labour Rebellion of 1938 and Its Aftermath* (The Hague: Martinus Nijhoff, 1978).

54. The Caribbean Labour Congress (CLC) was formed in 1945 and from 1947 under the leadership of communist Richard Hart vigorously promoted the formation of a self-governing West Indies Federation with dominion status. The CLC collapsed in 1953 under pressure of Cold War anticommunist campaigns, ending the hopes for an independent pan-Caribbean labor movement.

55. David P. Miller, "Joseph Banks, Empire, and 'Centers of Calculation' in Late Hanoverian London," in *Visions of Empire: Voyages, Botany, and Representations of Nature*, ed. David Philip Miller and Peter Hanns Reill (Cambridge: Cambridge University Press, 1996).

56. Davis, *Jamaica in the World*, 135. There were few strikes or "unrest" associated with the Jamaican bauxite mines, largely because they employed a relatively small number of workers and these workers were relatively well paid compared to other local industries, especially agriculture, and were thus easily replaceable. See Bolland, *Politics of Labour*; Evelyn Huber Stephens and John Stephens, *Democratic Socialism in Jamaica: The Political Movement and Social Transformation in Dependent Capitalism* (Princeton: Princeton University Press, 1986), 27.

57. Bolland, *Politics of Labour*, 617–21.

58. Ibid., 624–25.

59. Thompson, *Eye for the Tropics*. It was often the same corporations involved in commodity trading and tourism: ships laden with bananas or bauxite on the way north carried passengers on the return journey, while businessmen interested in investing in the region stayed at hotels owned by the multinationals and took their families on cruises.

60. Cresswell, in *On the Move*, discusses efforts to control the proliferation of a dance known as the shimmy in U.S. dance halls and ballrooms in the 1930s, as

its moves were considered to be overly lascivious and possibly "negro." See also Barbara Browning, *Infectious Rhythm: Metaphors of Contagion and the Spread of African Culture* (New York: Routledge, 1998).

61. Norman Washington Manley to Kaiser Bauxite Company, May 23, 1956, cited in Davis, *Jamaica in the World*, 189–90.

62. Davis, *Jamaica in the World*, 251.

63. Ibid., 229, 251.

64. Draft Newspaper Release & Draft Message to "Alcoa Works Managers, Sales Managers, et al.," September 29, 1960, HHC, MSS 282, Records of Alcoa, 1857–1992, box 11.

65. F. A. Billhardt, Alcoa Steamship Company, Inc., New York Office to Mr. L. Litchfield Jr., Pittsburgh Office, Re: Economic Study of Passenger Ships, Alcoa Steamship Company, Inc., September 22, 1960, HHC, MSS 282, box 11, Internal Correspondence.

66. F. A. Billhardt, Alcoa Steamship Company, Inc., New York Office, to Mr. F. L. Magee, Aluminum Company of America, Pittsburgh Office, Re: PAN-ORE Fleet, January 22, 1960, HHC, MSS 282, box 11, Internal Correspondence.

67. Stephens and Stephens, *Democratic Socialism*, 26.

68. Brennan, "Forecast," 86–89.

69. Stephens, "Minerals Strategies," 63–64.

70. Clive Y. Thomas, *Dependence and Transformation: The Economics of the Transition to Socialism* (New York: Monthly Review Press, 1974), 83.

71. For an argument against the Caribbean's capacity to "reach out beyond the extractive stage of production," see Sterling Brubaker, *Trends in the World Aluminum Industry* (Baltimore: Johns Hopkins University Press, 1967), a publication sponsored by the Ford Foundation–funded nonprofit Resources for the Future, Inc.

72. A typical smelter produces on average thirteen tons of carbon dioxide emissions per ton of aluminum, as well as the vast majority of the tetrafluoromethane and hexafluoroethane emissions worldwide. "Strip mining and [bauxite] ore processing produces about two and a half tons of wet mining wastes per ton of aluminum produced. It has historically led to severe soil erosion, as millions of tons of exposed earth and crushed rocks were left to wash into streams and oceans. Strip mining destroys whatever wildlife habitat has existed above the mine, and is difficult—if not impossible—to re-establish even with intentional revegetation" (Jennifer Gitlitz, *Trashed Cans: The Global Environmental Impacts of Aluminum Can Wasting in America* [Arlington, VA: Container Recycling Institute, June 2002], 17).

73. Peter Redfield, *Space in the Tropics: From Convicts to Rockets in French Guiana* (Berkeley: University of California Press, 2000).

74. Richard Price, *Travels with Tooy: History, Memory and the African American Imagination* (Chicago: University of Chicago Press, 2007). For an update on the Saamaka case before the Inter-American Court of Human Rights, see Richard Price, *Rainforest Warriors: Human Rights on Trial* (Philadelphia: University of Pennsylvania Press, 2011).

75. Ibid., 194.

CHAPTER 7
THE TRUE STORY OF AH JAKE: LANGUAGE, LABOR,
AND JUSTICE IN LATE-NINETEENTH-CENTURY
SIERRA COUNTY, CALIFORNIA

1. I am grateful for comments from seminar respondents and participants where this chapter made the rounds from 2009 to 2011: the Davis Center for Historical Studies at Princeton University; the Can We Seminar in the School of Social Science, Institute for Advanced Study; American Studies Seminars at George Washington University and the University of Southern California; and the Law and History Workshop at Columbia University. Special thanks to Dan Rodgers, Hendrik Hartog, Seth Moglen, Tyler Anbinder, Muneer Ahmad, and Judith Resnik for insights and suggestions.

2. There is no record of Ah Jake's full Chinese name. "Jake" is a Romanization of his surname, possibly *Zhou* (pronounced "Cheuk" in Cantonese) or *Zhai* ("Zak" in Cantonese); the appellation "Ah" is a familiar manner of address among laborers or friends, similar to "old" ("Old Jake") or "uncle," though "Ah" does not connote an age differential. Many Chinese laborers in nineteenth-century California were known to Euro-Americans only by this name form.

3. James Barrett, *Work and Community in the Jungle: Chicago's Packinghouse Workers, 1894–1922* (Urbana: University of Illinois Press, 1987); Gary Gerstle, *Working Class Americanism: The Politics of Labor in a Textile City, 1914–1960* (New York: Cambridge University Press, 1989); Lizabeth Cohen, *Making a New Deal: Industrial Workers in Chicago, 1919–1939* (New York: Cambridge University Press, 1990); James Barrett and David Roediger, "Inbetween Peoples: Race, Nationality, and the 'New Immigrant Working Class,'" *Journal of American Ethnic History* 16 (Spring 1997): 3–44; Gunther Peck, *Reinventing Free Labor: Pardones and Immigrant Workers in the North American West, 1880–1930* (New York: Cambridge University Press, 2000); Leon Fink, *The Maya of Morganton: Work and Community in the Nuevo New South* (Chapel Hill: University of North Carolina Press, 2003); Ruth Milkman, *LA Story: Immigrant Workers and the Future of the US Labor Movement* (New York: Russell Sage, 2006).

4. There is a considerable literature on Chinese native-place and lineage (clan) associations (*huiguan*, called "companies" by Westerners), which constituted the predominant form of social organization among the immigrants in the United States, but rather less on the sworn brotherhood societies (often known as "tongs," the Cantonese for *tang*, or "association"). See Him Mark Lai, *Becoming Chinese American* (Walnut Creek, CA: AltaMira Press, 2004); Yong Chen, *Chinese San Francisco: A Transpacific Community* (Stanford: Stanford University Press, 2000); L. Eve Armentrout Ma, *Revolutionaries, Monarchists, and Chinatowns: Chinese Politics of the Americas and the 1911 Revolution* (Honolulu: University of Hawaii Press 1999); Madeline Hsu, *Dreaming of Gold, Dreaming of Home: Transnationalism and Migration between the U.S. and South China* (Stanford: Stanford University Press, 2000); Adam McKeown, *Chinese Migrant*

Networks and Cultural Change: Peru, Chicago, Hawaii, 1900–1936 (Chicago: University of Chicago Press, 2001); Sue Fawn Chung, "Between Two Worlds: The Zhigongtang and Chinese American Funerary Rituals," in *The Chinese in America: From Gold Mountain to the New Millennium,* ed. Susie Lan Cassel (Walnut Creek, CA: AltaMira Press, 2002); Floyd Cheung, "Performing Exclusion and Resistance: Anti-Chinese League and Chee Kong Tong Parades in Territorial Arizona," *Drama Review* 46, no. 1 (Spring 2002): 39–59; Ko-Lin Chin, *Chinese Subculture and Criminality: Non-traditional Crime Groups in America* (New York: Greenwood, 1990).

5. Rodman Paul, writing in 1938, focused on political controversies over proposed (and ultimately unsuccessful) legislation for importing Chinese contract labor in the 1850s, but did not interrogate the assumption made by whites in the mining districts that Chinese were a race of "serfs." Rodman W. Paul, "The Origins of the Chinese Problem Issue in California," *Mississippi Valley Historical Review* 25 (September 1938): 181–96. The historiographic consensus that has held sway since the 1960s is that whereas Chinese were not exploited under formal indentures, an informal *intraethnic* system of contract labor and debt peonage served the same purpose. This argument originated with Gunther Barth's *Bitter Strength: A History of the Chinese in the US* (Cambridge, MA: Harvard University Press, 1964). Barth, a student of Oscar Handlin, used the Chinese case as the exception that proved the Euro-American norm of settlement and assimilation. Barth's claim rested on the highly selective use of quotes from newspapers and testimonies given before the California Senate and U.S. Congress (*Chinese Immigration: The Social, Moral, and Political effect of Chinese Immigration. Hearings before the California State Senate,* 1876; *Report and Hearings,* 1878; *Report of the Joint Special Committee to Investigate Chinese Immigration,* 44th Congress, 2nd Session, Senate Report 689, 1877). Barth, *Bitter Strength,* 24–28. Barth's interpretation has remained remarkably durable, even among scholars sympathetic to the Chinese, e.g., labor historian Alexander Saxton, *The Indispensible Enemy: Labor and the Anti-Chinese Movement in California* (Berkeley: University of California Press, 1971), 8; economic historians Patricia Cloud and David Galenson, "Chinese Immigration and Contract Labor in the Late Nineteenth Century," *Explorations in Economic History* 24 (1987): 22–42 (but see also Charles McClain's critical response, which betrays the frustrations in refuting the conventional view, *Explorations in Economic History* 27 [1990]: 363–78). In a thoughtful article comparing the Chinese labor question in the United States and South Africa, Matthew Guterl and Christine Skwiot acknowledge that it is "difficult—even now—to understand exactly how tightly bound the Chinese [in California] were." Guterl and Skwiot, "Atlantic & Pacific Crossings: Race, Empire, and the Labor Problem in the Late Nineteenth Century," *Radical History Review* 91 (Winter 2005): 40–61. Recent works by Asian Americanists on the "coolie question" focus on the "coolie" as a discursive figure and do not tackle the question of indentured labor, especially in California, as an empirical question. See Moon-Ho Jung, *Coolies and Cane* (Baltimore: Johns Hopkins University Press, 2006); Lisa Lowe, "The Intimacies of the Four Continents," in *Haunted by Empire: Geographies of Intimacy in North American History,* ed. Ann Laura Stoler (Durham, NC: Duke University Press, 2006). This essay is part of a larger

research agenda that aims to address the gap between Chinese American and U.S. labor history with analysis of both empirical data and racial discourse on the Chinese labor question, and in comparative study with Chinese mining labor in Australia and South Africa.

6. At the time of the trial, Ah Jake was in his early thirties. His testimony that he had mined with an uncle suggests that he could have come with the uncle as a boy, but not any younger than eleven or twelve years old, that is, old enough to work. The earliest he would have come would have been the late 1860s.

7. James Sinnott, *History of Sierra County* (Volcano, CA: California Traveler, 1973), 2:11, 202–4.

8. Ibid. U.S. Census data show that in the 1850s there were 400 Chinese living in a settlement northeast of the town of Goodyears Bar; in 1880 there were a few hundred remaining in the greater Downieville vicinity, including 100 at Goodyears Bar. On the Chinese mining settlement at Goodyears Bar, see http://www .goodyearsbar.com/?target=chinese.php (accessed March 11, 2010).

9. *People v. Ah Jake*, examination upon a charge of murder, reprinted in Albert Dressler, *California Chinese Chatter* (San Francisco: A. Dressler, 1927), 53 (hereafter cited as "examination"). By the late 1880s Goodyears Bar was "practically exhausted" of gold with mining in the district producing "indifferent results." "Report on Mineral Industries in the United States: Gold and Silver," in *Eleventh Census of the United States* (1890), 110.

10. *People v. Ah Jake*, examination, 51–52; *People v. Ah Jake*, transcript of testimony, December 12, 1887 (hereafter cited as "trial transcript"), 50–57, 61, 100, Executive Pardons, California State Archives, Sacramento, file F3659-13 (hereafter cited as Ah Jake pardon file).

11. *People v. Ah Jake*, examination, in Dressler, *California Chinese Chatter*, 51–52.

12. Ibid., 45.

13. Ibid., 44.

14. Ibid., 47.

15. Ibid., 50–51, 54–55.

16. Code switching with curse words is featured in the space cowboy cable TV series *Firefly* (first aired on Fox, 2002). The people who travel to the frontiers of outer space in the year 2517 speak English laced with phrases of Chinese profanity.

17. Downieville, Sierra County, California, enumeration district 98, in *U.S. Census of Population* (1880), 3 (accessed via Ancestry.com, August 18, 2010); Anita Kreitzman, "History of Shorthand," http://ncraonline.org/NCRA/History /History+of+Shorthand/ (accessed August 18, 2010).

18. W. C. Hunter, *The "Fan Kwae" at Canton: Before the Treaty Days, 1825–1844* (Shanghai: Kelly and Walsh, 1911), 60–62; Jonathan Spence, *God's Chinese Son* (New York: Norton, 1996), 7–8. Spence writes that when a comprador informs an American trader that a visiting official is expecting a large bribe, "'Mant-a-le [mandarin] sendee one piece chop. He come tomollo, wantee two-lac dollar,' everyone knows what he means." On etymology of *chop*, Amitav Ghosh, *Sea of Poppies* (New York: Farrar, Straus and Giroux, 2008), 521. Ghosh's historical novels about the opium trade, *Sea of Poppies*, and its follow-up, *River*

of Smoke (2012), include wonderful evocations of the pidgin languages spoken among lascars (South Asian seamen) and in Canton, respectively.

It should be noted that pidgin is a simplified contact language and not a creole, a mature language that is the primary language of a group, such as Gullah spoken in the Georgia Sea Islands, Jamaican patwah (*patois*), and Hawaiian pidgin. According to linguists, to be a true pidgin "two conditions must be met: its grammatical structure and vocabulary must be sharply reduced . . . and also the resultant language must be native to none of those who use it." R. A. Hall, Jr., *Pidgin and Creole Languages* (Ithaca, NY: Cornell University Press, 1966), vii.

19. I thank Teemu Ruskola for information on translators in nineteenth-century Chinese courts. On treaty writing, Lydia Liu, *The Clash of Empires: The Invention of Modern China in Modern Worldmaking* (Cambridge MA: Harvard University Press, 2004), 112. The treaty also notoriously banned use in any Chinese official documents of the Chinese word *yi*, meaning generally "foreigner" but translated by the British to mean "barbarian," to refer to the British government or persons. Ibid., 31–69.

20. The *Oxford English Dictionary* defines the verb "savvy" as "slang, *trans.*, to know; to understand, comprehend. Freq. used in the interrogative (= 'do you understand?') following an explanation to a foreigner or to one considered slow-witted."

21. Reverend William Speer, "Claims of the Chinese on Our Common Schools," *San Francisco Bulletin*, January 20, 1857. See also James F. Rusling, *The Great West and Pacific Coast* (New York: Sheldon, 1877), 303.

22. The opening scene in an episode of the television series *Deadwood* captures this dynamic: A white customer waves his hands and speaks in an exaggerated manner, telling the Chinese launderer to "washee" his soiled linens and asking if he wants to feed the human corpse in his wagon to his pigs, thinking this is what "heathens" do. The Chinese man's dignified bearing makes it doubly clear who in the scene is the real barbarian. "Deep Water," *Deadwood* (HBO), season 1, episode 2, first aired March 28, 2004. I thank Tyler Anbinder for bringing this scene to my attention.

23. Sarah Grey Thomason and Terrance Kaufman, *Language Contact, Creolization, and Genetic Linguistics* (Berkeley: University of California Press, 1988), 167–88.

24. Not until 1978 did the United States require federal courts to provide interpreters for defendants and witnesses whose primary language is not English (Court Interpreters Act of 1978, 28 U.S.C.S. § 1827). However, electronic sound recording of interpretation is not mandatory but at the court's discretion. Sec. (d) (2). Lack of translation and mistranslation are grounds for appeal, but the higher courts seldom find that translation errors reach the threshold for what they consider constitutionally an unfair trial.

25. *People v. Ah Jake*, trial transcript, 3.

26. Mary Frances Millard Hall and Sylvestor "Mike" Millard, "History of California Pioneer and Chinese Interpreter Jerome Millard" (unpublished typescript, 1973), in author's possession; quotes from letter by Jerome Millard, August 17, 1881, cited in ibid. On Millard's work for Charles Crocker, see also http://cprr .org/CPRR_Discussion_Group/2005/03/cprr-ah-henge-jmillard.html (accessed

August 18, 2010). I thank Alisa Judd for sharing photographs and information about her great-grandfather Jerome Millard.

27. *People v. Ah Jake*, trial transcript, 49–52.

28. Ibid., 78–80, 109–14.

29. Ibid., 120. I thank Gordon Bakken for clarifying that these strange instructions do conform to the California criminal code. In a fight situation, a person may be deemed to have acted in self-defense if he or she killed the initiator of the fight in the course of combat. However, if the initiator has been incapacitated by a blow or a fall and the other person takes advantage of the situation to then kill him or her, the state of mind is considered to have changed from self-defense to premeditation. The judge did not make these distinctions clear to the jury.

30. *People v. Ah Jake*, death warrant, December 23, 1887, Ah Jake pardon file; *People v. Ah Jake*, afternoon session of Superior Court, Sierra County, December 22, 1887, copy in Ah Jake prison file, Folsom Commitment Papers, California State Archives, Sacramento; *Mountain Messenger*, December 24, 1887, 2.

31. Letter from JA Vaughn to MD Baruck, August 15, 1888; letter from Rev. CH Kirkbride to Gov. Waterman, August 8, 1888; petition to RM Waterman from NB Fish, foreman, Robert Forbes, Samuel Tym, William Perrryman, Edward Perryman, William Box [1888]; petition to RM Waterman from William P. McCarty, October 12, 1888; petition to RM Waterman from L. Barnett, n.d.; petitions [1888, 1889]; all in Ah Jake pardon file.

32. Affidavit of Samuel C. Stewart, August 7, 1888; petition from FD Soward to Governor Waterman, August 18, 1888; both Ah Jake pardon file.

33. *People v. Ah Jake*, death warrant, December 23, 1887, Ah Jake pardon file; *People v. Ah Jake*, death warrant, July 24, 1888, copy in San Quentin Commitment Papers, California State Archives, Sacramento.

34. "Historic Sierra County Gallows," http://www.sierracounty.ws/index .php?module=pagemaster&PAGE_user_op=view_page&PAGE_id=28&MMN_ position=44:37.

35. Soward to Waterman, August 18, 1888, Ah Jake pardon file. On Downieville gallows, "History of Sierra City," http://www.sierracountygold.com/History /index.html.

36. Vaughn, however, told the governor that he did not know Ah Jake, either to make his appeal appear unbiased or because he was worried about retribution from local anti-Chinese elements, which campaigned against the employment of Chinese in the county. Ah Jake to Waterman, November 27, 1890; Vaughn to Baruck, August 15, 1888; both in Ah Jake pardon file.

37. For example, Victor Bouther, a farmer at Goodyears Bar, had met Ah Jake on the way into town on that fateful day. He gave Ah Jake a ride in his wagon and offered to carry his provisions back to Goodyears Bar. *People v. Ah Jake*, transcript of testimony, 99–100.

38. *People v. Ah Jake*, trial transcript, 52, 104–9; "A Curious Pardon," *Mountain Messenger*, December 1, 1888, 2.

39. The *Mountain Messenger* reported that Lo Kay paid out $100 in reward to Henry Hartling, who arrested Ah Jake. October 29, 1887, 3. *People v. Ah Jake*, trial transcript, 42, 98; FD Soward to Governor Waterman, September 1, 1889,

Ah Jake pardon file. On shared Hop Wo membership, *People v. Ah Jake*, examination, in Dressler, *California Chinese Chatter*, 55.

40. David Ownby and Mary Somers Heidhues, eds., *"Secret Societies" Reconsidered: Perspectives on the Social History of Modern South China and Southeast Asia* (Armonk, NY: M.E. Sharpe, 1993).

41. The 1902 Sanborn Fire Insurance Company map for Downieville, California, shows a Chinese quarter, at the end of Main Street, with four structures, the largest of which, a two-story building labeled "joss house," likely belonged to the Zhigongtang; and beyond, a few additional dwellings, including one marked "fem. bldg" (i.e., brothel) and "old and dil'd [dilapidated]."

42. Chung, "Between Two Worlds," 217–38; Cheung, "Performing Exclusion and Resistance." Cheung argues that the rituals of the Zhigongtang in North America, performed in the private spaces of their meeting halls, empowered Chinese laborers with masculinist, even supernatural, identities—their performances being a kind of offstage "weapon of the weak" that remained invisible to outsiders.

43. *People v. Ah Jake*, transcript of testimony, 105–7.

44. On mining cooperatives and sworn brotherhoods in the Pacific, see John Fitzgerald, *Big White Lie: Chinese Australians in White Australia* (Sydney: University of New South Wales Press, 2007), 56–80; David Ownby, "Chinese Hui and the Early Modern Social Order," and Mary Somers Heidhues, "Chinese Organizations in west Borneo and Bangka: Kogsi and Hui," both in *"Secret Societies" Reconsidered*, 34–88. The Borneo kongsi grew into federations, which controlled increasingly greater expanses of mining territory and became increasingly hierarchical with size. The original kongsi, however, were markedly egalitarian in structure and ideology.

45. "Report on Mineral Industries in the United States: Gold and Silver," in *Eleventh Census of the United States* (1890), 109.

46. California Mining Bureau, *Ninth Report of the State Mineralogist for Year Ending Dec. 2, 1889* (Sacramento, 1890), 22.

47. E-Tu Zen Sun, "Mining Labor in the Ch'ing Period," in *Approaches to Modern Chinese History*, ed. Albert Feuerwerker, Rhoads Murphy, and Mary C. Wright (Berkeley: University of California Press, 1967), 45–67. On merchant investor-managers in the United States, see Sue Fawn Chung, *In Pursuit of Gold: Chinese Miners and Merchants in the American West* (Urbana: University of Illinois Press, 2011), 16–18.

48. Most Chinese participating in the California gold rush came from agricultural regions in Guangdong province, but it is possible that some may have had mining experience there. Mining companies sometimes hired farmers for wages in the slack season. Sun, "Mining Labor," 50–51. Tin and iron sand mining organizations in Guangdong used placer techniques, which drew from Chinese agricultural water technologies. David Valentine, "Chinese Placer Mining in the United States," in Cassel, *Chinese in America*, 45.

49. Rossiter H. Raymond, *Statistics of Mines and Mining in the States and Territories West of the Rocky Mountains* (Washington, DC: Government Printing Office, 1872), 6. Raymond was likely describing not trade unions but guilds.

50. Walter Johnson, "Agency, a Ghost Story," in *Slavery's Ghost: The Problem of Freedom in the Age of Emancipation*, by Richard Follett, Eric Foner, and Walter Johnson (Baltimore: Johns Hopkins University Press, 2011), 8–30. See also Prasenjit Duara, *Rescuing History from the Nation: Questioning Narratives of Modern China* (Chicago: University of Chicago Press, 1997).

51. On anti-Chinese campaigns, see Jean Pfaelzer, *Driven Out!* (New York: Random House, 2007); in Sierra County and neighboring Plumas County, see *Mountain Messenger*, February–July 1886, passim; my analysis of employment patterns is based on Sierra County, *U.S. Census of Population* (1880).

52. "Letter from an Old-Timer," *Mountain Messenger*, June 12, 1886, 3.

53. RW Waterman, order of commutation of Ah Jake, November 14, 1888, Ah Jake pardon file; Folsom Prison Register 1882–1897, MF 1:9 (12), California State Archives, Sacramento. On March 1, 1890, for reasons unknown, he was transferred to San Quentin. San Quentin Prison Register 1880–1896, MF 1:9 (1), California State Archives, Sacramento.

54. F.D. Soward to Governor Waterman, September 1, 1889, Ah Jake pardon file; "Ah Jake's Case," *Mountain Messenger*, December 1, 1888, 2.

55. Ah Jake to Governor Waterman, September 14 and November 27, 1890; John McComb, warden of San Quentin, to R.W. Waterman, December 1, 1890. Spaulding was a grocer in Downieville and had signed petitions on Ah Jake's behalf. The warden reported that Ah Jake's conduct "while in prison has been good, never having been reported for punishment for violation of prison rules and has discharged his duties faithfully." Ah Jake also worked in the prison jute mill. B. Doughtery to McComb, December 1, 1890. All in Ah Jake pardon file.

56. Executive pardon, December 30, 1890, Ah Jake pardon file; San Quentin Prison Register 1880–1896, MF 1:9 (1).

57. At least fifteen Chinese prisoners in California received pardons between 1854 and 1885. California, *Journals of the Assembly and Senate*, 1853–85. Aggregate pardon data are included in the state prison director's reports, published in *Journal* appendices; names of prisoners pardoned appear in *Journals* as part of the governor's annual reports to the legislature.

58. In 1860, Song Ah Pong, who served four years of a ten-year sentence for murder in the second degree, was pardoned for good behavior and the governor's belief that the time served was adequate. California, *Senate Journal*, 1861, 51. Many whites received pardons for good behavior. The practice, which addressed both overcrowding in the state prison and the belief that the possibility of pardon promoted prison discipline, was similar to what we now know as parole. It was codified in 1864 with a law that granted a credit of five days for each month of "fruitful labor and good behavior," enabling an accelerated expiration of the prisoner's sentence. "Act to Confer Further Powers upon the Governor of This State in Relation to the Pardon of Criminals," April 4, 1864.

59. Ah Fong, serving a twelve-year sentence for murder in the second degree, suffering from consumption and close to death, was pardoned in 1868. *Senate Journal*, 1870, 68; Ah Lin, convicted of robbery, dying of heart disease, was pardoned in 1870. *Senate Journal*, 1871–72, 59.

60. Yung Toy, sentenced to seven years for robbery, was pardoned in 1869 after Shasta County residents petitioned that he was innocent. *Senate Journal*,

1873–74, 104. Legal historian Clare McKanna's study of homicide cases in seven California counties during the late nineteenth century also revealed that pardons and convictions vacated by appeals courts in Chinese cases often resulted from later revelations that Chinese witnesses, usually members of rival clans or brotherhoods, had perjured their testimony. Clare McKanna, Jr., *Race and Homicide in Nineteenth Century California* (Reno: University of Nevada Press, 2002), 32–51.

61. Doubt as to guilt was most commonly cited. "Doubt," pardon of Ah Yik, *Senate Journal*, 1871–72, 68; "Conspiracy," pardon of Ah Chee, *Senate Journal*, 1876, appendix vol. 4, 37; "Circumstances Have Come to Light," pardon of Ah Wong, *Senate Journal* 1871–72, 79.

62. Quoted in McKanna, *Race and Homicide*, 43.

63. Ko-Lin Chin, *Chinese Subculture and Criminality*; McKeown, *Chinese Migrant Networks*.

64. *People v. Hall*, 4 Cal. 339 (1854), California Statutes, chap. 70 (1863).

65. John Wunder, "Chinese in Trouble: Criminal Law and Race on the Trans-Mississippi West Frontier," *Western Historical Quarterly* 17 (January 1986): 25–41.

66. Antone Lavezzola to Albert Dressler, May 4, 1927, reprinted in Dressler, *California Chinese Chatter*, 60–61; John T. Mason to Albert Dressler, April 29, 1927, California State Library, Sacramento.

67. "The True Story of Ah Q" (1921), in *Selected Stories of Lu Hsün* (Beijing: Foreign Languages Press, 1960, 1972).

68. "Charlie Chan's Aphorisms: The Complete Sayings of Charlie Chan," http://charliechanfamily.tripod.com/id6.html. In fact Chan is speaking not pidgin but a parodic imitation of it.

69. Dressler, *California Chinese Chatter*, vii, viii. An illustration of Chinese laundrymen working in the "Sam Wo Wash House" in Sierra City shows one man smoking opium and another blowing (or possibly spitting) on a garment. Ibid., 32.

70. Louis Chu, *Eat a Bowl of Tea* (1960); Milton Murayama, *All I Asking for Is My Body* (1975); Maxine Hong Kingston, *China Men* (1977) and *Tripmaster Monkey* (1987); Lois Yamanaka, *Blu's Hanging* (1997). It should be clarified that Hawaiian pidgin and Chinese American or Chinatown pidgin are different languages. Also, whereas Hawaiian pidgin is indisputably a full creole language, Chinatown pidgin is arguably more of a contact language, although Kingston's work suggests a creolization of Chinglish as something spoken between immigrant parents and their American-born children.

71. Evelyn Chi'en, *Weird English* (Cambridge, MA: Harvard University Press, 2005), 110; see also Juan Li, "Pidgin and Code-Switching: Linguistic Identity and Multicultural Consciousness in Maxine Hong Kingston's Tripmaster Monkey," *Language and Literature* 13, no. 3 (2004): 269–87. More recently Chinglish has been embraced by Hong Kong and Chinese American poets, rapsters, and hip-hop artists as a subversive gesture against widespread ridicule (thanks to the Internet) of Chinglish as it appears on public signage and menus in China. Examples of poor or strange translations (sometimes the result of computer translation software) include "please bump your head carefully," "tender fragrant grass,

how hardhearted to trample them," and, in a hotel elevator, "please leave your values at front desk." Embarrassed Shanghai city officials determined to correct the English on public signage for the 2010 world expo. http://news.bbc.co.uk/2 /hi/8219427.stm (accessed August 18, 2010).

72. "Welcome to Goodyears Bar," http://www.goodyearsbar.com/?target =chinese.php (accessed August 18, 2010). In the 1920 census there were five Chinese—three cooks, one unemployed, and one gold miner in Downieville and in Goodyear's Bar. In 1930 there were two Chinese in Downieville and none listed in Goodyear's Bar.

CHAPTER 8
CREATIVE MISUNDERSTANDINGS: CHINESE MEDICINE
IN SEVENTEENTH-CENTURY EUROPE

1. I would like to thank the editors and the participants in the Davis Seminar (especially Benjamin Elman), the members of Karen Kupperman's Atlantic History workshop at NYU, and the fellows of the Cogut Center at Brown for their questions and suggestions. I would also like to acknowledge the stimulating conversation with Stephen Casper, who shared with me his enthusiasm for global history and medicine as well as his critical thoughts about the literature.

2. Harold J. Cook, "Global Economies and Local Knowledge in the East Indies: Jacobus Bontius Learns the Facts of Nature," in *Colonial Botany: Science, Commerce, and Politics in the Early Modern World*, ed. Londa Schiebinger and Claudia Swan (Philadelphia: University of Pennsylvania Press, 2005), 100–118, 299–302; Cook, *Matters of Exchange: Commerce, Medicine, and Science in the Dutch Golden Age* (New Haven: Yale University Press, 2007), 175–225. Also see the essay of Pamela Smith, "Knowledge in Motion: Following Itineraries of Matter in the Early Modern World" (this volume).

3. On ten Rhijne, see Cook, *Matters of Exchange*, 339–77.

4. Robert W. Carrubba and John Z. Bowers, "The Western World's First Detailed Treatise on Acupuncture: Willem Ten Rhijne's De Acupunctura," *Journal of the History of Medicine* 29 (1974): 376–78.

5. See, for example, the comment about how this is "no small puzzle" in Gwei-Djen Lu and Joseph Needham, *Celestial Lancets: A History and Rationale of Acupuncture and Moxa*, new introduction by Vivienne Lo (London: Routledge-Curzon, 2002), 271–76.

6. G.E.R. Lloyd, *Cognitive Variations: Reflections on the Unity and Diversity of the Human Mind* (Oxford: Clarendon, 2007). He has also published masterfully on comparative history, such as Geoffrey Lloyd and Nathan Sivin, *The Way and the Word: Science and Medicine in Early China and Greece* (New Haven: Yale University Press, 2002), and Lloyd, *The Ambitions of Curiosity: Understanding the World in Ancient Greece and China* (Cambridge: Cambridge University Press, 2002).

7. Mario Biagioli, "The Anthropology of Incommensurability," *Studies in History and Philosophy of Science Part A* 21 (1990): 183–209; Ian Hacking, *Historical Ontology* (Cambridge, MA: Harvard University Press, 2002), 168–72; How-

ard Sankey, "Kuhn's Changing Concept of Incommensurability," *British Journal for the Philosophy of Science* 44 (1993): 759–74.

8. In comparison to biomedicine, other kinds of medical learning seem to have basic likenesses, from an emphasis on health and the prevention of illness to ideas about the body and the causes of disease that include various kinds of fluids and powers. For a recent account of this kind, which looks for similarities between Chinese and earlier Western medical traditions, among others, see Roberta Bivins, *Alternative Medicine? A History* (Oxford: Oxford University Press, 2007). But between these "traditions" there are also fundamental differences: for example, while many ancient Greek writers discussed the four elements and the four causes, the contemporaneous *Huangdi neijing* discussed the five *wu-hsing*, or Five Agents, which are phases of change. While the Chinese five are sometimes said to be "equivalent" to the Greek four, and it is sometimes similarly said that Chinese texts described substances and processes equivalent to the Greek humors, blood, pneuma, and so forth, looked at from close up the systems are very different. See, for instance, Lloyd, *Ambitions of Curiosity*. It should be noted, too, that "Chinese" medicine can be as variable and contested as "Western" medicine, making all attempts to summarize "it" selective and partial: see, for instance, Paul U. Unschuld, *Medicine in China: A History of Ideas*, Comparative Studies in Health Systems and Medical Care (Berkeley: University of California Press, 1985), and Benjamin A. Elman, *On Their Own Terms: Science in China, 1550–1900* (Cambridge, MA: Harvard University Press, 2005).

9. Shigehisa Kuriyama, *The Expressiveness of the Body and the Divergence of Greek and Chinese Medicine* (New York: Zone Books, 1999), 21–22. Also see Elizabeth Hsu, "Towards a Science of Touch: Chinese Pulse Diagnostics in Early Modern Europe," *Anthropology and Medicine* 7 (2000): 251–68, 319–33, and Hsu, with Sima Qian, *Pulse Diagnosis in Early Chinese Medicine: The Telling Touch* (Cambridge: Cambridge University Press, 2010); and Roberta Bivins, "Expectations and Expertise: Early British Responses to Chinese Medicine," *History of Science* 37 (1999): 459–89.

10. I have developed further thoughts about translation and science for an introduction to Harold J. Cook and Sven Dupré, eds., *Translating Knowledge in the Early Modern Low Countries* (Zurich: Lit Verlag, 2012), 3–17.

11. Sanjay Subrahmanyam, "Connected Histories: Notes towards a Reconfiguration of Early Modern Eurasia," *Modern Asian Studies* 31, no. 3 (1997): 735–62; Subrahmanyam, *From the Tagus to the Ganges: Explorations in Connected History* (Oxford: Oxford University Press, 2005); Bénédicte Zimmermann, Claude Didry, and Peter Wagner, eds., *Le Travail et la Nation: Histoire Croisée de la France et de l'Allemagne* (Paris: Éditions de la Maison des Sciences de L'Homme, 2000).

12. Immanuel Wallerstein, *The Modern World System*, 2 vols. (New York: Academic Press, 1974–80).

13. Kristof Glamann, *Dutch-Asiatic Trade, 1620–1740* (Copenhagen: Danish Science Press/Martinus Nijhoff, 1958); Niels Steensgaard, *The Asian Trade Revolution of the Seventeenth Century: The East India Companies and the Decline of the Caravan Trade* (Chicago: University of Chicago Press, 1974); M.A.P. Mellink-Roelofsz, "A Comparative Study of the Administration and Trade of the Dutch

and English Trading Companies in Asia During the First Half of the Seventeenth Century," in *Dutch Authors on Asian History*, ed. M.A.P. Meilink-Roelofsz, M. E. van Opstall, and G. J. Schutte (Dordrecht: Foris, 1976), 430–53; K. N. Chaudhuri, *The Trading World of Asia and the English East India Company 1660–1760* (Cambridge: Cambridge University Press, 1978); Léonard Blussé and Femme Gaastra, eds., *Companies and Trade: Essays on Overseas Trading Companies during the Ancien Régime* (Leiden: Leiden University Press, 1981); Om Prakash, *The Dutch East India Company in the Trade of the Indian Ocean* (New Delhi: Oxford University Press, 1987).

14. But also see the notable works on South Asia by C. A. Bayly, such as his *Empire and Information: Intelligence Gathering and Social Communication in India, 1780–1870* (Cambridge: Cambridge University Press, 1996), and by Sanjay Subrahmanyam, such as *The Portuguese Empire in Asia 1500–1700: A Political and Economic History* (London: Longman, 1993) and *Merchant Networks in the Early Modern World* (Aldershot: Variorum, 1996).

15. Arjun Appadurai, *Modernity at Large: Cultural Dimensions of Globalization* (Minneapolis: University of Minnesota Press, 1996). See the excellent use to which this view has been put in, for instance, Kapil Raj, *Relocating Modern Science: Circulation and the Construction of Scientific Knowledge in South Asia and Europe, 17th–19th Centuries* (Delhi: Permanent Black, 2006).

16. R. Bin Wong, *China Transformed: Historical Change and the Limits of European Experience* (Ithaca, NY: Cornell University Press, 1997); Andre Gunder Frank, *ReOrient: Global Economy in the Asian Age* (Berkeley: University of California Press, 1999); Kenneth Pomeranz, *The Great Divergence: China, Europe, and the Making of the Modern World Economy* (Princeton: Princeton University Press, 2000).

17. For an important recent further step in the argument, see Jean-Laurent Rosenthal and R. Bin Wong, *Before and Beyond Divergence: The Politics of Economic Change in China and Europe* (Cambridge, MA: Harvard University Press, 2011); and Karel Davids, *Religion, Technology, and the Great and Little Divergences: China and Europe Compared, c. 700-1800* (Leiden: Brill, 2012).

18. Pamela H. Smith and Paula Findlen, eds., *Merchants and Marvels: Commerce, Science, and Art in Early Modern Europe* (New York: Routledge, 2002); Schiebinger and Swan, *Colonial Botany*; Lissa Roberts, Simon Schaffer, and Peter Dear, eds., *The Mindful Hand: Inquiry and Invention From the Late Renaissance to Early Industrialisation* (Amsterdam: Koninklijke Nederlandse Akademie van Wetenschappen, 2007); Cook, *Matters of Exchange*; Daniela Bleichmar, Paula De Vos, Kristin Huffine, and Kevin Sheehan, eds., *Science in the Spanish and Portuguese Empires, 1500–1800* (Stanford: Stanford University Press, 2009); Simon Schaffer, Lissa Roberts, Kapil Raj, and James Delbourgo, eds., *The Brokered World: Go-Betweens and Global Intelligence, 1770–1820* (Sagamore Beach, MA: Science History Publications, 2009); Siegfried Huigen, Jan L. de Jong, and Elmer Kolfin, eds., *The Dutch Trading Companies as Knowledge Networks* (Leiden: Brill, 2010).

19. Togo Tsukahara, *Affinity and Shinwa Ryoku: Introduction of Western Chemical Concepts in Early Nineteenth-Century Japan* (Amsterdam: J.C. Geiben, 1993).

20. On Floyer, see the entry on Floyer by D. D. Gibbs in the *Oxford Dictionary of National Biography* (Oxford: Oxford University Press, 2004), online edition at http://www.oxforddnb.com/; and Mark Jenner, "Tasting Lichfield, Touching China: Sir John Floyer's Senses," *Historical Journal* 53 (2010): 647–70.

21. Boleslaw Szczesniak, "John Floyer and Chinese Medicine," *Osiris* 11 (1954): 127–56; Mirko Drazen Grmek, *Les Reflets de la Sphygmologie Chinoise dans la Médecine Occidentale*, vol. 51: *Extrait de la Biologie Médicale, Numéro Hors Série* (Paris: Specia, 1962).

22. The most recent study of Floyer, which places his interest in the pulse in the context of his concern to use sensory evidence to develop new methods of diagnosis and treatment, is Jenner, "Tasting Lichfield"; also see Szczesniak, "John Floyer"; and Grmek, *Les Reflets De La Sphygmologie Chinoise.*

23. The knots tied in the rope were meant to be 1/120th of a sea mile (which was calculated at 6,120 feet), with the "sea glass" calibrated for a similar fraction of the hour.

24. John Floyer, *The Physicians' Pulse-Watch* (London: Printed for Sam. Smith and Benj. Walford, 1707), sig. A4.

25. Harold J. Cook, "Living in Revolutionary Times: Medical Change Under William and Mary," in *Patronage and Institutions: Science, Technology and Medicine at the European Court, 1500–1750*, ed. Bruce T. Moran (Woodbridge: Boydell, 1991), 111–35; Cook, "Markets and Cultures: Medical Specifics and the Reconfiguration of the Body in Early Modern Europe," *Transactions of the Royal Historical Society* 21 (2011): 123–45.

26. This is a classic philosophical divide in medical thinking, and the literature is extensive. For examples, see Owsei Temkin, "The Scientific Approach to Disease: Specific Entity and Individual Sickness," in *Scientific Change*, ed. A. C. Crombie (New York: Basic Books, 1963); Peter H. Niebyl, "Sennert, Van Helmont, and Medical Ontology," *Bulletin of the History of Medicine* 45 (1971): 115–37; and for an example of the physiological viewpoint in practice in eighteenth-century Germany, see Barbara Duden, *The Woman Beneath the Skin: A Doctor's Patients in Eighteenth-Century Germany*, trans. Thomas Dunlap (1987; repr., Cambridge, MA: Harvard University Press, 1991).

27. John Floyer, *Enquiry into the Right Use and Abuses of the Hot, Cold, and Temperate Baths in England* (London: R. Clavel, 1697), 81. He was also friendly with another physician, Edward Baynard, who published a short piece on a child's severe distress after swallowing two copper farthings, which was successfully treated by a cold bath: *Philosophical Transactions of the Royal Society* 20 (January 1, 1698): 424.

28. John Floyer, *The Ancient Phgerologeia Revived: Or, an Essay to Prove Cold Bathing Both Safe and Useful* (London: For Sam. Smith and Benj, Walford, 1702); Baynard's letter is at 207–77. For more on Baynard, see the entry by Mark Jenner in the *Oxford Dictionary of National Biography*. Floyer and Baynard soon found others coming to their support, as in Joseph Browne, *An Account of the Wonderful Cures Perform'd by the Cold Baths* (London: Printed for J. How, R. Borough, and J. Baker, 1707).

29. Floyer, *Physicians' Pulse-Watch*, 298–328.

30. Vivian Nutton, "Galen at the Bedside: The Methods of a Medical Detective," in *Medicine and the Five Senses*, ed. W. F. Bynum and Roy Porter (Cambridge: Cambridge University Press, 1993), 12.

31. Jean Fernel, *Two Treatises: The First of Pulses, the Second of Urines*, ed. and trans. Nicholas Culpeper and Abdiah Cole (London: Printed by Peter Cole, 1662), quotation from 1–2, with the words for pulses taken from 2–33.

32. For a fuller account of his possible motivations with special attention to his concern with using the senses fully in his investigations, see Jenner, "Tasting Lichfield."

33. Floyer, *Physicians' Pulse-Watch*, 425.

34. Ibid., sig. A5.

35. Ibid., 149.

36. Ibid., 336.

37. Ibid., sig. A7.

38. Ibid., sig. A7.

39. Ibid., 228. One of the works to which he refers was apparently Alvarez Semedo or Semmedo's *Imperio de la China* (Rome, 1642), with a French edition in 1645 and an English edition in 1655, the other probably the Dominican Louis Daniel Le Comte, who was published in English translation as *Memoirs and Observations . . . Made in a Late Journey through the Empire of China* (London, 1697).

40. Athanasius Kircher, *China monumentis, qua sacris qua profanis, nec non variis naturae and artis spectaculis, aliarumque rerum memorabilium argumentis illustrata* (Amsterdam: Jacob van Meurs, 1667); for an English translation by Charles D. Van Tuyl (1986), see http://hotgates.stanford.edu/Eyes/library/kircher .pdf (accessed July 8, 2011). On him, see Paula Findlen, ed., *Athanasius Kircher: The Last Man Who Knew Everything* (New York, London: Routledge, 2004). Floyer had received his knighthood for his services during the Tory reaction after the Exclusion Crisis: Jenner, "Tasting Lichfield," 652.

41. Jan Nieuhof, *An Embassy from the East India Company of the United Provinces to the Grand Tartar Cham Emperor of China*, trans. John Ogilby, 1669 (Facsimile; Menston: Scholar Press and Palmyra Press, 1972). It also had French, German, and Latin translations in 1665, 1666, and 1668, respectively. On this work, see Paul Arblaster, "Piracy and Play: Two Catholic Appropriations of Nieuhof's Gezantschap," in Huigen, de Jong, and Kolfin, *Dutch Trading Companies as Knowledge Networks*, 129–43.

42. Nieuhof, *Embassy*, 162–63. Floyer quotes from this text on 229 of his *Physicians' Pulse-Watch*.

43. For instance, see Eleanor von Erdberg, *Chinese Influence on European Garden Structure* (1938; repr., New York: Hacker Art Books, 1985); William W. Appleton, *A Cycle of Cathay: The Chinese Vogue in England during the Seventeenth and Eighteenth Centuries* (New York: Columbia University Press, 1951); and esp. Donald F. Lach, *Asia in the Making of Europe*, 5 books in 2 vols. (Chicago: University of Chicago Press, 1965–77).

44. Floyer, *Physicians' Pulse-Watch*, 337.

45. Arnold H. Rowbotham, "La Mothe le Vayer's Vertu des Payens and Eighteenth-Century Cosmopolitanism," *Modern Language Notes* 53 (1938): 10–14.

46. R. Po-chia Hsia, *A Jesuit in the Forbidden City: Matteo Ricci 1552–1610* (Leiden: Brill, 2010).

47. Most importantly in the encyclopedias of Athanasius Kircher and Nieuhof, *Embassy*, see its 106-page "An Appendix or Special Remarks taken out of Athanasius Kircher his Antiquities of China."

48. For a description of these editions, see David E. Mungello, "The Seventeenth-Century Jesuit Translation Project of the Confucian Four Books," in *East Meets West: The Jesuits in China, 1582–1773*, ed. Charles E. Ronan and Bonnie B. C. Oh (Chicago: Loyola University Press, 1988), 256–60.

49. The arguments about the *prisci theologii* of the Hermetic tradition have been put most forcefully by D. P. Walker, *The Ancient Theology: Studies in Christian Platonism from the Fifteenth to the Eighteenth Century* (London: Duckworth, 1972); and Frances A. Yates, *Giordano Bruno and the Hermetic Tradition* (New York: Vintage Books, 1969). For the view that the Jesuits also saw Confucius as one of the *prisci theologii*, Jonathan Israel, "Admiration of China and Classical Chinese Thought in the Radical Enlightenment (1685–1740)," *Taiwan Journal of East Asian Studies* 4 (2007): 1–25.

50. Lionel M. Jensen, *Manufacturing Confucianism: Chinese Traditions and Universal Civilization* (Durham, NC: Duke University Press, 1997), 111–33; Ina Baghdiantz McCabe, *Orientalism in Early Modern France: Eurasian Trade, Exoticism, and the Ancien Régime* (Oxford: Berg, 2008); Nicholas Dew, *Orientalism in Louis XIV's France* (Oxford: University of Oxford Press, 2009).

51. The literature on this subject is large. To mention just some of the work in English, see Daniel J. Cook and Henry Rosemont, Jr., "The Pre-Established Harmony between Leibniz and Chinese Thought," *Journal of the History of Ideas* 42 (1981): 253–67; Walter W. Davis, "China, the Confucian Ideal, and the European Age of Enlightenment," *Journal of the History of Ideas* 44 (1983), 523–48; Yuen-Ting Lai, "The Linking of Spinoza to Chinese Thought by Bayle and Malebranche," *Journal of the History of Philosophy* 23 (1985): 151–78; D. E. Mungello, "Confucianism in the Enlightenment: Antagonism and Collaboration Between the Jesuits and the Philosophes," in *China and Europe: Images and Influences in Sixteenth to Eighteenth Centuries*, ed. Thomas H. C. Lee (Hong Kong: Chinese University Press, 1991), 99–127; Julia Ching and Willard G. Oxtoby, *Moral Enlightenment: Leibniz and Wolff on China* (Nettetal: Steyler Verlag, 1992); D. E. Mungello, "European Philosophical Responses to Non-European Culture: China," in *The Cambridge History of Seventeenth-Century Philosophy*, ed. Daniel Garber and Michael Ayers (Cambridge: Cambridge University Press, 1998), 87–100.

52. Floyer, *Physicians' Pulse-Watch*, 232–33. For theological reasons, the Jesuits took the view that qi as known to the Chinese was a material substance distinct from spiritus, the latter of which could be properly known only following Christ's revelations: Qiong Zhang, "Demystifying Qi: The Politics of Cultural Translation and Interpretation in the Early Jesuit Mission to China," in *Tokens of*

Exchange: The Problem of Translation in Global Circulations, ed. Lydia H. Liu (Durham, NC: Duke University Press, 1999), 74–106.

53. For instance, Pierre Bayle thought the "atheistic" views of Spinoza were like the natural philosophy of "Eastern Countries": Pierre Bayle, *Dictionary*, ed. John Peter Bernard, Thomas Birch, John Lockman, et al. (London: 1734), 5:199.

54. Sir William Temple, *Miscellanea*, part 2 (London: Printed by J.R. for Ri. and Ra. Simpson, 1690), 334.

55. William Wotton, *Reflections upon Ancient and Modern Learning* (London: Printed by J. Leake for Peter Buck, 1694), 144–54, 152.

56. Floyer, *Physicians' Pulse-Watch*, 243.

57. Ibid., 258–97.

58. Ibid., sig. A7.

59. Copy of the *Specimen* in Queen's College, Oxford, shelf no. NN.s.62.

60. Floyer, *Physicians' Pulse-Watch*, 339–424.

61. Ibid., 340.

62. Ibid., 368, 422, 428.

63. Ibid., "An Essay to Make a New Sphugmologia, by Accommodating the Chinese and European Observations about the Pulse," 255–320.

64. Stanley Joel Reiser, *Medicine and the Reign of Technology* (Cambridge: Cambridge University Press, 1978), 96–98.

65. Floyer, *Physicians' Pulse-Watch*, vol. 2 (London: Printed for J. Nicholson, W. Taylor, and H. Clemenes, 1710), iv: "The Notion of a Circulation was very ancient; but before Hippocrates and Plato's time 'twas lost; yet there are some Passages in their Writings which seem to assert it."

66. The publication series was the Miscellanæ Curiosa (or Ephemerides). The group certainly deserves further study and is being investigated by Margaret Garber; at the moment, the best overall work remains Frances Mason Barnett, "Medical Authority and Princely Patronage: The Academia Naturae Curiosorum, 1652–1693" (PhD diss., University of North Carolina at Chapel Hill, 1995).

67. *Les secrets de la medecine des Chinois Consistent en le parfaite connoissance du Pouls*. (Grenoble: Phillipe Charvys, 1671).

68. Following the submission of the final version of this essay, the following important article was published: Puente-Beatriz Ballesteros, "Jesuit Medicine in the Kangxi Court (1662–1722)," *East Asian Science, Technology, and Medicine* 34 (2012): 86–162.

69. This is not the place for a further investigation of William Wotton's interpretation, but it suggests that he may well have been engaged in an anti-Jesuit polemic as much as a "modernist" agenda.

70. For a very revealing analysis, see Vicente L. Rafael, *Contracting Colonialism: Translation and Christian Conversion in Tagalog Society under Early Spanish Rule* (Ithaca, NY: Cornell University Press, 1988).

71. The literature on the early Jesuit mission is very large, but for recent views see esp. L. M. Brockey, *Journey to the East: The Jesuit Mission to China, 1579–1724* (Cambridge, MA: Harvard University Press, 2007); J. Gernet, *China and the Christian Impact: A Conflict of Cultures*, trans. J. Lloyd (Cambridge: Cambridge University Press, 1985); Jensen, *Manufacturing Confucianism*; D. E. Mungello,

The Great Encounter of China and the West, 1500–1800 (Lanham, MD: Rowman & Littlefield, 1999); Erik Zürcher, "Jesuit Accommodation and the Chinese Cultural Imperative," in *The Chinese Rites Controversy*, ed. D. E. Mungello (Nettetal: Steyler Verlag, 1994), 31–64.

72. See esp. Israel, "Admiration of China."

73. Floyer, *Physicians' Pulse-Watch*, 232–33.

74. Kircher, *China Illustrata*, pt. 3, chap. 1, Van Tuyl trans., 122.

75. In addition to the secondary sources cited above, see Qiong Zhang, "About God, Demons, and Miracles: The Jesuit Discourse on the Supernatural in Late Ming China," *Early Science and Medicine* 4 (1998): 1–36; Erik Zürcher, "Confucian and Christian Religiosity in Late Ming China," *Catholic Historical Review* 83 (1997): 614–53; Dauril Alden, *The Making of an Enterprise: The Society of Jesus in Portugal, Its Empire, and Beyond* (Stanford: Stanford University Press, 1996).

76. R. Po-chia Hsia, "The Catholic Mission and Translations in China, 1583–1700," in *Cultural Translation in Early Modern Europe*, ed. Peter Burke and R. Po-chia Hsia (Cambridge: European Science Foundation, Cambridge University Press, 2007), 39–51.

77. Readers can find their way into the extensive literature through Florence C. Hsia, *Sojourners in a Strange Land: Jesuits and Their Scientific Missions in Late Imperial China* (Chicago: University of Chicago Press, 2009), and Mordechai Feingold, ed., *The New Science and Jesuit Science: Seventeenth Century Perspectives* (Dordrecht: Kluwer Academic Publishers, 2003).

78. Pierre Huard, "La Diffusion de L'anatomie européenne dans quelques secteurs de l'Asie," *Archives Internationales d'Histoire des Sciences* 32 (1953): 269–70; for other examples, see Harold J. Cook, "Conveying Chinese Medicine to Seventeenth-Century Europe," in *Science between Europe and Asia: Historical Studies on the Transmission, Adoption and Adaptation of Knowledge*, ed. Feza Günergun and Dhruv Raina (Heidelberg: Springer, 2011), 213–19. Following the submission of the final version of this essay, the following important article was published: Noël Golvers, "The Jesuits in China and the Circulation of Western Books in the Sciences (17th–18th Centuries): The Medical and Pharmaceutical Sections in the SJ Libraries of Peking," *East Asian Science, Technology, and Medicine* 34 (2012): 15–85.

79. Hsia, "Catholic Mission and Translations," 46.

80. For Boym's biography, see Robert Chabrié, *Michel Boym: Jésuit Polonias et la Fin des Ming en Chine (1646–1662)* (Paris: Pierre Bossuet, 1933), with important qualifications by Paul Pelliot, "Michel Boym," *T'oung Pao* 31 (1935): 95–151; also Michel Boym, *Michael Boyms Bericht Aus Mosambik—1644 (Lateinischer Text, Übersetzung Und Kommentar)*, ed. Robert Wallisch (Vienna: Verlag der Österreichischen Akademie der Wissenschaften, 2005).

81. Kircher, *China Illustrata*; on the collaboration between the Jesuits in China and their Christian colleagues to spread news of the monument, which helped to make a case for the antiquity of Christianity in China, see Brockey, *Journey to the East*, 80, and David E. Mungello, *Curious Land: Jesuit Accommodation and the Origins of Sinology* (Stuttgart: Franz Steiner Verlag, 1985), 164–72.

82. Mungello, *Curious Land*, 167.

83. Ibid., 208–46; Walter Simon, "The Attribution to Michael Boym of Two Early Achievements of Western Sinology," *Asia Major* 7 (1959): 165–69.

84. Michel Boym, *Flora Sinensis* (Vienne: Matthæi Rictii, 1656).

85. Michel Boym, *Briefve Relation* (Paris: Sebastian Cramoisy, 1654). The appendix is mispaginated, numbered 72 to 75 despite being six pages in length.

86. Edward Kajdański, "Michael Boym's Medicus Sinicus," *T'oung Pao* 73 (1987): 162; Pelliot, "Michel Boym," 135.

87. Boym, *Briefve Relation*, 73; the medical work was described as "Medicus Sinicus seu singularis Ars explorandi pulsum & prædicendi & futura Symptomata, & affectiones ægrotantium à multis ante Christum sæculis tradita, & apud Sinas conservata; quae quidem ars omnino est admirabilis & ab Europæâ diversa" ("Chinese medicine, or the singular art of exploring the pulse and anticipating future symptoms and changes in patients, found out many years before Christ and preserved among the Chinese, which is indeed an entirely admirable art and distinct from that of Europe").

88. Cook, "Conveying Chinese Medicine," which critically synthesizes previous work and adds information from the Dutch connections.

89. See the account of Couplet sent in a letter of April 26, 1687, to Christian Mentzel, quoted in Eva Kraft, "Christian Mentzel, Philippe Couplet, Andreas Cleyer und die Chinesische Medizin: Notizen Aus Handschriften Des 17. Jahrhunderts," in *Fernöstliche Kultur: Wolf Haennisch Zugeeignet* (Marburg: N.G. Elwert, 1975), 187. Also see Paul Demaerel, "Couplet and the Dutch," in *Philippe Couplet, S.J. (1623–1693): The Man Who Brought China to Europe*, ed. Jerome Heyndrickx (Nettetal: Steyler Verlag, 1990), 117.

90. Michel Boym, Andreas Cleyer, and Philipp Couplet, *Clavis Medica ad Chinarum Doctrinam de Pulsibus* (Miscellanea Curiosa, 1686).

91. Noël Golvers, *François de Rougement, S.J., Missionary in Ch'ang-Shu (Chiang-Nan): A Study of the Account Book (1674–1676) and the Elogium* (Leuven: Leuven University Press, Ferdinand Verbiest Foundation, 1999), 530–31, 533–34.

92. Mungello, "Seventeenth-Century Jesuit Translation Project."

93. Demaerel, "Couplet and the Dutch," 102–11.

94. Ibid., 111–12.

95. Cook, "Conveying Chinese Medicine," 228, gives evidence for thinking that the work Cleyer sent to Amsterdam in 1681 was the Clavis, but I have now been persuaded that the comment by Willem ten Rhijne, that the ship was carrying a more complete version of "the Chinese work on the pulse," suggests that it was a more complete version of one of the texts printed in the *Specimen*, rather than anything written by Boym. This would also help to explain why Cleyer later complained that ten Rhijne and his friends had held up publication, the confusions of the printer, and why the sections were printed and paginated separately. The evidence is detailed in Cook, "Conveying Chinese Medicine," but also see esp. Kraft, "Christian Mentzel."

96. Herman Busschof and Hermann Roonhuis, *Two Treatises, the One Medical, of the Gout, . . . the Other Partly Chirurgical, Partly Medical* (London: Printed by H.C. for Moses Pitt, 1676); Cook, "Medical Communication in the First Global Age: Willem Ten Rhijne in Japan, 1674–1676," *Disquisitions on the Past & Present* 11 (2004): 16–36.

97. On ten Rhijne, see Cook, *Matters of Exchange*, 339–77.

98. Johannes Heniger, *Hendrik Adriaan van Reede tot Drakenstein (1636–1691) and Hortus Malabaricus: A Contribution to the History of Dutch Colonial Botany* (Rotterdam: A.A. Balkema, 1986).

99. Eva S. Kraft, "Frühe Chinesische Studien in Berlin," *Medizin Historisches Journal* 11 (1976): 121.

100. British Library, Sloane MS. 2729, fol. 73.

101. The manuscript, which contains some illustrations not printed in any other copy I have seen and is bound with a few additional materials that have been reviewed by Eva Kraft, is in the Staasbibliotek Berlin, MS Lat. 95. Floyer's copy was given to Queen's College, Oxford, where it remains as shelf mark NN.s.62.

102. The identification, by Pelliot, "Michel Boym," 140–41, is confirmed by Hannelore Müller, "'Specimen Medicinae Sinicae': Das 'Mai Chüeh' Oder 'Das Geheimnis Der Pulslehre' Und Die Rezeption Durch Europäer Des 17. Jhs" (MD, Ludwig-Maximilian-Universität, München, 1994). But Edward Kajdański believed some of the subsections were taken from the 1578 edition of Wang Shu-he's classic study of the pulse, Mai Jing: see his "Michael Boym's Medicus Sinicus," 169–70. On the original works, see Jean Borsarello, "Les 28 Formes Pulsatiles Pathologiques de Wang Chou Houo (267 Après J.-C.)," *Méridiens* 47–48 (1979): 37–48; and Wang Shou-He, *The Pulse Classic: A Translation of the Mai Jing*, trans. Yang Shou-Zhoung (Boulder, CO: Blue Poppy Press, 1997).

103. Kajdański, "Michael Boym's Medicus Sinicus," 180–83.

104. For a translation of this last section, see Colin B. Lessell, *Bibliotheca Medica de Asia Orientali, 1473–1900*, 2nd ed. (London: Samphire Press, 2007), 416–35.

105. For further discussion of this important subject, see Müller, "'Specimen,'" 40–43, and esp. Qiong Zhang, "Demystifying Qi."

106. Paul Uschuld has been particularly concerned to demolish this view, which remains common in Europe and America. See, for instance, his *Medicine in China: A History of Ideas* (Berkeley: University of California Press, 1985); and *What Is Medicine? Western and Eastern Approaches to Healing*, trans. Karen Reimers (Berkeley: University of California Press, 2009).

107. Floyer, *Physicians' Pulse-Watch*, 233–43.

108. On this point I agree fully with Mark Jenner, "Tasting Lichfield," although it should also be noted that Floyer was among those trying to find quantitative measures to substitute for qualitative ones.

CHAPTER 9
TRANSNATIONAL FEMINISM: EVENT, TEMPORALITY, AND PERFORMANCE AT THE 1975 INTERNATIONAL WOMEN'S YEAR CONFERENCE

1. Journalists and organizers referred to the IWY events as a global consciousness-raising session. Margaret Bruce, the head of the UN's Commission on the Status of Women, explained, "IWY, it is hoped, will result in a worldwide consciousness raising" (National Archives and Records Administration, College

Park, MD, RG 220, Records of the U.S. Center for International Women's Year; Subject Files, 1973–1975; A-AS; box 1, AAUW folder). The director of Mexico's IWY program, Gloria Brasdefer, similarly insisted that it was "not an homage to women" but rather a "consciousness-raising effort" (*Excélsior*, June 18, 1975, 1-B). See also *New York Times*, June 19, 1975, 41 and July 3, 1975, 1; *The Nation*, July 19, 1975, 36; *The Economist*, July 5, 1975, 72.

2. Bonnie Smith has pointed out that this proliferation of forms of women's activism requires us to consider feminisms in the plural. *Global Feminisms since 1945: A Survey of Issues and Controversies* (New York: Routledge, 2000). See also Myra Marx Ferree and Carol McClurg Mueller, "Feminism and the Women's Movement: A Global Perspective," in *The Blackwell Companion to Social Movements*, ed. David A. Snow, Sarah A. Soule, and Hanspeter Kriesi (Oxford: Blackwell, 2004). On earlier international women's movements, see, for example, K. Lynn Stoner, "In Four Languages but with One Voice: Division and Solidarity within Pan American Feminism, 1923–1933," in *Beyond the Ideal: Pan Americanism in Inter-American Affairs*, ed. David Sheinin (Westport, CT: Greenwood, 2000); Leila J. Rupp, *Worlds of Women: The Making of an International Women's Movement* (Princeton: Princeton University Press, 1997); Bonnie S. Anderson, *Joyous Greetings: The First International Women's Movement, 1830–1860* (New York: Oxford University Press, 2000).

3. Two other UN conferences the previous year had included NGO tribunes— the Food Conference (Rome) and the Population Conference (Bucharest).

4. Akira Iriye, *Global Community: The Role of International Organizations in the Making of the Contemporary World* (Berkeley: University of California Press, 2002).

5. For support from the Rockefeller Foundation, see the Rockefeller Archives Center (RAC), Rockefeller Brothers Fund, Series 3 (RBF Grants), box 461, Travelers Aid International Social Services of America—IWY Tribune 1975 folder and RAC, Rockefeller Foundation Archives, RG 13 (Projects), series 103 (International Organizations), Travelers Aid International Social Services of America NGO Tribune (1975–1975) subseries, box 10, folder 66. On John D. Rockefeller III's particular interest in the conference, see RAC, RG 5 (JDR 3rd Papers), series 3 (Office & Home Files), box 46, folder 281. On the Ford Foundation's support, see especially Ford Foundation Archive, grant no. 75-224. The Ford Foundation was in the midst of its own feminist consciousness raising. See Susan M. Hartmann, *The Other Feminists: Activists in the Liberal Establishment* (New Haven: Yale University Press, 1998), chap. 5.

6. Francesca Miller, *Latin American Women and the Search for Social Justice* (Hanover, NH: University Press of New England, 1991), 200. For their respective memoirs, see Domitila Barrios de Chungara and Moema Viezzer, *Let Me Speak! Testimony of Domitila, a Woman of the Bolivian Mines*, trans. Victoria Ortiz (New York: Monthly Review Press, 1978); Domitila Barrios de Chungara and David Acebey, *Aquí también, Domitila! Testimonios*, 1st ed. (Mexico City: Siglo Veintiuno Editores, 1985); Betty Friedan, "Scary Doings in Mexico City," in *"It Changed My Life": Writings on the Women's Movement* (Cambridge, MA: Harvard University Press, 1998).

7. Göran Therborn, *Between Sex and Power: Family in the World, 1900–2000* (London: Routledge, 2004), 103.

8. The geopolitical divide indicated here has been marked by various designations: North/South, West/non-West, industrialized/developing, and First World/Third World. For the purposes of this chapter, I mostly use the First World/Third World and industrialized/developing designations because the chapter's subjects used them most commonly. The constantly shifting use of terms, however, attests to the analytical limitations of each of these binaries.

9. Bina Agarwal, "From Mexico 1975 to Beijing 1995," *Indian Journal of Gender Studies* 3, no. 1 (1996): 88.

10. Carolyn M. Stephenson, "Women's Organizations and the United Nations," in *Multilateral Diplomacy and the United Nations Today*, ed. James P. Muldoon (Cambridge, MA: Westview, 2005), 214.

11. This diametric opposition echoes the early-twentieth-century European construction of the incompatibility of Marxism and "bourgeois feminism." See Marilyn J. Boxer, "Rethinking the Socialist Construction and International Career of the Concept 'Bourgeois Feminism,'" *American Historical Review* 112, no. 1 (2007): 131–58. This imagined synthesis offers an example of what Joan Scott has dubbed the fantasy of feminist history, conjured to fulfill an unmet yearning and to "assign fixed meaning to that which ultimately cannot be fixed." Joan Wallach Scott, "Feminism's History," *Journal of Women's History* 16, no. 2 (2004): 5.

12. B. S. Santos, "The Future of the World Social Forum: The Work of Translation," *Development* 48, no. 2 (2005): 17.

13. Mary Louise Pratt, *Imperial Eyes: Travel Writing and Transculturation* (London: Routledge, 1992), 4.

14. Diane M. Nelson, *A Finger in the Wound: Body Politics in Quincentennial Guatemala* (Berkeley: University of California Press, 1999), 348.

15. The description of Barrios de Chungara's experience at the IWY tribune appears in her coauthored memoir, Barrios de Chungara and Viezzer, *Let Me Speak!*, 198ff. Her account offers not a transparent recounting of events, however, but rather a quintessential example of *testimonio*—the witness-bearing representations that gained traction amid Latin American counterinsurgency campaigns of the 1970s and 1980s and that by the 1990s precipitated anxious debates about subaltern truth telling. On *testimonio* and its reconsideration, see especially John Beverley, "The Real Thing (Our Rigoberta)," *Modern Language Quarterly* 57, no. 2 (1996): 129–39; Diane M. Nelson, *Reckoning: The Ends of War in Guatemala* (Durham, NC: Duke University Press, 2009), chap. 4.

16. This representation coincides with what Clare Hemmings has dubbed "progress narratives" that see feminism as evolving from a liberal, racist past to a more enlightened feminist present. Clare Hemmings, *Why Stories Matter: The Political Grammar of Feminist Theory* (Durham, NC: Duke University Press, 2011).

17. *Excélsior*, July 1, 1975, 1.

18. Quoted in *El Universal*, July 1, 1975, 1.

19. *The Economist*, July 5, 1975, 72.

20. Judith Butler, "Contingent Foundations: Feminism and the Question of the 'Postmodern,'" in *Feminists Theorize the Political*, ed. Judith Butler and Joan Scott (New York: Routledge, 1992), 16.

21. *Xilonen*, June 30, 1975, 8. The anthropologist Ara Wilson similarly describes the inclusion of the term "sexism" among the 2005 World Social Forum's

hit list of global maladies as "a puzzling choice, an atypical reliance on liberal frameworks, perhaps a vestigial artifact of particular archives that inform textual production at the Forum." Ara Wilson, "Feminism in the Space of the World Social Forum," *Journal of International Women's Studies* 8 (2007): 13.

22. *New York Times*, June 19, 1975, 41.

23. Pacifica Radio Archives, *Betty Friedan versus the Third World* (sound recording; North Hollywood, CA: Pacifica Radio Archives, 1975).

24. William H. Sewell Jr., *Logics of History: Social Theory and Social Transformation* (Chicago: University of Chicago Press, 2005), 280.

25. See, in particular, Alain Badiou, *Being and Event* (London: Continuum, 2005); Sewell, *Logics of History*, chaps. 7 and 8.

26. Challenges to the imposition of normative and coherent meanings on historical evidence constituted one of feminist historians' most important interventions during the 1990s. See, in particular, Joan Wallach Scott, "The Evidence of Experience," *Critical Inquiry* 17, no. 4 (1991): 773–97 and Bonnie G. Smith, *The Gender of History: Men, Women, and Historical Practice* (Cambridge, MA: Harvard University Press, 1998).

27. For an account of the YWCA's role in transnational women's organizing, see Karen Garner, *Shaping a Global Women's Agenda: Women's NGOs and Global Governance, 1925–85* (Manchester: Manchester University Press, 2010).

28. Mildred Persinger, "Generations of Change: The United Nations International Women's Conferences" (roundtable presentation, Berkshire Conference on the History of Women, Amherst, MA, June 10, 2011).

29. Ibid.

30. *New York Times*, June 29, 1975, 2.

31. See, for example, Ford Foundation correspondence regarding grant no. 75-224.

32. MacDermot to Waldheim, March 6, 1974; Harris to MacDermot, April 4, 1974, both in International Women's Tribune Centre Archive, Sophia Smith Collection, Smith College, Northampton, MA, box 1.

33. Yuen-Li Liang, "The Question of Access to the United Nations Headquarters of Representatives of Non-governmental Organizations in Consultative Status," *American Journal of International Law* 48, no. 3 (1954): 434–50.

34. Francisca de Haan, "Continuing Cold War Paradigms in Western Historiography of Transnational Women's Organisations: The Case of the Women's International Democratic Federation (WIDF)," *Women's History Review* 19, no. 4 (2010): 547–73. For another discussion of the ICW/WIDF rivalry, see Mary Kinnear, *Woman of the World: Mary McGeachy and International Cooperation* (Toronto: University of Toronto Press, 2004).

35. While the UN had given $3 million for the population conference and allowed two years for planning, the IWY was planned in six months with an initial budget of $350,000. Judith P. Zinsser, "From Mexico to Copenhagen to Nairobi: The United Nations Decade for Women, 1975–1985," *Journal of World History* 13, no. 1 (2002): 146.

36. The issue of women's human rights would not secure a place in the UN's lexicon until the 1993 Vienna Human Rights Conference and was strengthened at the 1995 Beijing Women's Conference. Julie Peters and Andrea Wolper, *Women's*

Rights, Human Rights: International Feminist Perspectives (New York: Routledge, 1995).

37. Reporters noted that the North Vietnamese and South Vietnamese delegations made a point of appearing together at public functions during the conference. For example, *New York Times*, June 22, 1975, 48.

38. For a more elaborate discussion of reproductive-labor debates at the IWY events, see Jocelyn Olcott, "The Battle within the Home: Development Strategies, Second-Wave Feminism, and the Commodification of Caring Labors at the 1975 International Women's Year Conference," in *Workers across the Americas: The Transnational Turn in Labor History*, ed. Leon Fink (New York: Oxford University Press, 2011).

39. For a succinct summary of how these debates played out in the emblematic French case, see Joan Wallach Scott, *Parité! Sexual Equality and the Crisis of French Universalism* (Chicago: University of Chicago Press, 2005).

40. The question of whether NGOs have served women well in the ensuing decades, especially in poorer regions, has been a subject of intense debate. See esp. Sonia E. Alvarez, "Latin American Feminisms 'Go Global': Trends of the 1990s and Challenges for the New Millennium," in *Cultures of Politics/Politics of Cultures: Re-visioning Latin American Social Movements*, ed. Sonia E. Alvarez, Evelina Dagnino, and Arturo Escobar (Boulder, CO: Westview, 1998); Sonia E. Alvarez, "Beyond NGO-ization? Reflections from Latin America," *Development* 52, no. 2 (2009): 175–84; Breny Mendoza, "Transnational Feminisms in Question," *Feminist Theory* 3, no. 3 (2002): 295–314; Valentine M. Moghadam, *Globalizing Women: Transnational Feminist Networks* (Baltimore: Johns Hopkins University Press, 2005); Incite! Women of Color Against Violence, *The Revolution Will Not Be Funded: Beyond the Non-Profit Industrial Complex* (Cambridge, MA: South End Press, 2007).

41. "Wangari Maathai," in Dick Gordon, *Connection* (WBUR, August 1, 2005).

42. Materials on the founding of the Women's World Bank can be found in the Margaret Snyder Papers, Mudd Manuscript Library, Princeton University, and in the archives of the Ford Foundation.

43. See, for example, Eli Bartra, "Tres décadas de neofeminismo en México," in *Feminismo en México, ayer y hoy*, ed. Eli Bartra, Anna M. Fernández Poncela, and Ana Lau (Mexico: Universidad Autónoma Metropolitana, 2000), 40; Amrita Basu, "Globalization of the Local/Localization of the Global Mapping Transnational Women's Movements," *Meridians* 1, no. 1 (2000): 70; Myra Marx Ferree and Aili Mari Tripp, *Global Feminism: Transnational Women's Activism, Organizing, and Human Rights* (New York: New York University Press, 2006), 11; Jean Franco, *Plotting Women: Gender and Representation in Mexico* (New York: Columbia University Press, 1989), 184–85; Jane S. Jaquette, *Feminist Agendas and Democracy in Latin America* (Durham, NC: Duke University Press, 2009), 14; Yoshie Kobayashi, *A Path toward Gender Equality: State Feminism in Japan* (New York: Routledge, 2004), 33; Amy Lind, "Feminist Post-development Thought: 'Women in Development' and the Gendered Paradoxes of Survival in Bolivia," *Women's Studies Quarterly* 31, nos. 3/4 (2003): 229; Saba Mahmood, *Politics of Piety: The Islamic Revival and the Feminist Subject* (Princeton: Princeton

University Press, 2004), 3–4; Nima Naghibi, *Rethinking Global Sisterhood: Western Feminism and Iran* (Minneapolis: University of Minnesota Press, 2007), 76; Millie Thayer, "Transnational Feminism: Reading Joan Scott in the Brazilian *sertão*," *Ethnography* 2, no. 2 (2001): 248; Graham Willett, *Living Out Loud: A History of Gay and Lesbian Activism in Australia* (St Leonards: Allen & Unwin, 2000), 122–23.

44. Elizabeth A. Grosz, *Time Travels: Feminism, Nature, Power* (Durham, NC: Duke University Press, 2005), 1.

45. The strength of this alliance caught at least the U.S. State Department off guard. In communications regarding the nonaligned activities within the GA, Secretary of State Henry Kissinger and others predicted that fault lines would appear between oil-producing nations and the less-developed countries that particularly suffered from the oil embargo's inflationary effects. See, for examples, Secretary of State to Diplomatic Posts, May 14, 1974; State Department report on the Sixth Special Session of the UNGA, June 5, 1974; Secretary of State to Diplomatic Posts regarding 29th UNGA, August 22, 1974; all documents published in *Foreign Relations of the United States (FRUS)* E-14, pt. 1 (1969–76): docs. 13, 16, and 17.

46. *El Universal*, June 20, 1975, 1; *El Nacional*, June 18, 1975, 1; *El Universal*, June 19, 1975, 1.

47. For a particularly apropos example, see Friedan's account of her visit to Iran, "Coming Out of the Veil," *Ladies' Home Journal*, June 1975, 71, 98–103.

48. *El Nacional*, June 24, 1975, 7.

49. *Chicago Defender*, July 5, 1975, 6.

50. Jennifer Seymour Whitaker, "Women of the World: Report from Mexico City," *Foreign Affairs*, October 1975, 173.

51. *The Economist*, February 1, 1975, 33.

52. For a sanguine account of the Cuban Family Code's promise, see Marjorie King, "Cuba's Attack on Women's Second Shift 1974–1976," *Latin American Perspectives* 4, nos. 1–2 (1977): 106–19. For a historical perspective on how it played out in practice, see Johanna I. Moya Fábregas, "The Cuban Woman's Revolutionary Experience: Patriarchal Culture and the State's Gender Ideology, 1950–1976," *Journal of Women's History* 22, no. 1 (2010): 61–84.

53. Matthew Connelly, *Fatal Misconception: The Struggle to Control World Population* (Cambridge, MA: Harvard University Press, 2008), chaps. 7 and 8; Laura Briggs, *Reproducing Empire: Race, Sex, Science, and U.S. Imperialism in Puerto Rico* (Berkeley: University of California Press, 2002).

54. Memorandum of Conversation, Secretary's Luncheon Meeting with Outside Experts, Department of State, May 31, 1974, in *FRUS* E-14, pt. 1 (1969–76): doc. 15.

55. On "population control establishment," see Bonnie Mass, "The Politics of Population Control: Birth Control, Population Control, and Self-Help" (address, Harvard Medical School Women's Conference on Health, March 1975), Bobbye Ortiz Papers, Duke University Rare Book, Manuscript, and Special Collections Library, box 17, Subject File Latin America 2/4. On "indiscriminate birth control," see Barrios de Chungara and Viezzer, *Let Me Speak!*, 199–200. See also (among many other examples) the open letter from the Anti-Imperialist Women

Against Population Control, March 24, 1975, Ortiz Papers, box 17, Subject File Latin America 2/4; "Con engaños esteralizan a Mexicanonorteamericanas," *El Universal*, June 20, 1975, 3; "Forced Sterilization," *Sister: West Coast Feminist Newspaper*, June 1974, 8; "Controlling Reproduction," *What She Wants*, December 1974, 2; Sharon Lieberman, "The Politics of Population Control," *Majority Report 5* (May 31, 1975): 2.

56. Magdalena de Bastien, "¿Liberación Femenina? Como siempre, slogans y manipuleo," *Excélsior*, June 29, 1975, 2-C.

57. Many future IWY organizers were stunned to find that the agenda for the UN Population Conference had made no connection between fertility and women's status. Hilkka Pietilä and Jeanne Vickers, *Making Women Matter: The Role of the United Nations*, updated and expanded ed. (London: Zed Books, 1994), 77.

58. Ironically, Mexican President Luis Echeverría, whom most Mexicans hold responsible for the massacre during his tenure as Minister of the Interior, claimed that the UN had selected Mexico for the IWY conference because of its strong record on human rights.

59. Diana Taylor, *The Archive and the Repertoire: Performing Cultural Memory in the Americas* (Durham, NC: Duke University Press, 2003).

60. Ibid., 28.

61. Ibid, 28.

62. Although this idea has been elaborated fruitfully by feminist scholars over the past two decades, it is compellingly introduced in Judith Butler, *Gender Trouble: Feminism and the Subversion of Identity* (New York: Routledge, 1990).

63. *El Universal*, June 22, 1975, sec. 2, 4; *Washington Post*, June 22, 1975, A12.

64. Barrios de Chungara and Viezzer, *Let Me Speak!*, 199.

65. Sewell, *Logics of History*, 196.

66. Ibid., 341.

67. For a fuller discussion of these issues, see Jocelyn Olcott, "Globalizing Sisterhood: International Women's Year and the Limits of Identity Politics," in *Shock of the Global: The 1970s in Perspective*, ed. Niall Ferguson et al. (Cambridge, MA: Harvard University Press, 2010).

68. Barrios de Chungara and Viezzer, *Let Me Speak!*, 197.

69. Ibid., 203. Such descriptions serve as the archived version of knowledge production that Taylor discusses in *The Archive and the Repertoire* and offer unmistakably embodied performances that sustain a militancy grounded in gender complementarity.

70. Cindi Katz, "Lost and Found: The Imagined Geographies of American Studies," *Prospects* 30 (2006): 1–9.

71. Gayatri Chakravorty Spivak, "'Woman' as Theatre: United Nations Conference on Women, Beijing 1995," *Radical Philosophy* 75 (1996): 2–4.

72. Gayatri Chakravorty Spivak, "Can the Subaltern Speak?," in *Marxism and the Interpretation of Culture*, ed. Cary Nelson and Lawrence Grossberg (Urbana: University of Illinois Press, 1988), 271–316.

73. Marisela R. Chávez, "Pilgrimage to the Homeland: California Chicanas and International Women's Year, Mexico City, 1975," in *Memories and Mi-*

grations: Mapping Boricua and Chicana Histories, ed. Vicki Ruíz and John R. Chávez (Urbana: University of Illinois Press, 2008), 176.

74. Friedan, "Scary Doings in Mexico City," 449.

75. Ibid., 454.

76. For a more elaborate discussion of issues around sexuality, see Jocelyn Olcott, "Cold War Conflicts and Cheap Cabaret: Performing Politics at the 1975 United Nations International Women's Year Conference in Mexico City," *Gender and History* 22, no. 3 (2010): 733–54.

77. Barrios de Chungara and Viezzer, *Let Me Speak!*, 198–200.

78. *El Universal*, June 23, 1975, 4; *Excélsior*, June 25, 1975, 7-A.

79. Archivo General de la Nación (AGN), Investigaciones Políticas y Sociales, Caja 1163-A, vol. 1, Hoja 579–586; AGN, Dirección Federal de Seguridad, June 26, 1975, vol. 9-342-75, exp. 7, p. 156.

80. Norma Mogrovejo, *Un amor que se atrevió a decir su nombre: la lucha de las lesbianas y su relación con los movimientos homosexual y feminista en América Latina*, 1st ed. (Mexico City: Centro de Documentación y Archivo Histórico Lésbico, 2000), 67.

81. Mark T. Berger, *The Battle for Asia: From Decolonization to Globalization* (New York: Routledge, 2004), 51ff. Notably, the critic Michael Hardt compares the World Social Forum to Bandung. Michael Hardt, "Porto Alegre: Today's Bandung?," *New Left Review* 14 (2000).

82. Christopher J. Lee, *Making a World after Empire: The Bandung Moment and Its Political Afterlives* (Athens: Ohio University Press, 2010), 15.

83. See, for example, the essays in Antonia Finnane and Derek McDougall, eds., *Bandung 1955: Little Histories* (Caulfield East, Australia: Monash University Press, 2010); Lee, *Making a World after Empire*; See Seng Tan and Amitav Acharya, *Bandung Revisited: The Legacy of the 1955 Asian-African Conference for International Order* (Singapore: NUS Press, 2008).

84. Roland Burke, "Afro-Asian Alignment: Charles Malik and the Cold War at Bandung," in Finnane and McDougall, *Bandung 1955*, 27.

85. Vijay Prashad, *The Darker Nations: A People's History of the Third World* (New York: New Press, 2007), 45–46.

86. Katherine Ann Lynskey, interview of Mildred Persinger, Hollins University, Roanoke, VA, March 12, 2006, http://www1.hollins.edu/classes/anth220s06/lynskeyk/persinger_lynskey_main.htm (accessed June 9, 2009).

NOTES TO
ITINERANCY AND POWER

1. Aristotle, *Metaphysics*, book 11, sec. 1066a, in *Perseus Digital Library Project*, ed. Gregory R. Crane (Boston: Tufts University, updated February 7, 2012), available at http://www.perseus.tufts.edu/hopper/text?doc=Perseus%3Atext%3A1999.01.0052%3Abook%3D11%3Asection%3D1066a.

2. Talal Asad, *Genealogies of Religion: Discipline and reasons of power in Christianity and Islam* (Baltimore: Johns Hopkins University Press, 1993), 1–24.

NOTES TO
FROM CULTURES TO CULTURAL PRACTICES
AND BACK AGAIN

1. I thank Peter Brown, Dan Rodgers, Walter Pohl, Pavlína Rychterová, and in particular Jamie Kreiner for their generous support in translating the German thoughts and ideas behind this afterword into English and their as ever extremely helpful suggestions, comments, and corrections of earlier drafts of this essay.

2. See Klaus Amann, *Robert Musil—Literatur und Politik. Mit einer Neuedition ausgewählter politischer Schriften* (Reinbek: Rowohlt 2007), 63–84.

3. See ibid., 272, English translation by myself (with the support of Jamie Kreiner).

4. Ibid., 272.

5. Ibid., 106, 113.

6. Cf. the edition in ibid., 268–36.

7. See *Luhmann und die Kulturtheorie*, ed. Günter Burkert and Gunter Runkel (Stuttgart: Suhrkamp, 2003).

8. Günther Burkert, "Niklas Luhmann: ein Theoretiker der Kultur?," in Burkert and Runkel, *Luhmann und die Kulturtheorie*, 11–39.

9. Niklas Luhmann, "Kultur als historischer Begriff," in *Gesellschaftsstruktur und Semantik* (Frankfurt: Suhrkamp, 1999), 4:31–54.

10. See the still helpful overview in Jörg Fisch, "Zivilisation, Kultur," in *Geschichtliche Grundbegriffe: Historisches Lexikon zur politisch-sozialen Sprache in Deutschland*, ed. Otto Brunner, Werner Conze, and Reinhard Kosselleck (Stuttgart: Klett-Cotta, 1992), 7:679–774; one interesting example of one of many more recent studies on modern "culture" is Michael C. Carhart, *The Science of Culture in Enlightenment Germany* (Cambridge, MA: Harvard University Press, 2007). I owe the reference to this interesting study to Frederic Clark (Princeton).

11. Niklas Luhmann, *Die Kunst der Gesellschaft* (Frankfurt: Suhrkamp, 1997). Here and at other places where Luhmann discusses first- and second-order observations, he refers to the work of Heinz von Foerster; see his *Observing Systems* (Seaside, CA: Intersystems, 1981).

12. Luhmann, "Kultur als historischer Begriff," 32.

13. See ibid., 52–54.

14. Andrew Sartori, *Bengal in Global Concept History: Culturalism in the Age of Capital* (Chicago: University of Chicago Press, 2008). I thank Bhavani Raman for the reference.

15. Luhmann, "Kultur als historischer Begriff," 48.

16. See the discussion of cultural practices in Dan Rodgers's introduction to this volume.

17. Luhmann, "Kultur als historischer Begriff," 41; see also Dirk Baecker, *Die Form der Kultur* (Berlin: Stadtlichter Presse, 2006).

18. Peter Brown, *Through the Eye of a Needle: Wealth, the Fall of Rome, and the Making of Christianity in the West, 350–550 AD* (Princeton: Princeton University Press, 2012).

19. German historians have been discussing the question of how to use Luhmann's concepts for some time; see, for instance, *Geschichte und Systemtheorie*, ed. Frank Becker (Frankfurt: Suhrkamp, 2004).

20. See Plutarch, *The Malice of Herodotus*, trans. Anthony J. Bowen (Warminster: Aris & Phillips, 1992); Augustinus, *De civitate Dei*, ed. Bernhart Dombart and Alphons Kalb, Corpus Christianorum 47–48 (Turnhout: Brepols 1955), esp. books xv–xviii.

21. See the contribution of Peter Brown in this volume.

Index

Page numbers in italics refer to figures.

Abzug, Bella, 242
Acharya, Sudha, 262–63
Adalgisel Grimo, 105
The Adventures of Simplicius Simplicis-simus the Vagabond (Grimmelshausen), 67–68
advertising: and aluminum industry, 166, 169, *170*, 174–78, *177*; and Singer sewing machine in Lanka, 147–52, 321n68; and tourism in the Caribbean, 178–88, *182*, *184*, *185*, *187*, *188*
Africa: dance tradition, 26, 27, 30, 32, 57; and International Women's Year (IWY) conference, 262; martial skills, 32; tradition of aesthetic dueling, 33
African Americans: black–Irish exchange of dance forms in antebellum America, 14, 23–59 (*see also* challenge dance); cake dances and cake walks, 33; challenge dancers (*see* Juba, Master); and circulation of dance steps, 43–52; compatibility of African and Irish dance traditions, 26; contrast between African and Irish dance styles, *28*; dance among slaves and free blacks in early America, 25, 27, 44, 47; differing dance styles of house slaves and field hands, 41; interracial trade in lower-class districts, 53–54, *54*; juba (*nzuba*) dance, 27, 292n19; patting juba, 30, *36*, 39, *42*, 44; set dances (Irish sets, jubas), 33, *34*, 35, *36*; shared traditions of African and Irish dancers, 26–33
Afro-Eurasian ecumene, 120–21, 124
Agarwal, Bina, 242
Ah Fock, 208–9
Ah Jake, 18, 197–214, 330n2; background of, 199, 332n6; conviction and sentencing of, 206, 210; hearing on murder charges, 200–202; imprisonment, 210–11, 336n55; legal representation of, 205–6; life following pardon, 212–13;

limited knowledge of English, 205; pardon and release from prison, 210–11; self-defense argument, 201, 205; shooting of Wah Chuck, 199; support from white community, 206–7, 210
Ah Ting, 199–201, 205–6, 211, 214
air power, and aluminum, 165, 168–73, 175–76
Alami, Shahnaz, 251–52
Albertus Magnus, 114, 116–19, 310n33
Alcan, 17, 172, 183, 191
alchemy: Arabic alchemical texts, 117–19; and basilisk powder, 115 (*see also* cinnabar); cinnabar and Chinese alchemy, 120, 125–27, 307n7; and lizards, 115–16, 119–20; medieval European theory of metals, 116–19; potential links between Chinese and Arabic alchemical theories, 126–27
Alcoa, 17; advertising campaigns, 169, *170*, 174, 178 (*see also* advertising); and Afobaka hydroelectric dam in Guyana, 193; breakup of, 176; design department, 178; development of alloys and sheet metal, 171, 180; expansion into the Caribbean, 171–73; FORE-CAST Jet, 191; and tourism in the Caribbean, 171, 178–91; transport and aviation, 172, 175–76
Alcoa Steamship Company, 178–81, 190; advertisements of, *188*
Alfred of Sarashel, 118
almsgiving. See gift-giving, charitable acts, and justice from late Antiquity to the early Middle Ages
aluminum, 17, 165–93; advertising and industrial design, 166, 169, *170*, 174–79, *177*; and aesthetics, 168, 175; and air power, 168–73, 175–76; and architecture, 165, *170*, 176; bauxite mining in the Caribbean, 15, 166, 172–73, 189–92, 326n25; character-

aluminum (*cont'd*)
  istics of extractive industry, 167,
  324n7; development of alloys and
  sheet metal, 171, 180; development of
  smelting process, 169, 171, 325n17;
  electricity used in production, 169, 193,
  325n17, 326n33; environmental impact
  of extractive industry in the Caribbean,
  167–68, 192–93, 329n72; lightness of,
  165, 168–69, 174–75, 325n14; military
  uses, 171–72, 175–76; and modernity,
  166–69, 173, 175–78; and packaging, 325n11; promotion and publicity,
  165–66, 173–76; as "speed metal," 169,
  173–76; technological change as the
  result of newly available materials, 169,
  325n12; and tourism in the Caribbean,
  167, 171, 178–91; and transportation
  industry, 165, 169, 174–77
Amarasuriya, Hemaka, *149*
amator patriae, 88–89
Ambrose, Saint, 92, 96, 100
American Notes for General Circulation
  (Dickens), 24
Amsterdam, and vermillion production,
  207n4
Anderson, Benedict, 12, 62
Anderson, Robert, 47
Anim-Addo, Anyaa, 180
annona civica, 91
anthropology, 1–2, 7
Appadurai, Arjun, 9
Applegate, Celia, 12, 16, 60–86, 219, 275
Arabic alchemical texts, 117–19, 126–27
Arcades Project (Benjamin), 169
Aristippus, Henry, 117
Aristotle, 117–18, 267
Armitage, David, 180
Artzybasheff, Boris, 181–82, *182*, *184*
astronomy, 127–28
Augustine, Saint, 92, 100
Austria, 270–71
Avicenna, 118

Bach, Johann Sebastian, 62, 71–73, 81
Bacon, Roger, 310n30
Bandaranaike, Sirimavo, 242
Bandung Conference (1955), 256, 264–65
Baopuzi (*The Master Embracing Simplic-
  ity*; Ge Hong), 125
Barnum, P.T., 24, 53
Barre, Siad, 257

Barrera-Osorio, Antonio, 130
Barrios de Chungara, Domitila, 242, 265;
  and Brito de Marti, 244; difficulties
  traveling to IWY conference, 243–
  44; expectations of, 260; experience
  of poverty and repression, 261–62;
  Friedan–Barrios de Chungara confrontation (apocryphal anecdote), 242–44,
  246; performance of subjectivity, 259;
  testimonio of, 244, 263–64, 349n15
Barth, Gunther, 331n5
basilisk powder, 115
Basil of Caesarea, Saint, 92
Batavia (now Jakarta): and Jacobus Bon-
  tius's work, 216; and translations of
  Chinese medical works, 229, 234–38
bauxite mining, 166–68, 172–73, 181,
  192–93, 329n72
Bayly, C. A., 123
Bebbington, Laurie, 256
Beckert, Sven, 15
Beer, Johann, 64, 68–70, 299nn 22, 27,
  and 28
Beethoven, Ludwig van, 80
Benda, Franz, 66
Benjamin, Walter, 164, 169
Bennett, Louise, 189
Berger, Mark T., 264
Berlin, music in, 81, 84
Bertrand, Bishop, 105
Bessemer, Henry, 123
Bhabha, Homi, 4, 7, 8, 10, 270
Bible, the, 95–96, 99, 100
bicycles, 160, 163
Bingham, James R., *187*, 187–88, *188*
Bin Wong, R., 219
Būrūnī, Muhammad ibn Ahmad, 313n65
Bischoff, G. F., 80
*Bitter Strength: A History of the Chinese in
  the US* (Barth), 331n5
Bizet, Georges, 62
Blacking, John, 85–86
Bleichmar, Daniela, 130
blood, 113–14
Bloom, Jonathan, 311n49
Bohn Aluminum and Brass Corporation,
  176–77
Bontius, Jacobus, 216
*Book of Curious and Entertaining Infor-
  mation* (Tha'ālibī), 122
Book of the Art (Cennino), 112
Bourne, Frederick Gilbert, 149

Bowes, Kim, 97
Bo wu zhi (*Comprehensive Record of Things*; Zhang Hua), 120
boxing, 56–57
Boym, Michel, 230, 232–34, 237, 239, 345n80
Brahms, Johannes, 16, 60
Bratton, J. S., 47
Braudel, Fernand, 267
breakdowns (dance form), 26, 35, 37
Breathnach, Brendán, 32
British Guiana, bauxite mining in, 172, 183, 184, 326n25
Brito de Martí, Esperanza, 244
Bronze Age, 122
Brown, Peter, 13, 14, 16, 87–106, 269, 275–76
Brown, T. Allston, 55
Bruce, Margaret, 251, 347n1
Buddhism, 104, 145, 153–56, 322n86
Burbank, Luther, 8
Burke, Roland, 265
Burke, Timothy, 136
Burkert, Günther, 272
Butler, Judith, 245
Byam, Wally, 175

Caldwell, James, 50
California Chinese Chatter (Dressler), 213–14
California gold fields, 18, 197–214. *See also* murder trial of Ah Jake
Canavarro, Mary de Souza, 155
Carby, Hazel, 25
Cárdernas, Nancy, 263
Caribbean: aluminum production and marketing, 17; bauxite mining, 166–68, 172–73, 181, 192–93, 329n72; depictions of Caribbean people in advertising, 181–86; drug and weapons trade, 192; folk dance and music, 186–89; impact of mining, 167–68, 192–93, 329n72; independence movements, 186, 189, 190; labor force, 15, 183–84, 328n56; material culture, 189; and modernity, 179, 181, 188–92; offshore banking, 192; perceived backwardness of, 166, 173, 188–89; suppression of labor unions and social movements during the Cold War, 167, 328n54; tourism, 17, 167, 171, 178–92
Carleton, William, 23–24, 26, 32, 35–36

Caroline, Queen, 23–24
Carrol, T. M., *45*
Castells, Manuel, 9
celibacy, 93–94
Cennini, Cennino d'Andrea, 112–14
Ceylon. *See* Lanka
Ceylon at the Census of 1911 (Denham), 135
challenge dance, 14, 16, 23–59, 268; *babhta rince* (session of step dance), 297n94; board/shingle used in, 39, 44; brag dancing described, 24; circulation of steps, 43–52; clothing and adornment of dancers, 29, 30, 32, 57–58; and communal identity and self-assertion, 32; connection between looks and moves, 57–58; famous rivals, 24–26, 43–59; genealogy in America, 33–36; and humor, 33; informal dance matches at social gatherings, 26, 27, 29; between men and women, 27, 29; *moinín* dance, 29, 29; musical accompaniment to dancing, 58; regional variations, 39–40; spectators, 48, 50–51; stage challenges, 26, 51–52, 55, 59; street challenges and market dancers, 36–43, 58; tavern matches, 52–59; as a trade, 38–43; types of steps, 35–36, 40–41, 44; venues, 24, 32, 33, 36–39, 43, 47, 51–59. *See also* Africa; Ireland
charitable acts. *See* gift-giving, charitable acts, and justice from late Antiquity to the early Middle Ages
Chatterjee, Partha, 13, 148, 162, 164
Chettiars, Nattukottai, 320n53
Chi'en, Evelyn, 214
Chile, 256, 263
China, 10; alchemy, 125–27; Chinese workers in California (*see* Chinese workers in California); and connection between lizards and red pigment, 120; European interest in China in the late 17th and 18th centuries, 225–27; failure of Singer sewing machine sales techniques, 139; imitation gold made in, 314n71; Jesuit missionaries in, 15, 18, 226, 229–35; long history of science in, 314n84; medical systems, 18, 123–24 (*see also* Chinese medicine in 17th-century Europe); movement of trade goods, knowledge, technologies and people, 121–27, 221; potential

China (*cont'd*)
links between Chinese and Arabic alchemical theories, 126–27; as region of
interconnected trading zones and ethnic
groups, 219; steelmaking technology,
123, 312n56
China Illustrata (Kircher), 233
*China Transformed: Historical Change and
the Limits of European Experience* (Bin
Wong), 219
Chinese medicine in 17th-century Europe,
215–40; and Boym's *Clavis Medica
ad Chinarum Doctrinam de Pulsibus*,
230–31; and Cleyer's *Specimen Medicinae Sinicae*, 227–29, 234–38; and
incommensurable worldviews, 217–18;
and Jesuit translators of Chinese
works, 229–35, 237–39; and relative
ease of transmission of different types
of knowledge, 217–18, 239–40; and
*Les secrets de la medicine des Chinois,
Consistent en le parfaite connoissance
du Pouls* (anonymous), 230; and
Wotton's *Reflections upon Ancient
and Modern Learning*, 227–28
Chinese workers in California, 18; ethno-
race relations, 197–98, 207, 210;
murder trial of Ah Jake, 197–214 (*see
also* murder trial of Ah Jake); origins in
China, 335n48; and perjured testimony,
211–12, 337n60; position in labor
force, 198, 209, 331n5; secret brotherhood societies, 198, 208, 335nn 41, 42,
and 44; tong wars, 212. *See also* pidgin
Chinglish, 197, 200–201, 205, 214,
337n71. *See also* pidgin
chocolate, 130–31
choral societies and festivals, 16, 78–85,
301n57
Christianity: and change in meaning of
wealth, 104–6; changes in gift-giving
and charity between late Antiquity and
the early Middle Ages, 16, 87–106,
275–76; Christian gifts and "treasures
in heaven," 97–101; church wealth
as patrimonies of the poor, 101–3;
discourse of the rich and the poor,
87, 91–93; diverse social constituency
of Christian communities, 97–98;
and domesticity and respectability in
Lanka, 163; markers fostered (virginity, celibacy, etc.), 93–94; meanings

of blood, 113–14; nonreciprocal gift-
giving advocated, 93–95; "pastoral"
power, 89–90; and the poor as seekers
of justice, 95–96, 103; sacred relics, 12;
and separation of church and state, 90;
suspicion of music, 299n26
Churchill, Winston, 175
cinnabar, 109, 125, 127, 310n33, 314n77
circuses, and circulation of dance steps,
44, 46
Clark, Edward, 138, 143
*Clavis Medica ad Chinarum Doctrinam
de Pulsibus* (Boym), 220–32, 234, 239,
346n95
Cleyer, Andreas, 227–29, 234–38, 346n95
Clifford, James, 2, 61
clothing: of dancers, 29, 30, 32, 37, 48, 48,
57–58; dyes, 128–29, 307n2; and sewing machines in Lanka, 158–60, 161
cochineal beetle, 109, 128, 307n3,
316n113
Cohn, Leonard, 142
Cold War, 167, 328n54
Colombo, Sri Lanka, 140–42, 147, 155–57
Colonial Botany (Schiebinger and Swan),
130
colonialism, 7; "civilizing" mission, 148–
52, 162–63; consumption-production
dichotomy between colonizer and colonized, 134; science in colonial India,
315n103. *See also* Caribbean; Singer
sewing machine
community, changing models of, 87, 90–93
competition. *See* challenge dance; choral
societies and festivals
Compton, Harry, 40
Confucius, 226, 231, 235
Confucius Sinarum Philosophus, 226, 235
consumption: and market imaginary, 137;
modernity as desire for consumption of
modern commodities, 136; and sewing
machines in Lanka (*see* Singer sewing
machine); and Sinhalese nationalism,
152–53; teaching colonial inhabitants
to become modern consuming subjects,
136; in Zimbabwe, 136
Cook, Harold, 18, 130, 215–40, 275
Cooper, Frederick, 9
Copernicus, Nicholas, 128
cotton production, 15
Couplet, R. P. Philippe, 230, 232, 234–35,
237

creole cultures, 6, 7, 8, 337n70
Cresswell, Tim, 324n2, 328n60
Crosby, Alfred, 10
Cuba, 257
cultural friction, 10–14, 274. *See also* challenge dance; International Women's Year (IWY) conference; murder trial of Ah Jake
cultural practices: circulation of (*see* challenge dance; gift-giving, charitable acts, and justice from late Antiquity to the early Middle Ages; knowledge, transmission of; musical itinerancy and nation making); contingency of the concept of culture, 274–75; disembeddings and displacements, 12; examples, 11; fields of contest and collision, 13–14; first-order and second-order observations (Luhmann's conception), 272–77; "flow" of cultural materials and practices, 8–11, 120–24, 275; and interest in comparisons, 273–74; *Kulturpolitikskultur*, 270–71; objects in motion (*see* objects in motion); and power, 9, 13, 15, 16, 267–69; routes and itineraries, 12–13, 17, 267–69; study of cultural practices replacing study of place-rooted cultures, 11; translations and misunderstandings, 14–15 (*see also* Chinese medicine in 17th-century Europe; International Women's Year (IWY) conference; murder trial of Ah Jake)

Der Dacianische Simplicissimus (Speer), 69
dance, 14, 16; in Africa, 27, 30, 32, 57; *babhta rince* (session of step dance), 297n94; black–Irish exchange of dance forms in antebellum America, 23–59 (*see also* challenge dance); breakdowns, 26, 35, 37; cake dances, 33; in the Caribbean, 186–89; circulation of steps, 43–52; clothing and adornment of dancers, 29, 30, 32, 37, 48, 48, 57–58; commercial acts, 44–52, 55; compatibility of African and Irish dance traditions, 26; connection with boxing, 56–57; contrast between African and Irish dance styles, 27, 28; dancing for eels, 26, 41–43; dancing masters, 30, 32, 40; English dancers, 37; hornpipes, 35, 42, 44, 47–48, 48; in Ireland, 27,

29, 29, 30, 32, 33, 57; jigs (*see* jigs); juba (*nzuba*), 27, 292n19; and martial skills, 32; *moínín* dance, 29, 29; musical accompaniment, 30, 31, 58; percussive footwork, 30, 31, 35; reels, 35; screwpin dance, 23–24; *sean nós* dancing, 30, 41; set dances (Irish sets, jubas), 33, 34, 35; shared traditions of African and Irish dancers, 26–33; the shimmy, 328n60; shindigs, 32; spectators, 48, 50–51; types of steps, 35–36, 40–41
Danckert, Werner, 298n13
Dann, Otto, 76
Davies, Robert, 139, 145
Deadwood (television show), 333n22
de Alwis, Malathi, 162
de Certeau, Michel, 148
Declaration of Mexico, 249
Declaration on International Women's Year, 252
Dee, John, 129–30
de Grazia, Victoria, 13
de Haan, Francisca, 252
de Menonille, Nicolas-Joseph Thiéry, 128
Denham, E. B., 135, 136, 148
dental fillings, 312n56
de Osma, Pedro, 129–30
Depestre, René, 134, 160
de Seversky, Alexander, 175–76
de Silva, John, 153
De Voe, Thomas, 38, 39
Dharmapala, Anagarika, 155–56, 322n86
Diamond, John (Jack), 24–25, 43–44, 46, 48, 50–59, 296n89
Dickens, Charles, 24, 36, 53
disembeddings and displacements, 12
Dolaphillai, U. B., 156
Domosh, Mona, 148–50
Doordan, Dennis, 177–78
Downing, Thomas, 53
Drayton, Richard, 129
Dressler, Albert, 213–14
Duara, Prasenjit, 63
Dubois, Sylvia, 40–41
Dutch commerce, 130
Dutch East India Company (VOC), 216, 234–36
Dutch Golden Age, 215–16

Eiriksson, Thorstein, 106
Ellingham, Robert, 55
Elman, Benjamin, 314n84

An Embassy from the East India Company of the United Provinces to the Grand Tartar Cham Emperor of China (Nieuhof), 225
empire, 3–5, 7, 13
Ernst, Duke Johann of Weimar, 72
Europe: general interest in China in the late 17th and 18th centuries, 225–27; Jesuit missionaries in China, 9, 18, 226, 229–35, 237–39, 343n52; and the New World, 268; production of red pigments, 109–19; trade with India and China, 12, 219; views of disease, 123–24, 223–24. *See also* Chinese medicine in 17th-century Europe; gift-giving, charitable acts, and justice from late Antiquity to the early Middle Ages; musical itinerancy and nation making
Experiencing Nature (Barrera-Osorio), 130
The Expressiveness of the Body and the Divergence of Greek and Chinese Medicine (Kuriyama), 218
An Eye for the Tropics (Thompson), 181

Fasch, Carl Friedrich, 81
feminism, transnational, 18–19, 242–66; and role of states in social transformation, 256–57. *See also* International Women's Year (IWY) conference
Ferguson, James, 2
Ferguson's Directories (list of enterprises in Lanka), 158–60
Fernel, Jean, 223
Feyerabend, Paul, 217
Finn, Richard, 93
first-order and second-order observations (Luhmann's conception), 272–77
"flow," cultural, 8–11, 120–24, 275
Floyer, Sir John, 220–29; background of, 221–22; on Chinese philosophy, 226–27; and Cleyer's *Specimen Medicinae Sinicae*, 227–29, 234–38; defense of Chinese medicine, 227–29; *Physicians' Pulse-Watch*, 225, 229; pulse-counting method of diagnosis, 221–24, 239; pulse-watch innovation, 222–23; quest for information about Chinese methods of taking the pulse, 222, 225–29, 239; and Wotton's *Reflections upon Ancient and Modern Learning*, 227–28, 238
food crops, 121
Foster, George, 26

Foucault, Michel, 89, 105
France, musical culture, 71, 301n57
Frank, Andre Gunder, 219
Frankfurt, music in, 71
French Guiana, 193
Freu, Christel, 93
friction. *See* cultural friction
Friedan, Betty, 242, 256, 261–64; Friedan–Barrios de Chungara confrontation (apocryphal anecdote), 242–44, 246
From the Earth to the Moon (Verne), 170–71
Fuller, R. Buckminster, 175
functionalist social theory, 6
Futurist Manifesto (Marinetti), 174

Galen, 223, 225
Gamperaliya (*The Changing Village*; Wickramasinghe), 152
Gandhi, Indira, 255–56
Gaul, 88–89, 103
Geber. *See* ibn Hayyan, Jābir
Geddes, Norman Bel, 175
Geertz, Clifford, 2
Ge Hong, 125
Gerken, Peter, 65
German Winter Nights (Beer), 64
Germany, 81; and Austrian identity, 270–71; choral societies and festivals, 16, 78–85; German historiography of the 1990s, 9–10; musical itinerancy and nation making, 16, 60–86, 275, 302n69 (*see also* musical itinerancy and nation making); musician-authors, 67–70, 74–78
Gesellschaftsstruktur und Semantik (Luhmann), 272–73
Gienow-Hecht, Jessica, 302n69
gift-giving, charitable acts, and justice from late Antiquity to the early Middle Ages, 16, 87–106, 269, 275–76; change in meaning of wealth, 104–6; change in motivation of givers, 97–101; Christian discourse on the poor, 87, 91–93; and Hebrew Scriptures, 95–96; nonreciprocal gift-giving advocated by Christian teachings, 93–95; and "pastoral" power, 89–90; the poor as seekers of justice, not beggars, 95–96, 103; and second-order observations (Luhmann's conception), 275–76; shift from citizen/noncitizen distinction to rich/poor

distinction, 87–93; "treasures in heaven," 97–101, 105; "upward slippage" of image of the poor, 96, 97
Giroud, Françoise, 245
globalization, 5, 8–9
goat blood, recipes using, 113–14
gold: and alchemy, 115–16; gold pigments, 114; imitation gold made in China, 314n71
Goodyears Bar, California. *See* murder trial of Ah Jake
Goonesekere, P. F., 152
Gordon, Andrew, 139
Graham, Margaret, 171, 325n19
Great Britain: choral performances, 78–80; hornpipes as English dances, 35, 44. *See also* Floyer, Sir John
The Great Divergence: China, Europe, and the Making of the Modern World Economy (Pomeranz), 219
Great Lakes region, study of, 6–7
Greenland, Christian influence in, 106
Greer, Germaine, 241
Gregory the Great, 96
Gresset, Jean-Baptiste-Louis, 301n53
Grimmelshausen, Hans Jakob von, 67–68
Grosz, Elizabeth, 255
Group of 77 (G77), 249
Grundlage einer Ehrenpforte (Mattheson), 77
Gupta, Akhil, 2
Guterl, Matthew, 331n5
Guyana, 186, 190, 191, 193

Hachez-Leroy, Florence, 165–66
Hall, Charles Martin, 169, 171
Halleux, Robert, 117, 126
Halm, Friedrich, 60
Hamburg, music in, 71, 76
Handel, George Frideric, 78–79
Handler, Philip, 257
Harootunian, Harry, 153
Harrington, Bill "Liverhead," 56
Harris, Rosalind, 251
Hart, Richard, 328n54
Hartling, Henry, 334n39
Hartwell, Robert, 121
Harvey, David, 8–9
Harvey, William, 222, 224
Haspel-Hanss (Speer), 69
Hassler, Hans Leo, 300n37
Hässler, J. W., 74

Hatton, Charles, 228
Haydn, Franz Joseph, 79, 80, 301n58
health and medicine, 18; Chinese system, 18, 123–24 (*see also* Chinese medicine in 17th-century Europe); and chocolate, 131; differences between Chinese and Greek systems, 218, 339n8; European system, 114, 123–24, 223–24; and Jesuit translators of Chinese works, 343n52; materia medica texts, 125–27
Hemmings, Clare, 349n16
Herodotus, 277
Of Heroic Virtue (Temple), 227
Héroult, Paul Louis-Toussaint, 169, 171
Higgins, Mary Musaeus, 155
Hiller, Johann Adam, 79, 81
histoire croisée, 10, 219
history, changing study of, 1–19; cultures in motion in time as well as space, 271; disembeddings and displacements, 12; emphasis on cultural practices, not place-rooted cultures, 11; fields of contest and collision, 13–14; first-order and second-order observations (Luhmann's conception), 272–77; generativity of collisions, 13–14; German historiography of the 1990s, 9–10; global histories, 219–20, 239–40; itinerancy and power, 267–69; older analytical language, 6–11; power and structures, 15; routes and itineraries, 12–13; *Transfergeschichte*, 9–10; translations and misunderstandings, 14–15; Wallerstein's "world-system" approach, 219. *See also* cultural practices
Hodgson, Marshall, 120
Holst, Harry, 148
hornpipes, 35, 42, 44, 47–48, 48
Hortschansky, Klaus, 73–74
Howe, A. J., 205–6
Howe, Elias, Jr., 138
Howland, Douglas, 14
Hutar, Patricia, 248, 261
hybridity, 6, 7–8, 11, 274

ibn al-Birīq, Yahyā, 118
ibn Hayyan, Jābir, 118, 126, 310n29
ibn Shahriyar, Buzurg, 124
ibn Sīnā, Abū ʿAlī al-Husayn, 118
ice trade, 154
Imperio de la China (Semedo), 342n39
Incas, 128

India: European trade with, 12, 219; gemstones, 124, 312n61; home-rule movement, 13; and International Women's
Year (IWY) conference, 255–56; lack of
enthusiasm for Singer sewing machines,
139, 142, 144–45; red dye, 307n2;
science in colonial India, 315n103; as
source of "wonders," 124, 313nn 61,
65; steelmaking technology, 312n56
Indonesia, 121
International Women's Year (IWY) conference (Mexico City, 1975), 18–19, 242–
66; alliances, 255, 352n45; as contact
zone, 243, 266; and core issues vs.
political distractions, 253, 264; and the
Declaration of Mexico, 245–46, 249;
diverse expectations for NGO tribune,
250–51; divisions among participants,
242–43, 245–46, 249–50, 253, 257–58,
261–66, 349nn 8, 11 (see also specific
issues under this heading); and equality
and sexual difference, 253; expansion
of NGO tribune, 250–51; and family planning and population control,
257–58; fragmenting of issues, 252–53,
257–58, 263–65; Friedan–Barrios de
Chungara confrontation (apocryphal
anecdote), 242–44, 246; genesis of,
248–49; goals of, 246; hopes for consensus and unity, 244–45, 264; and lesbians, 263–64; and literacy programs,
253; media depictions of clashes, 246;
organization and agenda-setting, 249–
52; outcome and consequences, 246,
253–54, 264; parallel NGO tribune,
241–42, 249–52, 260–61; participants'
expectations, 260–61, 347n1; participants' frustrated aspirations for identification and recognition from other
participants, 262–65; and participants'
performance of political identities and
womanhood, 259–66; planning of,
261, 350n35; and power relations,
243; prominent participants, 242, 260;
and representation issues, 260–62;
and reproductive labor, 253, 258; and
role of states in social transformation,
256–57; role of temporality in imagining IWY as an event, 254–59; selection
of location, 258, 353n58; social life at
IWY gatherings, 260–61, 351n37; and
solidarity and unity implying exclusion
and reification, 245; structure of, 249;
and structures of conjuncture, 249,
252, 254; UN financial commitment to,
252, 350n36; as watershed in transnational women's activism, 247–54; and
world events and domestic events in
participants' home countries, 255–56;
and World Plan of Action, 245, 249,
252; and Zionism, 255. See also Barrios
de Chungara, Domitila; Friedan, Betty
Intorcetta, Prospero, 233–34
Ireland: dance tradition, 27, 29, 29, 30, 32,
33, 57; emigration from, 25; martial
skills, 32; tradition of aesthetic dueling,
33
Irish Americans: black–Irish exchange of
dance forms in antebellum America,
14, 23–59 (see also challenge dance);
challenge dancers (see Diamond, John);
and circulation of dance steps, 43–52;
compatibility of African and Irish dance
traditions, 26; contrast between African
and Irish dance styles, 27, 28; dancing
on a board or shingle, 39, 44; interracial trade in lower-class districts, 53–54,
54; patting juba, 44; shared traditions
of African and Irish dancers, 26–33
Iriye, Akira, 63
Isaiah, Prophet, 96
Israel, 253, 255, 256
Italy, musical culture, 71, 72
Iwanaga Sōko, 216
IWY. See International Women's Year
(IWY) conference

Jagan, Cheddi, 183, 186
Jamaica: bauxite mining, 172, 189–90,
192, 326n25, 328n56; independence,
186, 189, 190; John Canoe dancers,
187, 188; labor movement, 184; tourism, 181
Japan: imagined Japan as Asian beacon,
153–56; and modernity, 155–56; movement of trade goods, 121
Jerome, Saint, 96
Jesuit missionaries, 9, 15, 18, 226, 229–35,
237–39, 343n52
Jiagge, Annie, 262
jigs: as Irish dances, 35, 44; jig-dance
competitions, 24, 27, 29 (see also challenge dance); moínín dance, 29, 29;
Negro jigging, 25; origins, 25, 29; and
set dances, 35
John Chrysostom, Saint, 92

Johnson, Samuel, 222
Jones, Hugo, 97–98
juba (*nzuba*), 27, 292n19; patting juba, 30, 36, 39, 42
Juba, Master (William Henry Lane; Boz's Juba), 24–25, 37, 43, 45, 52–59
Judaism, 16, 94–96, 99
justice: murder trial of Ah Jake, 197–214; pardons in California, 336nn 57–60; the poor as seekers of justice, not beggars, 95–96, 103

Kaiser Aluminum, 175, 176, 178, 326n25
Kaplan, Caren, 175
Keating, B. J., 141
Kellman, Jordan, 316n113
Kelly, William, 123
Kerman, Joseph, 70
kermes beetle, 109, 307nn 2, 3
kinêsis, 267, 269
Kipling, Rudyard, 7, 10
Kircher, Athanasius, 225, 231, 233
Kirkbride, Charles, 206
Kissinger, Henry, 257, 352n45
Kitāb al-Ahjār (*Book of Stones*), 118
Kitab'ajayib al-Hind (*The Wonders of India*; ibn Sahariyar), 124
Kitab al-Shifā (*Book of the Remedy*), 118
knowledge, transmission of: flow of goods, knowledge, texts, etc. across the Afro-Eurasian ecumene, 120–24; and incommensurable worldviews, 217–18; and the New World, 128–31; relative ease (degree of "stickiness") of transmission of different types of knowledge, 12, 217–18, 220, 239–40, 275–76. *See also* Chinese medicine in 17th-century Europe
Ko, Dorothy, 120
Koselleck, Reinhart, 77
Kuhn, Thomas, 217
Kuhnau, Johann, 68, 70, 74–76
Kulturpolitikskultur, 270–71
Kuriyama, Shigehisa, 218

labor force, 12–13, 15; and bauxite mines in the Caribbean, 15, 167, 183–84, 328n56; and the Chinese in California, 197–98, 208–9, 331n5; and International Women's Year (IWY) conference, 253, 258; tailors and seamstresses in Lanka, 158–60
lac beetle, 307n2

Lactantius, 94
Lafontant, Jewel, 261
Lambert, David, 180
La Mothe le Vayer, François, 226
Lane, William Henry. *See* Juba, Master
language: Jesuit translations of Chinese works, 229–35, 237–39; pidgin and the murder trial of Ah Jake, 197–214; trading languages and pidgins, 14, 198, 203, 204
Lanka (Sri Lanka): and clothing, 161; consumers and users of sewing machines, 156–58; cultural characteristics, 145; ethnic and gender distribution of tailors and seamstresses, 158–60; and the imagined America and Japan as Asian beacons, 153–56; literacy in, 147, 320n64; media in, 147–53; and modernity, 136, 137, 150, 152–56, 162–64, 268–69; and nationalism, 137, 152–53, 164; perceptions of the U.S., 154–55; Singer sewing machines in, 12, 17, 134–37 (*see also* Singer sewing machine); trade with U.S., 154
Larison, C. W., 40
Latin America. *See* International Women's Year (IWY) conference
Laufer, Berthold, 313n66
Lee, Christopher, 264
Leipzig, music in, 71–72, 75, 79, 80, 81
Leontius, Bishop, 90
Leo the Great, 96, 100–101
lesbians, 263–64
Lester, Alan, 180
Let Me Speak! (Barrios de Chungara), 262, 349n15
le Vayer, François La Mothe, 226
Liedertafeln, 81–83
Lindbergh, Charles, 172
literacy, 147–48, 253, 320n64
lizards, 115–16, 119–20, 127, 309n21
Lloyd, Geoffrey, 217
Lo Kay, 200, 202, 204, 205, 208, 334n39
London, 13
Long Island, and black–Irish exchange of dance forms in antebellum America, 38–43
Lowe, "Uncle Jim," 43
Lower Rhine Festival, 80–81
Ludowyk, E. F. C., 160
Luhmann, Niklas, 19, 272–77
Luther, Martin, 299n26
Lu Xun, 213

Maathai, Wangari, 254
MacDermot, Niall, 251
Mackenzie, Shelton, 39
Maha Bodhi Society, 155, 320n64, 322n86
Maha Wiyawula (*The Great Confusion*; Sirisena), 161
Mahomet (black dancer), 23–24, 26
Manley, Michael, 191–92
Manley, Norman Washington, 189, 192
Mappa clavicula (*A Small Key of Handiwork*), 117
MacQueen, S., 141
Marcos, Imelda, 260
Marinetti, F. T., 174
market imaginary, 137, 152–53
Marks, Master (T. M. Carroll), 45
Maroons, 193
Masao, Maruyama, 155
Mason, John, 213
Masten, April F., 14, 16, 23–59
Ma Thi Chu, 256
Matters of Exchange: Commerce, Medicine, and Science in the Dutch Golden Age (Cook), 130
Mattheson, Johann, 72–73, 76–78, 300nn 50, 51
M'Cann, Bob, 23, 26
McKenzie, George Ross, 139
media: and International Women's Year (IWY) conference, 246; and Singer sewing machine in Lanka, 147–53. *See also* advertising
medicine. *See* Chinese medicine in 17th-century Europe; health and medicine
Mellett, Coleman, 63–64
men: men's choruses, 81–84; as retailers and buyers of sewing machines, 151; tailors, 158–60. *See also* challenge dance; Chinese workers in California; musical itinerancy and nation making
Mendelssohn, Felix, 79
mercury, 109–14, 116–19, 124–26, 307n7, 310n33, 312n56, 314n77
Meroux, Adolph, 202
Meteorologica (Aristotle), 117–18
métissage, 6, 8
Mexico City, international women's year gathering. *See* International Women's Year (IWY) conference
microfinance development programs, 254, 265
middle ground concept, 6–7, 10, 274

Miles, Joe, 57
Millard, Jerome, 205
Miller, Francesca, 242
Millett, Kate, 260
mimicry, 7, 14
minstrel shows, 25
Mintz, Sidney, 134, 168
mirrors, 126, 129, 130
missionaries. *See* Jesuit missionaries
Mitchell, John, 144, 146
mobility: and Aristotle's *kinêsis*, 267, 269; Cresswell's description, 324n2. *See also* knowledge, transmission of; objects in motion
modernity: and aluminum industry, 166–67, 169, 173, 175–78; and the Caribbean, 179, 181, 188–92; and Lanka, 136, 137, 150, 152–56, 162–64, 268–69. *See also* aluminum; Singer sewing machine
moínín dance, 29, 29
Mojekwu, Victoria, 262
Molyneaux, Tom, 57
mortar, waterproof, 315n94
Mo Tsing (*Treatise of the Pulses*; Wang Chou Houo), 236
Mount, William Sydney, 39, 40
Mozart, Wolfgang Amadeus, 62
Mukerji, Chandra, 315n94
murder trial of Ah Jake, 197–214; Ah Jake pardoned and released, 210–11; Ah Jake's self-defense argument, 201, 205; California code on premeditated murder, 206, 334n29; conviction and sentencing of Ah Jake, 206, 210; hearing on murder charges, 200–202; and perjured testimony, 211–12
music: in the Caribbean, 186–89; choral festivals, 16, 78–85, 301n57; in Europe (*see* musical itinerancy and nation making); history of music profession, 64–67; musical culture, 71; in the U.S. (*see* challenge dance)
musical itinerancy and nation making, 12, 16, 60–86, 275, 302n69; choral societies and nation building in the 19th century, 16, 78–85; court, church, and town employment, 64–66, 70–74; development of public performances, 74, 75; development of writings about music, 74–78; hard vs. soft national boundaries, 63; itinerancy as persistent

feature of musical life, 16, 60–61; and
musician-authors, 64, 67–70, 72–76,
299n22; musicians' guilds, 65; reputa-
tions of musicians, 16, 64, 66, 73; and
second-order observations (Luhmann's
conception), 275; and suspicion of music, 69, 299n26; transmission of knowledge, styles, and genres, 62, 66; trend
toward musical marketplace, 73–74
A Musician's Life (Weber), 8
Der musikalische Quacksalber (Kuhnau),
74–76
Musil, Robert, 270–71
Mussolini, Arnaldo, 168
Muybridge, Eadweard, 171
*The Mysterious Teachings on the Alchemi-
cal Preparation of Numinous Cinnabar*,
125

Nägeli, Hans Georg, 302n65
nationalism: Caribbean independence
movements, 186, 189, 190; German
nationalism (*see* musical itinerancy and
nation making); Sinhalese nationalism,
137, 152–53, 164
National Organization for Women (NOW),
256
Nelson, Diane, 243
networks, 9, 10, 11
Das neu-eröffnete Orchestre (Mattheson),
76
New York City: black–Irish exchange of
dance forms in antebellum America, 14,
16, 38–43; and International Women's
Year (IWY) conference, 250–52; sky-
scrapers, 165
Ngai, Mae, 14, 15, 18, 197–214
NGOs. *See* International Women's Year
(IWY) conference
Nieuhof, Jan, 225
Niewood, Gerry, 63–64
Nolan, Mary, 13
Norton, Marcy, 130
NOW. *See* National Organization for
Women
Nye, David, 174

objects in motion: chocolate, 130–31;
exchanges of technologies and people,
121–22; and first- and second-order
observations (Luhmann's conception),
275; food crops, 121; itineraries of

matter, practices, and ideas, 131–33;
and literature on "wonders," 124; and
meanings of practices and objects,
131–32; medical systems, 123–24 (*see
also* Chinese medicine in 17th-century
Europe); and the New World, 128–31;
and pigment making, 109–20, 125–28;
trade goods (rarities and staple goods),
121–22; weapons technology, 120–21.
See also alchemy; aluminum; Singer
sewing machine
obsidian, 129
Ojeda Paullada, Pedro, 261
Okoth-Ogendo, Opinya, 262
Olcott, Colonel, 153–55
Olcott, Jocelyn, 15, 18–19, 242–66
Old Testament, 95–96

Pahlavi, Princess Ashraf, 241, 252, 259,
260
painting, 112–13
Palladius of Autun, 105
paper making, 122, 311n49
Paris, 13, 80
Parker, Daniel, 257
Parsee community, and Singer Corpora-
tion, 143–44, 319n43
"pastoral" power, 89–90
Patell, Nusserwanjee Merwanjee, 140,
142–46, *143*
Patlagean, Evelyne, 92
Paul, Rodman, 331n5
Paul II, Pope, 128
Paulinus of Pant-y-Polion, 88–89, 102
Payne, Ethel, 264
Pekstok, Willem, 110, 207n4
Pelham, R. W., 51–52
Pennybacker, Susan, 13
Perón, Isabel, 255–56
Persinger, Mildred, 250, 265, 266
Pertchik, Harriet and Bernard, *185*
Philadelphia, and black–Irish exchange of
dance forms in antebellum America,
38–43
philosopher's stone, 119
Physicians' Pulse-Watch (Floyer), 222–23,
225, 228–29
pidgin, 197–214, 337n70; characteristics of
Chinese Pidgin English, 203; character-
istics of pidgin used in California, 203–
4; as contact language, 197, 333n18;
Dressler's *California Chinese Chatter*,

pidgin (cont'd)
213–14; and hearing on murder charges against Ah Jake, 200–204; pidgin in colonial trading ports of China, 198, 203, 204; stereotyped pidgin, 213
Pieterz, Francis, 159–60
pigment making, 109–20, 125–28, 275. *See also* red pigments; vermillion
Plants and Empire (Schiebinger), 130
Plutarch, 277
Der Politische Bratenwender (Beer), 68
Politische Näscher (Weise), 68
Pomeranz, Kenneth, 219
Pomerius, Julianus, 101
poor, the: church wealth as patrimonies of the poor, 101–3; gift-giving, charitable acts, and justice from late Antiquity to the early Middle Ages, 87–106; nonreciprocal gift-giving to advocated, 93–95; the poor as seekers of justice, not beggars, 95–96, 103; shift from citizen/noncitizen distinction to rich/poor distinction, 87–93
Porphyrius of Lepcis Magna, 88–91, 99, 104
power, 9, 13, 15; and International Women's Year (IWY) conference, 243; itinerancy and power, 267–69; "pastoral" power, 16, 89–90
Praetorius, Johann Philipp, 78
Prashad, Vijay, 265
Price, Richard, 193
Printz, Wolfgang Caspar, 68, 70, 229n28
Private Worship, Public Values and Religious Change in Late Antiquity (Bowes), 97
pulse, 18; Chinese practice of feeling the *mo*, 218; and differences between Chinese and Greek medical systems, 218; Floyer's investigations and ideas, 220–29, 239; pulse-taking in European medicine, 223–25; pulse-watch innovation, 222–23
Pulse-Watch. See Physicians' Pulse-Watch

Rabin, Leah, 253, 260
Radebaugh, Arthur, 176–77
Ragep, Jamil, 127, 315n96
Raman, Bhavani, 19, 267–69
Raymond, Rossiter, 209–10
Raynor, Henry, 65

al-Rāzī, Abū Bakr, 118, 126, 310n29
Rechter Gebrauch der Alchimei, 115
red pigments, 109–20, 125–28, 275, 307n2; association with blood and regeneration, 112–13; dye and the New World, 128–29; and gold pigments, 114; recipes/sources of, 109–12, 120, 307nn4 7, 316n113. *See also* vermillion
reels, 35
Reflections upon Ancient and Modern Learning (Wotton), 227–28, 238
Reichardt, Johann Friedrich, 74
Reimitz, Helmut, 19, 270–78
Relations de divers voyages curieux (Thévenot), 226
religion, 6, 11. *See also* Buddhism; Christianity; Judaism
ReOrient: Global Economy in the Asian Age (Frank), 219
Reynolds Metals, 173, 175, 176, 178, 326n25
Rhazes. *See* al-Rāzī, Abū Bakr
rich, the. *See* wealthy, the
Richmond, Bill, 57
The Rise of the Network Society (Castells), 9
Rodgers, Daniel T., 1–19, 271
Roger II of Sicily, 122
Rome, Roman society, 88–89, 91, 92, 94, 96
Roosevelt, Franklin, 175
Rostow, W. W., 166–67, 192
Rousseau, Philip, 97
Ryan, F. D., 211, 212

Sadat, Jehan, 241, 260
Sahlins, Marshall, 248
sailors, 13, 23, 24, 35, 50, 121, 124
Saliba, George, 127, 315n96
Sang, Edward, 144
Santos, Boaventura de Sousa, 243
Sapientia Sinica, 226, 233
Saragon, Katalina, 110, 307n4
Sartori, Andrew, 274
Schiebinger, Londa, 130
Schlessinger, Bert, 205–6
Schreck, Johann, 232
Schumann, Clara, 60
Schwartz, Seth, 94

science: and colonial India, 315n103; and creative misunderstandings, 14; and Dutch Golden Age, 215–16; exchanges between East Asian and European scholars, 221 (*see also* Chinese medicine in 17th-century Europe); incommensurable worldviews, 217–18; and itineraries of matter, practices, and ideas, 10, 109–33; long history in China, 314n84; vernacular science of matter and transformation, 116–19. *See also* alchemy; aluminum; health and medicine; red pigments

Scott, Joan, 349n11

screw-pin dance, 23–24

"scrying" glass, 129

sean nós dancing, 30, 41

second-order observations (Luhmann's conception), 272–77

Les secrets de la medecine des Chinois, Consistent en le parfaite connoissance du Pouls (anonymous), 230, 235

Der seltsame Springinsfeld (Grimmelshausen), 68

Semedo, Alvarez, 225, 233, 342n39

Sewell, Sandra Serrano, 262

Sewell, William, 15, 247, 260, 272

sewing machine. *See* Singer sewing machine

Sheehan, James, 67

Sheller, Mimi, 15, 17, 165–93

Shiming (Explanation of Names), 120

shindig, word origin, 32

Shōadyū Motogi, 216

"Signs Taken for Wonders" (Bhabha), 7

Silk Road, 123, 220

Der simplicianische Welt-Kucker oder abentheuerliche Jan Rebbu (Beer), 69

Sinarum scientia politico-moralis, 226, 233

Singakademie, Berlin, 81, 84

Singer, Isaac M., 138

Singer sewing machine, 12, 17, 134–64; Asian market for, 139–40; canvasser-collector sales system, 139, 144, 150–51; and circuits of communication (advertising, newspapers, trade cards, etc.), 137, 147–52; and "civilizing" mission, 148–52, 162–63; and clothing, 161; consumers and users, 156–58, 268–69; and cultural characteristics of Lankans, 145; development of, 138; diffusion in Lanka, 141–42; effect of climate on stocks, 145; introduction into Lanka, 140–41; main competitors, 138, 151–52; and market imaginary, 137, 152–53; market share and global spread, 137–39; and men as retailers and buyers, 151; and modernity, 136, 163–64, 268–69; and nationalism, 137, 152–53; and Parsee community, 143–44; paucity of data, 135–36; place of machine in the home, 161; and related skills (repair, recycling), 160; sales strategies in Lanka, 142–46; sales techniques and failure in China and India, 139, 144–45; tailors and seamstresses, 158–60; teaching colonial inhabitants to become modern consuming subjects, 136; unpopularity in India and China, 139, 142, 144–45; and women, 151, 160–64

singing groups. *See* choral societies and festivals

Sinhala Parabhavaya Natakaya (de Silva), 153

Sipila, Helvi, 261

Sirisena, Piyadasa, 161

Skwiot, Christine, 331n5

skyscrapers, 165, 170, 176

Smith, Bonnie, 348n2

Smith, Pamela, 17, 109–33, 275–76

Snider, Bartoldt, 65

Snyder, Margaret, 262

Solnit, Rebecca, 171

Somalia, 257

Soward, F. D., 206, 207, 211

Specimen Medicinae Sinicae, sive Opuscula Medica ad Mentem Sinensium (Cleyer), 227–29, 234–38, 346n95

Speer, Daniel, 68

Spirit of St. Louis, 172

Spivak, Gayatri, 262

Spohr, Louis, 80

Sri Lanka. *See* Lanka

The Stages of Economic Growth (Rostow), 166–67

Stanford, Leland, 171

steel manufacturing, 123, 312n56

Steinem, Gloria, 260

Stephenson, Carolyn, 242–43

Stewart, S. C., 201, 206–7

Stoler, Ann Laura, 137

Stout, William Bushnell, 175
Subrahmanyam, Sanjay, 2, 12, 219
sulfur, 109–14, 116–19, 124, 126, 307n7
Suriname, 171, 172, 193
Swan, Claudia, 130
Sweeny, Joel Walker, 31, 46–47

tailors and seamstresses, 158–60
taverns: challenge dancing, 24, 52–59;
    interracial trade in lower-class districts,
    53, 54, 54; Pete William's dance house,
    24, 34, 43, 53, 55–58
Taylor, Diana, 259
Telemann, Georg Philipp, 66
Temple, Sir William, 227
ten Rhijne, Willem, 216, 218, 235–37,
    346n95
Tereshkova, Valentina, 241, 253, 257
Terrentius, Johann Schreck, 232
Tha'ālibī, 122, 235, 311n49
theaters: and challenge dancing, 51–52,
    55, 59; and circulation of dance steps,
    44, 47, 50; and nationalizing culture,
    74
Theophilus, 115
Thévenot, Melchisédec, 226
Thimonier, Barthélemy, 138
Thomas, James, 44
Thompson, Krista, 181
tourism in the Caribbean, 17, 167, 171,
    178–92; and advertising, 178–88, 182,
    184, 185, 187, 188
trade, 12, 13, 121–22, 154, 219
trade cards, and Singer sewing machine
    advertising, 148–50, 149, 150, 321n68
trains, and aluminum, 165, 176
Transfergeschichte, 9–10
translations and misunderstandings,
    14–15; and Chinese medicine in 17th-
    century Europe, 215–40; difference
    between translation of written texts
    and oral testimonies, 204–5; and
    International Women's Year (IWY)
    conference, 242–66; and murder trial of
    Ah Jake, 200–205
transnational feminism, 18–19, 242–66.
    See also International Women's Year
    (IWY) conference
transportation industry, 165, 169, 176. See
    also aluminum
Trigault, Nicholas, 226
Trismegistus, Hermes, 231

Trouillot, Michel-Rolph, 179
Tsing, Anna Lowenhaupt, 10–11
Türckische Vagrant, 69
Turner, L. J. B., 157
al-Tusi, Nasir al-Din, 128

UNIFEM (United Nations Development
    Fund for Women), 254
United States: choral groups, 82–83,
    301n57; and flows of technology, 123;
    imagined America as Asian beacon,
    153–56; and International Women's
    Year (IWY) conference, 250–52,
    256 (see also Friedan, Betty); trade
    with Lanka, 154. See also African
    Americans; Alcoa; aluminum; challenge
    dance; Chinese workers in California;
    Irish Americans; murder trial of Ah
    Jake; Singer sewing machine

Valentin, Erich, 84
van Reede, Hendrik, 236
Vaughn, Jerome A., 206, 207, 334n36
Verdi, Giuseppe, 83
vermillion, 17, 109–20; association with
    blood and regeneration, 112–13; and
    Chinese alchemy, 120, 125–27; and
    gold pigments, 114; and medieval
    European theory of metals, 116–19;
    and movement of knowledge over
    geographic distance, 119–24; recipes/
    sources of, 109–12, 120, 307nn 4, 7,
    316n113
Verne, Jules, 170–71
Veyne, Paul, 92
Victory Through Air Power (de Seversky),
    175–76
virginity, 93–94
Vitruvius, 315n94
Vockerodt, Gottfried, 69
Der vollkommene Capellmeister
    (Mattheson), 77

Wagner, Richard, 84
Wah Chuck, 198–201, 205–9, 214
Waldheim, Kurt, 251, 252
Walker, Mack, 73
Wallerstein, Immanuel, 219
Walpole, Horace, 129
Wang Chou Houo, 236, 237
Waterman, Robert, 206, 210
Watson, Samuel, 222

wealthy, the: change in meaning of wealth, 104–6; church wealth as patrimonies of the poor, 101–3; gift-giving, charitable acts, and justice from late Antiquity to the early Middle Ages, 87–106
weapons technology, 120–21
Weber, Carl Maria von, 86
Weber, Gottfried, 80
Weber, William, 78, 79
Weise, Christian, 68
Were the Jews a Mediterranean Society? (Schwartz), 94
Werner, Michael, 10
Whaley, Joachim, 302n63
Whitaker, Jennifer Seymour, 256
White, Richard, 6–8, 10
Wickramasinghe, Martin, 152, 162
Wickramasinghe, Nira, 12, 17, 134–64, 268–69
WIDF. *See* Women's International Democratic Federation
Williams, Barney, 44
Williams, Pete, *34*, 43, 53, 55–58
Willis, Nathaniel P., 55
Wilm, Alfred, 171
Wilson, Ara, 349n21
women, 163; and competitive dance tradition, 27, 29; and domesticity and respectability in Lanka, 162–64; literacy in Lanka, 147, 320n64; and

Singer sewing machine in Lanka, 145, 147, 151, 158–64; transnational feminism (*see* International Women's Year (IWY) conference); women's choruses, 84
Women's International Democratic Federation (WIDF), 248, 251–52
Women's World Bank, 254
Woodruff, George, 140, 144
Woolf, Leonard, 148
World Plan of Action, 245, 249, 252
World Social Forum (WSF), 243
World War I, 171, 172, 325n19
World War II, 172, 191
Wotton, William, 227–28, 238
WSF. *See* World Social Forum

Young, Robert, 8
Yuan Cai, 121

Zelter, Carl Friedrich, 81, 83, 84
Zeppelin, Count Ferdinand von, 325n19
Zhang Hua, 120
Zheng, Andreas, 233
Zhigongtang (sworn brotherhood society), 208–9, 335nn 41, 42
Zimbabwe, consumption of personal care products in, 136
Zimmerman, Andrew, 15
Zimmerman, Bénédicte, 10